Aviation
in Canada

The Formative Years

In honour of the bush pilots, Jack!

Larry Milberry

Jan. 2010

OPAS D.H.61 Giant Moth G-CAPG *Goose* on the slipway at Sault Ste. Marie *circa* 1928. Of 10 Giant Moths built by de Havilland in England, three had Canadian careers. 'APG ended its days as a WWII training aid at the Galt Aircraft School. (Ontario Ministry of Natural Resources)

Aviation *in* Canada

The Formative Years

Larry Milberry

Library and Archives Canada Cataloguing in Publication

Milberry, Larry, 1943-
    Aviation in Canada : the formative years / Larry Milberry.

Includes bibliographical references and index.
ISBN 978-0-921022-21-3

1. Aeronautics, Commercial–Canada–History.
2. Aeronautics, Commercial–Canada–History–Pictorial works. I. Title.

HE9815.A3M55 2009   387.70971   C2009-903333-X

Design: James W. Jones, Iroquois, Ontario
Proofreading: Lambert Huneault, Windsor, Ontario; Rodger Levesque, Vancouver; Ron Pickler, Burlington, Ontario; William J. Wheeler, Markham, Ontario
Printed and bound in Canada by Friesen Printers Ltd., Altona, Manitoba

Published by
CANAV Books
Larry Milberry, publisher
51 Balsam Avenue
Toronto, Ontario M4E 3B6
Canada

(Title page) The great Canadian Airways Ju 52 "Flying Box Car" on the ice at Red Lake in the mid-1930s. For years CF-ARM, which always drew a crowd, was the biggest airplane in Canada. (Don Parrott)

(Above) The Fairchild FC-2 is symbolic of Quebec's bush flying roots. The first (G-CAGC) appeared in the summer of 1927. Through Centennial Year, the Canadian Aviation Heritage Centre in Ste-Anne-de-Bellevue, Quebec was working on this remarkable FC-2 replica. The CAHC came about largely with the support of Godfrey Pasmore, the son of Fairchild of Canada founder, Hubert Pasmore. (Pierre Gillard)

(Front Endpapers) Canadian government D.H.9A G-CYBF took part in the first trans-Canada flight. 'BF was part of the Imperial Gift donated by Great Britain after WWI. (CANAV Col)

In the Roaring Twenties amphibians were the choice of adventuresome millionaires. This Sikorsky belonged to Col Edward A. Deeds, whose interests included the Dayton-Wright Airplane Co., National Cash Register and Pratt & Whitney. Deeds' beautiful toy is seen during a stop at Sioux Lookout circa 1930. He mainly used the Sikorsky to serve his 200-ft yacht. (J.P. Culliton Col.)

A boyish C.A. "Duke" Schiller sits on the nose of a flying boat during his stint as an aviation mechanic in post-WWI America. Schiller soon was home in Canada, where he carved out a huge reputation as a pioneer bush pilot. (Fred Hotson Col.)

OPAS HS-2L bushplanes at home base in Sault Ste. Marie circa 1931. (J.P. Culliton Col.)

Vickers Viking G-CAEB – one of the most famous of Canada's early bushplanes. From 1922-26 it served anywhere from James Bay to northern British Columbia. (J.P. Culliton Col.)

Several Felixstowe F.3s were shipped to Canada as part of the Imperial Gift. Here is G-CYBT on the Red River during the 1920 Trans-Canada Flight. (K.M. Molson Col.)

The mighty D.H.61 Giant Moth was powered by a 500-hp Bristol Jupiter. G-CAPG, one of three Canadian examples, began with the Ontario Provincial Air Service in August 1928, then served stalwartly into 1941. (CANAV Col.)

(Back Endpapers) Western Canada Airways added Giant Moth G-CAJT in August 1928 for a Winnipeg-Moose Jaw-Calgary air mail and passenger service. But 'AJT was short-lived, crashing near Calgary on October 23. (William J. Wheeler Col.)

Hamilton Metalplane CF-OAH served the Ontario Provincial Air Service 1930-44, then continued for a few years with Northwest Airlines in Alaska. (CANAV Col.)

Ford Trimotor G-CATC operated briefly on the Victoria-Seattle-Vancouver triangle before disappearing in coastal waters on August 25, 1928. (Finlayson Col.)

Canada's pioneer airmen rest in cemeteries across Canada. In this Sioux Lookout plot lies WWI and Western Canada Airways pilot Paul A. Garten. On June 2, 1930 he was taxying Fokker G-CASF on Lake Seseganaga, east of Sioux Lookout. A heavy gust suddenly flipped the plane and Paul was drowned. In this 2007 scene, Richard Hulina of Slate Fall Airways and Bucky Wong visit Paul's grave. (Larry Milberry)

Western Canada Airways Laird mailplane CF-APW at its Winnipeg base. A few days later 'APW was lost here when the hangar burned to the ground. (William J. Wheeler Col.)

Flying the mail in early times was inherently dangerous work. Here lies the sad wreck of Travel Air mailplane CF-AJO, which crashed in March 1930 on W.F. Good's farm north of Kingston, Ontario. (Melville Good)

Another view of the incredible Viking – G-CAEB. (F.T. Jenkins)

One of the war surplus JN-4 Canucks flown in the early 1920s by May Aeroplanes of Edmonton. Such cheap, readily-available types gave a start to commercial aviation in post-war Canada. (CANAV Col.)

Contents

The *Silver Dart* replica takes flight at Baddeck on February 22, 2009. Why did it fly the day before the 100th Anniversary? Since Atlantic Canada winter weather was predicted to be fierce on the 23rd, the next best thing was the 22nd, which proved to be almost ideal. (Shawn Dunlop, Baddeck, NS B0E 1B0)

Preface

In November 2008 CANAV Books launched the first of its Canadian Centennial of Flight books, *Aviation in Canada: The Pioneer Decades*. Then, on February 22, 2009, national celebrations for centennial year commenced royally at Baddeck on Cape Breton Island, when astronaut Bjarni Tryggvason made several flights in a magnificent *Silver Dart* replica. Adding to the excitement, astronaut Chris Hadfield flashed by in the Vintage Wings F-86 Sabre resplendent in Golden Hawks colours, and Capt Tim "Donor" Woods of 410 Squadron performed in his Centennial of Flight CF-18 Hornet.

The *Silver Dart* is the result of years of dedicated volunteer effort by a group of technical and historical enthusiasts based in Welland, Ontario. Their association – AEA 2005 – honours the Aerial Experiment Association, formed in 1907 in Halifax to conduct powered airplane experiments. Headed by Alexander Graham Bell, the AEA included Canadians F.W. Baldwin, J.A.D. McCurdy, and Americans Glenn H. Curtiss and Thomas Selfridge. The AEA story is told in *Pioneer Decades*.

Aviation in Canada: The Formative Years follows naturally behind *Pioneer Decades*. It begins as Canada's new breed of aerial warriors returns after WWI. A few of these combat veterans soon were exploring peacetime aviation possibilities. *Formative Years* covers all their efforts, beginning shakily in the barnstorming world, then progressing, as more practical challenges appeared. Start turning the pages to see what progress they made in the first years. The highlight is the birth of bush flying in Canada in 1919. Airplanes are used to manage forest resources, spot forest fires, then assist in fighting them. From forestry, aviation branches naturally into aerial mapping, mineral development, Arctic exploration, fisheries and customs control, air mail, etc.

As always in the CANAV big picture, *Formative Years* came about through team

Astronaut Bjarni Tryggvason "on screen" during one of his *Silver Dart* flights of February 22. This image was captured by a airframe-mounted camera. Then, Bjarni with the Chief of the Air Staff LGen Angus Watt. (Larry Milberry)

Newsman Peter Mansbridge does the CBC "National" broadcast from the *Silver Dart* hangar on Bras d'Or Lake. (Larry Milberry)

effort. Of my many collaborators, Fred W. Hotson proved typically indispensable. At age 95 (but as energetic as men half his age) Fred always was available. It seems that, whatever the topic, he could dredge out a file of data and photos – stuff to make a researcher weep. Thanks to Fred, several important stories come to life in *Formative Years*, as with the coverage of Freddie Shaylor of Skyways Limited, and Wilson H. Clark of General Airways. In another case, Fred provided original album pages from his sidekick of decades past – the great aeronautical aficionado C. Don Long. Hugh A. Halliday provided his usual

support, in one case coming up with a hefty box of Ontario Provincial Air Service historic raw material.

Any serious author is always after that elusive "Eldorado". While researching for my first book 40 years ago, such gold mines as the Matt Berry diaries and Frank E. Davison papers came to light, neither having seen the light of day for decades. This time, two especially important collections surfaced. Thanks to J. Ellis Culliton, I had access to the papers and photos of his renowned bush flying father, J.P. "Jay" Culliton of NAME and the OPAS. Then, a phone call one day from

Baddeck's wonderful Alexander Graham Bell Museum in the dead of the 2009 Cape Breton Island winter. This is the planned future home for the AEA 2005 *Silver Dart*. (Larry Milberry)

Stephen McDonough led to the long-buried aviation treasures of his father, W.J. McDonough. The biographies of these monumental aviation figures appear for the first time in *Formative Years*.

Many photo sources have been used here, not the least of which is CANAV's own vast files. I started these more than 50 years ago, in the days when archives, museums and corporations happily answered their mail and sent out professional-quality prints for which there rarely was a charge. Sad to say, in the 2000s few such sources remain. Even worse, many archives and museums simple-mindedly envision their photo collections as "profit centres", charging ludicrous amounts for a history fan to acquire a single print. For this they should hang their heads in shame, especially since none of these "profit centres" actually makes any profit. Instead, the chief effect of their "pay or else" policy is to deny Canadians the enjoyment of seeing the photos which they, as sole taxpaying

proprietors, have full right. Happily, there are a few exceptions to the rule, including the Glenbow Museum and Lake-of-the-Woods Museum.

Among Canadian history publishers, CANAV has led the way in accurately crediting photographs. While most publishers were not bothering with credits 30 years ago, CANAV was burning the midnight oil trying to get an accurate credit for every photo that it published. This policy continues, as you can see. In the meantime, many Canadian publishers have emulated the CANAV style of accreditation. However, many old prints still have no known absolute point of origin. Such photos temporarily appear under the catch-all heading "CANAV Collection", "William J. Wheeler Collection", etc.

Routine duties during this project kept me returning to those many tried and true history sources, whether books, journals, newspapers, archives, museums, etc., and thousands of telephone calls, emails and

letters were sent and received, as questions arose and, ultimately, deadlines threatened.

Neither *Pioneer Decades* nor *Formative Years* can possibly cover their respective topic 100%. Because of this, for further information, serious readers must refer to the bibliography. Listed are many of the important aviation source books: *Canada's Flying Heritage*, *A History of Canadian Airports*, etc. cover or expand upon many topics not found elsewhere. Although many such books are out-of-print, used copies normally are available through internet-based book stores. All that you need do is Google your title and it likely will pop up. Geographically, the Canadian gazetteer is on the internet, so even the smallest natural feature, community, etc., may be pinpointed, should the reader be curious.

James Jones has done his usual fine work in getting *Formative Years* onto the printed page. A talented book designer and knowledgeable aviation enthusiast, James began with Aerographics in Ottawa, where design guru David O'Malley handed him the job of producing CANAV's 3-volume *Canada's Air Force at War and Peace*. As usual, many others assisted along the way, including proof readers Bert Huneault, Rodger Levesque, Ron Pickler and William J. "Bill" Wheeler. Through their diligent efforts, few typos will be found throughout this book's vast text and hundreds of captions.

Further sources of information, photos, etc. include (some of the fine citizens listed have passed on): Alaska State Archives,

On the other side of Canada, on April 25, 2009, the Centennial Heritage Flight performed at 19 Wing Comox. Flying the Snowbird Tutor was Capt Greg Wiebe, while Capt Tim "Donor" Woods flew the specially-painted CF-18, and Steve Will flew the Vintage Wings F-86 Sabre. Then, the Sabre in formation with the Snowbirds in "Big Wedge" formation during the same show. (Larry Milberry)

In recent years many outstanding restoration projects have contributed immensely to Canada's flying heritage cause. One of the top projects was Fokker Super Universal CF-AAM, seen here at Toronto City Centre Airport on August 29, 2003. Then, Don McLean, Clark Seaborn (team leader) and Bob Cameron, who got CF-AAM back into the air after a 60 year hiatus. In 2003 their masterpiece flew in a trans-continental air tour, then Clark donated it to the Western Canada Aviation Museum in Winnipeg. Much data about the AEA 2005 Silver Dart, CF-AAM, Vintage Wings, the Canadian Warplane Heritage, etc., may be found on the internet. (Larry Milberry)

Alberta Aviation Museum, Archives of British Columbia, Archives of Manitoba, Archives of Ontario, George R. "Bob" Ayres, Robin Brass, British North America Philatelic Society, Buffalo and Erie County Historical Society, Buffalo and Erie County Public Library, Brian Burke, Douglas H. Burt, Col J. Burwash, D.J. Cameron, Patrick Campbell, Canadian Airways Ltd., Canada Aviation Museum, Canada's Aviation Hall of Fame, Canadian Aerophilatelic Society, Canadian Aircraft Operator, Canadian Aviation Heritage Centre, Canadian Aviation Historical Society, *Canadian Aviation* magazine, T.A. "Rusty" Blakey, Samson Clark, Ralph Clint, Ray H. Crone, J. Ellis Culliton, DND Joint Imagery Centre, Bill Dunphy, Frank H. Ellis, John and Joyce Ellis, Jon Eriksson, Norman Etheridge, Fairchild Aviation Museum, Mike Filey, Robert Finlayson, George A. Fuller, Richard F. Gaudet, Pierre Gillard, Glenbow Museum, *Globe and Mail* "Canada's Heritage from 1944", Melville Good, J. Carter Guest, Robert G. Halford, Robert Hanshew (USN/HHC), Richard Hulina, A.T. "Tony" Jarvis, Joseph P. Juptner, George F. Kimball, Stanley N. Knight, Lake-of-the-Woods Museum, Library and Archives Canada, Arthur Limmert, Richard K. Malott, Al Martin, W.R. May, Stephen McDonough, T.M. McGrath, M.L. "Mac" McIntyre, Gordon McNulty, Jack McNulty, E.G. McPherson, Brian Milberry, Kenneth M. Molson, National Air Photo Library, National Museum of Science and Technology, National Museum of the United States Air Force, Natural Resources Canada/Atlas of Canada, Lori Nelson, Niagara Falls Public Library, Ontario Ministry of Natural Resources, Don Parrott, E. Parsons, Prince Rupert Archives, Robert S. Petite, Red Lake Museum, Royal Aeronautical Society, Clark Seaborn, W.F. Shaylor, G.R. Spradbrow, Don Starratt, E.W. Stedman, Brett Stolle (NMUSAF), Edgar Strain, G. Swartman, Rex Terpening, David J. Thompson, Tiptonville (Tennessee) Public Library, Toronto Harbour Commissioners Archives, Toronto Public Library, *Toronto Star* "Pages of the Past", United States Navy Naval History and Heritage Command, William J. "Bill" Wheeler, Elwood White, S.J. Woodham.

I should explain that measures here are in Imperial, since that was the system of the day. In order to maintain a fine-looking page, you will not be bothered by unsightly Imperial-metric conversions. You can quickly work these out if desired. Also, the taxpayer's pocket has not been picked in producing *Formative Years*. CANAV Books, being a serious publisher, has not so much as applied for a government grant. CANAV survives by producing fine-quality books which interested readers happily buy. It's "a business thing" that has worked for CANAV since 1981.

LARRY MILBERRY

Located in Ste-Anne-de-Bellevue on the MacDonald College Campus of McGill University, the Canadian Aviation Heritage Centre had several important Centennial of Flight projects. In June 2009 Pierre Gillard photographed this pair of 1909-vintage Bleriot monoplane replicas being created at the CAHC. Count Jacques de Lesseps made the first flight over Montreal on such a Bleriot.

VC heroes Bishop and Barker spent one exhilarating season doing airshows in high-performance Fokker D.VII war prizes. Likely due to problems keeping these advanced fighters serviceable, after 1919 there is little news of them in Canada. Here is Maj W.G. Barker, VC, in the D.VII that he flew in the Toronto-New York air race. Of the many D.VIIs brought to Canada, the only survivor in 2009 belongs to the Brome County Historical Museum in Knowlton, Quebec. (A.G. McLerie Col.)

The Birth of Civil Aviation

Basic Beginnings

With war's end in November 1918 Canadian society began adjusting to peacetime conditions. In Ottawa this included considering how aviation might be used for the national good. In *The Creation of a National Air Force*, historian W.A.B. Douglas explained how this process began: "The initial interest of men like J.A. Wilson and C.C. MacLaurin lay in converting the expansive potential of aviation, so clearly demonstrated in war, to constructive peacetime uses, a focus of commitment which coincided nicely with the prejudices of an unmilitary people tired of war and a government bent on economy."

In order to regulate aviation, the Canadian Air Board Act was passed in June 1919. The goal was to licence pilots, register aircraft and enforce Canada's first civil air regulations. The Act specified three aeronautical purposes: controlling commercial flying (to come under the Civil Aviation Branch led by Superintendent LCol J.S. Scott); overseeing civil government flying (under the Civil Operations Branch led by Superintendent LCol Robert Leckie); and conducting training (under the Canadian Air Force led by MGen Sir Willoughby Gwatkin). Vice-chairman of the Air Board, Col O.M. Biggar, announced that the organization's first task would be to regulate against the unsafe use of civil airplanes. He added

Immediately after WWI war surplus equipment and supplies flooded the market. Included were hundreds of cheaply-priced Curtiss JN-4 trainers. For years these would be the backbone of Canadian civil aviation. This trio, belonging to the Aerial League of Canada, is seen at the Willows aerodrome at Victoria on June 11, 1919. Nearest is C1293 named "Pathfinder II", later registered G-CABU, then lost on a daring flight to Prince Rupert. (Archives of British Columbia 18868)

that aerial surveying would be another key priority and that this work would be done by flying boats since, other than the Royal Air Force (Canada) training bases in southern Ontario, there were no airfields. Forestry patrols, police assignments and carrying the mail would be other aviation duties to evaluate.

Of the seven Royal Air Force (Canada) bases in Ontario, Ottawa supported only Camp Borden postwar. Camps Rathbun and Mohawk at Deseronto and Camp Beamsville reverted mainly to agricultural status. W.A. Bishop and W.G. Barker barnstormed for a couple of seasons from Armour Heights in north Toronto, then the place was developed as a housing estate. Camp Leaside in northeast Toronto became F.G. Ericson's base for a war surplus business. "Ericson Field" gradually evolved into Toronto's main airport, but little was spent on improvements. Camp Borden became the main flying base for the new Canadian Air Force, but remained largely unimproved for years. This view of a muddy-looking Camp Borden shows the extensive infrastructure, but with not a JN-4 in sight. Perhaps this was during the winter of 1917-18 when the flying had transferred to Texas. (DND RE15521)

Soon after the war, ex-military pilots began taking refresher flying courses at Camp Borden. This provided a cadre of licenced pilots for Canada's developing civil aviation scene. Most flight training was done on Avro 504Ks such as G-CYAT and 'EE. (George F. Kimball/CANAV Col.)

The Canadian Air Force was authorized on February 18, 1920 as a non-permanent entity to train former RAF members in flying and the trades, courses to be taught at Camp Borden. Personnel would serve part time and remain civilians, even if wearing the CAF uniform. Initially, some of those trained were seconded via the Civil Service Commission to the Civil Operations Branch for such flying duties as forestry patrol and aerial photography. By the end of 1922 some 1821 men had been trained and many operations conducted. But no new pilots had been produced, so a shortage of qualified men was looming, and no official air force flying units existed. The Air Board realized that a permanent air force – full time and military in nature – was needed. This led to the passing of the National Defence Act. Effective January 1, 1923, this brought the Department of Militia and Defence, the Canadian Naval Service and the Canadian Air Board under a new organization – the Department of National Defence. On March 12 of the same year the DND acknowledged that its request to King George V for approval to use "Royal" in designating Canada's air force had been approved. The Royal Canadian Air Force came into existence on April 1, 1924.

While pilots trained at Camp Borden, so did aviation tradesmen. Many were veterans, while others came with automotive or other mechanical trades. This class is shown training on Clerget engines as used in the Avro 504. (CANAV Col.)

The Barnstormers

Even though the term "barnstormer" is usually associated with the American flying circuses as portrayed in such Hollywood films as "The Great Waldo

Pepper", Canada had its own daredevil fliers – youthful veterans some of whom wore gallantry medals. Flying their war surplus planes from place to place, these always adaptable fellows were ready to do anything for a quick buck. Their normal routine was to turn up at some community event to sell rides. Flights might be charged at a set rate of $5.00 or so, but various gimmicks also were used – rides for a dollar-a-minute, a dollar-a-mile, a nickel-a-pound, etc. Stunt

Wartime flying hero Fred McCall became one of Alberta's great barnstormers. Here is his famous landing at the Calgary Exhibition of July 5, 1919. The Calgary *Herald* observed: "With the power suddenly lost from his machine, Capt. McCall was forced to choose as a landing either the race track, on which auto demons were speeding at breakneck speed, or the midway, crowded with thousands, or the centre pole and guy cables of the merry-go-round... It was a wonderful exhibition of daring aviation, quick thinking, and pluck." Neither McCall nor his young joyriders, Ronald and Herbert Richardson, were injured. Inset, Capt Fred McCall at Calgary in 1920 in his JN-4 G-CAAH. (DND RE64-1820, LAC C43976)

flying and wing-walking often were on the agenda and flying lessons and aerial photography were available. All this usually worked, so long as the weather co-operated and there were no serious breakdowns or accidents.

What made this life possible was that hundreds of war surplus planes were for sale at easy prices – $1000 or $2000 for a JN-4 in good condition. In one case, Canada's Victoria Cross heroes, W.A. Bishop and W.G. Barker, took over Armour Heights airfield in North Toronto, and began marketing JN-4s and carrying on their own flying circus. Meanwhile, Bishop went on the lecture circuit, and wrote *Winged Warfare*, an instant best-seller covering his combat days. On the local barnstorming scene, on September 18, 1920, Bishop and Barker held an open house at Armour Heights. One notice announced: "This Aerial Circus is guaranteed to be the finest display of flying ever seen in Toronto." The locals turned out, no doubt enticed by advertisements mentioning a display

of German war prize aircraft and offering flights "at reasonable rates in safe aircraft". Others were busy

on this scene, including the greatest of Canada's aviation wheeler-dealers, F.G. Ericson.

To improve barnstorming prospects, Bishop and Barker added this rare 2-seat Sopwith Dove. Based on a common wartime design, the Dove was typical of postwar British civil aircraft – it was nothing more than a modified Pup fighter. Here is the Bishop-Barker Dove in New York prior to delivery to Toronto, where it became G-CAAY. (CANAV Col.)

A display ad that he ran in the April 23, 1919 Toronto *Globe* offered JN-4s for sale at $2000:

Canadian pilots are buying Canadian planes for passenger carrying, advertising, aerial photography, fair exhibitions, forest survey and patrol. This is the big year for profitable local flying. Keep in the game and be ready for the wonderful aerial developments ahead. Canadian J.N. planes complete with OX5 90 H.P. motors and liberal spare equipment for immediate delivery. Wire or write to F.G. Ericson, 120 King St. E. Toronto, Ont.

On May 15, 1919 Ericson and US Army veterans Milton Elliott and O.M. Locklear, did wing-walking stunts over Toronto in a pair of JN-4s. A newspaper item noted how Locklear was filmed from a third plane "hanging from the landing structure", then deftly swinging from one plane to the next. This is the first known "change of planes" in Canada. (Elliott held the 17th Canadian

An International Aerial Transport JN-4 in Toronto – perhaps the plane from which a Heintzman phonograph machine was dropped in August 1919. With six JN-4s, IAT thrived for a few months, then faded. Its advertisement in the Toronto *Daily Star* of May 27, 1919 informed readers: "Flying at Armour Heights every day... Now is your opportunity to take a trip over Toronto. Ride with your friends. We are sending several planes up together to fly in formation. Safe, reliable planes, expert pilots. Straight smooth sailing, or stunts, as you wish... Take Metropolitan Cars to Stop 26." (CANAV Col.)

civil pilot's licence ever issued. He and Locklear would pursue barnstorming until it killed them.)

A few days later an advertisement in the Toronto press announced "Free Exhibition of Stunt Flying Sunday, June 1st, at 3 p.m. at Armour Heights ... Capt. Parsons Ex-R.A.F. Will Crawl All Over His Plane ... Passenger Flights Arranged by Appointment ... International Aerial Transport, Limited". H.J. Webster was listed as general manager of this outfit. On August 26 this company was involved in a publicity gimmick paid for by the Heintzman piano company. Carrying Gerhard Heintzman's wife, a JN-4 flew from Toronto to Hamilton in 42 minutes but, along the way, a Heintzman phonograph machine "accidentally" fell from the plane. According to Heintzman, the battered record player was recovered and, when tested, still played beautifully. It was put

on display at the 1919 Canadian National Exhibition.

On September 1, 1919 the Toronto *Globe* described the Labour Day weekend show put on at the CNE by W.G. Barker and his cohorts: "Every corner of the grounds was filled by excited spectators ... [they] were treated to some close-up views of the captured German Fokkers in which the pilots flew... The five machines reached the fair grounds in the form of a wedge with Lieut-Col. Barker leading. Over the grounds they went through a series of evolutions, wheeling and weaving in and out with beautiful precision..." This was first-class entertainment for the fair goers, but also was the sort of shenanigan that the Canadian Air Board Act was hoping to regulate.

Barnstorming in Canada was curtailed through WWI with the exception of a few Americans who continued until the US joined in the war in 1917. Texan pilot, Katherine Stinson, who had learned to fly in Chicago in 1912, was a popular barnstormer who always gave the crowd its money's worth. Here she is with her Matty Laird biplane in Brandon, Manitoba in July 1916. (CANAV Col.)

C282 *Winnipeg* – one of many JN-4s honouring Canadian communities that fund-raised to pay for them. *Winnipeg* carried pioneer airmen, did aerial reconnaissance during the Winnipeg general strike, and barnstormed around Manitoba until fading off in the early 1920s. (Pittaway Col.)

Canuck C282

Typical of surplus JN-4C Canucks built by Canadian Aeroplanes Ltd. was one sponsored during the war by the citizens of Winnipeg – C282. Sponsoring was a way for Canadians on the home front to directly support the war effort. In this case Winnipeggers were thanked by having the name of their city emblazoned in red on the side of their plane.

Built in August 1917, C282 was assigned to 89 Squadron at Leaside. Besides the daily grind of training, it completed the second official Toronto-Ottawa air mail service, Lt A. Dunstan flying that trip on August 26-27, 1918. Immediately after the war, some gift aircraft were returned to their host cities, as was C282. It initially was stored, then dusted off in June 1919 when the Winnipeg general strike turned ugly. Flown by a Capt Jones, it apparently made at least one reconnaissance flight over the city during the unrest. No further official use was made of it, and there is no suggestion that C282 be preserved historically. Instead, it was loaned in 1920 to wartime pilots A.A.L. Cuffe and G.A. Thompson of Canadian Aircraft Ltd., who used it in their Manitoba flying circus with "Winnipeg" painted out.

In May 1920, C282 was re-registered G-CAAO on behalf of CAL. On May 23 Reg Ronald and Frank H. Ellis pranged it in Gull Lake, Saskatchewan, as they

were preparing to do some 24th of May barnstorming. Once repaired, the plane was busy on the summer circuit. On June 20, W.G. Barker and Frank Ellis flew it to Dauphin, where Barker visited his family. Meanwhile, the loan agreement was extended by Winnipeg city council for a second year, but 'AAO was struck from the civil aircraft register in 1924 and not heard of again. A Canuck sponsored by Edmonton had a happier ending – nicely restored, it survives with the Reynolds-Alberta Museum in Wetaskiwin.

Canadian Aerial Services

Another early Canadian flying operation was R.B. Danville's Canadian Aerial Services, based at a field along Bois Franc Rd. in suburban Montreal. CAS planes, however, could land pretty well anywhere there might be some business. The company began in July 1920 with Avro 504 G-CAAE imported from the UK, then purchased a JN-4C from Bishop-Barker. J.H. St-Martin (pilot) and A.N. Goodwin (mechanic) were Danville's first employees. Services included hopping passengers, aerial photography, demo parachute jumping, racing cars at fairs, and there even were rumours about smuggling booze across to the US.

One day a fellow was killed upon walking in front of a JN-4 that was landing. After Danville and his pilots

spent the winter of 1920-21 taking a DND-sponsored refresher course at Camp Borden, he merged with a Montreal rival, R&W Air Service. The new arrangement, still under Danville's banner, had six planes operating from the R&W site, which included a surplus RFC canvas hangar. The big deal in the 1921 season was a film-making contract in the Adirondacks, where considerable stunt flying was done. This, however, was the final season for CAS. Danville briefly noted this at the 1969 Canadian Aviation Historical Society convention: "Canadian Aerial Services was not only the first concern of its kind to obtain a federal charter, but also one of the first to discontinue operations."

Danville now joined newly-formed Laurentide Air Service Ltd. On February 6, 1922 his original Avro G-CAAE completed the first flight to James Bay. Crewed by J.H. St-Martin and Roy Maxwell, it departed Cochrane (head of rail for the Temiskaming and Northern Ontario Railroad) at 1600, landed 40 minutes later at an HBC post to drop off some mail, took on a small load, then reached Moose Factory after a flying time for the day of 2:10 hours. One report noted how this flight "proved beyond a doubt that winter flying in this country with ski attachments is in every way as practical and safe as with a flying boat…"

Meanwhile, others were venturing into business using surplus JN-4s, including a company listed as Northern Canada Traders Ltd. NCT applied to register its plane on July 8, 1920. Of the company's five principals, the president was listed on the application as Ernest Lloyd Janney – the infamous founder of Canada's first "air force" in 1914. Little is known about this short-lived company, although its JN-4 – G-CADC – survived in other hands into 1926.

Swanning off to Tennessee

An off-beat story made the Toronto headlines in January 1921. *Daily Star* coverage began: "Buffalo, Jan.21. A Canadian military airplane was forced down just outside the city yesterday, smashing a strut on landing. Careening wildly, the plane came to a stop without overturning." The pilot explained that he was on official business – a flight to Memphis. He and his passenger then took the trolley into Buffalo. Next day, however, the JN-4, inscribed "Chypengarb", was seized by US Customs. Mr. Collins at Ericson Field in Leaside reported that the plane had taken off from there piloted by Lt Hamilton, who had his new wife along. Hamilton apparently had told Collins that they were on their honeymoon. Although the plane was still in RFC markings, Col Douglas Joy at Camp Borden said it "certainly is not connected to the Air Force", yet Hamilton reportedly had recently been on strength at Camp Borden. The press was full of such oddball flying stories in early post-war days. Unfortunately, there rarely was any follow-up, as with the "Chypengarb" story.

Western Go-Getters

Many a barnstormer ended with his plane a pile of rubble and lucky to be alive. In southern Alberta, Harry Fitzsimmons' experiences included having a prop shattered following a bird strike (then crash-landing) and having a plane damaged by a bull at a rodeo. He was able to end his days with a rare safety record and the claim that, "During our two years we never had a single instance where a passenger has not left our machine as an enthusiastic booster for aviation." He wrote about barnstorming in his memoir *The Sky Hobos*:

Ex-RFC JN-4 C590 of Roland Groome's Aerial Service at the field near Cameron St. and Hill Ave in Regina. This was Canada's first official "air harbour", its licence having been awarded by the Air Board on April 22, 1920. On May 14, 1920 C590 became G-CAAM. H.W. Doucette crashed it on September 27, 1923. (R.H. Crone Col.)

The reason I started these wing walking feats was that in 1920 we were late getting into the field and I found that most of my competitors were bidding for fair contracts. As a newcomer, I had to devise a scheme to beat them to it in order to keep my company in operation. Palmer and I then started to train quietly. One of our favourite places was over Henderson Lake when few people were around. We practiced the top and bottom plane work first and devised a set of signals. As we were both practical airmen, we knew the effect of strain and balance on the wings and how to work together. After I disappeared from sight underneath the plane, Palmer was to give me one minute and a half and, if at the end of that time I did not re-appear, he would figure that I was exhausted or otherwise unable to get back up. He was then to come down as close to the lake as possible, and pull the plane almost up to a stall. This would allow me to drop in the lake, and chances were that I would come out unharmed.

That was the plan – if we had used it, which we never did. As I have always been something of an athlete, the balancing and climbing came quite easily to me.

BE A BIRD
AN AEROPLANE
WILL VISIT
Glenboro
ON
June 14 1920
Passengers will be carried for
SHORT TRIPS
in a Canadian Aircraft Aeroplane. The First Person giving the Pilot on his arrival one of these bills will be taken for a Free Ride.
THE
CANADIAN AIRCRAFT CO. LTD.
43 AIKINS BUILDING, WINNIPEG

THIS BILL DROPPED FROM AN AEROPLANE
☞ PLEASE POST UP IN A PROMINENT PLACE ☜

This pen-and-ink by Frank C. Taylor shows a typical Western Canada barnstorming scene. Pilot Harry Fitzsimmons is holding his JN-4 steady as partner Jack Palmer does the wing-walking. This sort of act was great fun for the fair-going public. Not surprisingly, however, the Air Board frowned sternly upon such aviating. Wing walking proved, on the whole, to be self-regulating. Revenue was always iffy and death stared performers in the face every day. Most wing walkers smartened up before their luck or funds ran out. (CANAV Col.)

H.S. "Stan" McClelland was a Saskatoon exhibition pilot. Seeing a future in aviation, in 1919 he and partner H.L. Lobb brought the first war surplus JN-4s to Saskatchewan. On April 28 he took up Saskatchewan's first passenger – a woman. All likely would have gone well, except that someone had parked a car on the field. McClelland cracked up, but no one was hurt. The hat was passed, as sometimes happened in earlier ballooning days, and $200 reportedly was collected to help replace the plane. On May 3, 1920 Lobb was injured and passenger R.C. Hamilton killed when their JN-4 crashed while spinning over Saskatoon.

Roland Groome, McClelland's friendly competitor and a partner in the Regina firm Aerial Survey Co., recorded two "firsts": he received the first commercial pilot's licence issued in Canada, and his JN-4 G-CAAA (formerly RFC C-210) carried the first registration allotted by the Canadian Air Board. The historic date of registration was April 20, 1920. On May 19 Groome flew from Saskatoon to Regina, stopping en route for gas. Canadian Aviation Historical Society researcher Ray H. Crone commented about this: "In taking off from Davidson, the plane caught a barbed-wire fence and tore out a number of posts." Groome continued to

Roland J. Groome's Regina-based JN-4 G-CAAA was the first officially-registered civil aircraft in Canada. It had an ugly ending on June 6, 1926 when it crashed at Shaunavon, Saskatchewan. (R.H. Crone Col.)

A quartet of young WWI veterans during their CAF pilot refresher course at Camp Borden over the winter of 1920-21: Ewart Gladstone MacPherson (Canadian pilot licence No.12), Roland John Groome (No.1), Charles Raymond McNeill (No.41) and Howard Stanley McClelland (No.2). All became well-known prairie barnstormers. Notice that the fellows are proudly displaying their Canadian Air Force wings. In 2009 such an artifact was selling on the collector's market for at least $1000. (E.G. MacPherson Col.)

Stan McClelland's JN-4 ex-RAF C1049 at some barnstorming location. Then, one of Wop May's JN-4s at Grande Prairie, Alberta In another typical scene of the times. Some joyriding business likely was in the wind in both cases. (William J. Wheeler, W.R. May Cols.)

Regina, unperturbed. His 'AAA would survive until June 30, 1926, when pilot R.A. Hawman got into a spin near Shaunavon, Saskatchewan. Not wearing a seat belt, he was fatally thrown from the plane. In spite of such bad times and publicity, McClelland and Groome did much to bring aviation to communities across the prairies. Another post-WWI barnstormer in the west was Frank H. Ellis, author of Canada's premier aviation history book, *Canada's Flying Heritage*. Published in 1954, "CFH" remained in print into the 2000s. Ellis describes a typical barnstorming event: "When the great day arrived, the whole town was agog, and schools were sometimes closed to give the kids a chance to be on hand. Then, as the roar of our engine was heard, and we dropped low, flying at roof-top level along Main Street, the entire populace and all the dogs turned out, racing to the field."

Dancing with Death

The danger inherent in barnstorming again is illustrated by the case of an American daredevil named Reese. High over downtown Regina on October 19, 1921, he was transferring from one plane to another. From atop the wing of Roland Groome's JN-4, he was reaching for the bottom rung of a rope ladder dangling from the aircraft above. Just then he slipped and plunged to his death.

During WWI, John Lilburn Drummond of Spencerville, Ontario had flown B.E.2e bombers with 100 Squadron, and had about 350 flying hours by August 1920. At that time he and a partner, E.D. Eckardt, bought JN-4C G-CADI with which they expected to make some easy money by barnstorming. They rustled up a contract to fly at the Shawville fair in the Ottawa Valley. This went well, $90 being earned on September 22, their first day hopping passengers. Next day, however, proved disastrous, when the plane's controls somehow jammed. 'ADI spun and crashed, injuring Drummond and killing passenger E.G. Amey.

Several other accidents were investigated by the Air Board in these early days. On May 24, 1920 Albert C. Baker, an unlicenced pilot, was hopping passengers at Minoru Park, Vancouver. Carrying passenger E.H. Beasley, Baker got JN-4 G-CAAF into a spin, was unable to recover and crashed. Beasley died, while Baker was slightly hurt. The Air Board found Baker negligent, noting 17 infractions of the federal air regulations.

On July 16, 1920 A.E. Bingham, a pilot from Grand Forks, ND, was test flying the Renault-powered Avro 548 G-CABS from a field near Winnipeg. When his engine quit, Bingham flew into wires while attempting to force-land. He and his passenger were uninjured and the plane later was rebuilt as G-CACI. In time, editorials were railing against careless flying and governments were enacting stricter regulations. Most of Canada's barnstormers soon were out of business. In the case of Drummond and G-CADI, the Ottawa *Citizen* opined:

The aeroplane crash at Shawville is another reminder that there is a useful place for civil aerial transport, but none for stunting at fairs. Aviation can be demonstrated safe, perhaps as safe as motoring or train traveling on properly organized lines of service over distances... Perhaps the Canadian Air Board may find means to head off the possibility of public confidence being destroyed in aviation, as well as to safeguard unwary citizens from unnecessary risk in the air. It should be against the law to perform stunts in an aerial conveyance for hire, as it is to trespass on railway tracks or to speed on thoroughfares.

Anything for a thrill ... JN-4 G-CADF gets ready to tow a string of skiers at the Gray Rocks Inn in St. Jovite, north of Montreal. The Air Board would not have been amused. 'ADF was ex-RAF (Canada) C-123. Postwar it first had served with Price Brothers of Chicoutimi. (CANAV Col.)

Canada's First 25 Licenced Pilots, 1920*

In 1982 the Canadian Aviation Historical Society published K.M. Molson's well-researched list of the first 500 licenced Canadian civil pilots of whom the first 25 are listed here:

1. Roland J. Groome, Aerial Service Co., Regina, killed in plane crash
2. Howard S. McClelland, McClelland and Lobb, Saskatoon
3. Harry L. Lobb, McClelland and Lobb, Saskatoon
4. George K. Trim, Pacific Aviation Co., Vancouver
5. Frederick R. McCall, McCall-Hanrahan Air Service, Calgary
6. Frank Donnelly, McCall Aero Corp., Calgary
7. Wilfred R. May, May Aeroplanes Ltd., Edmonton
8. George W. Gorman, May-Gorman Aeroplanes Ltd., Edmonton
9. Earl L. McLeod, Holbrook & McLeod, Hanna, Alberta
10. C.M. Holbrook, Holbrook & McLeod, Hanna, Alberta
11. W. Frank Kirby, Western Aero Co., Moose Jaw
12. Ewart G. MacPherson, Western Aero Co., Moose Jaw
13. John R. Wight, Aerial Service Co., Regina
14. Edgar A. Alton, J.H. Smith, Brandon, Manitoba
15. Shirley J. Short, US barnstormer, US air mail pilot 1923-27. Killed on May 26, 1930 in a twin-engine Bellanca owned by the Chicago *Daily News*
16. Alfred A. Leitch, Airco Ltd., Winnipeg, later RCAF
17. Milton "Skeets" Elliott, US barnstormer. Killed in Los Angeles on August 2, 1920 along with fellow Hollywood stunt pilot Olmer Locklear. They had been doing a night stunt during shooting of the feature film Skywayman
18. Reginald B. Ronald
19. Fredrick J. Stevenson, Canadian Aircraft Ltd., Winnipeg, killed in WCA plane crash at The Pas
20. George A. Thompson, Canadian Aircraft Ltd., Winnipeg
21. Albert A.L. Cuffe, Canadian Aircraft Ltd., Winnipeg, later RCAF
22. Frank M. Bradfield, B&B Air Service, Niagara Falls
23. Rod B.J. Danville, Canadian Aerial Service Ltd., Montreal
24. Joseph Hervé St-Martin, Canadian Aerial Services Ltd., Montreal, killed in plane crash
25. Robert Leckie, Canadian Air Board, later RCAF

Pilot + his first affiliation

New York - Toronto Air Race

North America's first grand, post-WWI aerial extravaganza was a 1919 race between New York and Toronto. The race was conceived by aeronautical pioneer Chauncey "Chance" Vought and made possible by $10,000 in prize money put up by John Bowman, owner of New York's Commodore Hotel. Co-sponsors included the American Flying Club, the Aero Club of Canada and the Canadian National Exhibition. The Toronto *Globe* reported on August 26: "The race is being held mainly to prove the feasibility of a fast air mail service between Canada and the United States … which would also help wonderfully in the development of the airplane." Many aeronautical minds were quoted in the press in the coming days as to how important it was to establish Canada – US air links, and to keep pace with European aeronautics.

The race route was 522 miles from New York via Albany, Syracuse and Buffalo to Toronto, then back. Contestants could begin at either end. They could re-fly certain legs to improve scores, but had to finish by midnight of August 29. They began on the 25th in bad weather at both ends. At Toronto, planes started from Leaside's Ericson Field.

The wreck of Lt Austin B. Crehore's SVA (No.23) after its crash at Albany while en route to Toronto. Crehore was badly hurt. (National Museum of the US Air Force)

Twenty-seven aircraft left New York on the 25th, but none passed Syracuse that day due to weather. The Toronto *Globe* reported that the Canadian D.H.9 crew of Sgt Coombs and Lt Maurice Holland from Leaside was the first to land at Roosevelt Field at Mineola, Long Island, touching down on the 25th at 7:11 PM after 6:11 flying hours. Curtiss test pilot Roland Rohlfs in an Oriole, and US Army Maj R.W. Schroeder in a Vought, landed at 7:18 and 7:22. Holland reported about the weather and several aircraft had trouble: "The broken

New York-Toronto race participants at Buffalo. Nearest is Rohlfs' Curtiss Oriole (No.51). Right is Schroeder's Vought. No.55 is Sgt C.B. Coombs' USD-9A, No.56 is Capt C.W. Cook's Fokker D.VII, then W.G. Barker's D.VII (No.50), Duke Schiller's JN-4 (No.62) and an unidentified machine. (National Museum of the US Air Force)

machines at Albany reminded one of an aviation graveyard." When William Barker, VC, reached Mineola in a Fokker D.VII, much was made of his war wound to an arm and how, as the *Globe* wrote, "He brought letters … newspapers, and a bag of mail for Washington, in which was included a letter from Sir Robert Borden, Premier of Canada, to President Wilson." Another plane apparently was waiting to hurry this to Washington, while Barker quickly headed home.

On August 26 the *Buffalo Daily Courier* ran an air race photo spread showing the local Curtiss aerodrome. One view showed Red Cross women, "who served refreshments to aviators". Another featured a Canadian, Sgt C.B.B. Coombs – "first to arrive at Curtiss field". This showed him "trying to dodge crowds and snatch a bit of lunch" (none of the hundreds of photos taken that week in Buffalo and Albany seem to exist in either public library or historical society collections in those cities). The *Daily Courier* reported on the 26th:

For two hours and a half yesterday afternoon Buffalo held the center of the stage in the great Hotel Commodore International Airplane race and handicap contest … Between the hours of 1:24 o'clock in the afternoon, when Sergt. C.B. Coombs, piloting the DH-9A, thundered in from Toronto and hit the sod at Curtiss field, to the hour of 3:31 o'clock, when Lieut. Slater, piloting a DH-4, rose from the turf and bent his course east on the wings of a 30-mile breeze, the Queen City was the target of all eyes of two countries. Close to 5,000 persons … cheered the twelve fliers…

The *Buffalo Evening News* reported Lt M.J. Plumb, flying a D.H.4, as the first to start back to Mineola from Toronto, his first leg being the 65 miles to Buffalo. He arrived at 12:30 after 28 minutes, then set off for Syracuse at 1:07. The paper's front-page caption described W.G. Barker as flying "a German Fokker plane … with one hand" One by one, most of the entrants made it back to their starting points. The *Globe* of August 28 wrote:

A Liberty-powered Lowe, Willard and Fowler "LWF" at Leaside. (National Museum of the US Air Force)

JN-4s No.62 *Lorraine* and No.64 during the New York - Toronto race. That a JN-4 could survive this demanding return trip speaks well for the prosaic trainer and its 90-hp OX-5 engine. (CANAV Col.)

A good deal of interest was manifest yesterday in the arrival of Lieut. S.S. Moore ... who is one of F.G. Ericson's "stunt" pilots. He had entered the race in one of the old Canadian training "buses", the lowest powered type of machine competing, and his performance was consequently watched with keen anticipation by his friends here. They greeted his appearance over the field with enthusiasm, and when he landed at 1:34 p.m., after expressing his high spirits in a "loop" and a couple of "rolls", they crowded around the plane... He had covered the course in about fifteen hours and a quarter ... He was not too fatigued to treat a girl passenger to a number of thrills in a stunt flight later in the afternoon.

One Canadian in trouble en route was another of Ericson's men, C.A. "Duke" Schiller, the youngest entrant. Suffering from water in his fuel, he had to stop in Utica. He finally reached Mineola with his machine showing the effects of hail. On August 28 word came that Lt. H.T. Slater, having left Buffalo for Toronto on the 25th, was missing. According to the *Globe*, "the conclusion reached by local officials is that he has fallen into Lake Ontario and been drowned". Aided by boats, several aircraft began what may have been the first large-scale aerial search over Lake Ontario. Next day, however, the press reported that Slater had turned westward upon leaving Buffalo, and arrived later that day at his home base, Selfridge Field, Michigan. Many took umbrage at this, especially in view of the costly and risky search that had followed his "disappearance". Slater explained that he had to get home to tend a faltering engine.

By August 29, 54-56 aircraft seem to have taken part in the race. There had been mishaps, but no fatalities. Lt B.W.

Maynard in a D.H.4 took the Canadian National Exhibition Trophy for the fastest trip – 465.5 minutes. C.A. Schiller in a JN-4 and Col Barker in a D.VII each won cash prizes. Barker

had some forward-thinking comments about the experience:

The chief significance of the race is that it had demonstrated the danger of small airdromes and fast-landing machines. The need for roomy airdromes was amply illustrated at Albany, where five machines crashed on the small field, owing to their inability to come to a stop in the limited area. The disadvantage of machines which have high landing speed, when forced landings occur, has also been clearly shown. What we must have for commercial flying is a machine that will make about 125 miles per hours in the air, and will land at a speed of about 65...

Known Aircraft and Pilots – New York Air Race*

Type	Number	Pilots~
Avro 504K	1	Lawrence B. Sperry
Caproni Ca.3	1	Lt Philip Melville
Curtiss JN-4C, JN-4D, JN-4H	12	Lt Lloyd W. Bertaud, Wilson Campbell, Capt W.B. Chandler, Richard H. Depew, Maj A.H. Gilkeson, Charles S. Jones, Lt U.G. Jones, Maj J.L. Lyons, S.S. Moore, C.A. "Duke" Schiller, Capt W.R. Taylor, Lt Wallace Young
Curtiss Oriole	3	Bertram Acosta, James D. Hill, Roland Rohlfs
de Havilland D.H.4	19	Col Gerald C. Brandt, Lt William C.F. Brown, Col H.B. Claggett, Lt William T. Coates, Lt Harold H. George, Lt Daniel B. Gish, Maj E.R. Hasslet, Lt F.T. Honsinger, Lt Ross C. Kirkpatrick, Lt Belvin W. Maynard, Lt Robert F. Midkiff, Lt C.S. Osborne, Lt M.J. Plumb, Capt C.H. Reynolds, Lt John P. Roullett, Maj J.W. Simmons, Arthur R. Simonin, Lt. H.T. Slater, one unknown.
de Havilland D.H.9A	1	Col L.L. Breteton
Fokker D.VII	2	Col W.G. Barker, Capt H.W. Cook
Le Pere	2	LCol H.E. Hartney, Lt P.H. Logan
L.W.F.	2	J.M. Foote, Elliott W. Springs
S.E.5a	7	Capt Ray W. Brown, Lt Charles R. Colt, Lt John O. Donaldson, LCol H.E. Hartney, Lt Field E. Kindley, Capt Harry W. Smith, Capt Felix W. Steinle
Standard J.1	1	O.S. Palmer
S.V.A.	1	Lt Austin B. Crehore
USD-9A	1	Sgt Clarence B. Coombs
Vought VE-7	1	Maj Rudolph W. Schroeder
Total aircraft	**54**	

~2-seaters carried a crewman, the Caproni had a crew of three.
*Source: K.M. Molson's research for his CAHS paper "The New York-Toronto Air Race", CAHS *Journal* Fall 1971.

An S.E.5a departs Mineola. The race included seven on these little fighters, four of which did not finish due to mishaps. (National Museum of the US Air Force)

Barker's main complaint about the air race was how Capt Beatty of the Aero Club of Canada had conned him into carrying a letter from the Prince of Wales to President Woodrow Wilson. But this was only a publicity stunt to win media acclaim. No such letter was in the pouch carried by Barker, who commented: "I have since made inquiries and found that the Prince had not heard of the matter, and was very much annoyed over it."

Many other tidbits appeared in the local media during the week. One noted how three Fokkers bearing Iron Crosses had landed at Leaside, these likely being D.VII war prizes from Armour Heights or Camp Borden. A comparison of newspaper columns shows how one often disagreed with another as to the spellings of pilots' names, their nationalities, aircraft types, times en route, etc. As to Col Barker, from August 23

to September 6, 1919 he and wartime pilots Dallin, Hyde-Pearson and James were flying daily airshows in D.VIIs at the Canadian National Exhibition.

Anything like the New York-Toronto event, even local barnstorming, helped in laying the foundation for Canada's future in aviation. Ottawa was taking note of every event at home, and tracking overseas developments, especially in Great Britain and Europe. There, aviation's peacetime potential was being evaluated in a flurry of European route-proving and long-range endurance flights with such modified, war surplus types as Handley Page and Vickers bombers. Britain also was anxious to assist the dominions. It made generous gifts of airplanes and, in October 1919, its Controller-General of Civil Aviation, MGen Frederick Sykes, noted wisely from "across the pond" how aircraft might be used in Canada "to extend the influence of the railways", giving "an impetus to every branch of Canadian commerce". He specifically mused about an air link from Montreal to Canadian Pacific's Great Lakes steamship terminals from which passengers sailed to the lakehead, then reached Western Canada by rail. Sykes even urged communities across Canada to start thinking about putting in their own airfields. This was "pie in the sky" thinking, but shows that the wheels were turning.

Air Board Statistics
May 1 to October 31, 1920

Licenced aeroplanes	58
Floatplanes	4
Flying boats	8
Single-engine aeroplanes	70
Licenced commercial pilots	71
Licenced air engineers	60
Firms manufacturing aircraft	1
Firms operating aircraft	30
Flights made	18,671
Hours flown	6505
Average flight duration	21 min.
Passengers	15,265
Freight carried (lbs.)	6740
Aerodromes & seaplane bases	36
Total minor accidents	20
Total major accidents	14
Accidents involving death	5

As the years passed, the war surplus JN-4s began to fade, especially as designs such as the de Havilland Moth appeared. Each JN-4 had its own story. Tattered-looking JN-4 G-CABE began after the war with the F.G. Ericson organization. Ericson dealt in hundreds of JN-4s, whether Canadian or US in origin, or composite aircraft made from spare parts, rebuilt wrecks, etc. G-CABE first was with K.R. Kerr of Toronto in June 1925. It soon was sold to Jack Elliot of Hamilton, but at Chippawa, Ontario on August 22, 1927 was in an accident that killed passenger Stanley Bryusziewicz of Philadelphia and injured pilot F.W. "Fred" Hartwick of Hamilton. The wreck was rebuilt, joined the Leavens brothers in Belleville, Ontario in 1929, then was sold in Ohio in August 1930. Here it sits at the Leavens farm. (Alf Barton)

Alcock and Brown's converted Vickers F.B. 27 Vimy at Lester's Field at Quidi Vidi Lake outside St. John's. On June 14-15, 1919 it became the first aircraft to fly non-stop between the New and Old Worlds, completing the trip in 16:12 hours. First flown in November 1917, the Vimy was too late for wartime service. Basic specifications included: wing span 67' 2", length 43' 6.5", engines 2 x 360-hp Rolls-Royce Eagles, empty weight 5420 lb, gross weight 9120 lb. (LAC PA72433)

First Atlantic Crossings

Following the flight of the Vimy in 1919 came the first non-stop, east-west Atlantic aerial crossing. Although not involving Newfoundland or Canada directly, this event was closely watched by Ottawa and the world, for many in this era were anticipating great things for the airship in international travel.

His Majesty's Airship *R.34* had been launched in 1918. The war being over, however, it was loaned to the Air Ministry for endurance trials. After initial flight testing, on July 1, 1919 *R.34* was gassed to its limit with hydrogen, and fuelled with 6000 gallons of petrol. With 30 crew, early next morning it cast off from East Fortune, Scotland to cross to America.

By daybreak *R.34* was passing the Clyde and heading for open water. Twenty-four hours later it was half way en route, but headwinds were causing fuel anxiety. By the time the ship reached Labrador, it had been four days aloft and the crew was weary. Happily, *R.34* made destination after 108:12 hours. When it moored at Mineola, NY, a mere 140 gallons of fuel remained. In spite of a gruelling trip, *R.34* was in good condition. After refuelling, topping up with hydrogen from thousands of cylinders, and taking on other essentials, it cast off three days later. The return was made in 75:03 hours. All together *R.34* had covered 7420 miles at an average of 43 mph. Many aeronautical headlines were made in 1919, and the next decade would see more, as aviators sought successfully or tragically to conquer the Atlantic.

A fine painting of HMA *R.34* done by Canadian artist William J. Wheeler and presented by him to fellow CAHS member Jock Forteath, an *R.34* helmsman during the Atlantic venture. (Below) The great vessel being gassed by groundcrew using hundreds of cylinders. Then, *R.34* serenely aloft. (CANAV Col.)

America's Coup

With the war over, all aviation horizons were open so, when the London *Daily Mail* offered a £10,000 prize to the first who flew the Atlantic nonstop, aviators could not resist. Two well-financed teams quickly set up in Newfoundland, North America's nearest point to the Old World (departing from here assured aviators that they would have the Westerly Winds at their backs). Though not involved in the *Daily Mail* challenge, Canada understood how important aviation was going to be in its own future, so closely monitored events.

While the *Daily Mail* contenders prepared and fretted about a spate of hopeless weather, the US Navy also had an eye on the Atlantic, an interest closely linked to its new Navy Curtiss "NC" flying boat designed in Buffalo for anti-submarine warfare. Designated *NC-1*, the first example flew at Rockaway, New York on October 4, 1918. Three more NCs followed, but the war ended, leaving the fleet in limbo. A record-breaking flight of November 27, however, caught everyone's eye. Grossing 22,000 lb, *NC-1* carried 51 people on a single flight. Neither Curtiss nor the US Navy wanted to see such potential wasted and both sides knew of the *Daily Mail* challenge.

The US Navy now received permission to use the NCs on an independent trans-Atlantic attempt. They would fly the route planned in 1914 for the Curtiss *America*: Rockaway to Trepassey Bay in Newfoundland via

The Navy Curtiss *NC-4* – the first airplane to fly the Atlantic. Four "NCs" were built at war's end, the first flying from Jamaica Bay, NY, on October 4, 1918. The NCs were the largest US-built airplanes to date: wing span 126', length 68' 3", engines 4 x 400 hp Liberty, empty weight 15,900 lb, gross weight 27,400 lb. On May 8, 1919 three NCs departed to conquer the Atlantic. Two were lost en route, but *NC-4* reached Lisbon on the 27th. (US Navy NH44288)

The ill-fated US Navy blimp *C-5* moored near Quidi Vidi Lake. Then, an aerial view of the lake, looking eastward with the Atlantic Ocean just over the hills. The flat area on the left and near the mouth of the stream that enters the lake is where Rayham and Morgan crashed on takeoff. The *C-5* was moored in the same area but across the road (known today as The Boulevard). (K.M. Molson Col., EMR A4591-16)

Halifax, thence to the Azores, Lisbon and Plymouth. A USN destroyer would be positioned every 50 miles to aid in navigation and, if required, rescue. The flotilla (minus *NC-2* which had been damaged) took off at mid-morning on May 8, 1919. *NC-1* (LCMDR P.L.N. Bellinger) and *NC-3* (CMDR John Towers) made Halifax to refuel and rest overnight, but *NC-4* (LCMDR A.C. "Putty" Read) had to seek haven near Cape Cod. Engine repairs were made and it reached Halifax on the 9th to find the other NCs gone to Newfoundland.

Atlantic weather now kept the NCs at their buoys. A report of May 11, discussing the Navy's eagerness to get away, noted how "Commander Towers, the squadron commander, will not commit himself on this point, and refuses even to say whether he is awaiting the NC4." On the 15th *NC-1* and *NC-3* tried to get away, but menacing cross winds prevailed and the aircraft returned to shore just as *NC-4* arrived. About the same time the US Navy airship *C-5*, moored at nearby Quidi Vidi Lake at St. John's, was torn from its moorings. Two crewmen made a hasty escape, then *C-5* disappeared out to sea.

The NCs finally flew away at about 1800 hours on May 16. Several destroyers were passed, radio contact was positive if short-ranged, and all seemed fine until fog shrouded the sea. To get a bearing, LCMDR Bellinger landed *NC-1*, but the seas were so high that he could not safely get off again. Things went down hill as waves pounded *NC-1*. The steamer *Ionia* eventually rescued the crew, the destroyer USS *Fairfax* arrived, but *NC-1* was lost. Meanwhile, *NC-3* had taken a steer from a vessel which it mistook for a USN station-keeper, so it flew off course. CMDR Towers landed to try for a reliable bearing but, on touchdown, hit a swell, disabling two engines. *NC-3* then drifted for two days before Towers started his two good engines and taxied to Ponta Delgada in the Azores, arriving 52 hours after initially landing. The Toronto *Globe* of May 19 headlined its story "2 U.S. Planes Reach Azores NC-4 Arrives at Capital of Fayal Island in Excellent Form … NC-1 Is Safe – Third Machine Missing".

Although dogged by weather, *NC-4* and its 6-man crew had reached the Azores at noon on May 17 after a flight of 15:18 hours. Ten days later it made

NC-4 arrives in Lisbon on May 27, 1919. Four days later it was in Plymouth, England, from where it was shipped home. Displayed for a while in Central Park, NY, it was refurbished, made a goodwill tour in the southern US, then was placed in storage by the Smithsonian Institute. Today it is part of the collection at the National Naval Aviation Museum in Pensacola, Florida. (US Navy)

Lisbon, becoming the first airplane to fly the Atlantic. On May 31 it finally reached Plymouth. Back in Canada, J.A.D. McCurdy had followed the NC expedition. Now his comment of March 1910, while in Havana after his historic flight from Key West, rang especially true: "Although not disposed to make any wild calculations … I am seriously impressed with the possibility of making intercontinental, transocean flights by aeroplane."

The NC-4 crew at Lisbon on May 28, 1919: Chief E.C. Rhoads, Lt J.L. Breese, Lt W.K. Hinton, Lt E.F. Stone (USCG) and LCMDR A.C. Read. Missing is Ensign Rodd. (US Navy NH47280)

The Empire Answers

As the NCs were battling wind and wave, British contenders Harry Hawker, Kenneth Mackenzie-Grieve and their modified Sopwith Transport landplane *Atlantic* had been weather-bound in St. John's since early April. The crew had taken extra precautions – they would wear waterproof immersion suits and, mounted atop their rear fuselage, had a small lifeboat with provisions and survival gear. To lighten *Atlantic* and speed it on its way, their undercarriage would be jettisoned on lift-off. The test flight of *Atlantic* early in May was the first airplane flight for Newfoundland.

Also encamped in St. John's were Frederick P. Raynham and C.W.H. Morgan, whose aircraft was the Martinsyde landplane *Raymor*. The press kept an eagle eye on both teams, filing lengthy stories from St. John's,

sensationalizing them at every opportunity, e.g. the New York *Times* headline of April 12 blared "Planes Start Today on Win or Die Atlantic Flight".

Both British teams were downhearted when the NCs preceded them. Hawker and Mackenzie-Grieve, hoping perhaps to overtake "the Yanks", rushed into the air at mid-day on May 18. One reporter described the takeoff from their rough little Mount Pearl strip near St. John's: "Hawker got away in a lurching, 300-yard run, bumping hazardously over an uneven field …" A report in next day's Toronto *Globe* noted how they were "winging their way across the Atlantic tonight on the most perilous airplane flight in history" and expected to complete their mission in about 20 hours. The *Globe* added how Hawker's departure had "shattered" the hopes of Raynham and Morgan who, in panicking to get away the same day, crashed,

leaving Morgan badly injured.

Once the *Atlantic* had disappeared, the vigil began but, when word came, it was bad. The *Globe* headline for May 19 announced, "Argonauts of Atlantic Flight Fail to Reach British Coast". Much was made of the plane ditching a few miles off Ireland and how the Admiralty was claiming that the crew had been "picked up", but this was newspaper hogwash. By May 21 there still was no positive word and the press, always needing some angle, began blaming the Admiralty for not providing Hawker the same support that the NCs had enjoyed. Newspapers ranted on about patriotism, the Empire, brave young men being sacrificed, etc., while expressing disappointment that all the good leads had dried up. A May 21 report lamented how "Even the rumours which prevailed yesterday and last night have died down. There are no more reports like that which said the Sopwith

(Top and above) The doomed Sopwith *Atlantic* on May 18, 1919. Note the neatly-fitted lifeboat atop the fuselage. Then, Mackenzie-Grieve and Hawker in hand-me-down outfits soon after their rescue. (First 2 E.W. Stedman Col., Frank H. Ellis Col.)

The undercarriage of the *Atlantic* was jettisonned by Hawker after take-off, thus lightening and cleaning up the plane for its long flight. (LAC PA121883)

The Raynham-Morgan Martinsyde after its May 18, 1919 crash along the Quidi Vidi shore. The crowd milling around was typical for any aviation happening in these times. Following such a crash, a wreck often was scavenged by local souvenir hunters, but *Raymor* was well guarded and was soon rebuilt. (NMST 1908)

machine fell into the sea within sight of the River Shannon," as if any old rumour would do for a headline.

By May 23 the press had given up on Hawker and Mackenzie-Grieve, the *Globe* noting how "the loss of both brave explorers of the air has come to be sadly accepted" and how their fate "is no longer referred to or discussed". That King George V had sent condolences to Mrs. Hawker reinforced the sense that the pair was lost. Now the reporters camped in St. John's were writing glowingly about a new team just arrived to try the Atlantic in a Vickers Vimy. The *Globe* of the 23rd opened its item with "Other Airmen to Try Flight":

John Alcock and Albert Brown with team member Montague Couch (centre), while their Vimy was being erected at Pleasantville (Quidi Vidi) near St. John's. (CANAV Col.)

Captain Alcock, the Vimy bomber pilot, has arranged to take over the Sopwith airdrome on Mount Pearl, which is rapidly being denuded of all traces of the Sopwith expedition, for assembling the biplane which is expected late tonight on the Digby. From there he will fly "light" to Harbor Grace, provided he completes arrangements to share the

Handley Page field. Captain Raynham, amidst the hurried disassembling of the Martinsyde which crashed last Sunday, is still endeavoring by cable, to find a navigator competent both in that capacity and as an air pilot ...

Out of the blue, however, the press suddenly had a story to their liking – the international news of May 26 was all about Hawker and Mackenzie-Grieve being alive! Details of their salvation quickly spread. Soon after taking off, their radio equipment had failed. Their trip, however, ran smoothly in good weather, the *Atlantic* cruising for hours at 10,000 feet at 100 mph. But rain and rough skies took over, and the Sopwith's engine over-heated. Troubles endured through the night, then a new wall of weather loomed at sunrise of the 19th. Both men agreed that they could not last, so descended, scouring the roiling sea for a ship. When a freighter appeared, Hawker moved quickly, ditching just ahead of it. He and Mackenzie-Grieve launched their lifeboat and, after about

90 minutes, were picked up by the tramp steamer *Mary* en route from New Orleans and Norfolk to Scotland and Denmark. Hawker and Mackenzie-Grieve learned that they were 700 miles off Ireland and had covered about 1100 miles. A few days later they were aboard a Royal Navy vessel, then overnighted at Scapa Flow in the Orkneys. Hawker explained how the *Mary* had no radios, hence the long silence. He added that his 375-hp Rolls-Royce Eagle engine had been their salvation, since it had kept running even after the cooling system failed.

On May 28 Hawker and Mackenzie-Grieve were feted in London, met the NC-4 crew and received a £5000 *Daily Mail* "consolation prize". Each also received the Air Force Cross from King George V, this being the first award of a new decoration created for the RAF for "an act or acts of valour, courage or devotion to duty whilst flying, though not in active operations against the enemy". Next day Hawker made some unfortunate and ignorant remarks about the US Navy's stunning success with *NC-4*, stating how the American flight was hardly serious, since it had had so much support. Meanwhile, the *Atlantic*, which had remained afloat, was salvaged by the SS *Lake Charlottesville* and put ashore with its air mail at Falmouth.

The Handley Page, referred to above, was the 4-engine V/1500 *Atlantic* commanded by Vice-Admiral Sir Mark Kerr with the crew of Maj H.G. Brackley, DSO, DSC (pilot), Maj Tryggve Gran (navigator) and LCol E.W. Stedman, OBE

Views of the H.P. V/1500 during its June 10, 1919 shakedown flight at Harbour Grace. Powered by 4 x 375-hp Rolls-Royce engines, this was the largest aircraft entered in the 1919 *Daily Mail* trans-Atlantic challenge. (LAC PA22835, PA121926)

Alcock and Brown say goodbye to Newfoundland and prepare to face the Atlantic on June 14, 1919. (CANAV Col.)

(engineer). Others on the team included a telegraphist and a meteorologist. On May 2, 1919 the V/1500, modified with a 2000-gal fuel capacity and carrying radios and survival equipment, had left Liverpool aboard the SS *Digby*. Eight days later it was in St. John's from where it went straight by rail to Harbour Grace, about 20 miles from St. John's. There a rough 2700-foot strip was laid out. Brackley made a 5-hour test flight on June 13, but there was radiator trouble. Alternate radiators were en route aboard *Digby* but, due to fog, the ship only docked on June 14. By this time the Vimy had been assembled at Lester's Field, Quidi Vidi, and the airstrip made useable with the help of local people (property owner Charles F. Lester billed John Alcock $1345.10 for 2079 hours of labor at the going hourly rates of 40 cents and 330 hours at 25 cents).

On the day that *Digby* reached St. John's with Kerr's components, Alcock and Brown departed eastward. After 16:12 hours and 1800 miles, much in heavy weather, they landed in a bog near Clifden, Ireland, becoming the first aviators to span the Atlantic non-stop. "We have just come from Newfoundland", Alcock told the first of the locals to reach them. He later explained how their flight had been tough going:

We had a terrible journey. The wonder is we are here at all. We scarcely saw the sun or moon or stars ... for four hours our machine was covered in a sheet of ice ... An hour and a half before we saw land we had no idea where we were, but we believed we were at Galloway or thereabouts... Our flight has shown that the Atlantic flight is practicable, but I think it should be done not with an airplane or a seaplane, but with flying boats.

John Alcock and Arthur Brown received the £10,000 *Daily Mail* prize and were knighted by King George V. They were lauded everywhere, including in a Toronto *Globe* editorial of June 16, 1919:

The original Alcock and Brown Vimy as displayed today in the Science Museum in London, England. (Science Museum)

Their experience proved that a nonstop transatlantic air journey could be made ... [they] had the good fortune to reap the reward of their careful preparation, the staunchness of their machine and their own physical fitness and bravery... They have opened to all the world of commerce, science and travel, possibilities so great that the mind is almost dizzied by the vision of the aerial future.

Much was made of the boys being British, having a British airplane with British engines, and how "They have shown that the bulldog breed that held the seas and made the winning of the great war possible means to maintain the supremacy of the air." The editor then referred his readers to Rudyard Kipling's futuristic 1905 short story "With the Night Mail: A Story of 2000 A.D." describing the imaginative overnight voyage of a London-Quebec City mail-carrying airship. Unfortunately, in the ancient tradition of the Canadian media, the editor also made sure to take some ignorant jabs at the Americans, slagging their success with *NC-4*. The Alcock and Brown Vimy today is in the Science Museum in London.

Following the Vimy's success, Sir Mark Kerr scrapped his trans-oceanic

The mighty V/1500 after coming to grief at Parrsboro, Nova Scotia. It was repaired, made some trial flights in the US, then was wrecked in a landing mishap. (E.W. Stedman Col.)

plan and took the V/1500 to the US on some air freighting trials. This began with a July 4, 1919 flight to New York that ended in a crash-landing near Parrsboro, Nova Scotia. The aircraft was repaired over the next four months, made it to New York, conducted several flights carrying hefty loads, but was wrecked on landing one night near Cleveland, Ohio. Of the V/1500's stalwart crew, E.W. Stedman, settled in Canada and quickly rose to prominence in the RCAF.

Vimy Reborn

Generations after Alcock and Brown, Californian Peter McMillan decided to build a Vimy replica to re-enact some of the 1919-20 *Daily Mail* challenges.

Under the supervision of John LaNoue, components were fabricated in Australia and in Sonoma, California and, in less than two years, a new Vimy was ready. As much as possible the replica met Vickers specs, e.g. using cotton fabric covering, even though the fuselage was of metal framing compared to the original wood. Christened *Silver Queen II*, the aircraft flew at Hamilton AFB, California on July 30, 1994.

An experimental certificate of airworthiness was granted and, after the necessary tests, the Vimy flew to the UK aboard a USAF C-5A Galaxy. Peter McMillan now prepared to re-enact an historic November/December 1919 Vimy flight by brothers Ross and Keith Smith with two mechanics – the first

flight between England and Australia. The odyssey departed Farnborough on September 11, 1994. After many stops en route, *Silver Queen II* touched down in Darwin on October 22. From June 1 to July 29, 1999 it also covered the London-to-Capetown route flown in 1920 by the original *Silver Queen*.

Flown by Mark Rebholz and John LaNoue, *Silver Queen II* arrived at Oshkosh from California on July 23, 2001. Over several days and 37 flying hours en route, they had watched the weather closely, Rebholz explaining in Oshkosh's *AirVenture Today*: "Because of the airplane's low performance, weather and winds that aren't a problem for other airplanes will ground us." He explained about the dreadful visibility from the cockpit, and how the second crewman always occupied the observer's nose position to act as extra eyes. He also described the Vimy's large and difficult ailerons: "That was an attempt to improve the roll rate, but all it did was make the ailerons very heavy, and introduce a large amount of adverse yaw. A small aileron deflection in this thing requires a bunch of rudder to get it to turn." *AirVenture* explained how the skills needed to fly the Vimy were "typically those required to fly a low-performance tail-dragger that has very light wing loading." All this made anyone appreciate the realities of fighting a war in such a machine more than 80 years earlier.

The Vimy replica NX71MY taxies at Downsview during a June 1, 2005 visit to the Toronto Aerospace Museum. Following its trans-Atlantic crossing from Newfoundland on July 2, it was donated to the Brooklands Museum in England. For 2009 it was on based at Duxford for a final series of demo flights. Crewed by pilots John Dodd and Clive Edwards, the Vimy crossed on June 11 to Galoway, Ireland to commemorate the 90th anniversary of the Alcock and Brown flight. It flew back to Duxford on June 15, the plan being for it to retire permanently to Brooklands at season's end. (Larry Milberry)

Vimy pilots Mark Rebholz and Steve Fossett at the TAM. Fossett commented at this time how their Vimy was a very basic flying machine, not pleasant to handle, and not likely flyable on one engine. The great aerial adventurer Fossett died in a light plane crash along the California-Nevada border on September 3, 2008. (Larry Milberry)

A standard Vimy *circa* 1918, then *Silver Queen II* on the runway at Downsview on June 1, 2005. From here it flew to Ottawa, Quebec and St. John's, then conquered the Atlantic on July 2. (CANAV Col., Larry Milberry)

On May 24, 2005 *Silver Queen II* again was at Oshkosh in advance of the last of its great *Daily Mail* re-enactments – the Alcock and Brown crossing. Piloted by Mark Rebholz and Dan Downs, on May 25 it continued via London to Downsview in Toronto, where Steve Fossett joined the team. He already had twice circumnavigated the globe – by hot-air balloon and airplane. Fossett contributed $150,000 to the Vimy project.

Rebholz and Fossett carried on to Ottawa, Quebec and St. John's, from where they intended to fly the Atlantic, as had Alcock and Brown, on June 14. But technical problems and weather delayed them until late on July 2. Happily, the crossing was smooth and their landing on Connemara golf course at Clifden, Ireland, a good one. They had covered some 1500 nm in 17:00 hours. In 2006 Peter McMillan donated *Silver Queen II* to the International Society of Transport Aircraft Trading of Chicago, which handed it over to the Brooklands Museum of Weybridge, Surrey, UK, located on the very airfield where Vimys had been built in WWI.

First Trans-Canada Flight

Beginning immediately after the war, the press in Canada was enthusiastically reporting pretty well every aviation event. Typical was one of August 7, 1919, operated on behalf of the Aerial League of Canada, an organization formed in Vancouver in February of the same year. With sponsorship from the Vancouver *Daily World* and newspapers in Calgary and Edmonton, Capt Ernest C. Hoy, DFC, set off in a JN-4 at 0413 hours from Minoru Park, Vancouver. He flew via Vernon, Grand Forks, Cranbrook and Lethbridge to Calgary, where he landed in Bowness Park at dusk. This had taken 16:42 hours, including 12:34 aloft and was the first time that Canada's western mountain region had been over-flown. Feted and rested, Hoy set off for Vancouver on August 11, but only got as far as Golden, where he crashed on takeoff, so had to complete his journey by train.

Vimy Replica Specs	
Length	43' 6"
Wing span	68'
Height	16' 4"
Cruise speed	75 mph
Stall speed	40 mph
Empty weight	7642 lb
Gross weight	12,500 lb
Ceiling (at 9000 lb)	13,800'
Fuel	2400 lb
Power	2 x Orenda OE ea. 600 hp

Capt Ernest Hoy, first to overfly the Canadian Rockies, is seen at Bowness Park, Calgary during his historic August 7, 1919 trans-mountain venture. Then, Hoy departs for Vancouver on August 11. His trip had been organized by the Aerial League of Canada, an organization formed in Vancouver in February 1919. (CANAV Col., Glenbow Archives N16-625)

By far the most ambitious postwar Canadian civil aviation venture was organized by the Air Board – the first trans-Canada flight. Already contemplating future air mail, even passenger services, Ottawa was anxious to complete a cross-country survey. Such a flight would provide knowledge about geography and weather, and raise public awareness about air transportation. The venture commenced with HS-2L proving flights in July and August 1920 between Halifax-Roberval, and Halifax-Ottawa. The big flight finally commenced in Halifax on October 7, when LCol Robert Leckie and Maj Basil Hobbs took off in a Fairey seaplane to fly to Ottawa. Mechanical problems, however, led to a heavy landing on the Saint John River. The Fairey was a dead loss, so HS-2L G-CYAG came up from Halifax to replace it. By day's end Leckie and Hobbs had reached Rivière-du-Loup, landing on the St. Lawrence River in darkness.

On October 8 Capt H.A. Wilson delivered a Felixstowe F.3 flying boat from Montreal to Rivière-du-Loup, then took the HS-2L back to Halifax. Leckie, Hobbs and air engineer Heath now set off. After several hours of bucking headwinds, they landed on the Ottawa River to be greeted by such dignitaries as J.A. Wilson, secretary of the Air Board. Capt G.O. Johnson joined the crew. At 0830 next day they departed westward to trace the ancient canoe route once used by the *coureurs de bois*. They landed at Sault Ste. Marie at 1700.

On October 10 the F.3 crossed Lake Superior, passed the Lakehead and made Kenora for fuel. At day's end it was tied

Derived from a successful wartime line, the Fairey IIIC came too late for combat. This long-range version was in Newfoundland in 1919 to compete in the *Daily Mail* challenge. When Alcock and Brown settled that issue, it was acquired by the Canadian Air Board and stored in Montreal. The Air Board decided to fly the Fairey non-stop Halifax-Winnipeg on the first leg of its planned trans-Canada flight. The route was amended to Halifax-Ottawa and the plane set off on October 7, 1920. It barely had crossed the Bay of Fundy when mechanical trouble forced it out of the game. (DND RE11710-3)

The Trans-Canada Flight F.3 at Kenora's Government Dock on October 10. Such a red letter event drew most of the townspeople down for a look. Atop the hill beyond is Notre Dame church. Down the hill is the subway for road traffic going under the CPR tracks. To the right is the Matheson Street bridge. (Lake of the Woods Museum)

Trans-Canada flight F.3 G-CYBT attracts a crowd on the Red River near Selkirk, Manitoba on October 10, 1920. The Air Board was quick to replace its F.3s with HS-2Ls. In the case of 'BT, it was struck off strength in September 1922. (DND AH-88)

up on the Red River at Selkirk. On the 11th Leckie and Hobbs made the short hop up-river to Winnipeg, from where they entrained for Vancouver. Henceforth, D.H.9s would cover the prairies and mountains. Early on October 11, wartime pilots Capt J.B. Home-Hay and LCol Arthur Tylee, commander of the Canadian Air Force, took off from Winnipeg in G-CYAN. They were just passing Regina when engine trouble forced them down. G-CYAJ was rushed from nearby Moose Jaw, then Capt C.W. Cudmore and Tylee proceeded to Calgary. Finally, on October 13 Capt G.A. Thompson and Tylee departed in G-CYBF. Routing via Field and Golden, they were obliged by weather to stop near Revelstoke. On the 15th they reached Merritt, where they again were storm-bound. Finally, on the 17th they bashed through more weather to refuel at Agassiz and, later in the day, landed on the racetrack in Richmond, near Vancouver. In 11 days the pilots of the first trans-Canada flight had logged some 45 hours, covered 3265 miles and had demonstrated the feasibility of trans-Canada air operations. Even so, 20 years would pass before such flights would be common.

From Winnipeg the Trans-Canada Flight continued with D.H.9s. G-CYAJ, shown here, flew the Regina - Calgary leg. 'BF then finished the odyssey, going all the way to Vancouver. (DND)

Some of the D.H.9 men at Winnipeg with G-CYAN: Capt J.B. Home-Hay (pilot, front cockpit), mechanic Sgt W. Young (rear cockpit), Capt G.H. Pitt, mechanic J. Crowe, Capt C.W. Cudmore, mechanic J. McLaughlin and LCol A.K. Tylee. (DND)

Other Early Flights

Aviation headlines and stories became commonplace in immediate post-WWI times. One of these with Canadian content ended badly: On May 28, 1919 Mansell R. James, DFC, of Watford, Ontario, came first in a race from Atlantic City to Boston. He won the $5000 Pulitzer Prize, $1000 from the *Boston Globe*, and took the Pan-American Aeronautic Convention gold medal for the greatest distance flown – 340 miles. Sadly, though, James disappeared next day in his Sopwith Camel. He had been returning to Atlantic City, from where he planned to fly to Toronto via Cleveland and Detroit. During the war, James had flown Camels on 45 Squadron in Italy. The citation to his DFC of September 1918 notes: "An excellent scout pilot who has at all times shown great skill, courage and determination in attacking enemy machines. During a short period of time he has destroyed nine enemy aeroplanes." Hundreds of brave young wartime fliers would meet similar fates, as aviation around the world sought new roles in the peacetime environment.

In other early events involving Canada, on August 29, 1919 US Air Service pilot Maj J.W. Simmons and his passenger made the first non-stop flight from Toronto to New York in 3:44 hours. Routing via Fredericton, Quebec City and Montreal in an HS-2L, on August 26-28, 1920 Capt H. Allan Wilson completed the first Halifax-Ottawa flight.

In July 1921 Clarence O. Prest and Morton Bach set off from Mexico to fly a JN-4 to Siberia. Crossing Canada they made stops in Lethbridge and Edmonton on August 16. They continued to Hazelton and Prince Rupert, where their plane was wrecked in a wind storm. (The following summer Prest planned to fly from New York to Nome, Alaska. Having departed Dawson City, Yukon, he crashed in the mountains, but was rescued.)

On April 6, 1924 four float-equipped US Army Air Service Douglas Air Cruisers stopped at Prince Rupert after leaving Seattle on a 5-month round-the-world venture, but two aircraft were lost en route. On their return, the surviving planes crossed from Greenland to Indian Harbour, Labrador on August 31, refuelled at Pictou, Nova Scotia on September 3 and were back in Seattle on September 28. On August 12, 1925 two US Navy Loening amphibians under LCMDR Richard E. Byrd landed at Hayes Fiord on Ellesmere Island. This is noted as the first presence of airplanes in the Canadian Arctic. Frank Ellis' *Canada's Flying Heritage* is the best all-in-one source covering such long-distance flying relating to Canada.

Even by the mid-1920s aviation in Canada remained somewhat stymied, regardless of headline-grabbing events. Two key factors explained this. First, there were almost no purpose-built commercial or club airplanes on the market, only war surplus types that had to be adapted one way or another to peacetime uses. Second, nearly all pilots

had been trained for combat, not peace. The great Canadian bush flying pioneer, W.J. McDonough, addressed this in his 1930 book *Airmanship*. His wartime peers would have winced at his candid explanation:

It is sad, but true to relate, that a large percentage of present-day pilots (even amongst the best), are lamentably ignorant of the most elementary factors concerning aeroplanes and their proper maintenance. This situation has, of course, been largely created by the late war, which called for a particular type of pilot – a type of war machine, so to speak … Courage and implicit obedience were his essentials, but complete resourcefulness and adaptability to all and every situation, and a studied knowledge of his aeroplane and engine … were neither required nor expected… those who are contemplating taking up commercial aviation as a profession [should] realize the fact that the actual flying will be but a small part of the duties of the future commercial pilot who expects to command a good salary.

McDonough's assessment gradually would be appreciated. With the flying club movement, for example, a new breed of pilot would be trained for commercial flying, one that was adaptable beyond the "stick and rudder" part of things. Meanwhile, new aircraft designs were bringing welcomed safety to operations as well as improved profits throughout the industry.

The customized Prest-Morton biplane "Polar Bear" at Prince Rupert in July 1921. A Californian, Prest was doing air shows as early as 1909 in such places as Las Vegas. In spite of his devil-may-care life in aviation, he survived to 1954. Morton Bach operated a successful airplane design firm in Santa Monica, but must have been a character himself to join Prest on his zany Alaska adventures. (CANAV Col.)

Aeromarine, one of North America's earliest scheduled airlines, had a fleet of civilianized, ex-US Navy F-5s and HS-2Ls. The company survived for a few years, but its war surplus planes were impractical for long-service, and accidents brought devastating headlines. F-5 *Santa Maria*, seen in Toronto Bay during its visit of May 1921, may have been one of the 30 or so built by Canadian Aeroplanes Ltd. The inscription on the rear fuselage reads "U.S. Cuban Mail Service". (Toronto Harbour Commissioners Archives)

Commercial Aviation Inches Along

Commercial aviation in Canada initially moved at a snail's pace. Naturally, there was a "first" here and a "first" there, as in the case of one go-getter – Ervin E. "Ned" Ballough of Daytona, Florida. Ballough had been taught to fly in 1912 by Ruth Law. In 1917 he joined the RFC (Canada) as a mechanic, then earned his wings and instructed at Deseronto. Besides being a good aviator, he excelled in athletics, wing walking included.

Postwar, Ballough purchased a JN-4 in Toronto. Getting ready to return home, he scouted around for a last-minute opportunity and found a customer willing to pay to get a load of furs delivered in a hurry. On May 5, 1919 Ballough loaded 150 lb of raw furs. Flying via Watertown, NY, he delivered these to a client in Elizabeth, NJ. So far as is known, this was the first Canada-US trans-border commercial flight. Ballough later did photo-mapping for the city of Minneapolis, did air courier jobs for news agencies, patrolled power lines, flew in the 1927 New York-to-Spokane

There were many early experiments with commercial aviation in Canada, including an inaugural Estevan, Saskatchewan-to-Winnipeg of October 1, 1924. The ambitious flight was arranged to promote commercial development in Estevan, a growing agricultural and coal-mining centre. Here, F/L Edgar A. Alton of Winnipeg (Canadian pilot licence No.14) takes aboard a mail bag. Unfortunately, he did not get far in his Standard J-1 G-CACA. After only about 14 miles he had to land near Bienfait with engine trouble. On taking off again, he crashed, wrecking the plane. The mail later reached Winnipeg by train. Inset, one of the 1296 letters carried by F/L Alton. Such items are today classified by the aero-philatelists as "Canadian crash covers" and are especially collectable. (via Richard K. Malott)

air derby and, ultimately, became famous with Eastern Air Lines.

On a grander scale was a consideration in late 1920 by Canada Steamship Lines to run a fleet of large Vickers seaplanes on a Toronto-Montreal-New York summer service. Not surprisingly, this idea never left the board room, and it

In 1919 Britain's Controller-General of Civil Aviation recommended an air link between southern and northern Ontario and the prairies beyond. Long before the days of air travel across the area, the S.S. *Keewatin* was one of the great Canadian Pacific Railway vessels by which passengers could bridge the gap between Georgian Bay and upper Lake Superior (otherwise, the route was by rail). The coming of regular air service across Canada in the 1940s, then the completion of the Trans-Canada Highway around Lake Superior *circa* 1960, spelled the end of regular passenger steamships on the Great Lakes. The 350-foot, 3856-ton, 288-passenger *Keewatin* was built in Scotland in 1907. Here, it sails out of Port Arthur-Fort William on August 17, 1963, two years before retirement. In 1967 the grand ship, last of the breed on the Great Lakes, became a museum at Sauatuck-Douglas, Michigan. (Larry Milberry)

The "Aeromarine Aerial Cruiser" *Santa Maria* tied up at the Toronto Harbour Commission on Toronto Bay. The pride of the fleet, *Santa Maria* was christened on October 23, 1920, then inaugurated Key West-Havana service on November 1. In 2009 the THC building still served its original purpose. However, due to post-1921 land filling, it was by then far from the water's edge. (Toronto Harbour Commissioners Archives)

would be years before such operations came to Canada. In the US, however, airlines already were a reality and, in the case of Aeromarine Airways, there were Canadians involved. Formed in October 1920, Aeromarine was one of America's first scheduled carriers. Operations commenced with flights between Key West and Havana using ex-military flying boats. Mail and passengers were carried, the fare for the 60-minute flight (8 hours by sea) being $75.00.

On May 9, 1921 the company's "Aeromarine Model 75" *Santa Maria* left Keyport, New Jersey with 3 crew and 11 passengers to begin a Great Lakes tour. *Santa Maria* had begun as a Curtiss/Felixstowe F-5L, a type built in Toronto by Canadian Aeroplanes Ltd. in 1918. The Model 75 had been converted in Keyport for 11 passengers by Aeromarine Plane and Motor Co. For this occasion it would be evaluating potential summer business in the Great Lakes, when tourism was quiet in Florida. Piloting *Santa Maria* was Theodore L. Tibbs, formerly of Montreal and a wartime veteran.

Over the previous winter he had flown 96 trips between Havana and Key West. After stops at Albany, Lake George and Plattsburg, Tibbs headed for Montreal. The Toronto *Globe* reported in a May 10 story:

The Santa Maria, a 15-passenger aeromarine, arrived here tonight, three hours late on the final leg of the New York-Montreal flight from Plattsburg. The delay was caused by difficulties in securing the special highly volatile gasoline needed by aeroplanes. Capt. Tibbs, pilot in charge of the airship, stated tonight that the actual flying time taken for the trip from New York had been five hours 42 minutes.

The party on the airship included Hon. Edward E. Coffin, former Chairman of the United States Air Craft Board, and Mrs. Coffin, and Dr. Inches, Commissioner of Police, Detroit. The party proceeded to the Windsor

Canadian Theodore L. Tibbs flew with Aeromarine from October 1920 to May 1921. (CANAV Col.)

Hotel, where they were met by Governor Griesbeck of Michigan, and W.E. Metzger of the Detroit Athletic Club, who will go with the rest of the party on to Detroit.

The aeromarine took the water here at 5:10 and her speed was so great that she taxied down stream for a mile before her pilot could turn her back to the canal basin, her destination, and it was 6:30 before the party were brought ashore in a motorboat. She will set out tomorrow morning for Toronto and Buffalo.

In the September 1999 edition of *L'Avion*, the Montreal CAHS chapter newsletter, Quebec aviation historian George A. Fuller added to this story:

In the late afternoon of Tuesday, May 10th, 1921, Montrealers got their first look at a true airliner. Coming from the north, a big twin-engined biplane flying boat, painted white and black, took a wide circle over the harbour and made its final approach over the river downstream into the wind. It alighted between Jacques Cartier Pier and Île Ste-Hélène and ran about a mile before turning to follow the Montreal Harbour Board's tug, Sir Hugh Allan, which carried part of the welcoming committee. Near the entrance to the *Lachine Canal* it was taken in tow by a motor boat to a mooring site in calmer water close to the South Shore, off what was then known as the *Île-aux-Millions*. Its passengers were then taken by launch to a dock at the foot of McGill Street.

Meanwhile, the *Globe* of May 12, 1921 reported:

The Santa Maria is one of the 36 large seaplanes constructed by the Canadian Aeroplanes Ltd. for the United States Government at its Toronto factory at the corner of Dufferin street and Lappin avenue... This trip is in the nature of a demonstration to show the capabilities of the machine and to attract possible buyers. There is a possibility of some of these seaplanes being purchased for use in transporting prospectors and supplies to the newly-discovered Fort Norman oil fields.

After engine repairs in Montreal, *Santa Maria* departed on May 13, first making a hop to Lac St-Louis to collect nine passengers, then flying west to Belleville on the Lake Ontario shore. There it overnighted, then flew to Toronto on the 14th. The press was on hand as *Santa Maria* tied up at the Toronto Harbour Commissioners building. One newspaper story ("Giant Air Cruiser Visits Toronto, Makes Trip from Belleville in One Hour and Forty Minutes") noted: "There are two cabins on the Santa Maria, and the appointments are luxurious, the interior being in mahogany and silver. There are six comfortable reclining chairs in the forward cabin, while the after cabin is fitted up as a lounge and smoking room with accommodation for five and conveniences for card-playing and writing."

Capt Tibbs commented before leaving for Buffalo, "We could start a service between Toronto and Buffalo if Toronto were wet" (this was the era of prohibition in Canada). Aboard for Buffalo was LCol Thomas Gibson, president of the Aero Club of Canada. *Santa Maria* completed its mission in New Orleans on September 27, having covered 900 miles in 20 weeks. Next summer the company operated on the Great Lakes, including between Detroit and Cleveland, which

was dubbed "The Ninety Minute Line". For a $25.00 ticket, a passenger could fly this 95-mile route in 90 minutes, compared to slower rail at $9.00 or steamship at $5.00. In winter, the flying boats returned south to serve such routes as the "High Ball Express" – New York to Havana in two days via Atlantic City, Beaufort, Miami and Key West.

Although off to a promising start, Aeromarine failed in 1924. Since 1920 it had carried some 30,000 passengers on scheduled routes, thousands more on charters and sightseeing, but accidents marred the company's reputation, spoiling its motto: "Thousands of passengers carried. Not a single mishap." On July 9, 1921, for example, *Santa Maria* was taking off near the head of Belle Island in the Detroit River when it ran over a rowboat. Occupants Arthur Hettinger and Arthur Drischm were killed, and *Santa Maria* was towed to shore for repairs. Even worse, when the Model 75 *Columbus* foundered off Cuba in January 1923, four passengers died. On February 23, 1923 Capt Tibbs (no longer with Aeromarine) and Delos Thomas were lost while flying between Bimini Island and Stuart, Florida.

Air Charter Pioneers

While they barnstormed and traded in war surplus planes, Billy Bishop and William Barker also organized one of Canada's first air taxi services. Over the 1920 summer season, their 3-passenger HS-2Ls plied a busy route between Toronto Bay and the Muskoka resort area a hundred miles to the north (they also were selling war surplus material and had a contract painting streetcars for the Toronto Transit Commission, so were juggling various balls). This kept their names in the press, but the day came when the headlines were not so rosy. On

September 10, 1920 pilot, engineer and two passengers were aboard Bishop-Barker HS-2L G-CADB flying from Orillia to Toronto. Sad to say, their engine failed and they ended in the trees at Bickle's Wood, near Brooklin, Ontario. Pilot R.F. McRae and engineer R.S. Baker were hurt, but not passengers Leonard Cairn and William Thompson.

One newspaper quoted McRae as claiming that all would have gone well had a stand of trees not gotten in his way! Naturally, Bishop defended his operation, stating how an HS-2L could "volplane" (glide) quite a distance without power, adding: "I might say that since May 1 we have carried 2,450 people and have flown 30,500 miles without a breakage of any sort … the other day I read an account of five people being killed by motors in Toronto over one week-end." The following May there was further misery when HS-2L G-CADM force-landed in Lake Ontario. Then, on August 31, 1921 a Bishop-Barker hangar burned at Armour Heights with the loss of an airplane valued at $5000. Of the ditching, the *Globe* reported:

Running out of gasoline, a seaplane belonging to the Bishop-BarkerCompany and containing Col Barker, VC, and two other occupants, was compelled to light on the lake near Scarboro Bluffs and about a mile off shore yesterday afternoon. The party was bound for Belleville on a trial trip. The plane was one of the latest acquisitions of the company. It was thought that there was sufficient petrol to carry it to Oshawa for replenishment. The supply, however, gave out when the machine was over the lake but, fortunately, near enough to land to be observed by Constable Stevens, who telephoned the life saving station at Ward's Island.

One of the Bishop-Barker HS-2Ls. By the looks of the surroundings, it could be somewhere in the Muskoka area. (William J. Wheeler Col.)

A unique Bishop-Barker escapade took place October 17-19, 1919 when the company chartered two JN-4s to a provincial referendum committee. In an upcoming election, the public would decide on the wider sale of alcoholic drink; the committee was determined to get its booze message spread. Leaflets (dubbed "aerograms") were printed with a message reading in part: "October 20 is your day … Will you expose your own child to the temptation and misery of booze? Your vote will decide for home and country. Mark your ballot as shown on the opposite side of this message."

On October 17 a JN-4 crewed by Capt Pearson and Lt Kissock left Armour Heights to cover points west, while pilot Allan G. McLerie and mechanic Gifford began in the second plane from Peterborough. Each commenced with 30,000 aerograms to scatter over designated communities. On October 18 the Toronto *Globe* outlined Pearson's route of the previous day: "Leaving Armour Heights at noon they flew northward toward Newmarket, dropping their messages on the villages as they passed along. They alighted at various points for fresh supplies and were expected to make Barrie before nightfall. Today they will continue on their journey, touching at … Collingwood, Goderich, Sarnia, Chatham, London, St. Thomas, Durham, Windsor." Come October 20 and Ontarians turfed out the reigning Conservatives, elected a new United Farmers government and voted emphatically as the referendum committee had hoped.

Pioneer Forestry Project or Scam?

Immediately after the war, Canada's wood products industry realized that airplanes could be useful surveying forest tracts and watersheds, helping fight forest fires, etc. An early venture was a survey on coastal Labrador, part of the British colony of Newfoundland. According to some ambiguous and sensational press reports, the survey was organized by Capt Daniel Owen of Annapolis Royal, Nova Scotia. Owen was typical of hundreds of wartime veterans who would give civil aviation a try. Most had been in combat, so came home with valuable skills in the air. In Owen's case, he had served in the RFC

on 84, then 28 and 55 squadrons. While on a raid to Courtrai railway station in France on October 7, 1917, he and his observer, W. Osborne, had tangled with some fighters. Osborne shot down one in flames and sent another out of control. On another operation, Owen was injured by enemy fire, became a POW, then may have escaped, as he later was reported interned in Holland.

On behalf of the Southern Labrador Pulp and Paper Co. of Boston, in 1919 Owen acquired two JN-4s from F.G. Ericson of Toronto. The aircraft were under the "H.V. Greene Aerial Survey Company" banner (Greene seems to have been a Boston stock promoter – the details in such stories often are fuzzy after so many decades). The planes were shipped to Annapolis Royal and test flown by American pilots from an improvised airfield The 109-foot steamer *Granville* was chartered to support the expedition. When it sailed on July 7 under Capt I.C. Rhude, five pilots, two mechanics, a rigger, a forester, a physician, a cook, and two photographers were reportedly aboard.

At the same time, the "North American Securities Corp." was running newspaper ads hawking shares in the "Southern Labrador Pulp and Lumber Co.", claiming rights to 1.5 million acres of Labrador forest, etc. Owen and company gained much publicity in numerous Atlantic and national newspapers, which would have boosted interest in the scheme. There also was a plan to provide daily updates of the expedition's progress.

On July 20 the *Granville* anchored in Battle Harbour about 80 miles up the coast from the Quebec-Labrador boundary. The aircraft were put ashore and assembled on a beach, which also served as the airstrip for the JN-4s. It later was claimed that all the surveying was completed in 10 flying days with no major holdups. Owen is said to have taken the photos directly to Boston by boat, arriving on August 26. He noted that all the work was done using just one airplane, said to have been equipped with a radio.

Owen is said to have moved to Boston in the fall of 1919 where, according to the Nova Scotia *Spectator* of September 18, 1919, "he will make his future headquarters as president of at least two multi-million dollar corporations". But Owen mainly is noted as practicing law in Annapolis in the 1920s. In researching this

story, K.M. Molson noted that, other than Owen (who died in 1939), he had been unable to find anyone from the alleged expedition. The only "facts" had been those released by Owen and associates. Happily for them, these had been enthusiastically hyped by the newspapers, e.g., the claim that 15,000 photos had been taken by one plane in a few days (an impossibility). As to any follow-up by the "Southern Labrador" company, nothing seems to have taken place. In this case, one might be excused for wondering if the whole enterprise might have been nothing but a stock swindle.

Bush Flying: Quebec Leads

In March 1919 the *Canadian Forestry Journal* was lamenting how Ottawa was not supporting Quebec's plan to use airplanes in forestry, "even though public owned hydro-planes are lying useless in their hangars in Nova Scotia, and skilled pilots are kicking their heels and aching for some form of active service." Later that year the St. Maurice Forestry Protective Association was formed under the leadership of Ellwood Wilson, a Philadelphian and chief forester at the Laurentide Company of Grand-Mère, Quebec. Such a forward thinker was Wilson that, as early as 1906, he had proposed tethered balloons for doing forest inventories.

In 1919 Laurentide acquired on loan two of the ex-US Navy HS-2Ls stored in Dartmouth, Nova Scotia. How this door opened is explained in the Toronto *Globe* of May 2, 1919: "To render the enterprise possible, the Quebec Government and the St. Maurice Forestry Protective Association volunteered to pay the maintenance of machines and pilots. The Acting Minister of Marine and Fisheries, Hon. A.K. Maclean, accepted the proposal, and ordered the machines released from their sheds ..." From June 5 to 8 former RNAS pilot Stuart Graham, his wife and mechanic Bill Kahre delivered HS-2L A-1876 to Lac-à-la-Tortue at Grand-Mère. Their trip – Canada's longest cross-country flight to date – covered 645 miles over 9:45 hours at an average of 66 mph. A-1878 followed from Dartmouth and a useful flying season ensued. On July 7 an HS-2L crew became the first in Canada to report a forest fire from the air. Writing in the *Canadian Aircraft Operator* of May 1, 1980, K.M. Molson

Still carrying its US Navy wartime markings, the first St. Maurice Forestry Protective Association HS-2L (later G-CAAC *La Vigilance*) is launched at Dartmouth. Stuart Graham soon flew it to Lac-à-la-Tortue. (CANAV Col.)

described another detail of this first season – how one of the H-boats had become sluggish to handle:

The reason was that water was accumulating in the hull sponsons. In naval service the aircraft was intended to be beached and the sponsons drained by removing plugs below the waterline. This was not possible owing to the lack of a ramp. All flying stopped and everyone pitched in to complete the facilities. The hull was then drained and flying resumed on the 20th of July.

The great Canadian bush flying pioneer Stuart Graham. Here he is on the float of a CCA Waco *circa* 1935. (NMST 23470)

railroads and transmission lines could be planned, etc. On a single flight at 5000 feet, an area ¾ x 60 miles could be covered using a roll of 100 negatives. In the

Canadian Forestry Journal of January 1920 Stuart Graham summarized the overall process:

We have shown that fires can be sighted from the air and rapidly

reported or extinguished in an efficient manner ... We have proven the value of aerial photography and shown the cheapness of this method of mapping ... we have constructed the necessary station equipment for carrying out the flying with boat type machines and have found out and overcome most of the faults of these machines.

Nonetheless, the SMFPA dissolved so, for the new season, only the Laurentide Company conducted air operations. Its two H-boats had been overhauled in the previous winter, and now were registered under the Canadian Air Board as G-CAAC and ’AAD. In July 1920 Stuart Graham flew out a party to stake mineral claims, an event that is considered another "first" for the airplane in Canada. In September,

By season's end the H-boats had made 57 flights entailing about 80 flying hours. Great forest tracts had been sketched and some 380 photos taken using an Eastman K1 aerial camera. The SMFPA seemed pleased with the season's results, e.g. how a single mission could provide an observer a fabulous view of the country, its extent and accessibility. Trees could be classified by type, age, accessability; gravel and water supplies could be pinpointed; future dam sites, roads,

The famous G-CAAC hauled out for servicing at its Lac-à-la-Tortue base. The remains of *La Vigilance* and its full-scale replica are with the Canada Aviation Museum. (William J. Wheeler Col.)

A well-known photo of Laurentide HS-2L G-CACX showing the plane ready for a trip and everyone decked out with warm clothing and goggles. In the rear cockpit are engineer A.L. Harvey and pilot J. Scott Williams, MC, AFC, MiD. Postwar, Williams had served in the nascent Canadian Air Force. (CANAV Col.)

Graham took delivery in New York of a Curtiss Seagull, a new, smaller, more efficient type. The 1920 season resulted in 34 fires reported by air, and some 3000 aerial photos taken. Seventy flights and 150 flying hours were recorded. Bill Kahre received his air engineer's licence that summer, Stuart Graham his commercial pilot's licence in the fall.

Roy Maxwell replaced Graham as chief pilot for 1921. Formerly an RFC (Canada) instructor, in 1919 he and H.D. Wiltshire of Montreal had been barnstorming with two JN-4s in Hamilton. They did well at this and expanded into aerial filming. In 1920 Maxwell acquired HS-2L G-CAAZ via Aeromarine Engineering and Sales of New York. On August 7 he and engineer George A. Doan left Hamilton in 'AAZ on a filming job with two Ontario government men. On August 11 they reached Remi Lake at Moonbeam, near Cochrane, after 7:57 flying hours. Now began a series of return trips to Moose Factory. Each leg took 2 to 2½ hours compared to the best overland time of about two weeks on the 200-mile route. These were the first flights in Northern Ontario. Maxwell/

Quebec bush flying stalwarts Irénée "Pete" Vachon and Roy Maxwell. (DND RE64-3237)

Doan carried a provincial land surveyor, flew the first air mail in the region and made one of the early post-war ambulance flights in Canada by transporting an ailing trader from Moose Factory to Remi Lake. Another passenger on this experimental operation was Toronto *Daily Star* reporter/photographer Frederick G. Griffin, who was fortunate to make a flight to Moose Factory. Meanwhile, A.G. McLerie was Laurentide's new second pilot, and brothers Roméo and Irénée Vachon took over in maintenance. Roméo's profile was typical for the business. Born in Quebec in 1898, in WWI he was a mechanic in the Royal Canadian Navy. In 1920 he did some technical courses at Camp Borden, and took his first flying lessons there on the JN-4C.

Through 1921 the Laurentide Co. recorded 95 flights. On May 5, however, Roy Maxwell lost control of the Seagull. While he and Roméo Vachon escaped, passenger W.M. Bowden of Laurentide was badly injured. Regarding one survey of this season, Ellwood Wilson estimated that $20-$30 per acre was saved by using airplanes over ground parties. Even so, Laurentide decided that it was too expensive to run its own aircraft. The flying was taken over by a new company, Laurentide Air Service, which came into existence in March 1922. Roy Maxwell and H.D. Wilshire were in management, such well-known aviators

Laurentide's exotic Loening Air Yacht. Columbia University's first aeronautical engineering graduate, Grover Loening, was taught to fly by Orville Wright in 1911 and in 1915 became the first US Army Signal Corps aeronautical engineer. He introduced the Air Yacht in 1921, then built several for wealthy businessmen and air taxi operators. Powered by a 400-hp Liberty, this comfortable and speedy type carried "pilot plus four" at 125 mph. As a strut-braced monoplane, however, the Air Yacht made traditionalists nervous – in his next design, Loening returned to a biplane layout. G-CADV was delivered to Laurentide in August 1922. On the following June 2 it crashed after an errant fire extinguisher jammed the rudder bar, causing pilot Jack Caldwell to lose control and crash at Lac-à-la-Tortue. (William J. Wheeler Col.)

as B.W. "Bill" Broach, Donald B. Foss, Adelard Raymond and Hervé St-Martin shared in the flying, while Thomas Hall of Montreal-based Hall Engineering Works put up the capital. Laurentide forestry turned over to LAS its Lac-à-la-Tortue flying boat facilities. A Vickers Viking, a Loening M23 and another HS-2L were purchased. Through 1922 LAS had good success marketing its services to forestry and government clients in Quebec and Ontario.

Meanwhile, another forestry giant, Price Brothers of Quebec City, also under-stood the potential in aviation. Under chief pilot Harold S. Quigley,

from 1919 it operated three postwar Martinsyde floatplanes from Chicoutimi in Lac St-Jean/Saguenay country, but had its misfortunes. On August 18, 1920 P.B. Morency was flying Martinsyde G-CAAX at Lake Onatchiway. While was leaning down in the cockpit trying to place the chain, controlling tailplane incidence, back onto its sprocket, his machine stalled and crashed from 1000 feet. Morency and passenger T. Nesbitt (a photographer) were gravely injured, while passenger P. Gauthier died. On May 30, 1921 the same pilot crashed Martinsyde G-CADG when the plane struck a navigation buoy on takeoff at

In June 1921 Martinsyde floatplane G-CAEA was registered to Price Brothers, the huge forestry operation at Chicoutimi on Lac St-Jean. Sold a year later to Dominion Aerial Exploration, 'AEA was lost in a foolish accident on July 11, 1923. This type was powered by a 275-hp Rolls-Royce Falcon engine and, as a float plane, had a 4600-lb gross weight (roughly comparable to today's DHC Beaver). This view shows how the pilot sat behind the passenger/cargo compartment. (Frank H. Ellis Col.)

Martinsyde G-CAAX on duty from its Chicoutimi base. This is the plane that crashed disastrously at Lake Onatchiway. (CANAV Col.)

Chicoutimi (he and a passenger survived). Price Brothers then sold Martinsyde G-CAEA to Dominion Aerial Explorations, a company formed by Quigley. For the 1922 season (May 11 to September 15) 'AEA completed 67 flights for 124.5 flying hours, but it crashed at Chicoutimi on July 11, 1923, killing both men aboard. An enquiry concluded that John Oldham, the company air engineer, an unlicenced pilot, had been at the controls, and that he and passenger Lee Evans had been drinking at the time of the accident.

The Spanish River Pulp and Paper Co. also pioneered in forestry flying in Northern Ontario. In 1920 it operated the 2-seat Aeromarine 40L G-CABM, a former US Navy flying boat trainer. Flying 'ABM was George H. Simpson of Toronto, who had graduated in October 1915 from the Wright school in Dayton. He joined the RNAS where he served with distinction, including in the North Russia campaign in 1918. In July 1919 he and mechanic Beal were stranded after a forced landing on a small lake near Sudbury. After a week in the bush they walked out to safety, this being the first such case known in Canadian aviation. Some sort of business took Simpson to the US in 1921 where, on January 9, he crashed fatally in 'ABM near Tiptonville in northwest Tennessee. The Humbolt, Tennessee newspaper reported next day: "George H. Simpson, captain, whose home is in Toronto, Canada, and Carl Fisher, pilot, whose home is Dayton, Ohio … making a trip from Cincinnati to Memphis, are believed to have drowned when a plane … fell into the Mississippi River late yesterday. Negro laborers reported an explosion and a flaming plane fell into the river."

Keng Wah Escapade

Each new aviation venture in Canada seemed to blaze a different trail, but most press items focused upon forestry and mining. This served the purposes of China which, starting in 1919, was quietly training pilots over the Canadian prairies. This operation was Keng Wah Aviation of Saskatoon, managed by Stan McClelland. At the north end of Saskatoon, the school had a straightforward purpose – train pilots for Sun Yat-sen's army in China (in 1911 Sun Yat-sen, founder of the Kuomintang political movement, had become China's first modern-day president).

Equipped with JN-4s, the Keng Wah operation was financed by Sun Yat-sen's Chinese National League, which boasted 2 million members in the US and Canada. Douglas Fraser was the first

instructor, but he soon was let go, apparently for reckless flying, and replaced by Harry Lobb. Ray Crone noted in the CAHS *Journal* that: "Mr. Stanley Bing Mah was to interpret the instructions in theory of flight, airmanship and aero engines, which would be taught the Chinese students." Lim On of Saskatoon was the school's first graduate. A flight that he and mechanic Harry Rowe began to Calgary on April 6, 1920 ended with mechanical trouble at Biggar, Saskatchewan. Then, on May 2, a Keng Wah plane crashed, killing Bob Hamilton and injuring Harry Lobb. On May 9 Lim On also crashed. He was being assessed at the time by Maj L.S. Breadner of the Air Board, when his engine failed and he lost control on landing. C.R. "Ray" McNeill now was hired to instruct. Maj Basil Hobbs certified him on June 21 and he was granted pilot licence No.41.

In May 1921 McNeill flew a JN-4C over Vancouver during a big Chinese convention. About this time Lim On was flying in Hong Kong supported technically by Harry Rowe. Later news was that Lim On and two other Keng Wah graduates were fighting somewhere in China. Back in Saskatoon at least eight Chinese students trained through that season. However, Ray McNeill left the school to earn triple the pay as a parachuting barnstormer that summer. Roland Groome of Regina now took over as the Keng Wah chief instructor.

A typical scene during Keng Wah days in Saskatoon. When this operation ceased, JN-4 G-CABQ languished with a local Chinese farmer, then was sold in Alberta, where it flew as CF-ALE. In 1942 it was lost in a fire in Wayne, Alberta. The Keng Wah, Spanish Civil War and other such escapades represent informal Canadian involvement in other nations' affairs. In one case Canada allowed the export of fighter planes to one of the Spanish factions. Such activity continued into modern times as in Afghanistan, Former Yugoslavia, Iraq, Somalia and Sri Lanka. Canadians helped finance these conflicts and took part in the fighting. (R.H. Crone Col.)

In July 1920 JN-4 G-CABU was purchased from F.G. Ericson by the Victoria branch of the Aerial League of Canada. It then was sold to Vancouver Island Aerial Service and modified with floats at Yarrows Shipyard. W.H. Brown's daring mission far up the BC coast in 'ABU nearly cost him his life. (D.E. Anderson Col.)

However, on October 9 there was a disaster involving Groome, when the American daredevil Reese fell to his death from Groome's plane as he tried a stunt – stepping from one plane to another high over Regina.

Eventually, 17 pilots graduated from Keng Wah, one being Wu Hon Yen, a Kuomintang general in Saskatoon under an alias. A December 28, 1921 article in the Saskatoon *Phoenix* described funding for the Keng Wah school: "The [Chinese National League] has raised enormous sums in Canada and the United States for the support of the insurgent government, and the flying school ... is supported by the League as a means of supporting the same cause." In 1922 Keng Wah ceased operations. The Chinese National League sold its hangar, which was dismantled and erected elsewhere in Saskatoon. There were thoughts of re-starting in Esquimalt and Kamloops. At Esquimalt, the Commercial Aviation School began with JN-4 G-CACJ on floats. However, on February 24, 1923 pilot Hip Kwong crashed it on landing.

At least three West Coast JN-4s operated on floats. Aircraft C-1374 was still in RFC (Canada) markings when photographed. Float "mods" were done by local enthusiasts, were unregulated by government, and each JN-4 floatplane was unique, e.g. while G-CABU had a pair of close-fitting floats, C-1374 had a centre float with outboard sponsons. C-1374's floats reportedly were done by the Hoffar brothers, who were Vancouver boat-builders. (D.E. Anderson Col.)

West Coast Survivor

Born in Victoria in 1894, William Henry Brown, MC, was a bank clerk before the war. Having joined the RFC in April 1917, he flew S.E.5s in France with 84 Squadron beginning late that summer. A glance at his war record quickly reveals an intrepid man. The citation to his Military Cross notes:

Whilst bombing an enemy aerodrome his squadron was attacked by a formation of forty enemy scouts. He engaged one of these with the result that it dived straight to the ground. He was then attacked by another machine, and by skilful piloting he succeeded in firing at close range behind its tail, with the result that it fell on its back and went down out of control. Later, whilst leading a low-flying attack on enemy troops, he dropped four bombs from a very low altitude, scattering the enemy in all directions, and then at a height of 300 feet engaged them with machine gun fire. Shortly afterwards he attacked two enemy two-seater planes, crashing them both to earth.

Having eight enemy aircraft to his credit, Lt Brown returned to Canada in the spring of 1918. Before long he got into business with another successful wartime pilot, A.E. Godfrey, who operated Vancouver Island Aerial Service. On September 20, 1920 Brown was flying JN-4 G-CABU between Alert Bay and Prince Rupert, far from the comfort of Victoria. When his engine failed, he was forced to land, then 'ABU was battered by the waves and sank. Brown swam to an uninhabited island, but quickly realized that he would perish there, if he didn't act. He soon launched out to sea on a log, which he paddled as far out as he could into the shipping lanes. Happily, after a full day he was rescued by an Alaska-bound vessel.

Air Board Statistics for 1921

In its 1921 summary the Air Board quoted many commercial aviation statistics obtained, mainly, from reports submitted by the operators. A request for data had been sent out at year's end by L.S. Breadner of the Air Board, urging that "a special effort be made to supply as full and accurate details as possible". In all provinces 9153 passengers were reportedly carried. Saskatchewan led at 3622, reflecting the enthusiastic efforts of Regina and Saskatoon barnstormers Roland Groome, *et al.* Manitoba and BC were next with 1601 and 1110 passengers. PEI, apparently, had no passenger flights. Of 79,850 lb air mail carried in 1921, BC accounted for 75,000 lb on the experimental Seattle-Vancouver-Victoria service inaugurated by Edward Hubbard and W.E. "Bill" Boeing on March 3, 1919.

Canada by then had 35 licenced air harbours, seven having Customs service (there also were six government air harbours). There were 73 licenced aircraft of which 58 were landplanes, 6 floatplanes and 9 flying boats (there also were 36 Air Board civil aircraft). There were 79 commercial pilots (plus 14 Air Board pilots), 60 pilot-air engineers (Air Board 17), 46 private pilots, 1 airship pilot, 84 air engineers (Air Board 31) and 26 unlicenced mechanics.

Some 10,386 commercial flights were known to have been made for 4347 flying hours. Something called "total machine mileage" was estimated at 294,449 miles. Air Board aircraft made 1209 flights for 2200 flying hours. Accidents for the year totalled 10 (commercial) and 1 (Air Board), four of which involved fatalities (five killed, eight injured). For Breadner's survey the following companies responded:

Aerial Service Co.
Regina, Saskatchewan
Aircraft: 2 JN.4
Pilots: R.J. Groome and J.R. Wright doing passenger flying.
Total flights 360/Hours flown 40/Passengers 325

Aircraft Manufacturers Ltd.
Vancouver, British Columbia
Aircraft: 1 "Canadian Training Seaplane"
Pilot: A.E. Godfrey doing passenger flying.
137/90/103

Bishop-Barker Aero Ltd.
Toronto, Ontario
Aircraft: 1 HS-2L, 1 Sopwith Dove, 1 Avro 504K, 2 JN-4
Pilot: F.W. McCarthy doing passenger flying.

Brandon Aerial Service Ltd.
Brandon, Manitoba
Aircraft: 1 JN-4
Pilots: C.C. Casewell and C.F. Bennett doing passenger and exhibition flying, parachuting, advertising, photography, flying instruction.
521/117/407

C.R. McNeill
Fiske, Saskatchewan
Aircraft: 1 JN-4
Pilot: C.R. McNeill doing instruction.
330/330/200

A typical barnstormer's handbill *circa* 1919-20. (CANAV Col.)

Canadian Aerial Services Ltd.
Montreal, Quebec
Aircraft: 1 Avro 504, 5 JN-4
Pilots: R.B.J. Daville, J.H. St-Martin, H.D. Wiltshire, L.R. Charron, A. Raymond doing passenger and exhibition flying, parachuting, advertising, photography.
1049/396/954

Canadian Aircraft Co.
Winnipeg, Manitoba
Aircraft: 1 JN-4, 4 Avro
Pilots: H. Brookes and A. Francis doing

passenger and exhibition flying, newspaper delivery.
1250/212/1200

Colley Aerial Service
Toronto, Ontario:
Aircraft: 1 JN-4
Pilot: A.K. Colley doing passenger and exhibition flying, advertising.

Donald Brown
Yorkton, Saskatchewan
Aircraft: 1 JN-4
Pilot: Donald Brown doing passenger and exhibition flying.
115/66/115

E. Hubbard
Seattle, Washington
Aircraft: 1 Boeing B.1 flying boat, 1 CL45 seaplane
Pilot: E. Hubbard carrying US mail. (an American, Hubbard held Canadian licence No.108)
150/450/100

E.A. Alton
Winnipeg, Manitoba
Aircraft: 1 Standard J.1
Pilot: E.A. Alton doing passenger and exhibition flying. 300/175/300

E.C.W. Dobbin
Toronto, Ontario
Aircraft: 1 JN-4
Pilot: E.C.W. Dobbin doing passenger and exhibition flying, advertising.
250/101/210

Ericson Aircraft
Toronto, Ontario
Aircraft: 1 JN-4
Pilots: S.H. McCrudden, S.S. Moore, F.W. McCarthy doing exhibition flying, advertising, photography, ferrying.
150/75/75

Holbrook & McLeod
Hanna, Alberta
Aircraft: 1 JN-4
Pilots: C.M. Holbrook and E.L. McLeod doing passenger and exhibition flying.
650/533/600

Imperial Oil Co.
Edmonton, Alberta
Aircraft: 2 Junkers JL-6
Pilots: G.W. Gorman, E.G. Fullerton, G.A. Thompson doing transportation.
89/120/200

J.M. Landry
Quebec City, Quebec
Aircraft: 1 JN-4
Pilots: H.A. Laurie and G.L. Vezine
doing passenger and exhibition flying.
150/75/75

J.S. Williams
Vancouver, British Columbia
Aircraft: 1 JN-4
Pilot: J.S. Williams doing
passenger flying.
200/50/200

Laurentide Co.
Grand-Mère, Quebec
Aircraft: 2 HS-2L, 1 Seagull
Pilots: W.R. Maxwell and
A.G. McLerie doing photography,
fire patrol, timber cruising.
75/92/?

Lethbridge Aircraft Co.
Lethbridge, Alberta
Aircraft: 1 JN-4
Pilot: J.E. Palmer doing passenger
and exhibition flying, parachuting
and photography.
358/344/280

MacDonald Aero Service
Wallaceburg, Ontario
Aircraft: 1 JN-4
Pilot: D.S. MacDonald doing
passenger and exhibition flying.
115/35/105

McCall Aero Corp.
Calgary, Alberta
Aircraft: 1 JN-4
Pilot: P.J.A. Fleming doing
passenger and exhibition flying.

McCall-Hanrahan Aero Service
Calgary, Alberta
Aircraft: 1 Avro
Pilot: F.R. McCall doing
passenger and exhibition flying.
7/7/?

McClelland Aircraft
Saskatoon, Saskatchewan
Aircraft: 2 JN-4
Pilots: H.S. McClelland,
H.N. Hyslop and C.R. McNeill
doing passenger and exhibition
flying and parachuting.
2050/205/1800

In the fashion of the day, this prairie barnstorming JN-4 carries advertising, including for Moose Jaw Hardware. This practice long was shunned by post-WWII operators. Today, however, thousands of airliners around the globe again are flying billboards. (William J. Wheeler Col.)

Niagara Air Service
Toronto, Ontario
Aircraft: 1 JN-4
Pilot: F.M. Bradfield doing passenger
flying, advertising and photography.
273/48/249

Pacific Airways Co.
Seattle, Washington:
Aircraft: 1 HS-2L
Pilot: Anscel Eckmann doing passenger
flying, photography and instruction.
208/75/632

Plante Aerial Service
Montreal, Quebec
Pilots: H.R. Hillick and
J.A. Mondor doing passenger flying,
advertising and photography.
163/51/160

Price Bros.
Chicoutimi, Quebec
Aircraft: 2 Martinsydes,
1 "Canadian trainer"
Pilots: H.S. Quigley and
P.B. Morency doing photography,
fire patrol and timber cruising.
75/97/25

R.J. Groome
Saskatoon, Saskatchewan
Aircraft: 1 JN-4
Pilot: R.J. Groome doing instruction.
439/197/35

Rocky Mountain Aviation Transport
Banff, Alberta
Aircraft: 1 NT2B flying boat
Pilot: A.H. Sandwell doing
passenger flying.
35/6/65

Vancouver Island Aerial Transport Co.
Aircraft: 1 "Canadian Training Seaplane"
Pilot: A.E. Godfrey doing
passenger flying.
5/5/1

Western Aero Co.
Moose Jaw, Saskatchewan:
Aircraft: 3 JN-4
Pilots: E.G. McPherson,
H.C. Ingram and A.J. Adamson doing
passenger and exhibition flying.
882/294/737

The gaudily-painted Lethbridge Aircraft Company's JN-4 G-CABX. Registered in August 1920, it seems to have served for about four years, then its C of R lapsed. It re-surfaced in 1928 as G-CATE and survives in the Reynolds-Alberta Museum. (William J. Wheeler Col.)

Using a pair of tough little, all-metal Junkers F.13s, in 1921 Imperial Oil ventured far down the Mackenzie Valley in support of oil prospects. Dubbed *Vic* and *Rene*, the F.13s paved the way for aviation down this natural transportation corridor. Here sits Vic in a rare view at Prince Rupert, following its halcyon Imperial Oil days. *Vic* soldiered on into 1929, by when it was totally worn out. (Prince Rupert Archives)

The Lure of the Mackenzie

Oil Down the Mackenzie

As far back as the 16th century, explorers such as Martin Frobisher were seeking mineral riches in what now is Canada's Arctic. In 1578 Frobisher led an expedition of 15 ships and 400 men to Baffin Island to mine for gold. Two thousand tons of ore were hauled back to England, where it was found to contain nothing but worthless iron pyrites – fool's gold. In the 18th Century, Samuel Hearne of the Hudson's Bay Company sought copper on the tundra, while Peter Pond noted how the natives along the Athabasca River were using a gooey black substance oozing from the ground to patch their canoes. While no such early explorers found riches, incalculable profits awaited in the 20th Century. This all began in earnest soon after Imperial Oil discovered oil near Fort Norman, far down the Mackenzie River. Newspapers of the day ran such headlines as, "Great Oil Field Found in Northland", "Gas for 500 Years", and "Run Pipe Line to Bering Sea, Ambitious Project to Get Oil from Mackenzie Basin". Presaging much later developments in the Beaufort Sea, a CP despatch of December 8, 1920, continued: "Conveyance of the oil products of the Mackenzie River Basin to the Bering Sea by pipe line, from where it would be carried by tankers to the markets of the world, is an ambitious project for which sanction will be sought by a bill to be considered by Parliament at the approaching session." The route – across into the Yukon River system via the Rat and Bell rivers, thence to salt water – had been proposed in 1887 by Yukon commissioner William Ogilvie, so interest in Mackenzie Valley oil was

Imperial Oil's soon-to-be-famous Junkers, *Vic* and *Rene*, newly arrived in Edmonton from New York. Standing by the nose of *Vic* are Elmer Garfield Fullerton (pilot), H.S. "Dick" Meyers, Mrs. McQueen (wife of A.M. McQueen, Imperial Oil vice-president), Charles E. Taylor (Imperial Oil), George Washington Gorman (pilot) and William Hill (mechanic). (Glenbow Museum NA2303-1)

not so new. The Toronto *Globe* of August 22, 1919 reported further on Canada's new natural resource potential: "In Canada the development work of oil companies and the explorations by Government geologists are being carried on at top speed, with the view of putting this country among the large oil producers of the world. Much has been hoped for the rich, oil-bearing sands of the Mackenzie River country, and the work of the experts there during the next few months will be of the greatest importance …"

Just as attracted as big business was to the Mackenzie by the smell of oil were those in transportation. While the oil rush created an overnight boom for steamboat and barge companies plying the lakes and rivers in the watershed north from Fort McMurray, some were sizing up air transport possibilities. A news item from February 1921 was headlined "Air Routes to Far North Oil Belt Proposed": "F.G. Ericson, the Toronto birdman, has announced his intentions of operating a flying service between Great Slave Lake and Fort Norman on a commercial basis." Ericson had been chief engineer of Canadian Aeroplanes, then a dealer in war surplus and member of the Canadian Air Board.

The article also reported about a Mackenzie scheme by E.L. Janney, the very huckster who had organized the Canadian Aviation Corps in 1914. Predictably, his was an outlandish plan, as mentioned in one news item: "A

dirigible capable of carrying about thirty passengers will be put on the Edmonton-Mackenzie route, according to Captain Janney's plan, in March." A return fare of $1500 was quoted for Edmonton-Fort McMurray. (In these days Janney was up to various shenanigans. In early February 1921, for example, he was charged in Judge Coatsworth's Toronto courtroom with false pretenses in the matter of obtaining an aeroplane. Several weeks later the charge was dropped when Janney paid F.G. Ericson $2000 for the plane. In September, Janney was in jail in Lethbridge for embezzlement. There he began a lengthy hunger strike, ostensibly to protest prison conditions. This put him back where he always loved to be – on the front pages of the daily papers. An item in the Toronto *Daily Star* of September 1, 1921 reminded readers how Janney had " a splendid war record" (the opposite was true) and was in jail for a scam "to float an aircraft company to carry on commercial trading in the far north." Newspapers published Janney's rambling manifesto on September 24, after which the story faded. Once released, he continued with his larcenous ways in Canada and the US.)

Meanwhile, another northern aviation scheme had being promoted by RFC fighter ace, F.R. McCall, whose newspaper advertisement read:

Fly to Fort Norman in absolute safety and comfort for what it costs to hire guides and buy outfit. Flying time about eight hours each way. Two six-passenger Flying Boats of a stable, safe type, approved by the British Air Board, to be placed in scheduled service between Peace River and Fort Norman the first day of May. Capt Fred Robert McCall, DSO, MC, DFC in charge of actual flying.

Another hopeful in these stakes was W.R. "Wop" May, offering a flying boat service to Fort Norman from McLennan on Lesser Slave Lake. Operations would commence in June 1921 under the "Great Northern Service" banner. In the end, however, none of these enterprises got off the ground – to launch even one, would have cost a king's ransom, as illustrated by a study done by a Toronto mining company into opening a full-scale aerial expedition down the Mackenzie in 1921. The promoter in charge was Frank Egerton Davison, whose experience dated to the Yukon gold rush of 1898. From that time onward his name appears in connection with such mining interests as Ballarat Mining Co., Universal Gas and Oil, Precambrian Exploration and Development, the Yukon-Alaska Exploration and Development Syndicate, and Mackenzie River Oil. The latter was capitalized in 1921 at $5 million. Davison acquired 200,000 Mackenzie River Oil shares by trading 44 oil leases he held in Peace River country.

Since the new company was planning a geological expedition, Davison proposed airplanes and brought in R.H. "Red" Mulock to consult. He picked the right man, for Mulock had led in RAF bomber

operations and commanded the Canadian Air Force in England in 1918-19. He studied Davison's proposition, then reported on April 18, 1921:

The proposition must stand on its own feet from an earning point of view as far as fast transportation is concerned. The scheme proposed to sell high speed service and, if the traffic is available, should pay large returns, as speed is worth high prices and the public are always willing to pay for it within reason.

The great R.H. "Red" Mulock, DSO and Bar, CBE, who prepared the landmark northern air transport study for Frank Davison in 1920. (DND PMR71-404)

Mulock recommended the Felixstowe F.3 flying boat. First flown in 1917, the F.3 served the RNAS well in the anti-submarine and anti-Zeppelin campaigns. Built of wood, it had a wingspan of 102', fuselage length – 49' 2", all-up weight – 12,200 lb, top speed – 91 mph. Mulock touted its 2000-lb payload, so 10 passengers could be carried with baggage. With two 360-hp Rolls-Royce Eagles, it could get airborne in 20 seconds, climb to 9000 feet in 56 minutes, cruise at 70 mph and fly non-stop 800 miles. The F.3 seemed tailor-made for the Mackenzie Valley.

Mulock recommended a fleet of 5 F.3s (2 line and 3 spare), and that 8 pilots and 8 mechanics should each be paid a seasonal rate of $4000 and $3000 respectively. Other specialized help was budgeted at $7400, while food for 36 men for 180 days at $2 per day

would run a further $13,000. Fuel for 106 round trips at 1440 gallons per trip would add $152,640, oil $15,264, maintenance and administration $76,000. To this would be added $205,000 for the F.3s, buildings, tools and an HS-2L for the superintendent. Along with a contingency fund, financing the venture would require $500,000, including Mulock's 25% "reserve" cushion. He pointed out that money could be saved by efficient operations. For example, he budgeted 18 hours for each one-way flight, then explained how a tightly run mission could be completed in 11. In this way, his best budget for the air operation looked more like $375,000. Mulock now gave his client an airplane – steamship cost comparison. The steamship fare from Peace River to Fort Norman in 1921 was $77 as quoted by the Alberta and Arctic Transportation Co. Mulock figured the fare by F.3 at $300, but the F.3 didn't look so pricey when time was considered: 5½ days downbound by steamer, 9 days upbound, compared to 11 hours via F.3.

Mulock's exhaustive report was supportive of aviation for the Mackenzie River Oil expedition. Nonetheless, in 1921 Davison operated by steamer from Peace River. The only aviation connection was that geologist H.A. "Doc" Oaks had been an RFC pilot. That, and the fact that the field report from the summer's work included a photo of an Imperial Oil Junkers lying damaged at Fort Simpson. All things considered, however, Mulock's study illustrates that Canadian business was taking aviation seriously as it looked ahead in natural resource development.

F.3s of the type recommended by R.H. Mulock for a 1921 Mackenzie River expedition. These examples, photographed on August 28, 1922, were on Civil Government Air Operations from Victoria Beach on Lake Winnipeg. The aircraft recently had been equipped with radio transmitters. Early in August they had been able to radio news of several forest fires to the Canadian Signals Corps radio station at Norway House. Quick action by ground teams brought the fires under control. Unfortunately, F.3 G-CYEN was lost in an accident on September 8. The F.3 was a capable enough machine, but difficult and costly to maintain on remote operations. (DND)

Imperial Oil Buys into Aviation

While Frank Davison vacillated about a flying boat operation, Imperial Oil of Toronto brought in the first Mackenzie Valley oil, then rushed to consolidate its interests. In 1914 it had sent chief geologist Dr. T.O. Bosworth to investigate oil showings around Bear Island (today's Norman Wells) 1400 miles down the Mackenzie River Valley from the head of rail at Peace River, Alberta. Little more occurred until 1919, when some drilling was done. The following year, crews under Imperial Oil's Theodore A. Link struck oil at 783 feet.

To bridge the transportation gap between Peace River and Bear Island, Imperial Oil ordered two Junkers-Larsen JL-6 monoplanes from the dealer in New York. In November 1920 W.R. May and George W. Gorman travelled to New York to ferry the planes to Edmonton. Both were combat-tested Sopwith Camel pilots, Gorman on 73 Sqn, May on 209. A base was established at Peace River Crossing, where the planes arrived on March 5, 1921. Of this the Edmonton *Journal* announced, "Mammoth Mono-planes Are Being Fitted with Skis at Peace River", then noted how "The operation of shoving the wingless monster into its northern shelter was expedited by the volunteered assistance of a score of Peace River school children who undauntedly contrived to be present on the memorable occasion." The *Journal* added how each plane would fly with a pigeon to courier word in case of emergency.

The JL-6s were registered and christened G-CADP *Vic* and G-CADQ *Rene*. Elmer G. Fullerton would fly *Vic*. He had served in the Canadian

The Imperial Oil Junkers prior to their adventures down the Mackenzie. In the first view, Wop May poses with *Vic*. Then, a nice static view of *Rene*. (Glenbow Museum NC6-6063, NC6-60)

Imperial Oil Junkers pilots W.R. May and G.W. Gorman. (CANAV Col.)

Expeditionary Force 1916-18, in 1918, with the RNAS, and had instructed at Camp Borden. George Gorman was assigned *Rene*. William J. "Bill" Hill and Peter Derbyshire were hired as mechanics. H.W. Waddell was expedition surveyor, while Sgt Hubert Thorne represented the RCMP. Hill later described Thorne as, "guide, philosopher, friend and liaison man." He would be the first RCMP member to use an airplane on duty.

On March 22 each plane ferried 100 gallons of "aviation spirits" to Hay River to start a fuel cache (suitable fuel would be available at the Fort Norman refinery). The planes returned the same day to Peace River. On the 24th the expedition was under way, heading into country where no airman had ventured. The planes, with supplies for 10 days, soon became entangled in a blizzard. Descending to 500 feet, they groped along until reaching the Hudson's Bay Company post at Fort Vermilion, about 125 miles NE of Peace River. They sat out the storm until the 27th, then pressed on to Fort Providence, a further 325 miles. Here they got their first look at the Mackenzie River, where it spills from Great Slave Lake. What they saw caused morale to sink. A later report portrays this as being "… for miles and miles, a jumble of piled up, contorted and

Rene after being damaged at Fort Simpson on March 30, 1921. (LAC C36390)

hummocky ice and crusted snow, which promised inevitable disaster as the consequences of any attempt to land."

Safe landings were made at Fort Providence then, on March 30, *Vic* and *Rene* flew 140 miles to Fort Simpson. *Rene* cracked up on landing, wiping off the undercarriage and splintering its propeller. Bill Hill later wrote: "This was real serious business, 50 percent of our aircraft out of commission, no spares within 500 miles, and 300 miles short of our objective." *Vic* flew to a safer spot on the river, then *Rene* borrowed its propeller and skis, becoming the more airworthy of the planes, since "Vic's" engine needed attention. Now came word that there was no suitable fuel at Fort Norman after all, and only 75 gallons remained at Fort Simpson. *Rene* took off, but broke its propeller and a ski in the process. Now definitely stranded, at least the stranded aviators would be well-hosted by RCMP Sgt Thorne and his wife. They soon decided to make a replacement propeller, Bill Hill and a local HBC man, Walter Johnson, being in charge. In the June 1934 issue of *Canadian Aviation*, Fullerton described what ensued:

We learned that the Catholic Mission had a few oak sleigh boards, 10 feet long and 7 inches wide, which was just about the size we needed to make a laminated propeller, except for being about an inch too narrow... We further learned that moose hide glue was available ... also a number of large clamps ... and Father Decoux ... informed me that we could have the use of the Mission workshop... The first step was to collect the broken pieces of the two propellers and try to assemble sufficient of them together with

glue, to form one, or most of one, propeller, which could then be used as a pattern from which templates could be made.

This excerpt from Hill's later reminiscence adds to the details:

We collected bolts from boats, jacks from river steamers and everything that could be pressed into clamping service. We built a roaring fire in the shop stove and worked like mad in order to get our blank together, while wood and glue were hot... While the blank was drying, I set up a bench to act as a general template table and rigid bed on which to carve out the propeller. The templates were made from sheet steel, which had once served as a smoke stack on a small steamer on the river. I fitted a complete

William Hill while crafting *Rene's* new propeller. (LAC C36391)

template every six inches from boss to tip, so placed in slots in the workbench, that quick and accurate gauging could be done ... The work of chopping with hatchet and carving with drawknife and spokeshave went on daily, and we began to have a propeller that seemed adequate enough.

With a run-up, then a test flight on *Vic* on April 15, the propeller proved serviceable and work began on a second, which was tested on *Rene* on April 20. With word that the river was breaking up and with no hope of landing safely at Fort Norman, on April 24 the aircraft headed for Peace River. In the mad rush *Rene* broke through the ice and was hauled ashore by oxen. Its propeller was switched to *Vic*, which flew to a nearby lake as the Mackenzie began to buckle. Next day Gorman, Fullerton, Hill and Waddell flew non-stop in *Vic* to Peace River – 510 miles in six hours.

Continuing a month later with their original mission, on May 27 Fullerton, with Hill, Waddell and geologist Theo Link, flew *Vic* on floats to Fort Simpson. Link would report how, "The trip from Peace River to Fort Vermilion was made in 2 hours and 35 minutes. Last year I made the same trip by boat in 33 hours running time." On June 1 they reached Fort Simpson, then headed down river on the 2nd for Fort Norman. In *Canada's Flying Heritage*, Frank Ellis notes how there now was new trouble: "A bad radiator leak developed en route, necessitating a landing on the Mackenzie … two hours went by with their craft moored to a large ice block ashore, while Bill Hill did a repair job."

Late on June 2 *Vic* reached Fort Norman, but a float collapsed on landing and a wing was damaged. The crew improvised and, with local help, *Vic* was floated 50 miles downstream to Discovery Well. Gorman, travelling by water from Peace River, eventually arrived with parts. Later in August, *Vic* flew south to Fort Simpson to join *Rene*.

Even though the expedition had not met its goals as envisioned, looking to the future the results were enough to sell Imperial Oil on northern air transport. "Between the points the airplane spanned in its six-hour flight", the company concluded, "the fastest time by dog team is forty-five days. Air travel will be done." Two of the best accounts

of this saga are in Frank Ellis' *Canada's Flying Heritage* and in K.M. Molson's "Early Flying along the Mackenzie" in the CAHS *Journal*, Summer 1982. Molson provides some clarifying details in his summary:

One may ask why were all these troubles experienced after having obtained the best available aircraft and airmen ... The troubles experienced during the winter flying were attributed by G.A. Thompson in 1931 to unsatisfactory skis. There is little doubt that Thompson was right ... the skis were weak and of inadequate area ... which led to the early accidents... The summer troubles seem to stem from the fact that none of the pilots had any experience on water-based aircraft ... Why at least one experienced seaplane pilot was not hired is not known...

Vic was sold and ended in BC with a mining concern. In May 1922 wartime veteran G.A. Thompson ferried it from Edmonton to Hazelton, BC. On board with him was L.S. Bell of the oddly named Railway Employees' Investment and Industrial Association. This flight is the first one known to have crossed the Rockies carrying a civilian passenger. Through the season Thompson made many flights carrying sportsmen and prospectors, even some joyriders, but profits were slight. W.H. McCardell took over the flying in 1923, then the old Junkers was hauled ashore to languish for long years along the Skeena River at Hazelton. In 1928 R.F. Corless bought 'ADP and shipped it to Prince George for repairs, even though the Controller of Civil Aviation had officially condemned it. Undeterred, Corless pressed the old clunker into service, apparently to support a secretly located gold property in the Prince George hinterland. In a letter to the CCA of June 1929 Leigh Brintnell of Western Canada Airways revealed a bit of this strange tale:

We are operating at the present time at 6 Mile Lake, 12 miles from Prince George and, while there, noted that the old Junkers F.13, which the Imperial Oil used to have, has been reconditioned and is now flying again. Do not wish to make this an official complaint, but would like to submit these suggestions to you, so that you can take care of them, if you deem it advisable.

The machine has no official licence and, I believe, its former licence was G-CADP. The pilot flying it is an old time German war pilot and has no licence either. We have kept our engineers from examining this machine officially, as we did not wish to be implicated in any way in the event of a crash. Unofficially, we feel that this machine is very unsafe to fly, as half an aileron pulled away in the air the day before I arrived.

Fathers Ganey and Rahin of Fort Simpson display one of the famous "Bill Hill" propellers made by hand for the Imperial Oil Junkers. This 1935 photo includes RCAF S/L Dave Harding on the left, Dr. W.A.M. Truesdell on the right. (CANAV Col.)

Rene awaiting repairs at Fort Simpson in July 1921. *Rene* and *Vic* finally took off from here on August 21. When it struck a log while landing on the Peace River later that day, *Rene* was wrecked. Although salvaged, the rugged little Junkers never flew again. (Col L. Burwash Col.)

It seems likely that Brintnell was correct about "Herr Jorge" – probably Herr Wilhelm A. Joerss, then flying in northern BC, and whose name does not appear anywhere in the list of pilots licenced in Canada to July 1929. However, the Civil Aviation Branch in Ottawa does not seem to have taken action about this. Meanwhile, in the view of the Prince George RCMP, Leigh Brintnell probably was protecting his own turf. "Professional jealousy" is what the RCMP thought this was about.

On September 20, 1929 the Junkers had a hard landing on Stuart Lake. It was beached with plans to resurrect it the following season. Over the winter, however, vandals smashed the cockpit and hacked up the wings so badly that 'ADP finally was abandoned. An offer from Junkers to rebuild it *gratis* somehow did not interest Corless and, over the years, what was left of this famous bushplane was carted away, the engine going to a mine to run a compressor, etc. As to the propellers hewn by Hill and Johnson, one was located with the Oblate fathers and donated in 1938 to the National Research Council, then the guardian of Canadian aviation artifacts. In 1945 Frank H. Ellis, after years of following leads, discovered the second prop with the Gormans, who donated it to the NRC. Today, these artifacts are with Canada's national aeronautical collection in Ottawa.

J.M. "Jack" Clarke's Central Canada Air Lines operated briefly in Northwestern Ontario and Manitoba using Curtiss HS-2L G-CAFI. Here the pilot at Kenora's Government Dock takes on a bundle of newspapers, likely for local mining camps. Although CCAL lasted only a few weeks in 1926, this ex-US Navy HS-2L persevered, flying later with Patricia Airways of Sioux Lookout, Canadian Airways (Old) of Montreal and International Airways of Hamilton. In 1930 it migrated to Bermuda on a new career as CF-AEA. (Norman Etheridge Col.)

Flying Boat Entrepreneurs

Pacific Airways Co.

In 1921-22 Seattle based Pacific Airways Co. briefly operated a 7-place HS-2L in Washington and British Columbia. Records indicate that owner/operator Anscel C. Eckmann officially carried 525 passengers plus 1000 lb of cargo through 1922. His aircraft was N-CACM, christened "Blue Bird". His advertisements offered short joy rides at $5.00 a seat, and charters at $50 an hour from Seattle to Vancouver (90 minutes) and Seattle to Victoria (60 minutes). "No dust, no grime, no jolts" he promised his customers, along with an optimistic HS-2L speed – 90 mph. Pacific Airways was typical of many short-lived US HS-2L operators, some of which had Canadian links due to proximity to the international border. Some of these outfits also were in the trans-border rum-running business. For this an HS-2L was ideal, as it could take on a decent load from vessels waiting in international waters, then fly (usually at night) to its coastal destination.

The HS-2L was truly the backbone of postwar commercial aviation in Canada. Sturdily built and using a reliable 360-hp Liberty engine, the HS-2L fleet carried the load, especially in the rugged Canadian Shield areas of Ontario and Quebec. A typical HS-2L accommodated pilot, engineer, three passengers and a small amount of baggage. Shown is G-CAPF *Finch* of the Ontario Department of Lands and Forests. (Norman Etheridge Col.)

Alaska bush flying pioneer Roy F. Jones operated Curtiss MF N-ABCS *Northbird* in the Stewart, BC region beginning in 1922. His market in this remote area was the burgeoning mining sector. (Alaska State Library Ruotsala Col. P46-265E)

Laurentide's Curtiss Seagull G-CADL and HS-2L G-CAAD at Lac-à-la-Tortue in the autumn of 1920. Roy Maxwell crashed the Seagull at Grandes-Piles, near Trois-Rivières on May 4, 1921, while H.D. Wiltshire crashed the HS-2L at Tadoussac on August 4, 1922. (LAC PA89145)

Laurentide Air Service

Through 1922 Laurentide Air Service logged 688:20 hours. Much of this was for Ontario's Department of Lands and Forests, especially a vast survey from Lake of the Woods eastward to the Ottawa Valley and north to James Bay. On September 2, during one of these missions, D.B. Foss crashed HS-2L G-CAAC "La Vigilance" on takeoff near Kapuskasing. No one was injured, but the H-boat was lost. In the 1922-23 off-season, Roy Maxwell visited the US to buy a fleet of HS-2Ls. Eight were in service through 1923, flown by several new pilots, including Cecil J. Clayton, Roy S. Grandy, J.R. Ross, G.A. Thompson and J.H. Tudhope. All had solid wartime records, e.g. on November 30, 1916, Ross, flying a Short seaplane, assisted in sinking the German submarine UB-19, and Tudhope tallied several victories flying S.E.5s on 40 Squadron. In the Fall 1983 CAHS *Journal*, K.M. Molson describes some of the 1923 flying done by LAS:

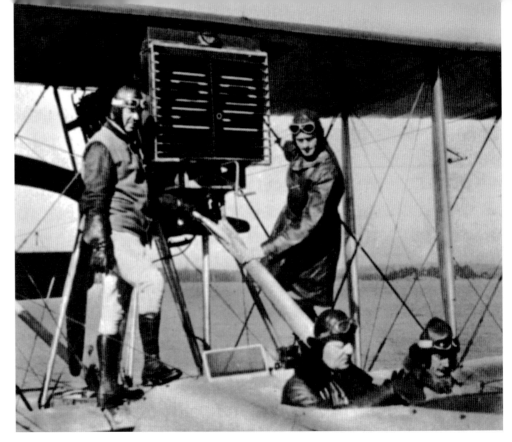

Leading figures from Canada's pioneer bush flying days: Roy Maxwell and C.J. "Doc" Clayton, on the deck of an OPAS HS-2L. Their passengers, a pair of government flunkies, await their thrill of a lifetime. (*The Firebirds*)

The most easterly operation was carried out from a temporary base set up at Manicouagan ... near Baie Comeau...

Owing to the limited range and capacity of the HS-2Ls, the operation had to be carried out by establishing gasoline and

The Laurentide Air Service maintenance facility receives some finishing touches at Trois-Rivières. Running down the berm to the St. Lawrence are tracks along which flying boats could be hauled. Note the HS-2Ls at their buoys in the river. (Norman Etheridge Col.)

food caches at suitable points in the interior. This was done by carrying 50 gal. of gasoline and 100 lb. of food on each flight. When the caches were complete, which took about a month, the foresters were brought in. Ground parties would check representative sections in each area, while other foresters would be flown in fan-like sweeps to sketch the timber. When the area around one cache had been surveyed, the group would move on to the next cache... In all, 160 hr. flying were put in over about three months, surveying an area which, it was estimated, would have taken 5-6 years to cover by ground parties alone... for the first time in Canada an aircraft was used to aid in carrying out an election. A man was flown to Moose Factory from Remi Lake in May to make preliminary arrangements. In June, Scott Williams flew the ballot boxes in and then out again following the

Typical of Laurentide's superb bush pilots was G.A. "Tommy" Thompson. A British ex-pat who had grown up in India, he began in the British air service in 1916. After emigrating to Canada postwar, he was involved in such pioneer ventures as the first trans-Canada flight, Imperial Oil's Mackenzie Valley expedition, and the Ontario Provincial Air Service. Later he served on the MacAlpine Expedition and rose in the ranks at Canadian Airways. (CANAV Col.)

Colin S. "Jack" Caldwell seemed to be everywhere in Canadian pioneer aviation days. In 1924 he participated in the Dayton, Ohio, endurance flight. Piloting a little Thomas Morse Scout, he covered one of the longest routes – 900 miles from Trois-Rivières to Dayton. In 1925-26 he flew the LAS Viking on remote prospecting operations. He pioneered on the Ottawa-Montreal-Rimouski air mail in 1928, and flew seal-spotting reconnaissance missions off Newfoundland 1925 through 1928. On June 20, 1929 Caldwell and his two passengers died when Fokker Super Universal CF-AEX flew into wires suspended across the St. Lawrence River at Montreal. (Norman Ethridge Col.)

provincial election... On 5 August ... Grandy flew an Indian treaty party out [from Moose Factory] making two trips in one day. Later, the Lieutenant Governor, the Premier of Ontario and party were also flown out. This was the first trip that had been made into the James Bay area by senior officials of the Ontario government.

In November 1923 Laurentide Air Service relocated from Lac-à-la-Tortue to Trois-Rivières. The season ended with 1480 hours having been logged, although two planes were lost (without casualty other than pilots' pride). Loening G-CADV crashed at Lac-à-la-Tortue on June 6, when a fire extinguisher came loose on takeoff and jammed pilot C.S. "Jack" Caldwell's rudder bar. On July 17 J.R. Ross crashed HS-2L G-CACV at Biscotasing, northwest of Sudbury.

Viking Prospector

Another early probe into Canada's North was with Laurentide's Vickers Viking G-CAEB. In 1924 pilot R.S. "Bob" Grandy and engineer B. McClatchey journeyed up the west coast of James Bay

G-CAEB, the famous Laurentide Vickers Viking at its summer base on Remi Lake near Kapuskasing, Ontario. Imported by Canadian Vickers of Montreal in June 1922, 'AEB had many incredible adventures all across the country, yet survived for a decade. (CANAV Col.)

One of Harold S. Quigley's Dominion Aerial Exploration Co. Norman Thompson N.T.2B flying boats. The first (G-CACG) was acquired in May 1924 from Rocky Mountain Aviation Transport in Alberta, where it had been used since the summer of 1921 on tourist operations. G-CAEL and 'EM were added in June 1924, but were sold to Jack Elliot of Hamilton two years later. Here is 'EL at Roberval with company personnel Emile Patrault, H.S. Quigley, H.F. McClellan, Jerry Lizotte and unknown. The N.T.2 first flew in 1917, then became the RNAS's basic flying boat trainer. Top speed about 85 mph. 100 to 150 NT's were delivered by war's end. Thereafter, civil examples served around the world. (K.M. Molson Col.)

as far as Attawapiskat. With them was an official from Ottawa visiting Indian reservations to distribute annual treaty money. An assignment that usually required an arduous canoe trip, this time several reserves were covered in about two weeks. The following year G-CAEB was on charter to a US exploration syndicate. It went by rail from Trois-Rivières to Prince Rupert, then was flown for about 100 hours by Scott Williams and Jack Caldwell throughout northern BC, the Yukon and Alaska, supporting prospecting parties.

Over the winter of 1925-26 'AEB was serviced at Sault Ste. Marie, then sent by rail to Edmonton, where the engine was overhauled. It went again by rail to Lac la Biche, Alberta from where it soon was on the wing, this time north of Lake Athabasca with the crew of Jack Caldwell and Irénée Vachon. Their task was supporting prospectors hunting for a rumoured gold deposit east of Great Slave Lake. Apparently, no gold was found, but the summer's flying ended safely.

After a few months in storage at High River, Alberta, 'AEB was shipped to Jericho Beach, Vancouver. More dormancy followed once the Viking's Rolls-Royce Lion engine was found to be badly worn. At last, in 1932 Capt Fred Clark purchased 'AEB for mineral exploration. It was airworthy by late summer but, sad to say, on a test flight of September 16, a fuel line burst and fire erupted. The pilot made a hasty landing in the Strait of Georgia, but 'AEB was lost.

Air Board Report 1924

The 1924 Air Board report begins with coverage of H.S. Quigley's Dominion Aerial Exploration Co. Founded in 1922, this company grew to prominence. Its two HS-2Ls had been reconditioned over the previous winter at Roberval, and three Norman Thompson N.T.2B flying boats were added. The N.T.2B (gross weight 3200 lb) used a 200 hp Hispano-Suiza that was more efficient than the 360-to-400 hp Liberty of the HS-2L (gross weight 6400 lb), and it climbed and cruised faster than an H-boat. Staffed by three pilots and five mechanics, DAE commenced forestry duties in late May on behalf of Price Brothers Ltd. First on the list of priorities was to cover any acreage overlooked the previous season, then the planes edged north into Mistassini country. "Much of this work was done in districts difficult to access," noted the report, which continued about work done beyond Lac St-Jean:

All supplies and gasoline were flown there from Roberval by H.S.2L machines, while sketching was done from N.T. boats. In this way the flying radius was doubled and the results obtained from the same amount of time in the air were greatly increased. The reconnaissance extended from a point about fifty miles north of Lake Peribonka … and reached as far as the river Bersimis … Several flights were next made north and east of

the Saguenay on the river Sault au Cochon for the purpose of making a preliminary sketch of the salient features of the district. During these flights a forester from one of the ground cruising parties, which would be working the district in the ensuing winter, was carried, so that he might gain a good general knowledge of the district, note the location of the most valuable timber, and map roughly the best routes to travel through the country.

In September the Parc Laurentide was surveyed for the Quebec government in order to upgrade existing maps. On this job the report noted how, "the better performance of the Norman Thompson boats was found to be of great use". Through 1924 DAE flew 346 hours on 240 flights. Fire patrols involved 140 hours, sketching and reconnaissance 180 and photography 26. Meanwhile, the Brock-Weymouth Co. of Philadelphia surveyed a proposed rail line in northern Quebec. This had begun the previous winter using a Fokker C.II. The CNR's chief engineer was pleased with the resulting maps: "For the production of a general contour map of a district, I believe that this Brock method would prove not only less expensive than any method used today from the ground, but that its accuracy would be far greater." For 1924 the Fokker flew 47:20 hours doing vertical photography over 167 sq.mi.

In 1925-27 this Fokker C.II, operated by Brock & Weymouth of Philadelphia, did photography in northern Quebec for the Canadian National Railway. The C.II traced its lineage to the Fokker D.VII fighter, and made its first appearance as the C.I air taxi. The cabin behind the pilot's open cockpit accommodated two passengers. The more advanced C.II, powered by a 185-hp BMW, proved very adaptable in aerial photography. G-CAEV (shown in this view at Camp Borden) later was sold to Jack Elliot, but was wrecked in a landing accident, when pilot Len Tripp hit a fence on landing at Hamilton. (RCAF RC1618, C. Don Long Collection)

Through 1924 Northern Air Services of Haileybury operated in the Ontario-Quebec Gold Belt, making 212 flights (169 flying hours) with an HS-2L. There were 470 fare-paying passengers, plus 22,580 lb freight and 1030 lb mail. NAS also had forestry contracts, one for Spanish River Pulp and Paper, whose report noted:

We use the aerial sketch method of survey for economy as well as for speed in obtaining required information... we are confident that we shall effect a saving of one-third of the cost of our regular 2½ per cent strip survey by this method. The map gives us more complete information of the areas of watersheds, the location of lakes

Having served Laurentide Air Service, G-CACT joined Northern Air Service in May 1925. Here it is somewhere in the Haileybury hinterland in one of the better HS-2L photos (originally a postcard). Pilot B.W. Broatch is third from the left. When the engine backfired at Haileybury on October 22, 1925, 'ACT ignited and burned to the waterline. Such fires were common in wooden aircraft covered in cotton cloth that also had layers of paint. Even worse, gas and oil normally were dripping from various points, and few crewmen considered smoking while refuelling to be a hazard. (CANAV Col.)

LAURENTIDE AIR SERVICE LIMITED
IN CONJUNCTION WITH
CANADIAN PACIFIC RAILWAY COMPANY
AND
CANADIAN NATIONAL RAILWAYS

The Laurentide Air Service Limited are operating daily a regular Air Transportation Service from Haileybury, Ont. and Angliers, Que. to Rouyn and Lake Fortune Mining District.

DAILY SERVICE
HAILEYBURY, ONT. and ANGLIERS, QUE.
to ROUYN and LAKE FORTUNE

Leave Angliers	-	8.00 a.m.	Leave Haileybury	-	8.00 a.m.
Arrive Osisko Lake	-	9.00 a.m.	Arrive Osisko	-	9.15 a.m.
Leave Osisko	-	9.30 a.m.	Leave Osisko	-	9.45 a.m.
Arrive Lake Fortune	-	10.00 a.m.	Arrive Lake Fortune	-	10.15 a.m.
Leave Lake Fortune	-	10.30 a.m.	Leave Lake Fortune	-	10.45 a.m.
Arrive Angliers	-	11.30 a.m.	Arrive Haileybury	-	12.00 a.m.

FARES :

ANGLIERS TO ROUYN OR LAKE FORTUNE - - Single, $40.00
HAILEYBURY TO ROUYN OR LAKE FORTUNE - Single, $60.00

PASSENGERS' BAGGAGE :
All Passengers are allowed 25 lbs. baggage free. Excess baggage 20c. per lb.

FREIGHT RATES :

Parcels not exceeding 100 lbs. - 20c. per lb. (Minimum Charge $2.50 per parcel)
Shipments over 100 lbs. and under 500 lbs. - - - - - 17c. per lb.
"   " 500 "   "   " 2000 " - - - - - 15c. " "
"   one ton and over - - - - - - 10c. " "

LIMIT AND SIZE OF BAGGAGE :
General limit of size is 36″ in length, by 15″ in width, depth or diameter.
Charges to be at Carrier's option by volume or weight on basis 40 cubic feet per ton.

Special Trips by arrangement to any District in Goldfields
APPLY
LAURENTIDE AIR SERVICE LIMITED
DRUMMOND BUILDING, MONTREAL, HAILEYBURY, ONT. or ANGLIERS, QUE.

ASSOCIATED WITH:
JAMES D. LACEY (CANADA), LIMITED
Drummond Building, MONTREAL.
TIMBER LAND FACTORS.   CRUISING—SURVEYING—AERIAL MAPPING.

The daily schedule as announced by LAS on July 10, 1924. An item in the Toronto *Globe* of July 26 reported that the Canadian Ingersol Rand Co. was planning to fly hardrock drills from Haileybury to Rouyn via HS-2L. A company spokesman explained how "a gasoline-driven portable air compressor can be transported to any part of the Rouyn gold field and completely assembled and in operation" within 36 hours. (CANAV Col.)

and type boundaries than we are able to obtain by our strip surveys and, although ground work is necessary to obtain an estimate of merchantable types ... this information can be obtained by sample plot surveys... We intend to continue the use of the aerial method of forest surveys.

According to the Air Board, Laurentide Air Service had a busy 1924 season. Commencing on May 23, points around the Gold Belt were served by an HS-2L. C.S. "Jack" Caldwell flew the first trip, his passenger, W.J. Hacker, becoming the first fare-paying customer on a scheduled Canadian air service. Two H-boats were added in June, allowing LAS to provide daily service. Flights were organized to meet the arriving CPR train at Angliers, Quebec, on Monday, Wednesday and Friday, then returned on following days to meet the outgoing train. On July 30 Haileybury, which had better facilities, replaced Angliers as the main air base. The fare to Rouyn, about 100 miles NNE of Haileybury, was $60. Baggage over 25 lb was 20¢ a pound. On September 11 LAS began Canada's first scheduled air mail service on this route.

On July 8, 1924 Laurentide suffered a setback. According to the next day's Toronto *Globe*, "One of the hydro-aeroplanes operating between Angliers and Rouyn goldfields ... was wrecked yesterday afternoon, when one of the wings of the machine struck a tree-top shortly after rising from Lake des Quinze. The machine crumpled and crashed in a heap in the flooded swamp lands adjacent to the lake." The pilot and passengers Robert Gamble and Charlie Shields of Haileybury escaped with minor injuries.

For the initial Quebec goldfields season (May 23 to November 15, 1924) LAS reportedly made 558 flights for 456 flying hours, carried 425 passengers, 55,485 lb freight, 8593 lb baggage and 780 lb mail (some 15,000 letters and telegrams). According to the company, its

W.J. Hacker (second from the right) was the passenger on what is considered Canada's first scheduled airline flight. On this occasion a Laurentide Air Service HS-2L operated from Angliers to Lac Fortune and Rouyn, Quebec on May 23, 1924. His companions from the left are renowned LAS pilots Roy S. Grandy, J. Scott Williams (recently released from the RCAF) and C.S. "Jack" Caldwell. For press purposes, LAS commenced scheduled service about two months later. (CANAV Col.)

A Canadian aero-survey landmark occurred in May 1924 when Fairchild of Grand-Mère acquired this Huff-Daland Petrel 5 exclusively for aerial photography. Manufactured in Pennsylvania, G-CAEK, which used a 180-hp Wright E-4 (a licence-built Hispano-Suiza), proved its worth for several years, finally fading by 1928. From the Petrel, Huff-Daland produced a line of crop dusters, the first aircraft exclusively manufactured for this specialty. Here, pilot Ken Saunders of Fairchild passes an aerial camera to his wife. A dog-drawn sled completes this fine, wintry Quebec scene. This photo illustrates the key features of Canada's national civil aircraft markings: large registration letters spread across the upper plane (the same for under the lower plane), bold side markings, and large "G" on the stabilizer and rudder. "G" indicated British Commonwealth, "C" indicated Canada. (NMST 1958)

goal for the 1924 Quebec goldfields season had been, "to prove the feasibility and advantage of aerial transport in a country of this nature ... and to stimulate public confidence in the use of aircraft." Besides goldfields business, in 1924 LAS reported 954 flights, 933 flying hours and 1020 passengers. Other business included aerial surveys for such clients as the E.B. Eddy, Spanish River, and St. Maurice pulp and paper companies, and the "joyriding" season from Bigwin Inn in the Muskoka region tallied 307 passengers. As to air mail service, the Air Board noted:

Express delivery of telegrams was a feature of the service. These could be sent from outside points, delivered to the pilot at either Haileybury or Angliers, taken to the mining camps, and a return message brought out to be telegraphed from either point to its destination all within a few hours... the service obtained recognition as a regular mail carrier by the Post Office Department and was authorized to carry mail bearing a special twenty-five cent stamp issued by the company.

In the winter of 1924-25 LAS continued Haileybury-Rouyn operations using ski-equipped D.H.9 G-CAEU. On January 24, however, Jack Caldwell crashed 'AEU in the bush between

Larder Lake and Rouyn. LAS soon folded, but not before it had made an indelible mark on Canadian air transport history. This is explained best by K.M. Molson: "While Laurentide Air Service disappeared, the traditions it established in Canadian bush flying did not. Its personnel spread through the industry to benefit it for years to come."

Operations in 1924 for Fairchild Aerial Surveys Co. (of Canada) Ltd. at Lac-à-la-Tortue, Grand-Mère, resulted in 1425 sq.mi. of map mosaics being produced in Quebec and Ontario. Projects included hydrographic surveys for the Quebec government, which wanted to boost hydro-electric output; and assisting the CPR, National Transcontinental Railroad, and Southern Abitibi Railway in route planning. Using a Standard J.1 and a Huff-Deland, 232 hours were logged on 138 flights. As well, 45 hours were purchased from Laurentide Air Service. Heading Fairchild in Canada was Ellwood Wilson, who had established the company in 1922 after discussions in New York with inventor and entrepreneur, Sherman Fairchild. Wilson grew interested in Fairchild's innovative aerial cameras, and his plan to design aircraft suited to photography. (Wilson's career would be highlighted by many honours. In 1942, for example, he became the first recipient

of a medal struck in his honour by the Canadian Pulp and Paper Association.)

In March 1924 Roy S. Grandy of Laurentide Air Service had undertaken pioneer seal-spotting flights off Newfoundland using a Baby Avro. (For the 1925-28 sealing seasons, C.S. Caldwell was the seal spotting pilot, apparently employed by the Bowring Brothers shipping and sealing operation of St. John's. Each season would re-emphasize the value of aerial reconnaissance to the sealing industry.) In 1924 the Air Board wrote of seal spotting:

On the first flight the ship was made fast to a good sheet of ice ... the plane put overboard, the tank filled with warm oil and no difficulty was experienced in getting away safely with one of the sealing crew [Jabez Winsor] as observer. After a flight of 70 miles on a triangular course at an average altitude of 2,000 feet, the plane turned and landed. No seals were observed, but ice conditions were reported... Some days later during a flight of an hour and a half, seals were observed... The plane was again hoisted on board and the ship steered towards the patch of seals observed. This information proved to be of greatest value as the seals seen were part of the main herd. A good catch resulted.

Canada's HS-2Ls

First flown at Buffalo, NY in October 1917, the Curtiss HS-1L anti-submarine patrol plane, powered by a 200-hp Curtiss engine, quickly was beefed up with a bigger wing, tail and 360-hp Liberty engine to become the HS-2L (most HS-1Ls were modified to "2s"). Production by Curtiss and its licencees totalled some 1218 aircraft by war's end. The US Navy had wartime units at home and in France, then kept the HS-2L on peacetime strength into 1926.

Postwar, the HS-2L proved indispensable in establishing Canadian commercial and military aviation. Some 46 civil and 30 CGAO/RCAF examples were registered, but there also were spare hulls, wings, etc. The first Canadian HS-2Ls were 12 ex-US Navy machines from Dartmouth: two went to the Laurentide Company for forestry beginning in the summer of 1919, the other 10 commenced Air Board duties a year later. Subsequent aircraft came from the US, where dealers such as Aeromarine in New Jersey targeted investors eager to get into commercial aviation. Aeromarine had a price of about $6000 for an HS-2L in fly-away condition. F.G. Ericson, busy with surplus JN-4 sales in Toronto, also marketed HS-2Ls from his New York and Baltimore locations. Other HS-2Ls were sold directly from the US Navy Salvage Section at such bases as Philadelphia and

Happily, HS-2Ls were well photographed wherever they appeared (Canadians in the 1920s-30s were as apt to be toting small cameras as people now carry cell phones). In these typical views, G-CAOQ of the OPAS is getting some servicing at the beach. Then, G-CAFQ of Canadian Airways (Old) is shown in another standard setting, likely serving prospectors or foresters. F.V. Robinson was piloting 'AFQ on June 4, 1927 when he was forced down by weather. He and his crew got ashore, but the plane was battered to pieces along the North Shore of the St. Lawrence. (Red Lake Museum, CANAV Col.)

Hampton Roads. The RCAF assumed control of the Air Board HS-2Ls in 1924, operating them on training and operational assignments into 1927. Thereafter, the fleet gradually shrank until all had been struck off charge by September 1928. Only one ex-RCAF aircraft was sold to a civil operator, G-CYGU becoming G-CARL in May 1928.

The interim list below is based on the solid work of John and Joyce Ellis of Peterborough. Using archival files in Ottawa, in the 1960s they researched each civil registration, then made their results available through the Canadian Aviation Historical Society *Journal*. Covering Canada's government-owned HS-2Ls was John A. Griffin, whose great work is *Canadian Military Aircraft Serials and Photographs*, published in 1969. For fans wishing more of this key story, *The Curtiss HS Flying Boats* by K.M. "Ken" Molson and A.J. "Fred" Shortt is mandatory reading.

Canada's Civilian HS-2Ls

Aircraft	Registered	Owner	Fate
G-CAAC	30-9-20	Laurentide Co.	To Laurentide Air Service, DBR 2-9-22 Fauquier, Ontario. Salvage 1968-69, remains on display Canada Aviation Museum
G-CAAD	30-9-20	Laurentide Co.	DBR Tadoussac, Quebec 4-8-22 hit log on takeoff
G-CAAZ	21-7-21	Canadian Aero Film Co.	DBF in hangar fire Burlington, Ontario 12-9-21
N-CACM	11-8-21	Pacific Airways, Seattle	7-place version dubbed "Blue Bird" that operated in BC and Washington. Returned to USA 5-22
G-CACS	26-6-23	Ontario Paper Co.,	Later Dominion Aerial Exploration. DBR 30 mi. north of Sept-Îles 16-7-26
G-CACT	16-5-23	Laurentide Air Service	Later Northern Air Service Syndicate. DBF Haileybury, Ontario 22-10-25
G-CACU	11-5-23	Laurentide Air Service	Certificate cancelled 16-6-24
G-CACV	17-7-23	Laurentide Air Service	DBR Biscotasing, Ontario.
G-CACW	1-6-23	Laurentide Air Service	Certificate cancelled 16-6-24
G-CACX	8-6-23	Laurentide Air Service	Later Northern Air Service Syndicate. Certificate cancelled 10-8-25
G-CACY	23-6-23	Laurentide Air Service	Certificate cancelled 16-6-24
G-CACZ	3-7-23	Laurentide Air Service	Certificate cancelled 16-6-24
G-CADB	12-7-20	Bishop-Barker Aeroplanes	DBR Brooklin, Ontario 10-9-20, crashed into trees after engine failure
G-CADM	25-10-20	Bishop-Barker Aeroplanes	Certificate cancelled 31-7-24
G-CADU	27-5-22	Laurentide Air Service	Written off causes unknown 10-8-25
G-CADY	15-6-23	Laurentide Air Service	Certificate cancelled 16-6-24
G-CAEY	2-6-25	Dominion Aerial Explorations	Certificate cancelled 28-2-31
G-CAFH	14-6-26	Pacific Airways	To Western Canada Airways Certificate cancelled 25-9-28
G-CAFI	10-5-26	Elliot-Fairchild Air Service	Later Central Canada Air Lines, Patricia Airways, Canadian Airways, Canadian Vickers, International Airways, J.A. Sanscartier who sent 'AFI to Bermuda in 1930
G-CAFP	6-7-26	Canadian Airways	DBR Stacker Lake, Quebec 11-10-27
G-CAFQ	6-7-26	Canadian Airways	DBR Kogaska, Quebec 4-6-27
G-CAGT	31-5-28	Canadian Airways	Certificate cancelled 14-3-30
G-CAHQ	18-5-27	Canadian Airways	Certificate cancelled 14-3-30
G-CANZ	12-6-28	Canadian Airways	Exported to Bahamas late 1929, lost at sea, certificate cancelled 28-2-30. The sole Canadian Vickers HS-2L modified with an improved wing, 5-person cockpit and known at CV as the "HS-3L"
G-CAOA	16-5-24	Ontario Government (OPAS)	Certificate cancelled 15-5-33
G-CAOA	16-5-24	Ontario Government (OPAS)	Certificate cancelled 15-5-33
G-CAOB	25-5-24	Ontario Government (OPAS)	Sank in Lake Superior off Gros Cap, Ontario 8-10-26
G-CAOC	22-5-24	Ontario Government (OPAS)	Crashed into trees at Savanne Lake, Ontario 16-8-24
G-CAOD	29-5-24	Ontario Government (OPAS)	Crashed on landing at Michipicoten Harbour, Ontario 12-6-25
G-CAOE	29-4-24	Ontario Government (OPAS)	Crashed taking off Snake Lake, Ontario 2-8-26
G-CAOF	23-4-24	Ontario Government (OPAS)	DBF Lac Seul, Ontario 27-6-29
G-CAOG	15-4-24	Ontario Government (OPAS)	Certificate cancelled 12-29
G-CAOH	31-7-24	Ontario Government (OPAS)	Crashed and sank Toronto Bay 27-4-24
G-CAOI	2-5-24	Ontario Government (OPAS)	Certificate cancelled 12-29
G-CAOJ	9-5-24	Ontario Government (OPAS)	DBR in storm, Fort Frances, Ontario 8-31
G-CAOK	16-5-24	Ontario Government (OPAS)	Certificate cancelled 15-5-33
G-CAOL	9-5-24	Ontario Government (OPAS)	Certificate cancelled 31-3-28
G-CAOM	29-4-24	Ontario Government (OPAS)	DBF Shebandowan Lake, Ontario 14-8-27
G-CAON	6-9-24	Ontario Government (OPAS)	Certificate cancelled 30-4-32
G-CAOP	31-1-26	Ontario Government (OPAS)	Crashed on landing at Fort Frances 10-30
G-CAOQ	31-1-26	Ontario Government (OPAS)	Certificate cancelled 15-5-33
G-CAOR	31-1-26	Ontario Government (OPAS)	Crashed on takeoff at Fort Frances 7-30
G-CAOS	31-1-26	Ontario Government (OPAS)	Crashed on landing Long Lac, Ontario 8-10-27
G-CAPE	15-5-28	Ontario Government (OPAS)	Crashed on landing Pays Platt, Ontario 4-5-31
G-CAPF	15-5-28	Ontario Government (OPAS)	DBR Twin Lake, Ontario 8-32
G-CARL	31-5-28	Canadian Airways	Ex-RCAF G-CYGU, certificate cancelled 29-10-29
CF-AEA	23-5-29	International Airways, later J.M. Clarke,	J.A. Sanscartier, shipped to Bermuda 10-30

A Canadian Airways HS-2L takes on the first trans-Atlantic mail from an ocean liner at Pointe-aux-Père off Rimouski on September 16, 1927. Piloted by H.S. Quigley and Stuart Graham, the aircraft then flew upstream to Montreal. In this way, the trans-Atlantic mail reached Montreal 2-3 days sooner than usual. (CANAV Col.)

G-CARL was the only ex-RCAF HS-2L to reach the Canadian civil aircraft register. Having served the RCAF since 1925, it joined Canadian Airways three years later, flying from the company's Roberval base. 'ARL retired and was scrapped at the end of the 1929 flying season. (Norman Etheridge Col.)

The HS-2L's hefty Liberty engine always kept crews busy with anything from minor daily tuning to back-breaking engine changes. Sometime the heavy work had to be undertaken far from the convenience of the hangar, but it always got done. (All, CANAV Col.)

CAF/RCAF HS-2Ls

Registration	Taken on Strength	Struck of Strength	Registration	Taken on Strength	Struck of Strength
G-CYAE	22-7-20	1-7-27	G-CYEF	17-11-21	10-8-23 Crashed
G-CYAF	22-7-20	2-8-24			Victoria Beach 26-6-23
G-CYAG	25-10-20	26-9-23	G-CYEJ	23-5-22	31-8-26
G-CYAH	25-10-20	26-11-24	G-CYEK	19-8-22	21-9-22 Crashed
G-CYBA	24-9-20	29-7-22			Roberval 21-9-22
G-CYBB	30-5-21	27-3-25	G-CYEL	2-9-22	12-8-25
G-CYDR	28-5-21	4-11-21	G-CYGA	13-10-24	1-7-28
G-CYDS	8-7-21	8-8-21	G-CYGL	8-6-25	9-12-26
G-CYDT	23-7-21	26-2-24	G-CYGM	19-6-25	1-7-28
G-CYDU	7-7-21	10-9-25 Crashed	G-CYGN	31-5-25	25-10-26
		British Columbia 23-7-25	G-CYGO	25-5-25	1-7-28
G-CYDX	27-6-21	26-1-24	G-CYGP	8-6-25	1-4-26
G-CYDY	19-7-21	1-7-28 Crashed	G-CYGQ	12-8-25	25-9-28
		Roberval, Quebec	G-CYGR	12-8-25	25-9-28
G-CYEA	12-7-21	9-4-23 Crashed	G-CYGS	12-8-25	8-5-28
		Vancouver 11-9-22	G-CYGT	12-8-25	1-7-28
G-CYEB	6-8-21	10-9-25	G-CYGU	12-8-25	13-4-28
G-CYED	27-9-21	1-7-28			Became G-CARL

"La Vigilance" Rises Again

Over the summers of 1968-69 a salvage team including M.L. "Mac" McIntyre of the CAHS, and Robert Bradford with several others from the National Aeronautical Collection were busy near Fauquier, Ontario dredging up what remained of the Laurentide Air Service HS-2L, which had crashed in September 1922. Rotted remnants of the hull and numerous metal parts, old tools, etc., were recovered and taken to the NAC at Rockcliffe. Another "archaeological dig" followed at Long Lac, Ontario, where G-CAOS had crashed in 1927. This resulted in such treasures as a Liberty engine, a radiator, and many more fittings.

Due to the good finds of metal components; locating in the US an original set of HS-2L wings, empennage, floats and struts; obtaining a suitable Liberty engine from the NAC's great friend, Cole Palen of Old Rinebeck, New York; plus a set of HS-2L drawings from the US Navy, in 1975 the NAC began work on a full-scale HS-2L. Building a completely new hull was the biggest challenge for the team, but all the heavy work was done by 1984. The magnificent HS-2L replica went on

This beautifully-crafted HS-2L composite replica was created by Canada's National Aviation Museum 1975-86. The preserved hull of the original aircraft sits under the replica's starboard wing. The details of this world-class project are covered in K.M. Molson's essential book *Canada's National Aviation Museum: Its History and Collections*. (J.W. Jones, Gordon McNulty)

display in 1986. Resplendent in the markings of Laurentide Air Service, and bearing its original civil registration, this HS-2L is a perpetual monument to Canada's bush flying pioneers. It also honours the museum's great curator from the 1960s, Kenneth M. Molson, his staff including A.J. "Fred" Shortt, and

Molson's successor, Robert Bradford. Without their tireless work, Canada would not have the supreme aviation history collection enjoyed today by all who visit it in Ottawa. No project vaguely resembling the HS-2L composite replica has been attempted by the museum since Molson/Shortt/Bradford days.

While flying boats dominated in Canada, where the nation's first "airports" were its natural lakes and rivers, there also was some commercial flying using wheel and ski planes, and the occasional float plane made an appearance. Canada's first twin-engine, civil plane is thought to be this one of a kind, float-equipped Dayton-Wright F.P.2. Owned by the Dayton-Wright Airplane Co. of Dayton, Ohio, it was chartered by the Spanish River Pulp and Paper Co. in the summer of 1922 for aerial forestry trials. It carried the joint US-Canada registration N-CAED. J. Scott Williams was piloting it on September 28, when a float collapsed on takeoff from Michipicoten Bay north of Sault Ste. Marie. 'AED was a wreck, although Williams was unhurt. (CANAV Col.)

Civil versions of the D.H.9 bomber also played minor roles, as with Laurentide Air Service (above) or G-EAQP, which F.S. Cotton operated in Newfoundland in 1921. (William J. Wheeler Col.)

On March 3, 1922 F.S. Cotton made the first known flight from Newfoundland to Labrador in this ski-equipped Martinsyde. His route was from Botwood to Battle Harbour, from where he continued to Cartwright. (E. Parsons Col.)

Jack Elliot's JN-4 G-CAFS said to be at Red Lake in the spring of 1926 (but 'AFS does not appear on the civil aircraft register until August). Elliot had a successful operation in Hamilton. He bought and re-sold many surplus JN-4s, built others from spare components, and marketed 3-seat conversions for private and barn-storming customers. He also collaborated with the Elliott brothers in Sioux Lookout in developing JN-4 skis. Flight training, aerial photography and advertising, and charter and exhibition flying kept Elliot busy into the 1930s. (NMST 08074)

Progress Far and Wide

Red Lake Gold Rush

By the turn of the 20th Century prospectors were criss-crossing the mysterious Canadian Shield in search of Eldorado – the mythical mother lode of gold. Impressive strikes were made in northwestern Quebec around Rouyn and Amos, and in adjacent Ontario. Transportation-wise, airplanes were the way to get around in this difficult land, so investors began to be attracted more into this niche market. In 1924 Laurentide Air Service set up a base on Lake Temiskaming near Haileybury. Business seemed brisk, but end-of-season profits were slim. The service did not resume following the spring thaw of 1925.

Jack Elliot – Red Lake's original bush flying pioneer. (Red Lake Museum)

Meanwhile, brothers Lorne and Ray Howey were striking pay dirt at Red Lake in distant northwestern Ontario. News spread around the world, resulting in a gold rush. People could reach the area by rail, but this still left them about 80 miles from Red Lake, several days travel by canoe in summer, or dog team and snowshoe in winter.

Jack Elliot, who had a successful flying operation in southern Ontario, decided to test the Red Lake market. In the spring of 1926 he sent two JN-4s by rail to Rolling Portage (today's Hudson) near Sioux Lookout. On March 3 Elliot

Elliot's JN-4s G-CADW and 'AEI being unloaded at Sioux Lookout in February 1926; then being serviced using an improvised double nose hangar. Attempting such an enterprise in Canadian Shield winter conditions shows what spirit imbued the country's young aviation community. 'ADW soon was wrecked near Hudson, but 'AEI survived the season. Following a later accident at London, it served the Leavens brothers of Belleville, then sat in storage until lost in a 1951 fire in Campbellford, Ontario. (CANAV Col.)

in G-CADW and Harold Farrington in G-CAEI made the first flights into Red Lake. On March 26 'ADW crashed, injuring pilot Howard Watt and passenger Jack Hill. Some locals rushed to the scene to drag the fuel-soaked men clear. Interviewed in hospital, Hill explained that the plane didn't seem to perform after takeoff. He later said that he would stick to the trail on future prospecting trips. In an upbeat case a few days later, Harold Farrington flew a seriously ill W.R. Stump out of the bush to medical assistance in Sioux Lookout.

In the short flying season before break-up, Elliot's operation carried 587 passengers and nearly 3000 lb freight and mail. In this period he was allowed by the Post Office to issue his own air mail stamps. Come break-up, however, he was grounded, since his ski-equipped JN-4s would not be practical on floats. (In March 1996 several aircraft commemorated Elliot's original flight by ceremonially overflying the same country.)

Jack Elliot's set-up in Hamilton in the late 1920s – he clearly knew the value of advertising! (LAC C61597)

The Curtiss Lark has its skis fitted on Ramsay Lake. (Jack McNulty Col.)

Patricia Airways and Exploration

Others appreciated the air transport potential in mineral development. In 1925 Toronto "Bay Street man" Frank E. Davison set up Patricia Airways and Exploration on the basis of 1000 shares each of $100. Among his partners were Sir Henry Pellatt of Casa Loma fame, Roy Maxwell of the OPAS, and Harold A. "Doc" Oaks – an RFC veteran, geologist and soon to be PAE's first pilot. Davison ordered a new Curtiss Lark (G-CAFB), which Curtiss pilot Charles S. "Casey" Jones, Roy Maxwell and Toronto *Daily Star* reporter Frederick Griffin delivered from the factory at Garden City, Long Island, to Buffalo on March 21, 1926. They covered the 330 miles at 100 mph, which Griffin described as "about as fast as anyone would want to go".

Air engineer S.A. "Sammy" Tomlinson with pilot H.A. "Doc" Oaks, the initial crew of the Curtiss Lark at Hudson. A wartime veteran, Tomlinson emigrated to Canada in 1924, working first with the OPAS, then being chief engineer at WCA. After a wartime stint in the RCAF, he served with CPA and Austin Airways. He passed on in 1973 and was inducted the following year into Canada's Aviation Hall of Fame. (William J. Wheeler Col.)

On March 25 Curtiss pilot Ed Ronne with Maxwell and Griffin flew the Lark to Leaside Field, where it was loaded with snowshoes, sleeping bags, rations, etc. for the ferry flight to Red Lake. Maxwell, engineer Sammy Tomlinson and Griffin were seen off at Leaside on March 28 by a crowd that included F.E. Davison and mining kingpin J.E. "Jack" Hammel. Two and a half hours later they landed at sunset on Ramsay Lake, Sudbury. "The little ship just swallows the distance," Griffin noted

The great Howey Mine that developed soon after the initial Red Lake gold rush of 1926. Since the highway to Red Lake (Hwy 105) was not completed until 1947, the community counted heavily on air transportation from its inception. To this day Red Lake remains an important northern aviation hub. (Red Lake Museum)

of this 225-mile leg. The plane's skis arrived by train next day, were fitted and test flown, but poor weather set in. It was April 2 before 'AFB continued, but it didn't get far – only a bit beyond Chapleau, since weather again intervened. The Lark reached Orient Bay on Lake Nipigon on April 8, then Sioux Lookout four days later – 23 days and 1700 miles from Long Island.

Under Doc Oaks the Lark went straight to work carrying passengers on

The famous Lark during summer operations. Through 1927 G-CAFB reportedly logged some 50,000 miles and carried 34 tons of freight and mail in Northwestern Ontario. (William J. Wheeler Col.)

Unknown principals and associates of Frank E. Davison's Toronto-based mining interests. The occasion was the December 1926 delivery of Stinson SB-1 Detroiter G-CAFW from Northville, Michigan to Leaside airport. The first of Eddie Stinson's renowned "Detroiter" series had flown the previous January. Davison bought three: G-CAFW, 'AGF and 'AJC. Powered by the 220-hp Wright J-5, these 6-seat utility planes proved efficient. Unfortunately, on June 16, 1927 'AGF was wrecked at Haileybury when a float collapsed on landing, but pilot Cumming and Fred Koehler of Stinson were uninjured. The wreck was sent for rebuild to Stinson. In June 1928 it joined newly-formed Great Western Airways of Calgary, this time as G-CANI. On July 19, 1934 it was wrecked at Cochrane, Alberta, while with Chinook Flying Service – Fred McCall had been taking off when his engine died. (Archives of Ontario)

the 1-hour route to Red Lake at a fare of $120 – a bargain considering time saved (it is said to have taken 12 days to break the first dog sled trail from Hudson to Red Lake). When the Howey Mine was established at Red Lake, company president J.E. Hammell claimed that by using the Lark, then Western Canada Airways' Fokkers, more than a year was saved in reaching production. Weather permitting, the Lark flew daily, until crashing at Hudson on September 12, 1927. Pilot J.R. Ross and three men from Jackson Manion Mines escaped. The wreck was sent to Canadian Vickers in Montreal for repairs, but was scrapped in the end. Meanwhile, Patricia Airways and Exploration had added Stinson Detroiters G-CAFW and 'AGF to its Red Lake and Haileybury-Rouyn markets. A report for 'AGF illustrates the effort expended on and the slim returns from a typical bush flying effort:

Patricia Airways' former Stinson G-CAGF in its later markings with Great Western Airways of Calgary. (G.R. Spradbrow)

Stinson SB-1 G-CAJC of Patricia Airways on winter operations. Eddie Stinson's beloved Detroiters brought the comfort of an enclosed cabin to air travel in North America. Northwest Airways became the first airline to operate this type. The "SB" series continued into June 1927, by when some 41 had been delivered. Stinson's monoplane "SM" series then arose. (William J. Wheeler Col.)

***Performance of No.2 Stinson
Under Pilot W.N. Cumming.
Installed in Service at Haileybury
on March 29th 1927.
In Service 18 Days out of 19 Days.***

Total flights	105
Passengers carried	160
Baggage	2076 lb
Express	81 lb
Mail	51 lb
Hours flying	50
Gas used	689 gal
Oil used	19 gal
Total flying hours for machine	55 hr 42 min
Total engine hours	73 hr 39 min
Total mileage flown with machine	5565
Revenue miles flown	5000
Total revenue	$3502.50

First Seaplane across North America

In 1927 Doc Oaks was the first to receive the Trans-Canada Trophy, instituted to commemorate the first trans-Canada flight by a single aircraft. This award came about after the American flying enthusiast, J. Dalzell McKee, proposed an expedition to Hudson Bay using his Douglas O-2B on floats. McKee, however, abandoned this, when the plane's performance at all-up weight with a 200-hp Liberty fell short (while at Sudbury in July 1926, the O-2B refused to get off the water).

Needing to get his plane to Douglas in San Diego for modifications, McKee decided to fly it there. He sought the assistance of the RCAF, which assigned an experienced advisor, S/L A.E. Godfrey (RCAF HQ realized that, by taking this opportunity, Godfrey would gain valuable experience in float operations). Arrangements were made for the RCAF and OPAS to assist McKee with fuel and other services. He and Godfrey departed Montreal for Ottawa on September 11, 1926. They took off again next day, but were forced down by weather, not reaching Sudbury until the 13th. Two days later they passed Sioux Lookout and reached Lac du Bonnet, Manitoba. En route they had made some precautionary landings to check their bearings. Much of the way they navigated by the "iron compass", as aviators called the train tracks.

J. Dalzell McKee's handsome Douglas MO-2 seaplane. Crewed by him and RCAF pilot S/L A. Earl Godfrey, in September 1926 the MO-2 became the first aircraft to fly across Canada, a heritage landmark that is thoroughly detailed in such books as *Canada's Flying Heritage*. (CANAV Col.)

Francisco, where the O-2B was left for a Douglas ferry pilot. In his report to RCAF HQ, S/L Godfrey later wrote:

I had never met Mr. McKee until an hour before the flight commenced. I found him to be a man of whom I cannot speak too highly ... a man of great initiative and a very hard worker, always ready to help in any situation no matter what is entailed, and never allowing any obstacle to stand in the way. We became fast friends, our trip and friendship being a thing that will always remain fresh in my memory.

J. Dalzell McKee and his crewmate A.E. Godfrey. (CANAV Col., DND RE17753)

Efforts to get away from Lac du Bonnet on the 16th proved fruitless after a float flooded. On the 17th, however, McKee and Godfrey reached Prince Albert, then were at Wabamun Lake near Edmonton next evening. Following the Thompson River, they reached Jericho Beach, Vancouver on the 19th. On the 22nd they started for San Diego, stopping first in Seattle, where they met Bill Boeing. Next day they made Eureka in northern California. On the 23rd they landed in San

In appreciation for help given by the RCAF, OPAS and Controller of Civil Aviation J.A. Wilson, McKee donated a silver cup – the Trans Canada Trophy, which became known simply as the "McKee Trophy". Most years since then it has been awarded to the Canadian contributing most significantly to progress in Canadian aviation. For 1927 McKee planned another tour: Montreal to Edmonton, north to Herschel Island, across Alaska, down the coast to Vancouver, then back to Montreal. Two Vedettes and the Douglas would be used, the latter by now having a 400-hp P&W Wasp "A" and redesignated MO-2B ("M" for modified). Among expedition personnel were S/L Godfrey and F/L A.T.N. Cowley. Godfrey test flew the Vedettes at Canadian Vickers on June 9, 1927. That same day McKee was landing Vedette G-CAGB on Lac la Pêche north of Montreal. His touch-down was hard, the plane broke up and McKee drowned. His great plans were finished

The Trans-Canada Trophy, Canada's perpetual memorial to its finest aviation citizens. (CANAV Col.)

and the remaining two aircraft ended on RCAF strength. However, the success of the initial McKee – Godfrey expedition strengthened the resolve of Canada's air transport visionaries, some of whom already were discussing the topic of transcontinental air travel.

McKee, Godfrey and the MO-2 en route over northern Saskatchewan. (CANAV Col.)

J.A. Wilson

Over the decades there has been some competition for the title of "father" of Canadian civil aviation. While several names may be mentioned in this regard, no individual deserves the appellation more than John Armistead Wilson. In 1936 the Controller of Civil Aviation, a branch of the DND, had field offices in Montreal, Toronto, Winnipeg and Edmonton. In charge was J.A. Wilson, whose deputies, A.T.N. Cowley and A.D. McLean, were responsible for the CCA's Air Regulations and Airways branches. Such other vital areas as the trans-Canada airway, radio and meteorological affairs, flight training, the flying clubs, and licensing of pilots and air engineers all were in Wilson's domain.

J.A. Wilson, Canada's long-serving Controller of Civil Aviation and top contender for the honourable title "Father of Canadian Civil Aviation". (CANAV Col.)

Raised and educated in Scotland, J.A. Wilson qualified as an engineer in 1901, then worked in India before emigrating to Canada. In 1910 he was with the Department of Naval Services and in 1918 helped organize the short-lived Royal Canadian Naval Air Service. In 1919 he joined the Canadian Air Board, from where he strove diligently to establish Canada as a leader in civil aviation. In 1922 he became Controller of Civil Aviation, after which he was busy promoting aviation in every possible commercial application. He was a driving force leading to the Canadian flying club movement, and instrumental in organizing pioneer air mail ventures in 1927-28. Ever since the 1920 trans-Canada flight, he promoted a national airway. As this inevitably took shape, he spent much time on inspection tours, making sure that schedules were being met, that work was being done according to contracts, etc. Writing in *Legion Magazine* March 2005, Hugh A. Halliday summarized this great man's accomplishments, noting in part:

Wilson's modus operandi throughout his career was to be industrious and informed. He was never a pilot, yet he flew often as a passenger to remote corners of the nation. In 1924 he travelled 16,000 kilometers by flying boat, and in 1934 he covered 24,000 kilometers, almost two-thirds by air, to review the state of airfields across Canada and in the Arctic. Wilson also took the public pulse at scores of air meets across the nation. He corresponded with soldiers, statesmen, celebrities and editors.

If there was an international conference on aviation, Wilson was sure to attend, usually to present a paper on Canadian aerial progress and to learn about developments elsewhere. He was equally at home with British planning of Imperial airship routes and American airline concepts that married large airmail subsidies to nascent airline development, allowing the latter to expand into a complex matrix of routes.

Wilson was transferred to the new Department of Transport in November 1936, still serving as controller of civil aviation. In that capacity he was named a director of Trans-Canada Airlines (later Air Canada) upon its formation. However, he remained in touch with the Department of National Defence, and in 1939 was largely responsible for mobilizing civil aviation as a component of Canada's war effort. Upon signing of the British Commonwealth Air Training Plan agreement on Dec. 17, 1939, his Department of Transport division was tasked with choosing and developing sites for training bases. Some of these bases were established at existing airfields; others sprouted from virgin farmlands; all were chosen according to strict standards that ignored political considerations and focused on service requirements. Many of the schools were organized by the flying clubs that Wilson and his colleagues had championed in 1928.

There was more. From the Department of Transport, Wilson co-ordinated meteorological, radio and airfield services. He was a key figure in organizing Ferry Command, itself responsible for thousands of aircraft being flown directly from North America to overseas theatres. Late in 1942 he attended a conference in London and helped plan a Canadian government Trans-Atlantic Air Service, a service that would lay the foundation for later transoceanic air services by Trans-Canada Airlines. Late in 1944, he attended the conferences that established the International Civil Aviation Association (ICAO), which ultimately established its headquarters in Montreal.

Accolades abounded. In 1945, Wilson was awarded the Trans-Canada Trophy ... In July 1946, he was appointed a Commander, Order of the British Empire (CBE). Two years later, the Norwegian government bestowed upon him their Cross of Liberation. He died in 1954, but death did not curtail his honours; in 1973 he was named to the Canadian Aviation Hall of Fame.

In getting around Canada to carry out their many CCA duties, J.A. Wilson's staff used a fleet of superb aircraft, whether the KR-34, Puss Moth, Rambler, Stearman (shown), Stinson or Waco. (William J. Wheeler Col.)

Western Canada Airways

Pilots and air engineers have always adapted to the economic times, changing jobs as conditions oblige, especially when employment fails. But one of Canada's pioneer operators began solidly and remained that way, providing employees from clerks to mechanics and pilots with long, steady, prosperous careers. This was Western Canada Airways, incorporated on December 10, 1926 by Winnipeg's James A. Richardson. In 1930 WCA would evolve into Canadian Airways then, about a decade later, into Canadian Pacific Airlines.

Seeing the need for transportation in the inaccessible north, in 1926 Richardson ordered some new Fokker Universals and hired H.A. "Doc" Oaks, then with Patricia Airways and Exploration. In late December he sent Oaks and C.A. "Al" Cheesman to Teterboro, New Jersey to collect the first Universal. This aircraft, G-CAFU *City of Winnipeg*, reached Hudson on Christmas Day and two days later Western Canada Airways was making money. Revenue by month's end totalled $180.

A Toronto *Daily Star* item of January 25, 1927 reported how the Red Lake Transportation Company at this time had 50 teams of horses hauling equipment and supplies on an ice road from Hudson to mines as far as 100 miles distant. Gas-powered tractors shared this work, but the airplane was increasing its influence, as noted by the *Daily Star*: "The giant five-passenger plane of Western Canada Airways Limited, which is operating from Hudson to the various mining fields, is giving … rapid transportation of men, supplies and even dogs into the north to help speed up the work." For January alone *City of Winnipeg* logged 87 hours, carrying 78 passengers and 5 tons of freight.." With all this activity, no one was surprised when Oaks and Cheesman set off by train for New York to collect another Universal. Meanwhile, the *Daily Star* of February 15 was describing the boomtown atmosphere in Hudson: "The hotels are filled to capacity … People … are optimistic now that mining machinery is being moved in and there are many rumours of still other mining companies … taking in large shipments of supplies before the break up." All this was only the beginning of what would become a long relationship between mining and commercial aviation.

Fokker Universal G-CAFU "City of Winnipeg" – the first Western Canada Airways plane. H.A. Oaks and S.A. Cheesman ferried it to Canada beginning on December 16, 1926 at Fokker in New Jersey and reaching the WCA base at Hudson on Christmas Day. So began a legacy that would end in the 1990s with Canadian Airlines International. Shown at Hudson with 'AFU are four of the men who brought WCA to the forefront during the Fort Churchill airlift of 1927: J.R. "Rod" Ross, Bernt Balchen, S.A. "Al" Cheesman and F.J. "Fred" Stevenson. An accident finally ended the extensive career of G-CAFU on December 17, 1939. (CANAV Col.)

The WCA "office" set up in January 1927 at Gold Pines by Harold Farrington. A great national airline would grow from this humble niche. (*Canadian Aviation* magazine Col.)

WCA got an early start promoting its services and its geographical domain. (*Canadian Air Review* Col.)

A superb view of WCA's original Fokker Universal G-CAGD, published here for the first time in any book. The pilot, wearing his leather face mask and goggles, would have praised the arrival in July 1928 of WCA's first enclosed-cockpit Super Universal. This photo also gives excellent details for any artist or modeller of the floats and fittings, the Wright J-4B engine installation, the engine exhaust and markings. (W.J. McDonough Col.)

Doc Oaks delivered G-CAGD to Hudson on February 26, 1927. Here is sits at Camp Borden, where Oaks cleared customs. The aircraft is on Fokker skis, which proved too narrow for bush work, so Oaks had the Elliott brothers of Sioux Lookout make up wider skis. Soon both Fokkers had been damaged, just as WCA took on the government contract to support development work at Fort Churchill. Repairs were rushed, Fokker No.3 G-CAGE was delivered in March, and the Fort Churchill contract was a success. (CANAV Col.)

Fort Churchill Project

In this period Ottawa, wanting to shorten the trans-Atlantic sea route for prairie grain, was planning a new harbour on Hudson Bay; engineers were anxious to start drilling through the ice at Fort Churchill. RCAF Fairchilds supported this work, then Western Canada Airways was contracted by the Department of Railways and Canals in March 1927 to fly men and materiel from the head-of-rail at Cache Lake on the Hudson Bay Railroad, 200 miles south of Fort Churchill. Since two WCA planes were unserviceable due to accidents, Fokker provided technical support, including Norwegian aviation pioneer Bernt Balchen, and the aircraft soon were back at work. Balchen stayed on as one of the work-a-day pilots, assisting chief pilot J.R. "Rod" Ross and Fred Stevenson. Work commenced on March 20 when two Universals left Hudson. Over the next month they shuttled back and forth in sub-zero weather between Cache Lake and Fort Churchill. The job was finished on April 17 and the planes returned to Hudson just days ahead of spring break-up. Eight tons of cargo and some passengers had been carried over 102 flying hours. In 1927 Ottawa announced that it would build its port at Fort Churchill. Part of the credit for this decision certainly could be claimed by James A. Richardson, his skilled and dedicated staff, and his two reliable Fokker Universals. In the Summer 1976 CAHS *Journal*, Bernt Balchen described some of the goings-on during the Fort Churchill job:

We started north from Hudson in the middle of March with the temperature down around -55°F... Al Cheesman flew in the plane with me and we followed Steve [Fred Stevenson] to Cache Lake... We were camped at the end of steel and we had some railroad cars with bunks... For one solid month the temperature never ... went above 45 below zero F. This was really the introduction of aircraft into cold weather operation in Canada... We were flying open cockpit planes with no heater ... One morning Steve was just getting airborne carrying a load of charcoal, a kitchen stove and a passenger from the survey gang for a flight to Fort Churchill. Steve got the plane off the lake, but it took longer than

A rare snapshot showing the rough camp and engineering emplacements at Fort Churchill in July 1928. Through the efforts of Western Canada Airways the year before, a major saltwater port soon arose on this site. (J.P. Culliton Col.)

normal. All of a sudden, he side-slipped down, hit sideways and washed out his landing gear... Ross and Steve got one of the rail cars and took the damaged gear with them to the railroad shop at The Pas [450 miles] and had a new axle and gear made. In 10 days they were back and had the plane flying again...

The July 15, 1932 (Vol.4 No.1) edition of *The Bulletin* – the Canadian Airway newsletter – tells more of the landmark project:

The Province of Manitoba is centrally located in the Dominion and extends 760 miles northward from the international

Fokker Universal G-CAGE "Fort Churchill" at Hudson in the spring of 1927. Beyond is Stinson Detroiter G-CAFW of Patricia Airways and Exploration. (Archives of Ontario)

Having joined WCA in March 1927, Fokker 'AGE, seen at Hudson, worked solidly through the coming months. But it would end very badly. While about to land at The Pas on January 5, 1928, it crashed, killing pilot Fred Stevenson. (J.P. Culliton Col.)

Fokkers 'AGD and 'AGE at Hudson over the summer of 1927. Then, a shipment of Royal Mail in front of the WCA office in Hudson, waiting for a plane to Red Lake. J.P. Culliton of the Hudson Bay Company stands on the right. The building beyond is the Bank of Commerce. (J.P. Culliton Col.)

boundary to lat. 60ºN... all railroads, with one exception, are confined to a belt some 160 miles wide along the southern boundary ... the agricultural area. The remainder of this vast territory is an expanse of bush, rivers and lakes without a single road. To negotiate it the traveller must have recourse to the canoe, steamboat, dog team or aeroplane... At that time Churchill was more "off the map" than Aklavik on the Arctic Ocean is today. On March 20th, 1927, the first move was made in transporting by air 20,000 lbs. of equipment and 12 men from Cache Lake, near Kettle Rapids … to Churchill, 200 miles distant. This work was to be done by "break-up" and 27 trips were necessary to accomplish the job. This was undoubtedly the greatest accomplishment in aerial transportation in Canada to that date.

The WCA fleet grew quickly. In this Gold Pines scene *circa* 1928 sit Universals G-CAFU and 'AIX, then Super Universal 'AFL. Each had a dark blue fuselage and yellow wings. While the Universal used a 200-hp Wright J-4, the "Super" had a 410/420-hp Pratt & Whitney Wasp. The advent of such reliable engines revolutionized commercial aviation throughout the Americas. The increased power of the Wasp raised gross weight in the 5-seat Universal from 4000 lb, to 5150 lb in the 7-seat Super Universal. (CANAV Col.)

G-CAFU at Gold Pines with two Fairchild FC-2s acquired in the fall of 1927. All are in WCA's original silver overall paint job with black trim. Gross weights for these types were 4000 and 3650 lb. Most FC-2s later were upgraded from the 200-hp Wright J-5 to the 300-hp J-6. Leigh Brintnell crashed G-CAIE soon after taking off from Hudson on the day before Christmas 1927; C.M.G. "Con" Farrell crashed 'AID at Regina on September 23, 1930. Both planes were destroyed, but the pilots escaped. (NMST 4769)

Founded in 1928, Canadian Pratt & Whitney soon established a gold-plated reputation for excellent engines and customer service. (*Canadian Air Review*)

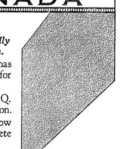
Later in 1927 WCA was on mining projects at Senneterre, Quebec, and north of The Pas. By October 4 Fred Stevenson, flying Universal G-CAGE from The Pas, had hauled 23 tons and 58 passengers on the biggest airlift to date in North America. For this solid work he received the U.S. Harmon Trophy for Canada. Sadly, the honour was posthumous – on January 5, 1928 Stevenson somehow got into a spin with 'AGE, and become Canada's first bush flying fatality.

Besides all the freight delivered, for 1927 Western Canada Airways flew 2500 fare-paying passengers. In 1928 it

Canada's great WWI fighter ace Donald R. MacLaren, DSO, MC and Bar, DFC. He returned home to pioneer in commercial aviation. (CANAV Col.)

CANADIAN VICKERS LIMITED

AIRCRAFT MANUFACTURERS

Land Planes — Sea Planes — Flying Boats — Amphibians

Designs
and
Modifications
for
Special
Requirements

Skiis
Floats
Repairs
Instruments
Service

Fokker Super-Universal

FOKKER SUPER-UNIVERSAL

CANADIAN CONSTRUCTION
UNDER EXCLUSIVE LICENSE

MONTREAL   Government
                  Contractors   **CANADA**

Canadian Vickers of Montreal built 15 Super Universals under licence from Fokker. These toiled stalwartly through the 1930s, contributing much to the development of Canada's sub-Arctic and Arctic hinterlands. (*Canadian Air Review*)

opened a flying school in Winnipeg, and absorbed Donald R. MacLaren's Pacific Airways. MacLaren, a wartime flier with 54 victories, had formed his company in 1925. Starting with an HS-2L, he earned most of his revenue from government fisheries contracts. Unable to finance expansion, however, he sold to James A. Richardson. WCA's new West Coast division added such equipment as two Boeing B-1Es and two Vedettes. Working mainly on fisheries, forestry and customs charters, the West Coast fleet tallied 445 flights in the first year.

Overall, WCA grew aggressively through 1928, ending the year with 27 aircraft, in spite of losing five in mishaps. Types on strength were: 9 Fokker Universals and 5 Super Universals, 3 Boeing flying boats, 1 Fokker F.VII trimotor, 1 HS-2L and 6 Avians, the latter used mainly in flight training.

One of the Boeing B-1 flying boats that served WCA so well on the West Coast. Duties ranged from air taxi to aerial photography, forestry surveying, prospecting support and fisheries patrols. G-CAUF joined the company in September 1928 under district superintendent D.R. MacLaren. It served into 1932, when it was retired and scrapped. This scene in Victoria Harbour with the Empress Hotel beyond easily reminds one of modern-day Victoria with Beavers and Twin Otters tying up daily. (William J. Wheeler Col.)

In its rapid fleet build-up through 1928, WCA purchased the 10-passenger Fokker F.VII-3m G-CASC. Powered by three Wright Whirlwinds, it was a modern airliner by any standards. First flown in 1925, the prototype "3m" won headlines by taking CMDR Byrd on an Arctic expedition in May 1926. More than 200 Fokker trimotors served around the world, 'ASC being the only Canadian-owned example. It was lost in a hangar fire at Winnipeg on March 4, 1931. (C. Don Long Col.)

More New Companies

New air carriers were regularly appearing on the Canadian scene. In June 1925, for example, H.S. Quigley formed Canadian Airways by taking over the operations of Dominion Aerial Explorations (K.M. Molson differentiates between Quigley's early Canadian Airways and James A. Richardson's later Canadian Airways by referring to the former as "Canadian Airways (Old)". Inevitably, operators were coming more under the influence of big business, as in June 1928 when International Airways formed by taking over Elliot Air Service of Hamilton. In January 1929 Interprovincial Airways took over the flying side of Fairchild Aviation Ltd. of Quebec. Two weeks later Canadian Vickers of Montreal acquired Canadian Airways (Old), Canadian Transcontinental Airways, International Airways and Interprovincial. Richardson, who was loath to see Canadian companies fall under US domination was instrumental in this (a takeover of International Airways by J.F. O'Ryan, president of the Aviation Corporation of America, apparently was imminent). In July 1929 the new consortium was named the Aviation Corporation of Canada. Only General Airways of Rouyn was excluded, perhaps since it held no air mail contracts.

The Aviation Corporation of Canada was controlled by the CPR, whose charter since 1919 included the right to operate an air service. All the earlier company names faded by June 1930 when everything was under a new umbrella name – Canadian Airways, headed by James A. Richardson. The CNR became a financial partner by year's end. Soon the

Fairchild FC-2 G-CATR of International Airways. With the financial backing of several wealthy investors, in the summer of 1928 J.V. Elliot formed this company. Within a few weeks Canadian Airways (Old) of Montreal was added. International Airways won the big air mail contracts from Montreal through to Toronto and Windsor. By year's end, however, it was pressed for funds, so accepted an offer from Victor M. Drury of Canadian Vickers. But Drury's plan was to re-sell his shares to J.F. Ryan of the Aviation Corporation of Delaware. Through the efforts of James A. Richardson, who wanted to see Canada's airlines controlled by Canadians, a new syndicate was formed that included himself, Drury, the CPR, et al. International Airways and other such firms as Canadian Transcontinental Airways were now safe from US control. (C. Don Long)

royal blue and orange planes of Canadian Airways, flying a Canada Goose logo, were familiar from Vancouver Island to Cambridge Bay, Red Lake, Chibougamau and the Magdalens. Although Depression times had set in, Canadian Airways was solidly financed, so had a chance of surviving until the economy picked up.

G-CART of St. Hubert-based Canadian Transcontinental Airways. Like 'ATR it also ended with Canadian Airways. In 1933 it was cannibalized. In that process, its wings were used to build a new Fairchild 71 CF-AUA. (C. Don Long Col.)

Under the direction of K.M. "Ken" Molson, in 1962 the National Aeronautical Collection in Ottawa acquired FC-2W-2 NC6621 from Aero Service of Philadelphia. The museum restored NC6621 in the colours of G-CART. (J.W. Jones)

The great 1920s Montreal airline was Canadian Transcontinental Airways. Three of its aircraft are shown in these fine Don Long scenes: Fairchild 71 CF-AAT, Loening G-CARQ and Stearman G-CARR. The Fairchild carries one of the early "CF" registrations, as introduced in 1929. Thereafter, the old "G-C" series was allowed to die a natural death. 'AAT was lost in a crash near Sioux Lookout on March 12, 1936. Pilot H.A. "Art" Schade escaped, but passenger Russell Broley was badly hurt. The Loening was on contract to the Quebec Liquor Commission and thought to be doing "rum running" patrols, when it mysteriously burned at Rimouski on the night of June 5, 1930. Stearman C3B G-CARR began with CTA in August 1928, about when Don Long photographed it with its flashy checkerboard colour scheme. In 1930 the entire CTA fleet moved to Canadian Airways, 'ARR remaining on strength into 1940. Thereafter it had a varied career in Quebec until it was wrecked taking off at Rivière-du-Loup in January 2, 1947.

Regional Carriers:
National Air Transport

While the Aviation Corporation of Canada spread its influence, independent carriers persistently cropped up. Some were short-lived, others somehow survived. One busy operator was National Air Transport, incorporated in Toronto on July 4, 1928 by wartime veteran Earl Hand, DFC. NAT began at the old Leaside airfield on the northeast edge of Toronto along the Don Valley, then moved west a few miles to Barker Field on Dufferin St. Buhl CA-5 Airsedan G-CATO and D.H.60 Moth G-CAUD were NAT's first planes, then CA-3C Sport Airsedan G-CATP was added, and NAT became a Buhl distributor.

In March 1927 Buhl-Verville of Detroit had become the first US aircraft manufacturer awarded a Department of Commerce "Approved Type Certificate" (in 1926 the ATC became mandatory, as the US sought to regulate aircraft design). The first B-V design, the 3-seat J4 Airster tandem cockpit sport plane, was a solid product, but few were sold. Then B-V reformed as the Buhl Aircraft Co. and began producing cabin "Airsedans" for the commercial market. First came the 5-seat CA-5, which fared well in the marketplace.

National Air Transport proved adept at getting in the news. This was important to keep the company in the public eye, so long as the news was good. Initial coverage appeared in July 1928 with a press release noting that NAT's 5-seat Buhl had great power and "the maximum of safety". On August 27, 1928, Earl Hand flew the air mail from Windsor to Hamilton in 'ATO, from where Jack Caldwell of Canadian Transcontinental Airways took it on to

National Air Transport's Buhl CA-5 G-CATO. Manufactured in Marysville, Michigan, 'ATO joined NAT in August 1928, then served well until lost in a hangar fire at Barker Field in 1935. The CA-5, similar in category to its contemporary, the Stinson Detroiter, had a wing span of 42', length of 27' 8" and gross weight of 3700 lb. Top speed was 120 mph and maximum range about 850 miles when fuelled with 90 US gallons of gas. A new CA-5 was priced at the factory at $12,500. (C. Don Long Col.)

One of the handsome Curtiss P-1B fighters (U.S.A.A.C. 27-75) of the 17th Pursuit Squadron visiting Leaside from Selfridge, Michigan at the time of the Cleveland air race in August 1929. (C. Don Long Col.)

Toronto in Fairchild 'AIP. On October 25 an NAT Moth and Buhl delivered some goods from Buffalo to Leaside for Tait Radio Sales. In those days, even such an ordinary charter was story enough to get into the local newspapers.

On August 28, 1929 NAT entered the 310-mile Toronto-Cleveland goodwill air race. Seven planes competed in the commercial category, Ed Johnston and James A. Crang each piloting an NAT Buhl. Hervé St-Martin of Skyways Ltd. came first in a Travel Air, winning $2000. Johnston flew G-CATP to a second place finish ($1200), while Crang came third ($800). The race was topped off by a gala at the Royal York Hotel attended by 300 guests, including members of the US Army's 1st Pursuit Group from Selfridge, Michigan, in Toronto performing at the CNE with their Curtiss P-1 fighters.

Over the winter of 1929-30 National Air Transport operated the Leamington-to-Pelee Island air mail. By this time the fleet numbered eight planes. Besides mail, NAT carried passengers, instructed students and served the mining and forestry industries from such locations as Haileybury, Kirkland Lake and Sudbury. In December 1929 two NAT planes

helped in an aerial search from Kingston for the missing tanker *John B. Irwin* (which later turned up). A news item of April 1, 1931 noted how NAT pilots Kelly Edmison and Frank Fisher had been supporting Sam Sainsbury's prospecting expedition to the remote Belcher Islands in Hudson Bay. In 1932 Toronto-Buffalo passenger service was inaugurated by NAT. In late January 1933 there was the story of NAT pilot Mike Poupore with Joe Lucas flying into remote Montrose Lake

from Gogama, Ontario, to evacuate a gravely ill Indian, Ignace Twain.

Getting onto the front page due to an accident is every air operator's worst dream. This nightmare visited National Air Transport on April 4, 1931 when D.H.60 Cirrus Moth G-CATI crashed at Sudbury, killing instructor Frank Murdoch and injuring his student, M.O. "Buck" Smith. Another prang was worse. On September 8, 1935 Maurice J. Welsh and Ronald Brooksbank were aloft in a Gipsy Moth when the aircraft fatally plummeted to earth in Richmond Hill, minus a wing. Next, on September 11, 1933 NAT's Buhl CA-6 Standard Airsedan CF-ACX burned on the water at Huntsville, Ontario. In a final blow, a November 12, 1935 fire at Barker Field destroyed Buhl Air Sedans G-CATO and 'ATP, Bull Pup CF-AQI and Moth G-CATF. The month prior, Earl Hand had run in the federal election as a Reconstructionist, but lost badly. National Air Transport now faded from the scene.

Buhl CA-6 CF-AAY of Norman Cherry's Prince Albert-based Cherry Red Airlines. It was wrecked in an accident on Montreal Lake while en route from Prince Albert to Lac La Ronge with Alva Malone at the controls. Anglican missionary G. Fisher, his wife and two children all were safe. Certified in 1929, the 6-seat CA-6 was powered by a 300-hp Wright J-6, compared to the CA-5 with its 220-hp J-5. Gross weight was 4200 lb and top speed 140 mph. (Joseph P. Juptner Col.)

Canada's Buhl Airsedans

Reg'n/Year	Type	Owner	Fate
G-CATP 1928	CA-3	NAT	DBF Toronto 12-11-35
G-CATO 1928	CA-5	NAT	DBF Toronto 12-11-35
CF-AAY 1929	CA-6	Cherry Red Airlines	Cr. Near La Ronge, Saskatchewan 5-10-29
CF-ACX 1929	CA-6	NAT	DBF Huntsville, Ontario 11-9-33
CF-AOZ 1930	CA-6	Brook Construction of Prince Albert, Saskatchewan	Cr. Near Norway House, Manitoba 22-9-35
CF-AQG 1931	CA-6J	Brook Construction	Cr. Emma Lake, Saskatchewan 21-6-33
CF-OAQ 1937	CA-6M	OPAS	DBR Caribou Lake, Ontario 23-7-45-45
CF-OAR 1937	CA-6M	OPAS	DBR Mishabashu Lake, Ontario 23-1-45
CF-OAS 1937	CA-5M	OPAS	Scrapped 1951
CF-OAT	CA-5M	OPAS	DBR Hawk Lake, Ontario 22-6-40

A Colonial Sikorsky S-38 amphibian about to power its way up the ramp from Toronto Bay. (Toronto Harbour Commissioners Archive)

Toronto to Buffalo

Toronto's first scheduled international passenger/air mail service was inaugurated in June 1929 by Colonial Western Airways, part of the Colonial Air Transport system, which had begun in 1926 between New York and Boston. Two high-performance, 10-passenger Sikorsky S-38 amphibians (NC9138 "Nonokas" and NC158H "Neekah") operated the new service from downtown waterfront terminals. Business offices were set up in Toronto's new Royal York Hotel and in Buffalo's Hotel Statler. The first S-38 left Toronto on June 29, the one-way fare being $17.50, return for $30.00, $14.00 one way if the traveller bought a book of tickets. Twice daily service then continued until late September. Business in Toronto was brisk all summer, especially in late August, when the Canadian National Exhibition was drawing tourists from New York State.

Chief pilot on the route was Owen J. O'Connor, a former US Navy flying boat man. On July 22 "Nonokas" sank in Toronto bay after striking a dead-head. After being salvaged, it was shipped back to Sikorsky in Bridgeport, Connecticut, while its replacement, NC198H, took over. A bit of fun was had on Labour Day, September 2, 1929 when Colonial's Charlie Maris, flying an S-38 on the scheduled run, unofficially raced a speedy Savoia-Marchetti S-62 from Buffalo, to prove which machine was faster. Both aircraft roared across the

Further views of Colonial Sikorsky activity at the Toronto Air Harbour in 1929. (C. Don Long Col.)

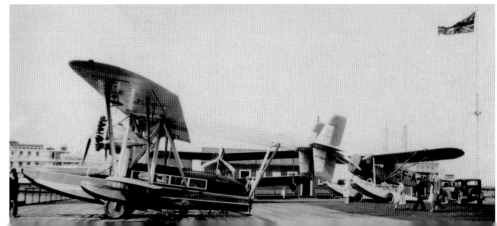

N9147, the S.62 that took part in the Buffalo-Toronto "race". Toronto's newly-opened Royal York Hotel is in the background. The S.62 mainly served as a military patrol plane. Basic specs (Sikorsky S-38 in brackets) were: length 40' 3" (40' 3"), wing span 54' 8" (71' 8"), gross weight 11,100 lb (10,500 lb), engine 1 x Asso 750 hp (2 x PW Wasp each 400 hp), top speed 137 mph (120 mph), max range 1250 mi. (750 mi.) (C. Don Long Col.)

Toronto waterfront in a photo finish and landed in the bay. Twenty minutes later Maris took off again for Buffalo, but his competition was done for the day, its engine unserviceable.

Although this service proved to be a great headline-grabber and everyone loved watching the S-38s coming and going, the handsome amphibians would not be back the following year. Passenger revenue proved to be scant, the mail contract insufficient to justify the operation (not to forget October 1929, which ushered in the Great Depression). Henceforth the Toronto-Buffalo air mail was carried by Canadian Colonial Fairchild FC-2W-2s based at Leaside airfield. In 1932 Ottawa cancelled most air mail service on account of the Depression. Only in June 1941 did Toronto-Buffalo service

re-commence, when American Airlines (formerly known as Colonial) put a DC-3 on the service. This continued later with the Convair 240 and DC-6, until Mohawk Airlines took over in June 1963 using Convairs.

Controller of Civil Aviation 1928 Report

In his 1928 annual report, Controller of Civil Aviation J.A. Wilson was upbeat: "The pioneer efforts of the years immediately following the Great War are now bearing fruit, and it is realized to-day in Canada, more than ever before, how important a factor aviation may be in the future growth of the Dominion." The Controller's report began with a chart illustrating civil aviation statistics.

The Controller focused on highlights – from the successful operations of the Ontario Provincial Air Service (by this time with 25 aircraft and a 1928 flying rate of 6227 hours), to how Western Canada Airways hauled more freight than all other Canadian air carriers combined, to Punch Dickins' first cross-tundra flight, to how the overseas mail had been sped by two days using RCAF aircraft delivering it to and from ocean liners. He noted how "283,000 pounds of mail were carried during 1928 under Post Office contracts without the loss or damage of a single letter."

Other Civil Aviation Statistics 1929

No. aircraft manufacturers	4
No. firms operating aircraft	81
Fights made	144,143
Hours flown	79,786
No. paying passengers	86,242
No. public seaplane ports	10
No. private seaplane anchorages	15
Total aerodromes land and sea	77
Total all aeroplanes	445
No. single-engine aeroplanes	281
No. multi-engine aeroplanes	2
No. floatplanes	119
No. flying boats	37
No. amphibians	6
No. licenced pilots	349
No. pilot-engineers	96
No. air engineers	212
No. unlicenced mechanics	150

Civil Aviation Statistics – 1925-1928

	1925	1926	1927	1928
Operating firms	8	14	20	55
Hours flown	4091	5860	12,070	42,500
Passenger miles	446,648	631,715	1,424,031	3,000,000
Freight (lb)	592,220	724,721	1,098,356	2,400,000
Mail (lb)	1080	3960	14,684	316,650
Licenced airharbours	34	34	36	44
Licenced aircraft	39	44	67	264
Commercial pilots	36	38	72	250
Private pilots	7	9	9	148
Air engineers	55	65	74	200

For West Coast operations, especially government fisheries duties, Western Canada Airways operated HS-2L, Boeing B-1 and Vedette flying boats. Seen in a typical coastal inlet setting is Boeing CF-ABB "Pintail". With a length of 32' 7", wing span of 39' 8", empty weight of 3220 lb and gross weight of 5000 lb, this type roughly equalled the much later coast plane, the DHC-2 Beaver. They were even comparable in horsepower: the Boeing's 420 to the Beaver's 450. While hundreds of 60+ year old Beavers still fly, wooden 1920s aircraft rarely lasted very long. First on strength in March 1929, CF-ABB toiled into 1935, then went for scrap. (NMST 1080)

G-CASK – the famous Super Universal in which Punch Dickins overflew the tundra in 1928. As shown in Robert Bradford's renowned painting honouring this historic event, the Western Canada Airways Fokkers of the day had a yellow wing with black registration letters, and a dark blue fuselage with white registration letters. (CANAV Col.)

More Iconic Figures

Punch Dickins

The roster of pioneer Canadian aviators bulges with the prominent names, mostly of men who had trained in wartime. From 1926 onward, many of these gravitated towards Western Canada Airways, Clennell H. "Punch" Dickins included. Born in Portage la Prairie in 1899, in 1916 he

Punch Dickins as a youthful yet experienced WCA pilot. Many of Canada's original bush aviators posed for such studio portraits, decked out in their Arctic finery. They were as much heroic figures then, as astronauts would be generations later. (CANAV Col.)

joined the infantry in WWI, then transferred to the RFC. It was over the front in France that he learned his most valuable lessons in airmanship, November 4, 1918 being a typical day. Flying a 211 Squadron reconnaissance D.H.9, he and his observer, 2Lt A.M. Adam, were attacked. They quickly shot down the enemy leader, about which the combat report succinctly observes, "This E.A. went on fire and broke up, the pilot leaving the machine in a parachute which did not open." As another enemy passed overhead, Adam also sent it down in flames.

The war over, Dickins joined the Canadian Air Force. He served at stations and detachments across Canada until January 1928, when he moved to WCA. That year LCol C.D.H. MacAlpine, head of Dominion Explorers, and his companion, Richard Pearce of *The Northern Miner*, chartered WCA Fokker G-CASK for a northern expedition. His crew was Punch Dickins and engineer William Nadin. For plane and crew, MacAlpine paid $75 daily, plus $1.50 a mile.

The party left Winnipeg on August 28, routing via Norway House, Churchill, Baker Lake, then across more than 800 miles of tundra and boreal country to Stony Rapids on Lake Athabaska. Next, they headed for Fort Fitzgerald, but landed out of gas on the Slave River. Happily, a barge came by with drums of fuel and 'ASK continued to as far as Fort Smith, thence home to Winnipeg on September 9 via Fort Chipewyan, Stony Rapids, Reindeer Lake, Cold Lake (Manitoba) and The Pas. The expedition logged 37 flying hours, covered 3965 miles and was the first by air over the tundra. This brought Dickins the 1928 Trans-Canada Trophy. That year he logged 1035 flying hours (half that would have been a busy year for any pilot).

Punch Dickins continued in aviation as a manager at Canadian Airways, help establish the CPR's Atlantic Ferry Operation in WWII, then enjoy a lengthy career with de Havilland Canada. His many honours along the way included the Distinguished Flying Cross (1917), McKee Trophy (1928), OBE (1935), Order of Canada (1968) and Member, Canada's Aviation Hall of Fame (1974). Punch Dickins' career is chronicled in numerous books, especially *Canada's Flying Heritage*, *De Havilland in Canada* and *They Led the Way*.

The sort of daunting natural terrain over which Punch Dickins, his passengers and G-CASK flew on their daring 1928 mission. (W.J. McDonough Col.)

Walter Edwin Gilbert

Former S.E.5a fighter pilot Walter Edwin Gilbert returned to aviation in 1927. He began by taking the RCAF refresher flying course at Camp Borden, which many wartime "retreads" were doing in this period. Beginning on April 8 under F/L Elmer Fullerton, he flew Avro 504Ks, doing all the basic exercises – "getting the feel" of once again being in the air. Exercises appear in his log book as "Turns and Landings", "Figure 8s", "X-wind Landings", "Forced Landings", "Gliding Turns", all very basic, but essential in the refresher process. The course, which totalled 11:45 hours, ended with a 30-minute solo in Avro 504 "EG" on May 27. P/O Gilbert now was posted to Cormorant Lake, Manitoba with "C" Flight, 5 Squadron, flying initially on June 17 in Avro Viper float plane G-CYGI.

Gilbert's duties were mainly on fire patrol in the Viper and the 2-engine Varuna flying boat. Besides fire patrols and searches, his log shows flights testing engines and wireless radios. Many patrols were cut short by snags or weather, as on July 15. Having patrolled in Viper "GG", Gilbert noted, "Forced landing Herb Lake. Broken oil pump drive shaft". On August 4 in Varuna "ZT" he had six passengers for a flight which he described as "Weight carrying test". This would have strained the under-powered Varuna and certainly was not a very clever undertaking by today's standards. On October 5 he flew a Vedette for the first time, going up in "GW" with F/L Sadler for 20 minutes, then soloing for 15 minutes.

One of Canada's all-time great pioneer aviators – Walter Edwin Gilbert. Having trained in the RFC (Canada) in 1917, he instructed in the UK, then fought over France in the S.E.5. Sent home with injuries, in the early 1920s he was active in the RCAF and in BC's nascent flying club movement, then got belatedly into commercial flying. Gilbert received the Trans-Canada Trophy for 1933, was inducted into Canada's Aviation Hall of Fame in 1974 and passed on in 1986. Here he is in the usual studio portrait, then in a more work-a-day setting. (CANAV Col.)

The summer done, P/O Gilbert returned to Camp Borden, his total peacetime flying being 74:30 hours. Through the winter of 1927-28 he flew various Avros on wheels and skis. On January 13, 1928 he flew a Fairchild FC-2 for the first time. Through this period his flight commanders and examiners included such WWI veterans as S/L George Brookes, F/L F.J. Mawdesley and F/L C.M. McEwen.

Come spring, Gilbert again was posted to Manitoba, this time on Vedettes, mainly doing photography. The season ended on October 25 when he flew "YB" to Winnipeg "to lay up for the winter", as he noted in his log.

Walter Gilbert now decided to leave the RCAF for a job with Western Canada Airways. On his first day of flying (December 18, 1928) he was on charter from The Pas to Pelican Narrows in

A Canadian Vickers Vedette (left) and a twin-engine Varuna, types flown by Walter Gilbert during his RCAF days in 1927-28. (William J. Wheeler Col.)

Fokker Universal G-CASF commanded by Herbert Hollick-Kenyon. He spent until March 10, 1929 mainly on mining charters, then was posted to Vancouver, commencing work on March 23 with Donald R. MacLaren in Boeing B-1E G-CAUF. There were several days of practice flying on 'UF and Vedette 'UT, then Gilbert began work on April 8. Log book excerpts show the variety of duties flying B-1Es CF-ABA and 'ABB. To begin, there was much photography and joy riding. Then came mining trips from Stewart and fisheries patrols from Swanson Bay (it was MacLaren's policy to keep a new pilot close to home, watch his progress, then gradually entrust him with the more demanding flying up the coast and in the mountains).

Fisheries missions meant trying to ensure that boats were working within specific distances from the mouths of rivers, that fish were being taken in season, and that nets were legal as to length and webbing. Patrols also inspected spawning grounds and transported fisheries personnel. One claim was that a single air patrol equalled the work of 40 patrol vessels. In its December 1934 edition, *Canadian Aviation* magazine reported that fisheries inspector D.S. Cameron had logged some 2300 patrol hours since 1923. In 1967 Walter Gilbert recalled this era:

A fisheries inspection scene *circa* 1930. The WCA Boeing might have been on operations with the large patrol vessel, perhaps checking out the smaller boats. In modern times, Canadian Forces Auroras were doing much the same work. (CANAV Col.)

I spent about ten months in all ... I had the remarkable experience of going into every hole and corner on the British Columbia coast... The fisheries patrol was just in its infancy, then. Don MacLaren was superintendent of the Western Canada Airways BC division and we had a very, very pleasant life, and a lot of fun. The salmon poachers had been having their own way with surface craft, because practically every fishing boat was faster than the old patrol boats the fisheries officers had ... They could recognize them coming miles away by the sound of their engines, and they'd immediately take their nets in and get out of the prohibited areas until the boats went away again...

Well, we beat that situation by taking advantage of the deep inlets that make up most of the BC coast. We knew where they were poaching. We'd come up the next inlet,

perhaps five or six miles away just on the other side of the mountain range that separated the two, then climb quickly and just suddenly appear over the top. We carried an 8 x 10 roll-film oblique camera and we'd catch them cold. We'd photograph the poachers from reasonably low elevation with some known object in the background. Then we'd land and take their papers ... They soon became used to that, and they'd team up to make it a little more difficult for us.

Then we started another racket. One of the fisheries patrol boats, if the weather was calm, just lay to, well off shore. We would spend the night tied up to her, and leave just at the first gray dawn, and come in and repeat our performance. We let the word be spread around that we had new equipment and were flying all night. That practically squelched the poaching for that year.

In January 1930 Walter Gilbert transferred to Edmonton, flying initially with C.H. "Punch" Dickins in Super Universal CF-AFL on January 21. Two days later he moved to Fort McMurray with the same plane. Break-up having commenced, on March 31, 1931 Gilbert flew south to Edmonton. With time on his hands he made up his log book, noting his peacetime flying hours to March 8, 1930 as 698:45. He would continue in aviation through the 1930s, but had other interests as well. In 1939, for example, he published a flying memoir, *Arctic Pilot*. During WWII he served with CPA at Vancouver, then Edmonton. In 1945 he and Russ Baker formed Central British Columbia Airways. Equipped with such types as the Beech 17, Junkers and Norseman, the company prospered, especially with government forestry work. Walter Gilbert left aviation in 1949. For a time he and his wife operated a fishing lodge, then settled in Washington state, where Walter did well in real estate.

From Walter Gilbert's Logbook, 1929

Date (1929)   Mission

April 18   Oblique photos Stave Lake area. Washed out.
            Camera operator Faulkner frost bitten.
April 18   Low scenics. Fraser River, Stave Falls.
April 26   Verticals for BC Electric over Fraser River. Also 5 obliques of base.
April 28   Sunday passenger joy-rides.
            Practice formation with RCAF for airport propaganda flight.
May 4   Charter trip to head of Narrows Inlet.
May 6   Photos of Rotary gathering in Stanley Park.
May 9   Victoria. Photos while awaiting D.R. MacLaren.
June 23   Charter to Deep Cove regatta. 5 passengers.
June 25   No.1 Fisheries. Major Motherwell. Lower Fraser
July 4   Vancouver to Swanson Bay via Campbell River, Alert Bay, Laredo Inlet.
July 5   Swanson Bay to Prince Rupert. Very bad visibility, 2:30 hours.
July 6   Stewart to Penguin Lake for Consolidated, 10,000 feet, 2:00 hours.
July 14   Stewart. Joy-riding (29 passengers).
July 19   Reconnaissance. Terrace highway. Mr. Gwyer passenger.
July 29   Stewart. Over Bear Creek divide and down Nass River to Mill Bay,
            thence to Prince Rupert. E.S. Holloway passenger (power corporation).
August 8   Fisheries. D.S. Cameron. Landings: Swanson Bay,
            Butedale, Lewis Channel, Keyell Bay, Ursula Channel,
            Butedale, Swanson Bay. 2:30 hours.

Stanley N. Knight

Stanley N. Knight was born in England on August 6, 1906. The family emigrated to Sudbury, Ontario but, with the father's death in 1919, returned to England. Stanley, however, came out again in 1924. He worked in Sudbury as a meter reader and electrician then, at age 20, was hired by Roy Maxwell of the OPAS. Beginning at Sault Ste. Marie as an "applicant air engineer" in February 1927, he worked in all areas, no doubt starting by pushing a broom. Gradually he learned his trade, from helping to overhaul Liberty and Cirrus engines, to rigging aircraft, repairing floats and hulls, etc. Knight later described the OPAS hangar as one of the best, having a superb slipway for the cumbersome HS-2L, marvellous shops, and every

HS-2L "Raven", wrecked at Fort Frances in 1929. Knight and pilot Ed McKay came through this close call. Then, Stan Knight (right) with his pilot, Ed Ahr, while they were crewing an OPAS HS-2L at Kenora the previous summer. (Stanley N. Knight Col.)

In 1927 Stanley N. Knight began in aviation as an eager young gopher around the main OPAS base at Sault Ste. Marie. He finished years later, a revered figure who had "done it all" in the bush and Arctic, and in such top positions as maintenance head at Central Aircraft during WWII. In retirement he roughed out an accurate memoir, and enjoyed the Canadian Aviation Historical Society during its grass-roots heyday. (Stanley N. Knight Col.)

tool required. There even was a blacksmith, Tommy Lake, who made all the spanners and other tools needed in maintenance. Knight recalled: "The main floor of the hangar ... could accommodate the assembly of two H-Boats with all wings on, and a third with the centre section and the extensions..."

Stan Knight had his first airplane ride in the summer of 1927, going in an H-Boat to Sudbury with pilot Terry Tully. The following summer he was stationed at Kenora with HS-2L pilot Ed Ahr and Gipsy Moth pilot Alex McIntyre. The "Gipsy" was from the first batch recently delivered from the UK and was, according to Knight, underpowered on its heavy Short floats.

Over the winter of 1928-29 Stan Knight studied for his air engineer's licence (granted in the spring), then was base engineer at Fort Frances with pilot Ed McKay. They lost HS-2L G-CAOR "Raven" on takeoff one July day, when it hit an 18-foot deadhead. Recalled Knight, "It ripped a hole down the right side of the hull under my seat some 2 feet wide and 8 feet long." Later in 1929 Knight was suffering from wanderlust, so contacted former OPAS mechanic, Tommy Siers, at Western Canada Airways. Siers was pleased to hire Knight to work at his base on the Red River near Brandon Avenue, and at Stevenson Field.

Knight soon transferred to Fort McMurray as Walter Gilbert's engineer on Super Universal 'ASN. The following narrative is a general reminiscence which Knight gave to Larry Milberry circa 1970. For some clarification, Walter Gilbert's log book entries for this June-July 1930 period are included, but these can be bit vague – as with many early bush pilots, few details were entered:

Air Engineer's Memoir

A pilot and engineer were very close. You were dependent on each other for so many things ... due to circumstances you were together day and night for weeks on end. At McMurray we operated off the snye across the junction of the Athabasca and Clearwater rivers. This was at Waterways, the end of steel about four

Stanley Knight with Walter Gilbert in Fokker G-CASN

Date (1930)	Route	Time (hrs.)
June 19	Edmonton - Fort McMurray	3:00
June 20	to Fort Simpson	6:50
June 21	to Fort McMurray	6:50
June 25	to Gordon Lake return	1:00
June 26	Fort McMurray to Fort Simpson	6:45
June 27	to Arctic Red River	6:05
June 28	to Fort MacPherson	0:25
June 29	to Aklavik	1:20
June 30	local joyriding	0:10
July 1	to Herschel Island and Fort Good Hope	6:20
July 2	to Fort Fitzgerald	7:45
July 3	to Fort Smith and Fort McMurray	3:10
July 4	to Wabasca and Edmonton	3:30

In early bush flying days, Cooking Lake near Edmonton was one of Canada's key aviation hubs. Flights operated from here down the Mackenzie River Valley as far as Aklavik, even into the Arctic islands. In this June 1930 Cooking Lake scene, recorded by air engineer Doug Burt, several classic bushplanes await assignments: Curtiss C-1 Robin CF-ALY of Consolidated Mining and Smelting, Super Universals G-CASN and 'ASM of WCA (often crewed by Gilbert and Knight), then Bellanca CH-300 Pacemakers of Commercial Airways, CF-AKI being nearest to the Fokkers.

miles from McMurray. We carried passengers and freight right down to Aklavik, but also served places from Fond du Lac to Stony Rapids, Snowdrift to Fort Reliance, Great Bear Lake, Coppermine, etc. A typical trip was one we made on floats in June and July 1930.

Leaving McMurray [June 20] our first call was Fort Chipewyan, a trading post due north on the shore of Lake Athabasca and at the headwaters of the Slave River. Next stop was Fort Fitzgerald about half way down the Slave. "Fitz" was quite a thriving community, as it commanded the only portage between Waterways and the Arctic Ocean. From here all the freight for the North had to be hauled across the portage – a road about 18 miles long ending at Fort Smith. Here was found the only hotel north of McMurray.

Our stop at Fitz was always accommodated by Moreys Bros. General Store. There was an attic over the store where we could stretch our "scratchers" (eiderdowns) out on the floor. The Moreys were very grand people and there was never any question of where we were going to stay. At many points where we called, it was almost embarrassing trying to decide at whose place we would stay, as the folks were starved for news of what was going on "outside". After supper there was always a gabfest where the women (what few there were) could put in their requests with us for little things that were unobtainable at the HBC.

Fort Resolution on the southeast corner of Great Slave Lake was next along the way and was considered a metropolis. Here, the hospitality of Carl Murdoff, the WCA agent, was enjoyed. Many games of bridge were played at Carl's and the evening highlight was "Amos and Andy" on his radio, one of the few in town. At five minutes to air time, a regular following of about 15 Indians would come in very quietly, sit on the floor in front of the radio, listen to the 15-minute show, rise, thank Carl very much, then disappear into the night.

Once at Fort Resolution a terrific 2-day blow threatened our aircraft. I had to take the caps off the floats and scuttle the Fokker in 4 feet of water to save her from breaking up on the dock. I spent the rest of the season getting rid of the sludge that had gotten into the floats that night.

Hay River, a small trappers' settlement on the southwest corner of Great Slave Lake, came next on our journey. Leaving here, we flew north down the Mackenzie River to Fort Providence. It had a large Catholic mission school and everyone welcomed us with open arms. Fort Simpson came next. Found at the junction of the Liard and Mackenzie rivers, the Royal Canadian Corps of Signals had a radio station here. This was one of only four such stations north of Edmonton, the others being Fort Smith, Fort Resolution and Aklavik. At Fort Simpson we always stayed with the signallers. As everywhere

en route, there was a fuel cache here that was kept well above the high-water level. This was about the muddiest place for refuelling, which usually took 2 or 3 barrels for our Fokker. Winter at Fort Simpson also was misery, as tons of snow had to be shovelled just to find the fuel drums, then they had to be hauled down to the Fokker on a sleigh.

Flying onward we next visited Fort Wrigley, a small post on the west side of the Mackenzie, then we flew on to Fort Norman, quite a large settlement. Just below the town is an island where the oil wells are situated. At Fort Norman we slept in an old half-built trapper's shack. This was nothing unusual, given how our business was somewhat of a circus. Leaving Fort Norman we went down the Mackenzie to The Ramparts, a narrowing

A typical summer aviation scene at the confluence of the Mackenzie and Liard rivers at Fort Simpson *circa* 1928. Aviation fuel is cached in drums along the beach to be used as needed. Aircraft are NAME's Fokker G-CARK (wrongly marked as to the hyphen), and Fairchild FC-2W-2 G-CATL, then WCA's Super Universal G-CASM. (W.J. McDonough Col.)

This 1929 aerial view shows how Fort Simpson hugged the bank of the Liard River. The old HBC post is lower right. (J.P. Culliton Col.)

Modern-day shipping and aviation at Hay River, NWT on July 13, 1992 – a Carter Air Twin Otter rests as the barge tug *Johnny Hope* passes. These twin modes of transport have been interacting along the Mackenzie system since the Imperial Oil expedition of 1921. (Larry Milberry)

... about 400 yards wide where the entire volume of the river rushes through the channel. This is spectacular to see from the air. Down river we would land at Fort Good Hope. Due to the effects of The Ramparts, this place has very poor conditions for tying up an aircraft. We always tried to avoid a long stop at Fort Good Hope, from where we set off for Arctic Red River. On this leg we crossed the Arctic Circle into "the land of little sticks" beyond the tree line.

At Arctic Red River, which turned out the darkest and finest muskrat furs in the NWT, we usually showed our appreciation for the hospitality with the odd jug, but this time we brought a couple

of cases each of tomatoes and celery. As we neared Arctic Red River we had to leave the river due to heavy smoke from a muskeg fire. We landed after midnight, but there still were a few people to meet us under the Midnight Sun. Since we were so thirsty, we each started sucking on nice, fat tomatoes. The local priest came by and I offered him one, which he could not refuse. I tossed it to him, he caught it, began polishing it, then wrapped it in a handkerchief. "Aren't you going to eat it?" I asked. "No," he replied. "That would be a sacrilege. I haven't seen a tomato in seven years!" Arctic Red River was home port to the old HBC vessel "Distributor", one of the best-known

boats on the river. She was an old stern wheeler that would plug along and load cordwood every few miles for fuel. Also of interest here was how the sled dogs were staked out along the river, left to molt and howl the summer away.

Now we crossed over to Fort McPherson, then on to Aklavik, in the Mackenzie delta and about 45 miles from the Arctic Ocean. Here there were the usual folks – a prosperous group of Eskimos, the missionaries, the RCMP, and the signallers. The Eskimos had their own schooners and were wealthy by anyone's standards. Mostly they trapped white fox in winter, then fished and loafed through the summer. While we were here, the Signals and RCMP requested a flight on July 1 to Herschel Island, just off the Yukon coast. Once airborne we found the Beaufort Sea off the Mackenzie delta to be full of drift ice. Arriving at Herschel Island we landed on some clear ice. To my knowledge this was the first commercial flight ever to this location. We were warmly welcomed and left the locals with newspapers and half a case of eggs.

Soon after returning to Aklavik, we headed for home. One leg was to Hunter Bay on the northeast corner of Great Bear Lake, where we had a fuel cache, and Dominion Explorers, a base. Gasoline at this point costs a fantastic sum. It is cached here in 10-gallon drums. After refuelling, we started over the worst piece of country I have ever seen. A forced-landing in this area would have been a bit lumpy, as our route had very few lakes and small ones at that. Finally, you raise the Coppermine River which is white water all the way to tide water, so impossible to land on.

In 1930 G-CASK, stranded during the MacAlpine search, was recovered at Dease Point and flown out. 'ASM assisted with this, then was assigned to support an expedition under Maj L.T.

An August 19, 1995 view at Cambridge Bay showing the hulk of Roald Amundsen's 292-ton *Maud*. From 1918-24 Amundsen traversed the Northwest Passage in the *Maud*. The ship later was sold to the Hudson's Bay Company, re-christened *Baymaud* and refitted as a supply ship. In 1926 it froze in at Cambridge Bay, then was left there until it sank in 1930. The previous year its radio room had been used to transmit news that the MacAlpine party was safe. On the distant shore in this view, where MacAlpine rescue mission Fokkers and Fairchilds once sat, is a Beaver on its summer contract. (Larry Milberry)

A south-looking photo of modern-day Coppermine taken on August 22, 1998 from a Buffalo Airways C-46 delivering some heavy equipment. The town sits on fluvial deposits at the mouth of the Coppermine River. Note the annual supply barge off-loading at the government dock. In his memoir for 1930 Stan Knight mentions the HBC supply ship *Bay Chimo* being here on similar duties. (Larry Milberry)

Burwash to locate the magnetic North Pole and search for evidence of the ill-fated Franklin expedition of the mid-1840s. Gilbert and Knight began on August 14, flying to Dease Point to salvage 'ASK. With them were pilot W.J. "Buck" Buchanan and engineer Tommy Gilmore, who would fly out 'ASK. Stan Knight described this:

WCA Super Universal 'ASK as Stan Knight and company found it at Dease Point, where it had been left to the elements a year earlier. (K.M. Molson Col.)

On our arrival at Dease Point ... the aircraft was sitting on the beach as though it had been left there the day before. It had been washed around by the shallow tides until it was broadside to the shore. It had a single rope on the tail post and the summer engine cover was in place. Shortly after we landed, a group of Eskimos appeared and were very curious about our intentions. These were the people responsible for saving the entire MacAlpine party, teaching them to build a hut out of muskeg sods, supplying fish which kept the party alive, etc. We found out that these folks loved sugar, which we soon ran out of. The same for cigarettes, as there seemed to be no non-smokers among the Eskimos. We left next morning for Coppermine, at which point Buck and Tommy left for the south with G-CASK.

Knight's diary continues with a description of Coppermine. This settlement had first been visited by air on September 1, 1929, when Pat Reid and Jimmy Vance landed here while on a mission from Baker Lake and Bathurst Inlet. At Coppermine, Gilbert and Knight needed to ensure the availability of fuel for their Burwash trip:

Here the Department of Marine and Fisheries were building a radio station. In port were a few schooners, one of which was to take gasoline from Coppermine across to Cambridge Bay and Gjoa Haven. The Eskimos of Coppermine were far behind their brothers at Aklavik. Coppermine has a small government hospital that was well-used by the natives.

The Hudson's Bay Co. "Bay Chimo" had docked, so everything was hustle and bustle, for the boat visited the coast only once a year from Vancouver. It brought all the supplies and one staggering figure was the cost of coal – $110 per ton laid down at Coppermine. In town was Dick Finnie on assignment from Ottawa to get all the information he could on Eskimo

folklore and, along with this, pictures. He immediately went to work on Walter Gilbert to let him accompany us to the magnetic North Pole. This was agreed, but we had to review our entire load and eliminate a lot of things to make up for Dick and his camera equipment.

Next day [seemingly August 16] we taxied about 3½ miles out on the gulf to take off on our great adventure. Gil poured the coal to the engine, but there was no evidence of the aircraft getting up on the step. I looked back along our path to see a trail of smoke, then Gil cut the power and we returned to shore. We soon realized that we had a major failure in one cylinder. We had to work fast, as the "Bay Chimo", having the only radio in town, was sailing in two hours for Bathurst, thence to Vancouver. I stripped off the cylinder and found that the head of the piston had completely collapsed. "Bay Chimo" sent my message to Winnipeg via Churchill requesting a cylinder and piston, then sailed. Later, Winnipeg was able to ask Dominion Explorers at Hunter Bay to take the spare parts to Walter Gilbert at Coppermine. It was almost like magic that around 1:30 next day Stan McMillan appeared from Hunter Bay, paid his respects, delivered the parts, and apologized for having to rush back to Hunter Bay.

After getting his engine torn down, Stan Knight found that he had another damaged piston. He and Gilbert agreed on doing a temporary repair, then flew to Hunter Bay to beg more parts. With Maj Burwash (Finnie had taken a schooner for Gjoa Haven), they set off, but landed after a bit to see how things were holding together. This proved prudent, for Knight found that his engine was about to fail again. Now they were stranded and it was late in the season. They hauled the Fokker onto the beach, set up a tent, settled in and contemplated a miserable future. Then, several days later their spirits soared when Buck Buchanan and Tommy Gilmour, passing by in 'ASK, spotted

their stranded buddies and landed.

With them they had a new engine, and installation began immediately. Gilbert, Knight and Burwash then left in 'ASK to intercept the *Bay Chimo*, so they could retrieve their aerial camera (put off the Fokker when Finnie had joined the expedition, and greatly needed for Burwash's purposes). According to Gilbert's log, they flew to Coppermine then, on August 25, to the bleak settlement of Bernard Harbour to await the ship. With no place to beach, 'ASK had to be anchored, but a storm blew in that kept Gilbert and Knight watching over their plane for days. Finally the *Bay Chimo* arrived, the camera was retrieved and 'ASK flew to Cambridge Bay on September 4, 1930. En route, Stan Knight began photographing the south shore of Victoria Island. Using the dates from Gilbert's log book, the trip unfolded this way:

Walter Gilbert's 1930 Franklin Trip

Date	Route	Time (hrs.)
August 25	Coppermine to Bernard Harbour	0:50
September 4	to Cambridge Bay & Peterson Bay*	6:50
September 5	to Boothia & Victoria Point	3:25
September 6	to Terror Bay & Peterson Bay	2:20
September 7	to Whitebear & Cambridge Bay	4:35
September 8	to Coppermine	4:00
September 9	to Fort Fitzgerald via Hunter Bay, Rae, Fort Smith	8:20
September 10	to Fort Chipewyan & Fort McMurray	2:20

* also called Gjoa Haven

'ASK overnighted at Peterson Bay on September 4, then traced the east shore of King William Island, over the Matties Islands and up the Boothia Peninsula:

The mystic landscape nearby Gjoa Haven on July 16, 1992. These same features were over-flown and perhaps photographed by Stan Knight during the 1930 Burwash Expedition. The plane here is DC-4 C-GPSH of Buffalo Airways. On a resupply mission to Gjoa Haven from Yellowknife, the crew was enjoying all the comforts they could desire, compared to a drafty, noisy Fokker. In charge was the great master of the DC-4, Capt Jim Smith. Assisting were his sprog co-pilot Sean Loutitt and crewman Gregg Elliott, both recently "promoted" from sweepers of the hangar floor. Such ambitious young aviators still come up through the ranks just as Stan Knight had done 65 years earlier. (Larry Milberry)

We circled the approximate location of the magnetic North Pole and, by this time, our compass was going crazy. We left there and proceeded North with the idea of flying to the Northeast Passage, but soon struck heavy fog... On returning, we swung westward over to Lady Jane Franklin Point on the northwest corner of King William Land. This, according to Burwash information, was the point where Franklin's party had finally abandoned their ship and taken two whale boats across the ice to the shore of the north end of the island. We chose a small, brackish, ice-free lake on the island, landed and tied up. We split into two parties and made a tour of that area. Finnie went with Burwash, while Gil and I went together.

On our return to camp Gil and I started to get supper ... Burwash came in and told us of having found a cairn ... In the bottom, which it appeared had been rifled since it was set up, was a piece of what was a navy coat, a piece of hemp rope, a gadget for tightening the lanyard on the side of a tent, and a piece of Cardiff coal. These may seem like insignificant things, but they were completely foreign to the area that we were in, and obviously had been left by the party when they landed...

It was too late in the day when we had a look at the cairn to continue back down to Gjoa Haven... I had the job of getting the oil out of the aircraft. I spent about an hour and a half sitting on the cross-bar of the float with oil cans, getting the

oil out. Already a thin scum of ice was evident on the edge of the lake... Before going to bed our old friend Burwash, who had boasted of walking the Arctic coast from Bathurst Inlet to Coppermine with nothing but a tea can and living off the country, was set back when we served up the supper that we had for him. It wasn't many moments later that he decided that he wasn't very hungry.

Next morning (September 6) Burwash and company explored down the west side of the island. After tramping the shore for about two hours, they found no sign of human presence and returned to Peterson Bay. Next day they continued to Cambridge Bay and were in Coppermine on September 8. The expedition had taken the airplane to its farthest northern point in Canada, although hadn't come close to the Magnetic North Pole, then situated about in the middle of Prince of Wales Island. Along the way Stan Knight had photographed much of the country. "This should prove of great assistance",

he wrote, "in doping out at least sketch maps," On the 9th 'ASM flew to Fort Smith where the Fairchild camera fell into the river. Knight grabbed it just as it sank and RCAF photo techs encamped nearby overhauled it before the Fokker departed next day for Fort McMurray. A large backlog of mail and freight awaited, so it was right back to the grind.

Having described summer operations, Stan Knight turned in his memoir to winter flying. Not surprisingly, he began with the predominant issue – keeping the oil flowing at 40 below. He noted how, for winterization, oil lines, fuel lines and tanks would be "lagged", i.e. rapped in asbestos insulation: "If you ever let the oil jell in the system, you were licked. Due to the lagging, you couldn't put heat around it to soften it up to get it out. Consequently, any stop in winter operations of more than 45 minutes called for dropping the oil and keeping it warm." This task has been described many times, but Stan Knight's coverage of general winter operations is exceptional:

Traditional transportation down the Slave River in 1925 – dog teams set out from Fort Smith. Note the stern-wheeler drawn up for the winter. Aviation soon began to make its mark in this remote area. (CANAV Col.)

The start of the day in winter flying was a pretty arduous business. You hopped out of your scratcher onto a floor that was just like ice, got your clothes on, and started down, in the case of McMurray, to the snye, where the aircraft was sitting out, usually under the moon. The engine was frozen solid – you could chin yourself on the prop and it wouldn't budge. First, you got your fire pots going. Then you got under the cover with a cigarette and sat it out, depending on the temperature. It was usually an hour to an hour and a half before your engine would limber up enough to make a start. You knew that you were making progress when the frost gradually came out of the cylinders, turned to water and started to drip. But you were never safe for a good start until you could bounce the prop and hear the tappet ring responding in the nose section.

At this point the pilot usually appeared with your oil, at least Gil always did – this team was a close corporation and the oil was generally looked after by the pilot. He would get it heated on the stove in the hangar or wherever we were overnighting. Our heavy load was usually left in the aircraft overnight, then the perishables would be loaded just before starting. By this time we were properly suited up. We always flew with sweaters and parkas, ski pants and either heavy boots or mucklucks, the Indian type with moose hide bottoms and the Hudson's Bay duffel leg.

For flying, we had to be very cautious about surface conditions on landing. In the early years our aircraft used a rubber bungee undercarriage. These would freeze solid and serve little purpose in shock absorbing. Later, we moved to oil and air cylinders, and oil with a spring in the cylinder, all improvements over earlier arrangements.

When you stopped for the night, one thing that was absolutely essential was to get your skis off the snow. If you left the aircraft on the surface it would freeze solid. You would have so much frost and snow on the bottom of your skis that you would spend half the day getting that straightened out. The solution was to get the skis up onto a couple of logs. One day we were landing on the Sloan River in the Northeast corner of Great Bear Lake. It was minus 52°F and we were looking forward to getting warmed up in a trapper shack that we knew about. Our

landing seemed normal until everything went black and we realized that we were up to the wings in "feather snow". Gil kept the engine running and we blew the snow away with slipstream, running up and down the ice for three quarters of an hour to clear all the feather snow and have a strip available for taking off later...

One morning at Coppermine it was frigid and a terrific wind was in the making. This, from the local boys, indicated a blow which might last for 10 days. We had to get out of town since, on the Arctic shore, there were no means of anchoring an aircraft. With my two tiny plumber pots it seemed as though I was trying to heat my engine with a cigarette lighter. Then one of the local lads came down with a big snow knife and built a snow wall around the fuselage and the nose, and it was no time before the engine was warm enough to proceed. Of course there was the quick shuffle of getting the oil from the store stove, bringing it down, pouring it in, priming your engine, loading your gear in and whipping the engine cover off. Then, since it was thought very poor economy to sacrifice 85 lb of useful payload on an aircraft battery, I had to wind up the inertial starters to get them going to start the engine. That day we made it off and flew to McMurray.

On another occasion we had a charter from Coppermine to the igloo settlement of Stapleton Bay some distance beyond Bernard Harbour. As usual, our compass served little purpose and, in winter, you could never tell where the sea ice began and the shore left off. It was just a case of taking a line on something, and starting out. We climbed high, sat over Coppermine and took a rough direction bearing for Bernard Harbour, which we reached in about an hour, then turned for Stapleton Bay. But there was a terrific ground drifting going on below and we were unable to follow the dog sleigh trails, so had to land back at Bernard Harbour and asked the RCMP for a guide.

Our Eskimo was a bright lad who had never flown, but he adjusted his sights to our speed and directed us along a path that seemed like a radio beam, bringing us straight to Stapleton Bay. We would never have found it without him. Returning, we were supposed to pick up Dick Finnie at Bernard Harbour, but Gil decided against this, due to the rough

landing ground there. Finnie would have to get back to Coppermine by dog sled. He sure got his native colour and experiences the hard way.

On December 23 Gilbert and Knight were at Fort Fitzgerald ready to fly a party of miners to Edmonton. This was everyone's ticket out for Christmas. As so often happens in aviation, however, nothing is for certain. While taxiing his Fokker to test for the safest takeoff run, Gilbert got onto a thin top layer of ice and broke through a foot to the main layer:

That washed out our flight and I went back to town, procured a team of horses and spent the rest of the day working with timbers getting the aircraft out of the water and back on top of the overflow ice. After much heavy going we succeeded and, next morning, were bound and determined to get through to Edmonton. We got away and, in spite of getting into heavy snows, Gil had taken careful bearings and we broke out where the Athabasca River empties into Lake Athabasca. At this time I got out the old Hudson's Bay Co. river captain's map, our only Athabasca map that had any detail. We flew right down over the water and I kept watching and telling Gil which way to turn. Suddenly, out of nowhere we flew into the bright sunshine. We both heaved a sigh of relief, leaned back, and Gil started to pull for height.

Then, without warning, the old girl blew dry on gas. With no choice Gil pushed the stick forward and landed in the snow on the river. He immediately set out looking for gas, while I looked over the engine, as we could not understand where our gas had gone. Gil hailed a lad heading with his dog team to the Hudson's Bay post. Meanwhile, I found the cause of our trouble – our altitude fuel mixture control had given up. Although the control was properly set, nothing was happening at the engine end. I fixed this problem, Gil got back with fuel and we took off for McMurray, gassed up there, then flew on to Edmonton. Arriving there on Christmas Eve, I'm afraid we acted up a little in that we went down Jasper Avenue at about 200 feet, burned up the joint, then went over to the airport and landed. We had made it for Christmas, but I don't know of any time we had used up so much luck and worked so hard to meet our goal.

Fairchild FC-2 G-CARE joined NAME in June 1928, then served reliably until the company ceased operations in 1932. With their outstanding Pratt & Whitney and Wright engines, the basic Fairchild utility plane, introduced in 1926, brought efficiency, economy and safety to the Canadian commercial aviation scene. (W.J. McDonough Col.)

Northern Aerial Mineral Exploration

Statistics from 1926 emphasized the growing bond between forestry, mining and aviation. At the request that year of the Topographical Surveys Branch of the Department of the Interior, some 59,000 sq.mi. were photographed from the air and 58,000,000 acres were patrolled, Besides this, 259 fires were detected, of which 256 were fought with aircraft assisting. Meanwhile, prospectors, trappers, missionaries and government officials in the North were coming more and more to appreciate the airplane.

In 1928 Northern Aerial Mineral Exploration formed in Toronto under mining kingpin John E. "Jack" Hammell (1876-1958). Among his partners in this venture was Winnipeg-based James A. Richardson, who took a 25% share. Hammell, who as a lad had tried boxing and newspaper reporting as careers, already had brought more capital into mining than any other Canadian. In 1915 he had backed a prospecting push in Northern Manitoba that resulted in mines that would produce some 70 million tons of copper-zinc ore.

NAME was intent on getting in on the ground floor of future mineral development in Canada's Precambrian Shield. It was certain that the new mines in places such as Flin Flon, Red Lake and Rouyn were only the tip of a mineral wealth iceberg. To NAME the key to unlocking more such natural treasuries lay in air transportation. In 1928 Jack Hammell described his vision of aviation:

Previously unpublished views of NAME's Fokker Super Universal G-CARK leaving the snye at Fort McMurray some time over the summer of 1928. Flying this day was H.A. "Doc" Oaks, who had on board company prospectors Simmonds and Morrison. (W.J. McDonough Collection)

The greatest new agency for the development of the enormous mineral and other natural resources of the Canadian North is the modern, high-powered, long-range airplane... *The airplane, when used by men of the vision, experience and training demanded, will do more in the next five years to speed up Northern development than any other single factor in the last fifty years...*

We believe we can double [a prospector's] work efficiency. First, by taking him into new areas in a few hours instead of several weeks. Second, by keeping him well supplied with food, tools, explosives and contact with skilled engineers and

John E. Hammell pictured in NAME's 1928 annual report. One of his pilots, Jay Culliton, later recalled of Hammell: "He more or less kicked off the development of Red Lake when he sponsored and developed the Howey mine. He was a rough, tough, and at times, loud man. Beneath this gruff exterior he was kind and considerate, and quite a good head. One day he turned to me and rather gruffly said, 'I have signed over 500 shares of Howey to you. Write the office for your certificates'. At the time the stock was worth a fraction over $1.00 per share. Little did I know that, within a year or so, I would be working for his company ..."

In establishing NAME in 1928, Jack Hammell and "Doc" Oaks hired the best pilots and engineers available in Canada (most were RFC or RNAS veterans). One day they were called together for a photos session. In the line-up are J.R. Humble, Francis Bell Barager, Arthur Massey Berry, Harold Anthony "Doc" Oaks, Clarence Alvin "Duke" Schiller, Silas Alward Cheesman, James Durkin Vance, W.J. "Jack" McDonough, G.M. Wadds, Frank Fisher, T. Caddick, Jay P. Culliton and Charles Frederick Kelson Mews. When they donned their head gear, the arrangement changed. Standing are McDonough, Schiller, Vance, Oaks, Berry, Barager, Culliton, Wadds and Fisher. In front are Humble, Cheesman, Caddick and Mews. (CANAV Col.)

Good details are shown in this sharp winter view of a NAME Fairchild. Then, one of the NAME gang refuelling a Fairchild. Someone would hand-pump the gas from a 45-gallon drum – note the refuelling nozzle and wobble pump attached to the drum. The fellow up top would pour the gas into the wing tank through a funnel lined with a chamois to filter out water or particles. (W.J. McDonough Collection)

NAME Fleet – 1928

Type	Registration	Delivery Date
de Havilland		
D.H.60X Moth	G-CARU	August 1
Fairchild FC-2	G-CARA	May 23
Fairchild FC-2	G-CARE	June 5
Fairchild FC-2W-2	G-CARJ	July 17
Fairchild FC-2W-2	G-CATL	August 23
Fokker Super Universal	G-CARK	July 11
Loening Amphibian	G-CATM	August 7

A NAME Fokker at Fort Resolution, on the south shore of Great Slave Lake. As usual, the townsfolk have come down to check out the aviation action. (W.J. McDonough Collection)

Anthony "Doc" Oaks, Silas Alward "Al" Cheesman, William John McDonough, Thomas Mayne "Pat" Reid, Clarence Alvin "Duke" Schiller and James Durkin Vance, most being wartime men. Cheesman and Schiller had come to NAME from Aeromarine Airways, one of America's first scheduled airlines. Mechanics were Thomas Caddick, Paul Felson and J.R. Humble. Two apprentice pilots were described as unlicenced mechanics: C.F.K. Mews and J.P. Culliton. The latter doing extra duty as the clerk at NAME's Winnipeg base.

Matt Berry's Diary

Born in 1888, A.M. "Matt" Berry grew up in the Ottawa Valley. He served overseas with the CEF, then transferred to the RFC, trained as a pilot, then came home to instruct on JN-4s at Deseronto. The war over, Berry tried ranching, then the white-collar world, but finally was drawn back to aviation. After finishing a Camp Borden refresher course, he received pilot licence No.330 on May 25, 1928.

The timing was ideal – NAME was forming and Doc Oaks was looking for good pilots. He quickly grabbed Matt Berry,

H.A. "Doc" Oaks in a studio photo contrasting with the typical "bush pilot at work" image. (W.J. McDonough Col.)

checked him out and assigned him to camp support duties in Northwestern Ontario. Berry would have been elated at this and made sure to record by diary the details of his season. These records came to light about 1975 when an archivist at

---

geologists who can assist him in his exploration and surface operation. We can make the company's small planes literally 'the prospector's taxicab' in the North, and with our larger planes we will overcome the problem of rapid transport of men in numbers, supplies in bulk and machinery of considerable capacity.

In 1928 NAME took on the Northwest Territories, joining such other players active in that vast areas the Lindsley syndicate of Toronto, supported by Col MacAlpine's Dominion Explorers Ltd; Cyril Knight Prospecting Co. of Toronto; Consolidated Mining and Smelting of Trail, BC, which had its own aviation department; and the Nipissing Mining Co. of Cobalt, Ontario. The latter had a party of four prospectors under H.S. Wilson. These tough characters travelled hundreds of miles by canoe and on foot from Great Slave Lake to the Hudson Bay coast. At the same time, Nipissing prospector Don Cameron led a small party north from Churchill by boat. Arrived at their destination in early July, Cameron's men seem to have been the first prospectors in the region since 1710, when the Hudson's Bay Company sent in a small party to seek precious minerals (all those men perished on Marble Island off Rankin Inlet).

NAME's first annual report describes accomplishments which, even today, would not easily be matched: "The flying was done in practically all parts of northern Canada from Ungava to the Yukon, planes usually working in pairs. Thirty-seven gas caches have been established throughout the north, which will meet our requirement for 1929... During the season we had only one minor engine failure, a broken crank shaft, which has been replaced by the

manufacturers." For 1928 the fleet covered 100,576 miles at an operating cost of $75,336. Eight pilots, 4 mechanics and one clerk comprised the aviation department. Hammell explained how so much had been done, even though his planes were not all available at the start:

We have seven planes, equipment, gas in caches and supplies on hand to the extent of $234,144.54… it should be remembered that we did not get our first 200 h.p. Fairchild plane until towards the end of May. The second small Fairchild was delivered early in June, the Fokker and first large Fairchild in the middle of July, the Loening and Moth the first part of August and the second large Fairchild in the latter part of August.

NAME's routes extended from Landing Lake in the Yukon, across to Sudbury and around to Fort Harrison on the east coast of Hudson Bay. The report listed pilots as Frank Bell Barager, Arthur Massey "Matt" Berry, Harold

---

Fairchilds and Fokkers were the core of the Northern Aerial Mineral Exploration fleet. Here is NAME's Fairchild FC-2 G-CATT motoring along at Norway House, Manitoba, as an RCAF Varuna waits at a buoy. Acquired from Canadian Vickers in November 1928, 'ATT had a short life. While landing at Millidge, north of Dryden, Ontario, on July 2, 1930, it caught fire and was lost. Pilot Duke Schiller was uninjured. (J.P. Culliton Col.)

the Provincial Archives of Alberta showed Larry Milberry a box of unaccessed papers and photos. This turned out to be the Matt Berry collection. Diary entries commence on July 15, 1928 with Berry and Al Cheesman being en route from Sudbury to Long Lac. As Berry described their day, he admitted how they had been wandering around, groping for the "iron compass" (as did many of his aviation contemporaries, Berry had a tendency to criticize fellow pilots):

Leaving town, Cheesman over-looked the railway and we flew too far to the South and were temporarily

The legendary S.A. "Al" Cheesman in Western Canada Airways days. While a mechanic with the OPAS, in 1927 he accepted an offer from Doc Oaks to join WCA. That December they ferried the first new WCA Fokker from New York to Hudson, Ontario. In 1929-30 Cheesman was on loan to Hubert Wilkins for the first Antarctic aerial mission. (H.A. Oaks)

lost. He kept trying to pick up the road by a course slightly South and West until I was convinced we were well South of the track and suggested flying due North ... This we did and had no other difficulty. We arrived at Long Lac at 8:30 PM and docked at the Provincial Air Station, where Capt. Dawson was in charge.

Next day the flight continued: "We reached Hudson at 3:00 and docked at Western Canada Airways. Fred Greaves, the veteran cook for the company, shouted to us to come up for a lunch and gave us a dandy... am to board at the Western Canada camp. A fine bunch of boys." Since he had been away from aviation after some years, Berry was still agog at everything, adding on the 16th:

Looking back over the trip out, it certainly was a marvellous experience. Until one takes such a journey by air, they can have no conception on the immensity of this country of ours. I was particularly struck by the mining possibilities of the district from Sudbury out, as it seems incredible that such a tremendous stretch of rough rocky country can't be chuck full of minerals.

Berry's first working trip was on July 17 to Favourable Lake, north from Hudson on the Ontario-Manitoba border. There, prospectors Murray and Stewart had made a find:

I wanted to see them and also take in some grub. It was 260 miles up, so I needed a big load of gas but, nevertheless, the Fokker took off nicely. I got my first view of the country over which I expected to

Tom Caddick formerly of Imperial Airways, emigrated from the UK after WWI. His assistants at NAME in 1928 were Jack Humble and Paul Felson. Paul drowned later at Savant Lake. (Culliton Col.)

be flying shortly, and it certainly presents a lot of difficulties to the inexperienced pilot. A few such trips and I think I will be quite OK, as I am getting onto the hang of following the waterways ... We found Murray and Stewart in good spirits, but looking for mail, which we didn't have.

Ken had some wonderful samples of lead and silver ores, tremendously rich, but he was not very enthusiastic. Thinks the body of ore not big enough to get excited about. Al took him up in the Fokker to look at the territory north... He is convinced he is in the right district and will have a mine shortly. Al let me fly the ship both ways and I had a great time. We ran into a lot of smoke and had to come down to 500 ft. to see the ground. We passed over one big fire at Deer Lake and

A.M. Berry (left) and air engineer Frank Harley with their Canadian Airways Junkers loaded, by the looks of it, with fur bales. (Glenbow Museum)

FC-2 G-CARA – the old "crock of a Wright" that Matt Berry was moaning about on July 19. This busy scene at Churchill shows 'ARA, a damaged plane, another half sunk at its mooring and a Super Universal farther down the shore. The damaged plane is NAME FC-2W-2 G-CARJ, which Berry had bent while landing on October 10, 1928. (W.J. McDonough Col.)

A rare views of FC-2 G-CARE. NAME called this type a "small" Fairchild (220-hp Wright J-5 engine). A "big" Fairchild (FC-2W-2) used a 410 or 420-hp P&W Wasp. Here, Jack McDonough and Jack Humble are at the left. (W.J. McDonough Col.)

odd looking kite, but has wonderful performance. Great interest in this addition to our fleet. Al flew it down to Sioux Lookout in evening to show it around." The 21st found Berry in Winnipeg readying to fly north and five days later he was in Churchill.

August 27: *Paul and I up at 3:00 A.M. to get ship off beach at high tide intending to leave for Pas to get remainder of grub. Turned out wet and blustery just as we were cranking up, so Pat [Reid] thought we had better stay put… we got away at 2:00 when tide was up again. Arrived Pas at 7:30 on nonstop flight, tired and stiff and ready for bed.*

August 29: *Ready to start but timing it so as to reach Churchill at high tide. Took a real hot bath, had lunch and pushed off at 12:00. No sign of Vance and R.E. before we left. Got in just right and found Pat and Duke in just ahead of us. Made a*

had a wonderful view of it. We were flying at 3000 ft. and great columns of smoke were at least a thousand ft. above us.

(On the 19th W.J. McDonough and engineer Tom Caddick arrived in a NAME Fairchild.) *Both glad to get back to civilization and good things to eat. Cheesman said to McDonough that he was picked to go on the Mackenzie River expedition, so "Mac" is all upset and trying to work things so he can get hold of the Wasp Fairchild that Doc Oaks is bringing out, and leave me with this crock of a Wright that he has used up in work here. I am sitting tight to see what happens.*

(On the 22nd J.E. Hammell and his manager and chief pilot Doc Oaks were in Hudson.) *Oaks in bad humour this A.M. Hammell wanted to get to Red Lake, so McDonough loaded R.E. [FC-2 G-CARE] with two of them and heavy baggage, about 700 lb. Stiff breeze blowing and tried twice to get off water and couldn't. Porpoised her tremendously. Oaks very sore at display. Transferred passengers and load to R.J. and Doc flew them in himself. In the evening flew R.E. into Sioux Lookout with practically same load as in morning, and gave Mc a lecture on taking off. Mc peeved.*

As the engine in G-CARE had gone to Winnipeg for overhaul, Berry and the crew spent some time improving their dock at Red Lake. There was excitement on August 15: "Famous Loening arrived at

Hudson with Younger [Geoffrey A. Younger] at helm and Duke Schiller and Paul Felson as passengers. Very

NAME's exotic Loening amphibian "Sourdough" bobs at the dock at Sioux Lookout, then is seen at an air display, perhaps at Winnipeg. In 1925 Grover Loening introduced the 2-seat OL-8, precursor of this unorthodox design. The OL-8 combined a hull – Loening's so-called "slippery float" – upon which sat a cabin to which wings and engine were attached. A set of wheels was housed in the hull. Powered by a 400-hp Liberty, the OL-8 served the US Navy, which admired its versatility, ruggedness and performance. Loening's assistant, Leroy Grumman, now designed the 4 to 6 passenger Loening Air Yacht based on the L-8. The new type was introduced with great fanfare at the 1928 Detroit Air Show. Powered by a 410-hp P&W Wasp, Air Yacht basic specs were: length 34' 8", wing span 45' 8", empty weight 3730 lb, useful load 2170, payload 1150, gross weight 5900, max speed 116 mph, fuel 140 US gal., range 570 mi. Wings and fuselage were mainly of spruce with some aluminum support fittings with everything fabric-covered. The wheels were hand-cranked up and down. Fly-away price from the factory on the East River in New York City was $24,700. Besides G-CATM there were three other Canadian-registered Loening Air Yachts. (CANAV Col.)

In 1928 there was no permanent settlement at Fort Churchill, Manitoba, the only sign of lasting human occupancy being the ruins of the HBC's 18th Century Fort Prince of Wales. Every pilot coming into this remote area in 1928 would have dipped a wing towards the fort and maybe taken a quick snapshot. Here's the place on July 19, 1973 – more or less as the NAME fellows would have seen it 45 years earlier. (Larry Milberry)

terrible landing close in and was relieved to find no one saw us coming in, so didn't mention it.

August 30: Got away for Chesterfield at 7:30 and had to fly at 250 feet to keep under the mist and low clouds... Most barren looking country imaginable, not a sign of life anywhere except for gulls, geese, ducks and white whales.

August 31 (Baker Lake area): All a very desolate looking place and one wonders how any human could eke out an existence on such an inhospitable stretch of barren rock. My admiration for the Husky [Inuit] increases daily, as I see what he has been up against.

September 3 (Baker Lake): Beached plane at Revillon Freres and found Dickins

with Super Fokker ahead of me. He and Col. MacAlpine as passenger touring the country. Had come up from Mistake Bay by Ferguson and Kazan rivers and were going to Lake Athabasca via Thelon river, then back to Winnipeg. We had the honour of having the first plane in Baker Lake last trip and Dickins is second.

September 6 (Baker Lake): Very strong wind from S.W. Not fit for plane on the water so, as we think Leith was delayed by rain and wind, I didn't pull out, but left buss on the beach. Tides are receding and leaving her high and dry. Tried to stop a leak in a pontoon yesterday by using rosin mixed with seal oil and I think it worked.

September 7 (re. prospectors): Tom [Tom B. Cowan] and Joe [Joe Rutherford]

blew in this afternoon. Couldn't get up the [Thelon] river with boat, so going to leave it here and have me put them in up stream, where they will walk back. Took Bill and St. Paul for a tour of inspection up the Princess river and the upper lakes. Pretty fast water, but they are going to try it with the canoe.

September 10: Took Dick Reid away up the Quoich river, taking the right hand branch to the first big lake, where I left him with all his equipment. Very rough country covered with light fall of snow, but to me it looks like a marvellous place for prospecting. Very rocky shores, so we had to assemble canoe from plane and paddle stuff to shore. Dick seemed quite content, but I hate to leave him alone in such a place.

September 14: Got a good start and took Bill and Shearer about 40 miles North into a good big lake where the formation looked good. We got off with them and found lots of mineralization and formation even better than we hoped for. Crushed some rock and found excellent tailings. Lowe thinks it's gold. Everything looks so good we think it's best to bring Tom and Joe in to make a thorough search. Quite calm after dinner and we couldn't get off the water. First time R.J. had refused to take a load for me. Dumped Lowe and our grub and a lot of equipment and got off.

September 21: Gales from the N.W. with practically steady snowfall all morning. Temperature just below freezing. Not fit for flying at all. Arthur and I went hunting ptarmigan about

After flying up the Hudson Bay coast from Churchill on August 30, 1928, Matt Berry noted in his diary: "Very forbidding looking shoreline, rocks everywhere and very little shelter." This modern view of the Chesterfield Inlet area, taken by Michael Mushet on July 19, 1973, illustrates Berry's description.

The standard type of air-transportable, sectional, cedar-strip canoe that was essential for NAME prospecting operations. (W.J. McDonough Col.)

10:00 and came back with 15 ... loads of fun, though it was very hard work tramping through the soft snow. Thought of trying to make Joe's camp in the afternoon, but the wind was very high and the visibility poor, so we thought better of it. Still no sign of schooner [the "Patrick and Michael"] and everyone is worried. Arthur imagines all manner of catastrophes have overtaken her, but I fancy the captain is still just delaying purposefully. This is making it very hard to get our camp together for the winter, and it looks as if we will have to bring in the prospectors for unloading the schooner and erecting the hut. In a little over a week we will have to be thinking of beating it back to civilization ... [Arthur] suggested yesterday that, if Hammell sends in a plane this winter, that I come back with it. Am not so sure I would like the job particularly, as there would be no hangar, or even nose hangar, for taking care of the ship, and it would be a big undertaking to put up anything after the snow comes.

Unfortunately, *Patrick and Michael* had burned in Chesterfield Inlet, but Jack Hammell was able to look on the bright side: "Although the boat is lost, it accomplished our purpose. We have established supply depots and flying bases on both sides of Hudson and James Bay, there being fifteen of these in all, and a camp on each side of the Bay where we have two years' provisions stored ... the Hudson's Bay Company's boats can take care of us in future…"

September 22*: Worked on the engine all day. No luck until we tried changing one set of plugs and then got her rolling at 6:00 P.M.*

September 24: *Got off water by 2:00 and ran for Joe's camp. Missed their lake and landed in one farther North. Finally got to their camp and discovered they had flown. Found notes saying they had started to walk for Baker Lake on twenty-first. Can't understand why they were out of fuel, as we took up seven gals. and they were only in camp seven days. Gathered up their equipment and beat it for Bill and Shearer. Lowe had a hell of a time – got his feet wet and hands very cold and was thoroughly miserable. Found Bill and Shearer rolled up in their eiderdowns and quite comfortable – lots to eat but reduced to burning their tent poles for fuel. Mighty rough on the lake,*

NAME schooner *Patrick and Michael* in St. John Harbour. (W.J. McDonough Col.)

but the ship took off nicely with a big load. Rather rotten landing at Baker Lake. Joe and Tom haven't come in yet.

September 25: *No sign of Joe and Tom and we are worried. I think we should take a couple of Huskies to the old camp and let them follow the old tracks South.*

September 26: *Fog and low mist this A.M., but we took the buss and went up the Thelon looking for Joe and Tom. Dick and Bill came along with Lowe. Went up the river 30 or 40 miles, then inland East. Engine cut over first lake and we came down to find a plug had worked loose and blown out. Soon made repairs and got off again, but fog got so bad we were forced to return without seeing any sign of the boys. Decided to let Bill go out with a native and try to trail them back.*

September 29: *Up early for a good start [for Chesterfield], but there was a heavy fog over the lake, and we couldn't get off. Tried to make it at 10:30, but couldn't get through, so came back and*

FC-2W-2 G-CATL with Loening 'ATM at Chesterfield Inlet over the winter of 1928-29. Note the *Patrick and Michael* in the distance at the left. (CANAV Col.)

NAME purchased FC-2W-2 G-CATL from Fairchild in August 1928. Here it is by the marooned *Patrick and Michael*. When NAME folded, 'ATL was sold to Canadian Airways. On January 31, 1933 pilot P.B. Calder and engineer W.B. Nadin were en route in it from Fort Rae to Cameron Bay on Great Bear Lake when a wing failed. Both men died. (J.P. Culliton Col.)

worked on the motor. Parson Smith asked us for lunch and we were just about going when Paul saw someone on the shore. We watched through the glass, but couldn't make out who it was till he was quite close, and then it was Tom – all alone! He was in bad shape and broke down telling us Joe had died three days out of camp, or on Sept. 24th. He realizes now how very foolish they were in ever leaving the tent in such weather. Says it was Joe's idea, as he seemed determined to get back ... Lowe upset. Expects Hammell in on the plane coming through. They find the schooner's back is broken and she is doomed. Cargo nearly all off and a day or two will finish it ... Bill and the Huskies came into camp. They had lost the tracks at the North end

of big lake and hadn't seen Joe's body, but had found Tom's rifle and compass.

September 30: *Beautiful day, first we have had for a long time. Got Bill and Toopic ready to go and find Joe's body, but when tried to crank the buss, the starter broke. Tried swinging prop by hand and with a rope, but couldn't get a kick out of her ... Staff and Bill got pie-eyed on Bob's rum, and Bill and Toopic running amuck and speaking lots of English. Staff cooked a bannock and we got two tins of beefsteak and onions out of the store and had dinner at Bob's.*

October 1: *Saw Tom in the evening and appeared much better and quite cheerful. His feet are bad yet, but the*

parson says they are improving steadily. Wore my new koolitang for the first time, and don't find it any warmer than my old canvas coat. Good protection for the face, however.

By October 4 the party was preparing to break camp. Holes in the floats of G-CARJ were patched and, on the 9th, Matt Berry flew Tom Cowan back to Churchill, where the harried prospector would have yet another terrifying experience.

October 10: *Cook gave us breakfast at 6:00 and the boys looked after Tom. Started at 7:00 but the DISASTER complete. The engine picked up a spray and quit, and when we settled in the water, the right pontoon sank almost immediately. Plane rapidly settled tail first, so I got the boys out on the front of left pontoon, which helped some. Saw motor boat shoot out from dock and was mightily relieved. Sinking fast when they pulled up to us and tried to take us in tow. Pulled Tom through window, as door was locked. He protested loudly, but plane was straight on end by this time.*

The wreck was towed ashore, then Doc Oaks arrived on the 12th to fly out Cowan. The others spent the next few days stripping down the plane for shipment south, where it was rebuilt (it would be destroyed the following August 9 while being flown by Frank Barager). On October 15 the Toronto *Globe* ran a story headlined "Prospector Tells of Fight for Life in Blinding Storm", giving the details in Tom Cowan's words. (The paper failed to mention that poor Tom had had both legs amputated due to freezing. NAME held the prospectors reponsible for their own misery, explaining how they had broken a basic rule – always stay put in any such predicament. Frank Hammell summed up this sad episode, saying "These things are unavoidable. It's the luck of the trail!"):

We were left about a month ago to prospect at a point about 50 miles north and west of Baker Lake, 200 miles west of Chesterfield Inlet. The plane that left us was to return for us in three days, but on the third day a blizzard started up, and we knew that no plane could fly in such weather. This lasted three or four days and, in the end, we decided that we

Two NAME men check out the *Patrick and Michael*. (J.P. Culliton Col.)

PROSPECTOR TELLS OF FIGHT FOR LIFE IN BLINDING STORM

Two Crawl for Hours Through Raging Blizzard

(Special Despatch to the Globe.)
Winnipeg, Oct. 14.—Out of the vast waste spaces of Canada's Northland comes another epic story of a fight for life by two men, that, in the case of Joe Rutherford, veteran prospector, whose relatives lived in Ontario, ending in death. He fell on the trail with his pack on his back and his face to the blizzard through which the men were forcing their way on their hands and knees. The other, Tom B   ~ lives in Toron¹⁻

might as well walk back to Baker Lake. And so we set off. We had plenty of grub, and there was really no need for us to start, but we were tired of waiting for the weather to clear.

It was hard going in the teeth of a strong wind, and by the third day things were pretty bad, as we threw away our eiderdowns and all unnecessary equipment. We were crawling on our hands and knees against the wind that day, and I had broken trail for about 500 yards when I took shelter behind a rock. Joe was a good bit back … After sheltering for the best part of an hour, I started back to look for Joe, and I found him lying 200 yards away on the track with his pack on his back. I turned him over and saw he was dead. I then took a bannock from my grub

and threw everything else away including my compass which was no good in that mineralized district anyway.

October 17 (back to Matt Berry's diary): *Nice mild, quiet day, but I didn't do much except hang around camp and mend some socks and underwear. Going to wash, but Bob wanted the tub. Paul and Shearer were out along the beach and found my ivory crib board, a bunch of tools, two pictures, the crank and gas hose.*

October 19: *Paul and Shearer found my camera in the sand and also my safety razor and old army knife as well as 51 cartridges for the 32. I went down later and found Arthur's thermos bottle about 20 yards off shore. Cleaned up camera in evening and it appears in fine shape and will be O.K. if shutter is not injured. Luck is surely with us and I still hope to find Tom's and Paul's bags.*

October 21: *Had the ptarmigan for dinner today and they were fine. The boys seemed to enjoy everything. We had ptarmigan with gravy and lots of dressing, mashed potatoes, creamed green peas, lemon pie, strawberry preserves, currant bread and cake and tea. Pretty fair chuck for the Barren Lands say I.*

On November 16 Matt Berry was flown out to Deer Lake, then proceeded to The Pas and Winnipeg by train. Soon he was on leave in Toronto and preparing for NAME's 1929 season. Meanwhile, another sad story had filtered out of the Arctic. On October 5, 1928 H.S. Wilson's Nipissing Mining party had reached Winnipeg with news of having

discovered the remains of explorer Jack Hornby and two companions. Having missed the caribou migration, they had starved along the Thelon River. Other news came from RCMP SSgt A.H. Joyce of Chesterfield Inlet – his report to RCMP Commissioner Starnes in Ottawa stated: "Just returned with party of four; fruitless search for body of Rutherford… must be covered as whole country now is under mantle of snow. Nothing can be done."

NAME continued through 1931 then, on account of the stringent economy, folded the following year. Its aviation assets were sold to Canadian Airways. No mine ever resulted from all NAME's efforts in the Keewatin (it would be 1957 before any mine opened in the district – the North Rankin Nickel Mine, a property staked in 1928 by the Cyril Knight party).

In 1932 Matt Berry joined Mackenzie Air Service. In 1936 he was awarded the Trans-Canada Trophy and, in 1937, joined the Northern Transportation Co., a branch of Eldorado Gold Mines. During WWII he managed 7 AOS at Portage la Prairie, then was with CPA in charge of building airstrips from Fort McMurray to Norman Wells to support construction of the Canol Pipeline. In 1944 he oversaw building the road between Yellowknife and its airstrip, then had contracts improving the airport. From 1949 he operated Territorial Air Service, then took over George Pigeon's Yellowknife Airways, until selling both to Associated Airways in 1951. Matt Berry finally left aviation, but remained busy in construction and mining. He died in Edmonton on May 12, 1970 and was inducted into Canada's Aviation Hall of Fame in 1973.

In spite of the millions spent and the lives lost exploring in the 1920s-30s, to this day only one mine ever has appeared on the Keewatin District coast of the NWT. In this view from July 1973 the mine's abandoned headframe towers over the hamlet of Rankin Inlet. Opened in 1957, this operation lasted only into 1962. (Larry Milberry)

Pat Reid

Born in Northern Ireland in 1895, Thomas Mayne "Pat" Reid served on flying boats in the Royal Naval Air Service. For gallantry under fire while his skipper was attacking a German submarine, Cpl Reid was awarded the Distinguished Flying Medal on September 21, 1918. Postwar, he was with Handley Page's pioneer air transport operation, then emigrated to Canada, where he joined the Ontario Provincial Air Service. After two years on general duties, he was selected by Roy Maxwell for pilot training. His first instructional flight was with T.B. Tully in HS-2L G-CAOA at Sault Ste. Marie on September 16, 1926. "Time in Air 1:05, Circuits of St. Mary's River, General Flying Instructions", noted Reid in his log book this day. So began what would be an auspicious flying career. Reid soloed on the same plane on September 29, on his 12th flight.

In November and December, Pat Reid was on an RCAF course at Camp Borden, training with F/O Trim and F/Ls Harding and McEwen on the Avro 504K. He flew 34 exercises, completed all the classroom lectures and was signed off as "Passed" by F/L G.S. Brookes. F/L A.T. Cowley of the CCA bureau tested him in 'AOA at Sault Ste. Marie on April 22. Cowley endorsed his log book "All flying tests for commercial air pilots certificate. Passed except cross country and night flight". His total flying to date was a bare 37:25 hours yet, as far as Roy Maxwell was concerned, he was qualified on the mighty HS-2L. Reid was granted pilot licence No.234 on May 17. Summer operations, however, would see his log book bulge by season's end to 336:05 hours – the figure he entered after ferrying HS-2L G-CAOK from Trout Mills, near North Bay, to Sudbury on October 15.

Over the 1927-28 off-season, Pat Reid was recruited by Doc Oaks of NAME. On May 12-13, 1928 Oaks checked him out in Wright-powered FC-2 G-CARA in Toronto Bay. On May 14 there was another flight with Oaks, who mainly was checking out another new pilot, W.J. McDonough. Seven further flights followed, then Oaks assigned Reid to take 'ARA north. He set out on May 25, 1928, flying to Sault Ste. Marie in 5:20 hours. He spent several days here, likely visiting old friends. On May 30 he had a

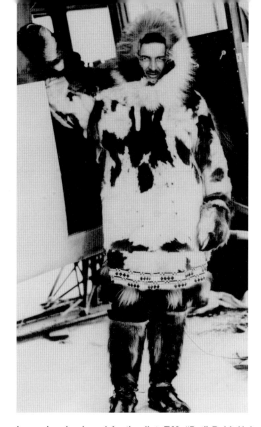

Legendary bush and Arctic pilot, T.M. "Pat" Reid. He's shown first in typical Arctic gear, then on a claim near Coppermine in 1929, hammering off a sample of pure native copper. (Giff Swartman, J.P. Culliton Col.)

6:50-hour flight to Hudson, then pushed on to his summer base at The Pas via Winnipeg and Lac du Bonnet. From The Pas most days were spent supporting prospecting at such locations as Cold Lake, Granville Lake, Loonhead Lake, Nelson House, Pelican Narrows and Reindeer Lake.

On August 2 J.P. Culliton checked Reid out on P&W Wasp-powered FC-2W-2 G-CARJ, after which 'ARJ became *his* plane. But this was short-lived – on August 25 Duke Schiller checked Reid out at The Pas on NAME's new Loening G-CATM. Next day he, Schiller and prospectors Cowan and Reed, started for Churchill in the Loening. Going via

Thicket Portage, they were 5:25 hours airborne that day.

From Churchill, Schiller and Reid pressed on to Chesterfield Inlet on August 29, this time with prospectors E. St. Paul and W. Scott. The flight took 5:15 hours, then they had to rush back to Churchill next day. Weather kept them down to 500 feet en route, but it was a speedy trip of 4:35 hours. Next day they were on the same course north, with prospectors Cowan, Reed and Rutherford. So it would go for Pat Reid in this inhospitable land (he soon would see first hand how the country dealt with those daring enough to test it – poor Cowan and Rutherford would pay the price).

NAME's Loening on the Hudson Bay east coast near Port Harrison. This powerful and exotic airplane would have been a handful to manage for the best of pilots, especially operating in such inhospitable country "a thousand miles from nowhere". Pat Reid and Duke Schiller were the key pilots on this NAME machine. (J.P. Culliton Col.)

Doc Oaks' Fokker G-CARK frozen in along the east coast of James Bay during NAME's December 1928 trip into that forbidding country. (J.P. Culliton Col.)

On September 2, Reid and Schiller flew the Loening from Chesterfield Inlet south to Moose Factory, thence up the east coast of James Bay and Hudson Bay to the Richmond Gulf area. Having visited several field parties, Reid was back in Winnipeg on September 23, noting in his log "Completion of summer operations". On December 10, 1928 W.J. McDonough checked Reid out on Fokker Super Universal G-CARK, then he was posted to Sioux Lookout with FC-2W-2 G-CATL.

A special winter operation took place in December 1928 involving FC-2W-2 G-CATL and Super Universal 'ARK with pilots Pat Reid and Doc Oaks, and mechanics Ken Murray and C.F. Kelson "Kel" Mews. Their mission was to bring 13 NAME men back to civilization after a season's prospecting in the remote Richmond Gulf area. Along with Oaks was NAME official Col Jack Leckie, plus some mail for the HBC. The aircraft left Sioux Lookout of December 27, flew to Longlac, Remi Lake near Kapuskasing, then to Moose Factory (Anglican missionary George Morrow and his wife joined Reid's flight at Remi Lake). On December 30 they left for Rupert House, but had to land miles apart on the ice in terrible weather. Oaks later explained: "The visibility was nil ...

Ice conditions to terrify any northern pilot. This surface was encountered during the 1928-29 NAME Richmond Gulf expedition. "Shoal ice on James Bay" is the caption in Jay Culliton's album.

We were not sure of our location and landed seven miles north of Rupert House." Their predicament proved dire, as reported in the Toronto *Daily Star* of January 1, 1929:

[Oaks] was about half a mile from shore on an open stretch of ice exposed to a three or four hundred mile sweep of wind. In an attempt to get the aeroplane closer to shore for better protection, one ski broke through the crust ice and was damaged. The machine gradually settled down into about two feet of water. A couple of hours went by with the other

ski slowly sinking. Then the tide went out and the plane froze in solid.

The crew and the parson and his wife cooked emergency rations with a blow torch and settled down for the night. In the morning ... it was 40 below, a steady blizzard blowing, the aeroplane with one ski broken, frozen in to the axles, and nothing outside but white, snow-blown waste.

[Oaks] set out on foot to try and locate Rupert House, and after walking about seven miles along a bleak coast, saw the outline of Sheerich Mountain. From this landmark he recognized that

Dog teams from Rupert House starting back to shore after bringing out supplies, equipment and manpower to rescue Doc Oaks and his Fairchild. This was one of many pictures taken during the expedition by the likes of Doc Oaks and Pat Reid even though, at this time of year, there were few hours of daylight suitable for photography. (J.P. Culliton Col.)

NAME's pair of winged Trojans after safely reaching the company's exploration base at Richmond Gulf on January 11, 1929. Then, the planes back at Moose factory next day with the 13 prospectors. In his photo album Jay Culliton captioned this picture: "Moose Factory. Oldest post of the Hudson's Bay Co." (all, J.P. Culliton Col.)

Mechanic Ken Murray (seated) with pilot Pat Reid and their Fairchild somewhere along their Richmond Gulf route.

he was north, not south, of the post. When he got back to the plane he discovered that Mews had gone to the post with an Indian trapper who happened to pass by. It was New Year's Eve and just about midnight a dog team arrived and took the Rev. Morrow and his wife back to Rupert House.

Hudson's Bay Co. factor J.W. Harris sent the dog team after hearing Mews' tale, then provided equipment and men to salvage and repair Oaks' plane. Both planes later proceeded, making stops at Eastmain (January 8), Fort George and Great Whale (9th) and Richmond Gulf (11th) from where the NAME crew was flown out to Moose Factory on the 12th, thence to Remi Lake. Back at base in Sioux Lookout, Reid continued with normal operations, but also took some advanced instruction with W.J. McDonough in Moth G-CARU, aerobatics included.

There was no shortage of culture shock as the White aviators and local Eskimo first met. The NAME fellows would have been aghast at the sight of this humongous whale being butchered at Repulse Bay.

Many Eskimos and James Bay Cree saw their first airplanes, even their first Whitemen, when Dominion Explorers, NAME and WCA flew into the James Bay and Hudson Bay region in 1928. Whites and natives all were mutually curious, but friendly. Jay Culliton captioned this photo of Pat Reid and friends, "Pat and an Eskimo family at Hopewell Narrows."

Tundra Rescue

On April 7-8, 1929 three NAME planes departed Sioux Lookout. Piloted by Duke Schiller, Jimmy Vance, and Matt Berry, they were bound for Chesterfield Inlet to support the summer's exploration. The season proceeded normally, until Schiller, mechanic Jack Humble and prospector Tom Creighton disappeared late in July north of Chesterfield Inlet. On August 3 Pat Reid began searching, making several flights each day – on the 3rd and 4th, for example, he was out four times each, usually with spotters. On one trip of the 8th he had four Eskimo spotters for a search along the Quoich River. Finally, on August 10, while 50 miles WSW of Wager Bay, Reid and his three spotters located the missing party. They landed to get the story of how the men had run out of gas and been 15 days trekking back towards Baker Lake. When the weather cleared next day, Reid flew everyone out. On August 16 he flew Schiller and Creighton 120 miles out to collect Schiller's Loening. All it needed was gas and it was back to work.

All along, NAME president J.E. "Jack" Hammell had been confident that this story would end happily, commenting in a press article of August 9: "Duke Schiller isn't a greenhorn … I'm expecting that they'll find their way out of this all right… Duke Schiller knows the air and Creighton is one of the best woodsmen in the country. They carried food for a month and unless they have been injured in a crash they will be able to find their way out … They've only been missing a couple of weeks." (The famous Quebec flier C.R. Troup was missing at the same time east of Seven Islands on the Quebec North

When NAME folded, Pat Reid became an ambassador for Imperial Oil, flying throughout Canada promoting its aviation products. In those days the company maintained a high public profile in aviation and Reid was revered wherever he went. From 1931-34 he often travelled in Imperial Oil's Puss Moth CF-IOL, then in its Beech 17 and Stinson Reliant. Shown is the Puss Moth, then Pat on the float of the Beech 17.

Shore. As with Schiller, there was no concern. One report noted that Troup had been missing for *only* nine days.) On September 12, 1929 Reid departed Coppermine, making Fort Norman in 5:00 hours. In the following days he pushed on, making Edmonton on the 16th, then reaching Sioux Lookout on the 20th and going straight back to regular flying. Some assignment found him in Alaska where, on December 31, 1929 he was test flying Fairchild 71 NC153 ("Machine & Engine OK"). His year ended with 312:40 hours flown.

In 1931 Pat Reid left NAME to join Imperial Oil as a corporate pilot. He took part in the 1931 Trans-Canada Air Pageant, but his log book is unspecific, and not even filled out by himself. Primarily, he was flying the Imperial Oil D.H. Puss Moth CF-IOL, doing a lot of fly-ins and airshows anywhere from Atlantic Canada to the West Coast. For all his good efforts, Reid received the

McKee Trophy twice – 1942 and 1943. After the war Reid continued in aviation product sales with Imperial Oil. Sadly, he and his wife died when a TCA North Star was lost in a mid-air collision over Moose Jaw on April 8, 1954.

On August 25, 1929 Duke Schiller was landing the Loening at Thicket Portage, Manitoba, when he stalled and crashed. Luck was with Duke, but not with his beloved "hot rod". Here it is partially submerged, then with its engine being salvaged. (J.P. Culliton Col.)

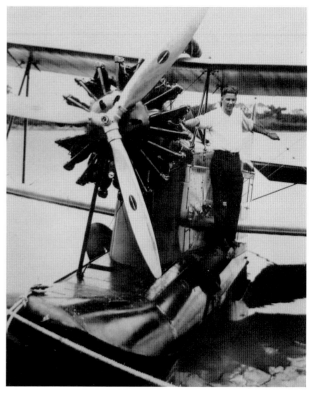

No fan can get enough of "oddball" airplanes and many books feature this topic alone. Although the Loening had distinctive looks, it was admired by most operators. It had plenty of power (this alone would endear it to any bush pilot) and carried a good load at a speedy pace (just what the operator wanted). There's no doubt what these NAME men would have thought about their own Loening G-CATM: Jay Culliton, the always colourful Duke Schiller, Matt Berry, that other NAME eccentric – Al Cheesman, and Paul Felson. (J.P. Culliton Col.)

J.P. Culliton

John Patrick "Jay" Culliton (1903-87) was born in Sault Ste. Marie, where his father was in plumbing and heating. In 1906 the family moved to Fort William. His boyhood seems to have been almost idyllic, including summers working aboard the renowned Canadian Pacific Great Lakes pass-enger fleet, and in the Canadian Car and Foundry shipyard. Following high school and a course at business school, in February 1920 Culliton was employed as a stenographer by the Hudson's Bay Company.

Recognized there as a solid type, he was promoted to assistant accountant. Then, anxious to know more about the trading, he transferred to the HBC post at Long Lac. Before long he was posted

farther north to Fort Hope, 125-miles by snowshoe and toboggan. En route, they slept out for six nights in minus 50 weather. Years later Culliton recalled of this journey:

Through the 20th Century, Fort William and Port Arthur, at the head of Lake Superior, comprised the economic centre of a vast region. From here great vessels carried prairie wheat plus forest and mineral products down the Great Lakes system, eventually to global markets. Finished goods arrived from down the lakes for trans-shipment by rail throughout western Canada. Great factories and yards turned out paper, ships and railway rolling stock. Aviation thrived especially in WWII, when Fort William produced some 2300 combat aircraft. Many young men from the Twin Cities would find their life's work in aviation, in the bush, with the airlines or in the RCAF. One such was Geoff Wyborn, who took this excellent view of Fort William late in the 1930s, then went on to have a stellar career in bush flying. (William J. Wheeler Col.)

Jay Culliton (above right) with friend Bob Lamb during one of his HBC postings in the mid 1920s. Then with some mates at a portage on the Root River north of Sioux Look while heading for Lake St. Joseph (J.P. Culliton Col.)

I learned later that this was my trial. The Indians had fully expected that I would "Hudson Bay it" by riding on the toboggan, and they kept expecting me to give in and take the easy way, as was my privilege. I was glad I stuck it out, and I am certain that this helped me immensely, in dealing with them, from then on.

At Fort Hope, Jay Culliton would learn much of the trading world and the native people inhabiting this remote part of Ontario, e.g. how Indian canoemen transported all the post's supplies by water from the railway tracks, passing over 25 portages, and how each bundle or box was carefully tracked by summer helpers positioned at the various portages. Eventually, each man on the transportation team was paid by the pound and by the distance he had travelled. Early in 1926 Culliton transferred to the HBC post at Hudson, where one of his jobs was to manage water transportation:

When I arrived in Hudson, the Red Lake gold rush was ... still gathering momentum. Prices were high, and there was never enough of anything to meet the demands of the gold seekers... Tents, equipment, and people of all types were spread along the shore for half a mile on each side of the little railway station. There were only three stores, including the Hudson's Bay Company, a couple of commercial fishing businesses, and one other water transportation company. Buildings were popping up all around; more docks were being built, and a second hotel was almost completed.

The Hudson's Bay Company had two motor boats, a couple of York boats, and a considerable number of large freighter canoes to take care of the water transportation of freight to the northern Posts being serviced through Hudson. The town was called Hudson, but the Post Office was named Rolling Portage.

Supplies for the posts at Osnaburgh and Cat Lake went up the Root River to Lake St. Joseph, and on from there. Lac Seul was, of course, supplied through Hudson, as was Red Lake, Pine Ridge (later changed to Goldpines), Woman Lake, Pikangikum, and several other outposts in that part of the country.

The pressure for supplies and equipment to be transported to the Red Lake

area was such that the company decided to expand its water transportation business, and carry freight other than for their own posts. They purchased, and had shipped to Hudson by rail, additional towing launches. Carload after carload of fir planking was brought in from British Columbia, to be used to build large freight scows, similar to those being used on the Mackenzie River. Several expert scow builders were brought from Waterways and the Peace River...

The Howey mine had been proved, and it required the transportation of additional heavy equipment. Other mines were in the process of being developed, and these too were requiring equipment

From Jay Culliton's album – an HBC team gets under way from some post, heading for Red Lake with supplies and a train of canoes.

and supplies. *Prospecting parties, with canoes, equipment, and other supplies were imposing further demands for transport... Other companies were formed to get in on the transportation, and anything that could float and carry a couple of men and their supplies was pressed into service.*

It was exciting, but hectic. We were working sixteen hours a day every day. The Hudson's Bay Company store had the Post Office in one end of the building, and our staff had to look after that. We were run ragged serving in the store, checking incoming supplies for our store and those for transportation to other posts and outposts, filling requisitions received from persons and companies in the bush, and making up our own requisitions to order what we were selling and shipping. In addition we had to check the freight being moved by scows, and make up bills of lading for the loads...

The summer of 1926 was extremely busy, but I think that the winter was even worse. With the lakes frozen, the freight movement almost dried up. Prospectors and others suffered from this lack of transportation. It was unbelievable the number of people who would arrive on the trains to go to Red Lake and adjacent areas... All had one thing in common – gold fever. Many were experienced prospectors from various places in North America, but there were many others who didn't have a clue. Dogs of all breeds and sizes were tied to dock posts, cribs and building foundation posts along the shoreline. Any size or breed of dog could demand a good price. We couldn't keep enough toboggans, snowshoes, or winter type clothing in stock

Jay Culliton was in Hudson when the first aircraft arrived – Jack Elliot's JN-4s, Patricia Air Transport's Lark and Western Canada Airways' Fokkers: "These aircraft were flown from dawn to dusk when weather permitted, and carried mountains of freight out of Hudson." Culliton describes the type of ingenuity that was required for aviation to survive in this rugged area:

When one of the Fokker Universals suffered a collapsed undercarriage at Goldpines, Al Cheesman, as senior air engineer, had to go in to assess the extent of the damage, and list the parts

necessary to repair it ... Al worked a couple of days improvising, as he could, with some lengths of wood cut from the bush. He wired, bolted, and nailed together the ski undercarriage. He then tested it by taxiing around on the ice...

The following day was cloudless. Al warmed up the engine and did a bit more taxiing, at various speeds. It felt so good that he gave it full throttle, got it into the air and pointed toward Hudson. He climbed to about 3000 feet and kept on going, following Lac Seul... Al reasoned that, if he was going to do some bouncing on the landing, and perhaps collapse the undercarriage and even write off the aircraft, he would do it where it could not be seen ... He figured the best place was on the side of the

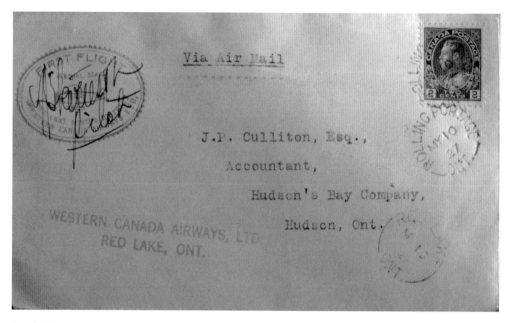

A valuable first day cover from the mail flown between Rolling Portage and Red Lake on May 10, 1927. The scrawled pilot's autograph belongs to F.J. "Fred" Stevenson. This is confirmed by K.M. Molson who noted that, on that day in Western Canada Airways history, Stevenson flew WCA's first air mail to Red Lake. This would have been from Rolling Portage, a post that was located near today's Ear Falls at the northwest tip of Lac Seul. (J.P. Culliton Col.)

island, hidden from the crowd. He made, he said, a very smooth landing, and taxied the aircraft back to the base. It was not long after that that Al received his pilot's license.

The gold rush at Hudson brought business in many forms. Culliton describes one way in which aviation could spin off some profits to the HBC:

The rate for freight, or anything, was $1.00 or $1.25 per pound to Red Lake. When the Fokker Universals came in, the rate dropped a bit. With the smaller aircraft each person was weighed when purchasing a ticket, and paid the rate.

Occasionally ... a passenger would realise that he was going to be sitting in an open cockpit aircraft, so would decide to buy a heavier coat or parka, or an additional one. The passenger would hike up to the store, purchase the parka, and return to catch the plane. There would then be a further delay, until he was again weighed, and paid the extra amount for the added weight of his new parka.

In September 1927, when Al Cheesman was sent to Fairchild in Farmingdale to take delivery of a new Wright-powered FC-2, he invited Jay Culliton along as an assistant. They took the train to the Lakehead, then boarded the SS *Hamonic* for Windsor, from where they continued by rail to Toronto and New York. At Fairchild, salesman and pilot Dick Depew was their host. After a few days, their aircraft, G-CAID (the first of the new "4-longeron" FC-2s), was handed over. Equipped with floats, they set off up the Hudson River Valley, stopped in Montreal then made Ottawa. There the RCAF was most anxious to look over 'AID and mooch a demonstration flight if possible. After his ride, S/L J.H. Tudhope didn't want to let the plane go (Tudhope and all at RCAF HQ were impressed and soon had their own FC-2s).

Cheesman and Culliton continued to Sudbury to pick up Doc Oaks, who was anxious to put the plane to work. On

Delivered from Fairchild in September 1927 by Al Cheesman with HBC passenger Jay Culliton, FC-2 G-CAID sits on the ice at Hudson. (J.P. Culliton Col.)

G-CAID during a medevac of July 4, 1928 (location unknown). Normally this plane would have been on floats in July, but may have been changed to wheels for this mission. In the caption of this photo in his album, RCAF P/P/O George Kimball noted, "Fairchild in which Holly brought in an injured mining man from mining fields 7/4/28." In the end this FC-2 was lost on September 23, 1930 in a Regina crash which pilot C.M.G. "Con" Farrell survived.

October 3 Leigh Brintnell delivered WCA's second FC-2 – G-CAIE. On the day before Christmas he had an engine failure and wrecked 'AIE. His trip that day had been to play "Santa Claus" by delivering a load of booze to Red Lake.

Happily, not one bottle was broken as Brintnell succeeded in gently putting 'AIE into the trees.

Meanwhile, Jay Culliton had joined Northern Aerial Mineral Exploration Ltd. in Winnipeg, working at first in space shared by NAME with WCA on its Red River base at Brandon Avenue. Initially, NAME had Loening G-CATM and Moth G-CARU. These were at Winnipeg airport, where W.J. McDonough was instructing neophytes Frank Fisher, Kel Mews and George Wadds (who would not complete his course). Anxious to get into flying, Culliton asked Doc Oaks if he could join this group. This was allowed, so long as he kept up with his chief duty as storesman. McDonough gave Culliton his first flying lesson in 'ARU on November 6, 1928. He soloed on January 9, 1929 after 13:50 hours of dual instruction. In this period NAME's Loening flew over to a small Winnipeg strip where Rod Ross had an aircraft servicing base. It was switched over there to skis, then Cheesman and Culliton took it on a test flight, which didn't go perfectly:

After gaining a bit of height, Al made a few medium turns to the left and right. Everything appeared to be O.K. We were making signs of satisfaction and relief,

The wreck of FC-2 G-CAIE from which Leigh Brintnell walked away. (J.P. Culliton)

Instructor Jack McDonough (front left) with his first NAME student pilot group: George Wadds, Jay Culliton, Frank Fisher and (front) Kel Mews. Then, Moth G-CARU on which the students trained under McDonough, a highly-qualified, ex-RAF instructor. (J.P. Culliton Col.)

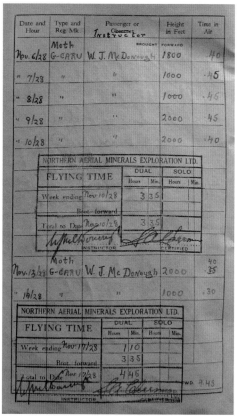

The first page of entries in Jay Culliton's carefully-kept log book includes his first 40 minutes in G-CARU under Jack McDonough. Note the certification signatures – McDonough and Cheesman. (J.P. Culliton Col.)

grinning at one another through the communications hole that joined the passenger cabin to the pilot's open cockpit above. We had not been flying long when, during a fairly steep turn, the nose of each ski went down about forty-five degrees. Al tried everything to bring them up to their normal position, but to no avail. He kept motioning to me that I should climb out the side windows and try to pull the skis up to the safe nose up position. His signals to me could not be misunderstood and neither could my hand signal to him.

We had not taken on very much fuel. When Al figured we were almost out, he headed for the strip, believing, as I did, that we were in for a bust-up. He lined up well back and came in with a bit of power on. We dropped lower and lower, until we were about fifteen or twenty feet above the ground. The skis were still nose down. As Al cut the engine I braced myself. At what seemed to be the last second, the skis suddenly responded to the pull of the shock cord, and righted themselves and we landed smoothly.

In these early NAME days, the Winnipeg staff had one thing in common – they were dedicated and seemingly addicted to hard work. They also were notorious partiers when opportunity arose, which it seemed often to do – their apartment on Sherbrooke Street was a busy little hub in off hours. There also could be shenanigans in the air, as when Duke Schiller lost his licence for flying below roof-top level down the main street of Port Arthur.

The new company badly needed a proper base in Winnipeg. Doc Oaks was working on this, when some real estate sharks, getting wind of NAME's plan to buy just the right piece of land, made an end run, bought the land themselves, then doubled the asking price. Oaks would not fall for this scam, so moved

Views of the NAME Loening being fitted at Winnipeg with skis, then out on the frozen Red River. (J.P. Culliton Col.)

NAME to Sioux Lookout, building a fine new base on Abram Lake. Included were a hangar, engine shop, office and stores building, carpenter shop, a shed for gas and oil, assay office, five cottages, a large mess building and a dock and slipway. Doing nearly all this work was MacDonald Brothers Sheet Metal of Winnipeg. Run by brothers Grant and Ed MacDonald, this company also had the licence to manufacture Edo floats, recognized as the best products on the market. NAME made the move to Sioux Lookout in January 1929.

On January 18, 1928 Culliton flew to Sioux Lookout with Al Cheesman, where his training continued under Cheesman and Frank Barager. On January 10 he took his first lesson in the NAME Avro Avian (G-CANP), Matt Berry being his instructor. For February they put in 20:05 hours. Later, Val Patriarche and Pat Reid also helped train Culliton in the Avian. On April 9 he and Reid took 'ANP 240 miles to Red Lake and back in 4:35 hours. On May 9 Culliton first flew on floats. F/L J.M. Shields of the CCA then came into town to test and pass him for his

licence. Of this period, Culliton recalled how the company hired a young fellow as a cook – a local boy, Bob McInnis: "He was a good worker and Tom Caddick took him on as an apprentice mechanic. On his own, Bob took flying lessons … He went on to fly in the bush for a number of years, ending up with Canadian Pacific Airlines."

With his pilot's licence, Jay Culliton now was sent on his first assignment to far off northern Quebec – flying G-CARU, he spent several weeks supplying prospectors in the region around Senneterre. By the middle of September his log book showed more than 150 hours. Also in the region was Brian Blasdale flying NAME's Avian G-CANP. One June 2, 1930 he wrecked 'ANP on a lake near Gogama.

When he broke a leg playing baseball, Jay Culliton spent five weeks in a hospital. There he met Ruth, one of his nurses, and before long the pair married. Many other changes ensued, an unfortunate one being the 1930 decision to split NAME into aviation and exploration branches. Oaks was so dismayed at this that he left NAME.

NAME's hangar rises near Sioux Lookout early in 1929. The first aerial view shows the hangars and shops in 1929. Five staff cabins are to the left. The local road beyond became Hwy 72. Abram Lake is in the foreground, Pelican Lake is the other side of the road, with Moosehorn Bay top left. When NAME folded in late 1931, this fine base was taken over by the OPAS, which used it until March 24, 1989. On that day a heavy snow load on the roof brought down the old hangar. The second aerial (inset), showing the same geography, was taken in March 2009. (J.P. Culliton Col., Richard Hulina)

Date and Hour	Type and Reg. Mk.	Instructor Passenger or Observer	Height in Feet	Time in Air
			BROUGHT FORWARD	22·30
July 11/29	Moth G-CARU	J. A. Cheesman	1500	·25
" 15/29	"	Solo	2000	·45
" 16/29	"	"	2000	·25
" 19/29	Avian G-CANP	J. A. Cheesman	1200	·15
				24·20

NORTHERN AERIAL MINERALS EXPLORATION LTD.

FLYING TIME	DUAL		SOLO	
	Hrs.	Min.	Hrs.	Min.
Week ending July 19/29	18	45	3	45
Brot. forward		40	1	10
Total to Date	19	25	4	55

INSTRUCTOR J. A. Cheesman CERTIFIED

1930	Avian G-CANP	Capt. A. M. Berry	1500	·55
Jan. 10	Moth G-CARU		1500	·45
" 15	"	"	1500	·45
" 16	"	"	1000	·25
" 17	"	"	1500	·40
" 18	"	"	1500	·35
" 21	"	"	2000	·20
			FWD	28·00

Jay Culliton was determined to make his way in aviation. At Sioux Lookout he logged a few hours of training with Al Cheesman in July 1929, a few more later with Matt Berry.

Jay Culliton (left) with Brian C. Blasdale. Culliton labelled this photo in his album "On our holiday", that being the summer of 1930 when he had Moth G-CARU (shown) in the Senneterre district, while Blasdale had Avian G-CANP in and around Temagami country. The "holiday" was not quite perfect for Blasdale – his bad landing of June 30 wrecked the Avian. Blasdale had been Jim "Dazzy" Vance's mechanic at Baker Lake during the MacAlpine search. Stranded with airplane problems, the pair joined a group of seasoned tundra people and trekked overland through the Arctic winter all the way to Churchill. (J.P. Culliton Col.)

Into mid-1930 word was getting around that NAME was in trouble. For all its great efforts, no paying mine had been established. Jay Culliton last flew for the company on September 25 – a trip with Al Cheesman in FC-2 G-CARA. NAME folded, although everyone soon found a job elsewhere.

Jay Culliton got on with the OPAS as a junior pilot, commencing work on February 15, 1931 at Sault Ste. Marie. He would do little flying in 1931, being mainly kept busy around the base at the Soo. The following year, however, he was busy, mainly doing fire detection patrols and supression flights, Moth

G-CAPC being his usual plane. Eventually he was posted to Sioux Lookout, where he would spend most of his OPAS career, rising to be district superintendent. Through all those years his base was the same solidly-built one that NAME had established in 1928.

A southeastward view of Sioux Lookout *circa* 1924. Established in 1912, the town by this time was a prospering transportation hub and trading centre on the shore of Pelican Lake. About mid-photo are the narrows connecting Pelican Lake and Abram Lake. In 1929 NAME built its modern air base near the narrows. The big lake at the top left is Minnitaki. This grand view gives a sense of why waterborne planes ruled in Canada's northland well into modern times. The earliest aerial visitors to this area were Civil Government Air Operations, Ontario Provincial Air Service and Laurentide Air Service HS-2L, F.3 and Viking flying boats. Sioux Lookout's first runway, installed in 1935, was part of the Trans-Canada Airway, but rarely hosted an airplane. (J.P. Culliton Col.)

This closer view of Sioux Lookout in the same period looks east-northeast. Below is the head of Pelican Lake, the town pavilion being the large building on the beach. Ahead are the CNR yards, the roundhouse being prominent. (J.P. Culliton Col.)

Looking northward *circa* 1930 with the Western Canada Airways hangar lower middle and the pavilion adjacent. WCA became Canadian Airways in 1930, then CPA in 1941. In the early 1950s CPA abandoned most of its bush operations. The Sioux Lookout base was sold to Transair, operating such aircraft as the Norseman and Bellanca Airbus. The rail yards are clearly seen, including an overpass and the coal dock to the right. The tallest building centre is Sioux Lookout school where all grades were taught. The old hospital sits just left of the coal dock. (J.P. Culliton Col.)

Sioux Lookout on March 29, 2009. Service industries today provide most employment for the town's 5000 citizens, but forestry, transportation and tourism remain vital to the economy. (Richard Hulina)

Starratt of Hudson

Northern Transportation Company of Hudson, Ontario was founded in 1926 by Robert W. Starratt. His company soon became a model among bush operators. A transplanted New

R.W. "Bob" Starratt – one of the north's great transportation inno-vators and entrepreneurs. First with Northern Transportation, then Starratt Airways and Transportation, he served his customers by land, sea and air. (CANAV Col.)

Brunswicker, Starratt had home-steaded in Alberta before settling in Hudson. There he began in water transportation with a motorized canoe. Business boomed with work from the Hudson's Bay Company, and much general freighting connected with the Red Lake gold rush. Starratt added barges to supply mines and exploration camps in summer, and horses (later, tractors) to haul sledges over the ice in winter. Costs were high, mainly due to portages. However, Starratt reduced costs from $250 a ton in 1926 to $60 in 1934. In *Canadian Aviation* magazine of October 1934 a brief profile lauded the company:

[Starratt] started with a Gipsy Moth, in January 1933 added a J-6 Travel Air, in May a Wasp Travelair, in September a Fox Moth and in March and May 1934 two Super Fokkers... last winter he flew 275 tons of freight to the mining camps in the

A typical scene at Starratt's *circa* 1935. Taxiing out is Travel Air CF-ABF. It served the company from 1932, but burned on a lake between Hudson and Pickle Lake on October 24, 1935 after catching fire in flight. Nearest are a Fox Moth and a Moth, possibly Starratt machines, although Harold Farrington at this time had his own Fox Moth nearby at Sioux Lookout. Beyond is OPAS Fairchild 71 CF-OAM, which later would be resurrected from a wreck to become CF-OAP. The biggest plane here is the famous OPAS workhorse – D.H.61 Giant Moth G-CAPG "Goose". (Norman Etheridge Col.)

Pilot Harold Farrington with Starratt's first airplane, Moth CF-AGX, acquired in October 1932. Then, the Moth being readied at Hudson. The coup top was a local mod for reducing the discomforts of sub-zero operations. Among the Moth's many useful duties was liaising with company barge trains in summer and tractor trains in winter. Little is known of individual aircraft colour schemes, however, in 2009 Don Starratt of Hudson recalled CF-AGX at one time being painted "international" orange and "RCAF" yellow. It served with Starratt for 11 years, then had numerous owners, including A.V. Giauque of Yellowknife in 1945-47. CF-AGX today is with the Reynolds-Alberta Museum in Westaskiwin in Alberta. (Don Parrott Col.)

Also painted orange and yellow, Travel Air SA6000 CF-AEJ served Starratt 1935-43. It last was heard of *circa* 1955 in Seattle. Then, Starratt Fox Moth CF-APO after a mishap. 'APO served Starratt 1933-36, then migrated to northern Saskatchewan. (Norman Etheridge)

district. Bulky items included three mine cars and a complete mine hoist to Red Lake for the Mackenzie Red Lake Gold Mines, an assay furnace for Pickle Crow Gold Mines at Pickle Lake, and a 14-foot shaft for J.M. Consolidated Mines at Woman Lake...

Northern Transportation originally specialized in barge and tractor trains. (Arthur Limmert & Bill Dunphy Cols.)

This summer's operations started with 300 tons of freight ... and extensive passenger service is done as well. The Gipsy Moth is the liaison ship ... keeping headquarters at Hudson in constant touch with the entire ground organization ... If there is a breakdown, the pilot takes the mechanical staff and what repair parts are needed to the scene. Should a man be hurt, the Gipsy Moth is the air ambulance...

Taken from a postcard of the day is this 1939 view down Starratt's dock of Fairchild 82s CF-AXD and 'AXL and Beech 18 CF-BGY, the first of its type in Canada. The Fairchilds were in the company's orange and yellow colours, while the Beech was dark blue overall. (J.W. Jones Col.)

A mid-1930s advertisement listing Starratt's bases and its variety of equipment. (CANAV Col.)

A little philatelic gem that was posted at Hudson in 1938. (J.P. Culliton Col.)

Starratt Airways grew steadily through the 1930s, adding such types as the Super Universal and Travel Air. The company merged with CPA in 1943, but a new Starratt Airways was formed post-war by brothers Dean and Don Starratt (sons of R.W. Starratt). They continued into 1984, when they sold to Glenn Tudhope. In 2009 Tudhope Airways still was operating from the waterfront originally developed by Bob Starratt in the 1920s. That year it's workhorse still was the Found FBA-2C originally purchased by Dean and Don in 1965.

The Ski Kings

One of the early problems for bush operators was finding suitable skis. K.M. Molson concluded that inadequate skis were chiefly responsible for the wintertime woes during Imperial Oil's 1921 expedition. The problem would be resolved by brothers Carman and Warner Elliott of Sioux Lookout, well-known in their area as builders of boats, toboggans and sleighs.

Some of the first flying in Northwestern Ontario was in 1925, when mining promoter Jack E. Hammell requested some airlift from the OPAS to support development of the Howey brothers gold claims at Red Lake. Five aircraft were loaned and 15 tons of supplies flown in from Kenora, a distance of 125 miles. Over the winter of 1925-26. Jack V. Elliott of Hamilton had his JN-4s operating off the ice at Hudson, doing a good business to and from Red Lake. Elliott would have used either surplus skis from former RFC (Canada) JN-4s, or improvised skis. That spring "Doc" Oaks began operations from Hudson with his Curtiss Lark, flying passengers to Red Lake at $90 one-way. The following winter he helped

James A. Richardson launch Western Canada Airways with several new Fokker Universals. All these types used skis, none of which held up very well under rough conditions.

Doc Oaks seems to have been the first to talk to the Elliott brothers about skis. They had the right idea from the outset, their design having a sharp up-curve on the nose to ride over snow and ice obstructions, and brass sheathing on the bottom. Several types of wood were evaluated, white ash being found most durable. The brass, obtained from a US foundry, had a high copper content, since this formula worked best in winter conditions. Test skis of various lengths, widths and thicknesses were built. The final product was 5-ply with one layer transverse to the four lengthwise ones. Each layer was steamed and pressed into shape, then the layers were glued with the best marine glue. A sheet of aluminum was applied to the bottom ply, then the brass was fitted using copper rivets. Coats of varnish followed.

Once the Elliotts had perfected their designs, they submitted drawings to the Department of Civil Aviation. These were approved after much test and evaluation. Orders soon came in from

Starratt Airways Travel Air CF-ABF and (opposite page, top) the great Canadian Airways Ju 52 CF-ARM at Red Lake in the mid-1930s. It's a sure bet that both planes were sitting on "Elliott Boards". (Don Parrott Col.)

Canadian operators everywhere, including in 1931 for the great Canadian Airways Ju 52. Then, with the Elliott fame spreading, came orders from the US. Admiral Byrd put "Elliott boards" on his Ford Trimotor on a 1929 Antarctic expedition, then on his Curtiss Condor for a 1933 expedition. In the summer of 1937 an order even came from Japan Airways. Elliott skis eventually were mass-produced during WWII for such types as the Tiger Moth and Norseman. The Elliott brothers always worked in strict secrecy. Few visitors were allowed into their shop, and ski production photos are unknown.

Cross-Border Connections

The 1920s was a landmark era everywhere for commercial aviation. No sooner was WWI done, than governments and entrepreneurs began evaluating and developing plans. Europe, the UK and US led, along with such other aeronautical powerhouses as Russia, China, Japan and several South American nations. Small in population, but almost obliged by their vast land masses and the need to link distant outposts to main business and population centres, Australia and Canada made their own small contributions. (The old idea that Canada invented bush flying is poppycock. Canada was "small potatoes" in the global picture, although its unique air activities regularly made local headlines.)

In 1919-20 Canada's only commercial or private airplanes were war surplus types – Avro 504, Curtiss JN-4, Curtiss HS-2L, etc. The nation had no aircraft industry and the Controller of Civil Aviation was on a critical learning curve. Initially, most air activity was unregulated. As the need for commercial aircraft grew, Canadian operators looked almost exclusively to American suppliers. Imperial Oil of Edmonton purchased its two new JL-6s through a Junkers representative in New York. As other types became available, Canadians started travelling regularly to US factories to take delivery. At Bellanca, Buhl, Fairchild, Fokker, Ford and Stinson they would meet the great personalities. Such Canadians as Doc Oaks, Al Cheesman, Jay Culliton, Roy Maxwell, Duke Schiller, Sammy Tomlinson and Roméo Vachon would shake hands with the top American pilots and technical men, and certainly chatted on occasion with the grand entrepreneurs themselves – Walter Beech, Giuseppe Bellanca, Sherman Fairchild, Tony Fokker, Grover Loening, Bob Noorduyn (in his Fokker days), Eddie Stinson, etc. In one case, in September 1927 Al Cheesman and Jay Culliton travelled to Fairchild on Long Island to accept a new FC-2 – G-CAID. There they were hosted by Richard H.

"Dick" Depew, Fairchild's renowned salesman and test pilot. Cheesman likely made at least one flight with Depew to get the feel of the FC-2.

Dick Depew already was legendary. Having learned to fly in 1911 at Maurice Farman in France, he was awarded FAI pilot licence 641. During WWI he was an Army flying instructor and Curtiss test pilot. Postwar he managed the Curtiss field at Mineola, then spent a year running the big Curtiss operation in

The great Fairchild pilot Richard H. Depew, who had soloed at age 19. At the time of his death in 1948, his log book showed that he had flown some 160 airplane types. (Fairchild Museum)

Argentina. From 1923-32 he had top positions with Fairchild, including test pilot, chief pilot, and vice-president.

Depew became the 211nd aero mechanic licenced in the US, and its 188th transport pilot. Canadians were fortunate to have first-hand connections with the likes of Depew. These auspicious relationships helped Canada's blossoming aeronautical culture. Adding to this process would be such worthy roles as supporting international long-distance fliers – Charles Lindbergh, Italo Balbo and a host of others.

For the company Christmas card one year, Spence-McDonough Air Transport featured a cheery, fully-equipped prospector hauling FC-2W-2 CF-AAO across the ice. This aircraft had begun in 1929 with Dominion Explorers, then ended with Canadian Airways when Spence-McDonough folded. In 2009 former Spence-McDonough air engineer Rex Terpening recalled CF-AAO having a medium red paint job. (W.J. McDonough Col.)

William John McDonough

In any aviation biography, depth and accuracy of coverage depend on the material available to the author. Sometimes the subject may be interviewed – an ideal situation, since everything from log books to diaries, correspondence, scrapbooks and photographs may be scrutinized with the person's assistance. Even if a subject has passed on, a researcher may be fortunate to find relevant material, such as the 1928 Matt Berry diary; boxes of old business records, as in the case of Frank E. Davison, etc. Often, however, the details of a life's work may be scant, especially if memorabilia has been disposed of following death.

While this book was being readied, the author heard from Stephen McDonough, the son of William John and Winifred McDonough. Stephen had been reading Fred Hotson's *De Havilland in Canada* and wanted to contact Fred to learn more about his father's days at de Havilland Canada. Soon, he invited Larry Milberry to look through his father's material, which long had been dormant in the basement of his home. Thanks to this opportunity, the brilliant aviation career of William John "Jack" McDonough can be told – how a sharp-minded young man's career evolved from training to wartime service; then, how an ocean liner trip to the New World provided the opportunity of a lifetime.

W.J. McDonough was born in Moseley, Warwickshire on September 26, 1898. As a boy of 15 he joined the Imperial Army, serving at first in the King's Own Yorkshire Regiment. Details about these days are skimpy, but it is known that he fought at Loos, then (March to May 1916) at Vimy Ridge, where he was wounded.

In December 1917 McDonough remustered to the Royal Air Force. The following years are interpreted here mainly through McDonough's detailed log books. This begins with the first entry in his "Army Book 425 Pilot's Log Book". It was May 18, 1918 at a Scottish aerodrome and the entry shows John McDonough's first flight as an RAF Cadet at No.18 Training School. With instructor Lt E.A. Simpson, he took a 15-minute familiarization flight in Avro 504 B4350. "Straight Flying. First Ride" is how he succinctly put it.

Now came the demanding grind through basic RAF flight training. Takeoffs and landings busied McDonough on the next few flights then, on May 25, he started branching out – "Turns and a spin" are listed for this flight (his 6th) in B4350. This simple entry reflects the big steps taken in training since 1914, when spinning an Avro 504 was considered suicidal, let alone looping one (which McDonough did on May 26). Flying proceeded almost daily. On May 31 he notes "12 Landings" with Lt Simpson, all in 25 minutes. Then, on June 7, following only 17 lessons, he soloed in D4417.

The term "Aerobatics" occurs first in McDonough's log book on June 14. He flew his first cross-country in D8297 – a 70-minute return to Stonehaven and home. Aerial photography was introduced on June 19, he tried his first Immelman manoeuvre on June 26, and had his first go at "Aerial Fighting" on July 1 in D8297. His lengthy cross-country of July 7 took him to Aberdeen and home in 1:10 hours. On July 8 he flew twice: a short trip in Avro D7752 practicing landings, then his first flight in a fighter – 30 minutes in Sopwith Pup B7575.

At last ready for operational training, McDonough left 18 TS with 40:05 hours, 29:40 being solo. He now joined 32 Training Depot Squadron at Montrose, near Dundee, Scotland, flying initially on July 9 in a Pup. Then began a demanding course on Avro 504s and Pups. He did his first air firing from Avro D8297 on July 19, then had his first accident (Pup B7575) on the 20th – "Crashed on Drome", McDonough noted. For the 24th he flew with Lt Donaldson in 2-seat Camel B7371, then soloed the same day in B4037. Gunnery commenced, as did formation flying.

For August 1918, McDonough flew the Camel 30 times, his longest trip being 85 minutes in E1443 on August 13 ("Formation. Firing. 150 Rds"). By September 18, his last flying day at 32 TDS, he had logged 81:55 hours. He now proceeded to No.4 Fighting School, where he made 13 Camel sorties, honing formation flying and air firing. From here,

W.J. McDonough as a young wartime pilot with an R.E.8, then with an S.E.5a. He often flew these types on test and ferry assignments. (McDonough Collection)

McDonough was posted to test and ferrying duties at No.1 Aeroplane Supply Depot at Marquise, France. He flew his first sortie on October 8 in Camel H7099. Henceforth, it is clear from McDonough's log book that he was born to fly, always ready to go up at a moment's opportunity, especially to add some new type. On October 11 it was no surprise that he flew the R.E.8 then, on the 13th, Armstrong Whitworth F5802 and a D.H.4. His A.W. flight ended in a forced landing after 40 minutes. He flew the F.E.2b on the 16th, the Bristol Fighter on the 30th, but generally was on Camels and R.E.8s. On November 7 he flew Bristol Fighter 5817 for 20 minutes, R.E.8 7057 for 10 minutes, then Camel 7098 on a 3:30 hour cross-country which ended badly: "Crashed in Dark", he noted in his log book. One muses about such succinct entries.

On Armistice Day, November 11, 1918 McDonough tested R.E.8 7187, about which he logged the comment "Overheating". On the 16th his undercarriage collapsed while taxying S.E.5 6370. For a test on Camel 7263 on the 23rd, all he had to say was "Hopeless". He force-landed D.H.9 1162 at Saidre on the 26th. On December 12 he headed to England in R.E.8 2870, but force-landed at Calais after 1:15 hours. For December he flew 27 times in 9 different types: the "Big" A.W., B.E.2e, Bristol Fighter, Camel, D.H.9, Dolphin, R.E.8, S.E.5 and Snipe.

On February 13, 1919 McDonough flew Bristol Fighter 5821 to England with Dr. Thorne as passenger. For the 22nd he logged "Attempted to cross Channel" then, two days later, noted "To Marquise from England", a 30-minute flight. Two more "firsts" in his log are the (February 25) Sopwith Salamander, and (March 3) the enemy's dreaded Fokker D.VII. On April 10 he was in England and on May 3 was demobilized, having flown 251:20 hours in the course of the one year since his initial familiarization trip.

In the spring of 1920 Jack McDonough sailed for America. This was the dawn of US Air Mail Service, a time when aircraft still were unreliable for civil use. Mail routes, navigation and weather reporting all were sketchy, yet pilots were expected to press on with the mail. For this a heavy price would be paid. Such prospects did not faze

McDonough, who must have had some sort of incentive regarding a job with the USAMS.

On March 20, McDonough flew initially in America, taking up a Farman at Mineola, Long Island. Some JN-4D training flights at Philadelphia and Washington came next, then air mail pilot Harry Huking converted him to the D.H.4b on May 16. On May 26-27 Max Miller, one of the greatest air mail pilots, took him on a check ride from Cleveland, Ohio to Bellefonte, in Pennsylvania's rugged Appalachians. Their plane was a converted Martin MB-1 bomber of which the US post office had six. They landed in one piece on Bellefonte's Clinton Country Club (four USAMS MB-1s soon were lost in crashes).

F/O McDonough flies Bristol Fighter 2871 on a message pick-up exercise at Aboukir, Egypt in March 1921. (W.J. McDonough Col.)

McDonough carried his first mail on May 29 in D.H.4 No.92, but this was inauspicious: "Lost my way, blown off course. Landed at Copely and again at Lorain. No gas, damaged propeller and bottom wings." His next trip was on June 1 from Cleveland to Buffalo, but he had engine trouble. On the 3rd he was operating D.H.4 No.60 from Bellefonte to Cleveland and again had a rough time: "Lost my way. Engine dud, Ship total wreck". But there was worse to come. On June 22, after flying Curtiss "R" No.42 for 2:30 hours from Cleveland to Bellefonte, he had a terrible experience: "Weather awful, crashed in mountains at Petersburg". (This town is on the Pennsylvania – Ohio border south of Youngstown.)

We don't know whether he was fired or quit, but in August 1920 Jack McDonough no longer was with the USAMS. Instead, he had joined a company called International, operating at Burlington, Vermont and Lake Placid, NY. Next, he moved to P.H. Huffman's company, United Aircraft Inc., operating at Lynn and Weston, Massachusetts in September. Both outfits were barnstorming with Avro 504s. On a typical trip, on September 12 McDonough flew five short joy-riding hops at Weston.

By now McDonough had good reasons to regret his New World foray. Perhaps in sackcloth and ashes, he visited the British embassy in Washington, likely seeking to re-join the Royal Air Force. About this prospect he probably was encouraged by the military attaché for, on January 1, 1921, McDonough sailed home to a solid new future. After some refresher flying at RAF Station Northolt (near London) and Shortwick (near Liverpool) on the Avro 504, Bristol Fighter and D.H.9, he was posted to Egypt in May 1921. By this time he had logged 549:30 hours.

In Egypt, McDonough qualified to instruct and was promoted to OC "B" Flight No.4 Flying Training School at Abu Sueir at Ismailia. Here he taught students on the Avro 504, Bristol Fighter and D.H.9, but also did considerable test flying. His log is replete with engine failure and force-landing entries, as the desert wore out airplanes. On occasion, McDonough took up the station hack –

Camel E6302. This was a busy and enjoyable time that included many flights to Cairo and a deployment to Jordan. The tour ended with a flight in Bristol Fighter 1160 on November 16, 1922, by which time McDonough's log book showed 829:15 hours.

Back on the old Avro 504, Jack McDonough commenced flying at Northolt on February 2, 1923. After a few days, he joined the instructing staff at No.1 FTS at Netheravon (near Salisbury) and in May was on the Bristol Fighter training flight. For a trip of November 7 in Avro 9380 he surpassed 1000 flying hours – high time for any pilot of the day. June 24 – 29,1924 he flew Avro E3136 in the RAF Pageant. This included the "Standard Avro Race", an 8-mile course with, as the program stated, "a flying finish past the Royal Box".

In these days McDonough mainly was flying the Snipe and the D.H.9, e.g. 2-seater Snipes 6482, 6529, 6613 6840 used in fighter conversion. Beginning in October, he added such types as the D.H.53, Fairey Fawn and Vickers Vimy. While flying D.H.9 J7090 on December 22, 1925, he and F/L Thomson crashed at night, but apparently were unscathed. His next flight was on the 29th in an Avro with the notation "To find J7090".

On July 17, 1924 F/O McDonough submitted his assessment of the various shortcomings of the dual-control D.H.9a trainer. This report illustrates his test pilot mind, and his stature at 1 FTS. He commented in part: "Stick too short. Rudder bar too far away from instructor's seat. Poor visibility ahead. No master ignition switch in instructor's seat. … seat prone to slide about … Machine generally very heavy fore and aft as well as laterally. Rudder bar had insufficient clearance from cockpit flooring…" Once local modifications were made, McDonough tested the improved aircraft, but remained critical: "Slightly higher seating position. Longer control column. Raised rudder bar box and cut-out slots for foot movement giving much more comfort in rudder control. … No master switch which, it is suggested, is most necessary. Visibility better but not as good as on the Westland conversion. Machine generally very heavy and sluggish laterally." November 22 through January 15 he made at least 26 test and evaluation flights mainly in D.H.9 J7008, but also J7054 and J7090. J7008 may have been a refined D.H.9

In the early 1920s Jack McDonough learned much about airmanship flying the de Havilland D.H.4 and D.H.9 with the US Air Mail Service, and with the RAF over Arabian deserts and the UK, and with Northern Air Lines. These D.H.9s are seen in a UK setting. Notice the spare wheel carried beneath the fuselage. (Samson Clark)

with recent mods by Westland, including "Harrison Gear", which improved stick-and-rudder control. McDonough was pleased:

All oil leaks have now been stopped… The seat position has now been greatly improved and is also adjustable 3"… The back stick has been lengthened 1"… The master switch has been placed in the Instructor's seat … The cowling and fairing for the back seat provides good visibility and comfort. In my opinion the machine is superior to dual D.H.9a's now in use in the service.

By March 1925 McDonough was out of the RAF, and chief pilot flying the 3-seat D.H.9 G-EBJX at Stranraer, Scotland, for Northern Air Lines Ltd. His log entries note 900 lb being about maximum for cargo, but loads as small as 50 lb were entered. McDonough also carried the occasional passenger. For May alone he flew 52 trips each of about 50 minutes to local centres. He began flying the 4-seat D.H.50 G-EBFN in

early May, this being a new commercial type based on the D.H.9.

In September 1925 McDonough joined the Midland Aero Club of Birmingham. In landing this job he had the backing of Mr. Scott-Scott, Chairman of Northern Air Lines, who wrote to the MAC on September 9, 1925: "We cannot speak too highly of Captain McDonough's capabilities … we should not dream of losing his services except in the circumstances in which the company finds itself … it has not, at present, sufficient funds to continue its operations." Henceforth, McDonough was busy instructing on the D.H.60 Moth. His 5th log book commences on August 21, 1926 by which date he had 1683:55 hours. That week he was in Bournemouth with Moth G-EBLT competing in the Light Aeroplane Club Instructors' Scratch Race, a 2-lap, 10-mile race with a £20 first prize. A new plane for McDonough in this period was Westland Widgeon G-EBRL, which he flew first on November 15, 1926. For the July 30, 1927 King's Cup Race,

D.H.50 G-EBFN which Jack McDonough flew for Manchester-based Northern Air Lines. 'BFN later operated in Western Australia into 1935. (Royal Aeronautical Society)

The Westland Widgeon III which McDonough flew to a second place finish in the prestigious King's Cup Race of July 1927. Powered by a 120-hp Cirrus, the handsome Widgeon lost the market to the D.H. Moth and only 26 were built. Perhaps for nostalgic reasons, in August 1929 McDonough imported Widgeon CF-AIQ. He flew it briefly from Winnipeg, then sold it to P.F. Osler, the first of several western owners. In 1946 'AIQ was converted into a snowmobile at Prince Albert. (W.J. McDonough Collection)

a 360-mile circuit starting at Hucknall Aerodrome, McDonough placed 2nd overall in 'BRL in 5:15:49 hours – £100 (1st place went to W.L. Hope in a Cirrus Moth: 5:50:14 hours, £200). With a Moth flight of September 10, 1927, McDonough passed his 2000th hour.

In April 1928 Jack McDonough, with 2139:15 hours recorded in five log books, made another risky career move – he emigrated to Canada. He immediately travelled to Ottawa to nose out flying jobs. He visited J.A. Wilson, who welcomed him genuinely, then directed him to some RCAF type down the hall, who feigned a lack of interest (a disgraceful yet common Canadian attitude towards immigrants from "the old sod"). This fellow wasn't impressed by any Englishman's achievements, reminding McDonough that this wasn't the desert: "Different conditions, my man", said "The Omnipotent One", as McDonough christened the ignorant functionary. Luckily, though, he was deemed acceptable and sent to Camp Borden for evaluation. Here, from April 30 to May 4, he flew twice in Avro Lynx G-CYBM" with F/O George Brookes, and once in Moth G-CAKO with F/O Dave Harding. But this sojourn was not a highlight for McDonough, who wrote later of Camp Borden: "It was a burial ground for the living. The smell of postwar decay was in the air. Senior officers, reduced in rank and skating on the thin ice of peacetime retrenchment, were bellicose at the advent of capable young men thirsty for knowledge." Yes, Camp Borden would have been a shock for any "Brit" familiar with the RAF's modern air stations that thronged with airplanes and young men eager to get ahead. McDonough's general impressions

of Canada were powerful, but Camp Borden, declining after years of caretaker maintenance, was too much for him.

One happy event for McDonough at Camp Borden was meeting Herbert "Bertie" Hollick-Kenyon, with whom he would have the best of times. One day they set off on the train from Angus to Toronto to scout out jobs at a new company – Northern Aerial Mineral Exploration. Next morning they were interviewed by H.A. "Doc" Oaks, who impressed them with his sharpness, even if he was abrasive. "Oaks knew his job and what he wanted," recalled McDonough. And so he did, and he hired both men.

Next day McDonough met a short, stocky fellow at NAME who shouted at Oaks "When the bloody hell are we going to get those planes?" It was NAME's president – Jack Hammell himself, who now changed gears: "Who the hell is this!". Oaks explained that it was McDonough, a new pilot. "Christ, are we hiring choir girls?" snapped the

old boy, disapproving of McDonough's city slicker garb and telling him to get on with things, but to leave his "ballet dress" behind.

On May 13 McDonough rendezvoused with Doc Oaks and Pat Reid on Toronto Bay to check out on the company's new Fairchild FC-2 G-CARA – what McDonough described on first sight as "a suitcase with wings". This would be his first go with a waterborne plane, and Oaks insisted that he do the flying. McDonough had neither a clue nor a choice. Improvising, he started the motor, taxied clear of all the pleasure craft in the bay, got airborne, flew a bit around Toronto, then got back onto the bay. Oaks called his efforts "lousy", but McDonough was getting the message. Reid was kinder, saying, "Nobody got hurt and that's a pass in my book." This was a tough but honest gang, and McDonough liked that.

On May 14 McDonough was on duty – training and doing joyrides. For the 19th he noted in his log, "3 flights, 8 passengers". A few days later he was given a $100 bill and sent to Fairchild at Farmingdale, Long Island to collect a new machine (FC-2 G-CARE) to deliver to Hudson. Taking along W.F. Bullock of the London *Daily Mail*, he flew to Montreal in 4:50 hours then, next day, made Toronto in 4:30. June 6 they proceeded to Sault Ste. Marie (4:10) then, on the 8th, to Hudson (5:15). Two days later McDonough began his bush flying career, carrying 450 pounds of freight to Gold Pines in 'ARE in 2:40 hours return. Henceforth his log shows daily mileage flown, likely since he was being paid by the mile, along with a base

A Toronto Bay familiarization flight in G-CARA was Jack McDonough's introduction to NAME. This FC-2 would survive until an accident with M&C Aviation at Lac La Ronge, Saskatchewan on June 19, 1937 – on takeoff it lost power and crashed, but pilot A.M. Campbell survived. (W.J. McDonough Col.)

salary. Gold Pines trips for June 19 are listed as 8:00 hours/600 miles.

In July 1928 McDonough was on FC-2W-2 G-CART supporting exploration camps from Nipigon to Favourable Lake in Northwestern Ontario. On August 9 he left Winnipeg solo in Fairchild G-CARA "Clara", bound for Fort Simpson. Carrying his personal kit, extra fuel and oil, grub and a few spares, he routed via The Pas, Cranberry Portage, Île-à-la-Crosse, Fort McMurray and Fort Resolution. The trip proved as terrifying as any over the Jordanian desert. Once, when needing fuel, he set down on a lonely lake where, as "Clara" bobbed and drifted, he poured fuel into his wing tank, started up and got away for what he later called his "Destination Dubious". Near sundown, he landed to find himself in Fort McMurray. He again topped up his fuel, had a quick meal and, by midnight, was off again. Years later he would recall the final leg of this trip:

Up the Athabasca River, past Chipewyan, then the junction of those great rivers the Peace and Slave. Northwest hour after hour, Clara rattling happily along, our ground speed 90. Gazing with awe on the mighty Mackenzie ... It was nearly six in the morning when you reached the Liard just south of Simpson and saw two tents on the south shore pitched close to a new Fokker Super Universal. You had made the NAME base camp.

In two days McDonough had covered some 2000 gruelling miles. He was dead tired, so not too impressed when Doc Oaks growled, "What's been the hold-

The NAME sub-base at Gold Pines in June 1928. From this rough and ready set-up aircraft were despatched to camps over a vast region. (W.J. McDonough Col.)

up?" Oaks then gave McDonough a hand-done map and instructed him to fly up the Nahanni River for about an hour. He then was to turn up the Flat River for what he called Landing Lake, which he described as "about the only place you can get down in that country with any hope of getting out again with these jalopies." It was high mountain country but, when McDonough asked if a fully loaded FC-2 could climb to the 8000 feet needed, Oaks only replied, "That's for you to find out, Mac." (In a September 2004 paper, Nicholas C. Larter of the NWT Department of Resources, Wildlife and Economic Development describes this same country: "In this rugged, remote area the mountains rise to as much as 2500 m from the 700-900 m Flat River valley floor, but generally the mountain tops average ca. 2100 m in elevation." The "Landing Lake" as named by Doc Oaks might be today's Seaplane Lake in that same region at about N61° W126°.)

Next morning McDonough and his engineer set out. "Clara" got them to 9000 feet, but over the roughest of Yukon country, the engine quit. Down they glided between canyon walls but, just as things looked hopeless, McDonough got the engine going and they made Landing Lake. Oaks came in next day, left the Fokker and reminded McDonough to look after it: "It'll be everything between you and a 300 mile walk, if you break it." Then Oaks departed with "Clara" and McDonough began the daily routine of hauling supplies from Nahanni Butte to the headwaters of the Flat River to supply NAME prospectors searching for gold. There also were many trips to Fort Simpson. All this soon got into McDonough's blood – from nature's wonders to the camaraderie and the pure fun of flying.

On September 17 Doc Oaks sent McDonough to pick up the mining engineer who would take over district operations. The trip to Fort Fitzgerald and back took 4:15 hours, McDonough returning with three passengers and 500 pounds of freight. The new boss turned out to be a rugged, one-eyed fellow who

The NAME colour scheme is thought to have been orange fuselage and wings with royal blue empennage, lettering and trim. Here NAME FC-2 G-CARE sits on winter gear with tarpaulin in place for daily engine servicing, pre-start warming, etc. Following the demise of NAME, L.F. Stewartson of Fort William acquired 'ARE. Next it became CF-MAH with the Manitoba Government Air Service. It toiled for the MGAS until May 28, 1943, when it burned at the dock in Lac du Bonnet. (W.J. McDonough Col.)

The daunting terrain that greeted the aviator who dared to challenge the Nahanni River Valley in 1928; then the fair haven at journey's end – Landing Lake. (W.J. McDonough Col.)

started by calling the set-up, "A tourist camp and look at them pansy faces," then telling the prospectors to clear out and get to work.

All prospecting ended with the first snow. McDonough headed east in C-GARK from Fort Fitzgerald on September 20, routing Fond du Lac to Fort McMurray, Edmonton, The Pas and Hudson, where he landed on the 30th. Now he was assigned to instruct at NAME's flying school in Winnipeg. This commenced on November 4 with a familiarization flight in Moth G-CARU. Next day he took on his first two students, J.P. Culliton and C.F.K. "Kel" Mews.

Looking east along Portage Avenue in Winnipeg during the mid-1930s. Nearly everyone who worked for WCA or NAME would have known this fine western city and strolled this famous street any chance they got. (J.P. Culliton Col.)

Another take from the 1928 NAME "family portrait" series – one where the photographer had not yet called his subjects to attention. Standing are Jack McDonough, Duke Schiller, Dazzy Vance, Doc Oaks, Matt Berry, Frank Barager, Jay Culliton, G.D. Wadds and Frank Fisher. In front are Jack Humble, Al Cheesman, Tom Caddick and Kel Mews. Tales of these men were legend, from flying combat in S.E.5s, H.P. O/400s, etc., to peacetime aviation in all its variety. In one case, from June 23-26, 1919 Vance crewed on an O/400 from Lympne, England to Cairo. This record-breaking flight had plenty of excitement and on the final leg from Crete had as a passenger none other than T.E. Lawrence – "Lawrence of Arabia". For this mission Vance received the Air Force Cross. But death lurked at all times in aviation. While landing Dominion Explorers' Fairchild 71 CF-AKX on Hunter Bay on July 14, 1930 Vance crashed and was drowned (prospector Monte Priske survived). Duke Schiller would die in WWII while ferrying a PBY Catalina from Bermuda. Kel Mews eventually joined CPA. On March 4, 1966 he was the co-pilot on DC-8 CF-CPK "Empress of Edmonton". Aboard for the 3-hour Hong Kong-Tokyo leg were 64 passengers and crew. While landing in bad weather at Tokyo, 'CPK crashed short of the runway. Mews, then age 59, was one of the 54 fatalities that dreadful evening. (J.P. Culliton Col.)

The sort of scene down on the dock that was so common in NAME days. It would be great to know who all these people were and what their business was. Few, however, labeled their photos as to whom, where or when. Here, Doc Oaks is third from the right. This likely is one of his parties going to or arriving from some camp via NAME Fairchild. (W.J. McDonough Col.)

Fairchild 71 CF-ABM of Consolidated Mining and Smelting after a dunking at Churchill. Then NAME's FC-2 G-CARA being salvaged from a similar predicament, location unknown. The normal cause for such a mishap was leaky floats – inspection plugs could come adrift, or floats could be holed in shallow waters. To get a waterlogged plane back into service took much effort by the air engineers and helpers. (W.J. McDonough Col.)

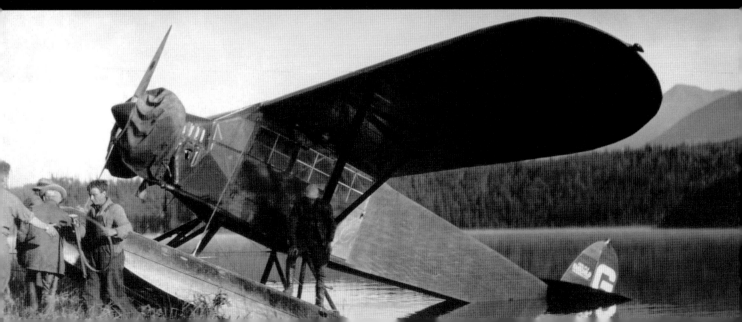

NAME Super Universal G-CARK with engineer Jack Humble on the left. Notice how the fellows are in hip waders, which was standard kit for float operations. Jack McDonough had 'ARK on the Nahanni expedition over the summer of 1928, then delivered it back to Hudson on September 30. Dazzy Vance and Brian Blasdale then took it north to Baker Lake on the MacAlpine search. Damaged there in a fierce gale of October 17, it was stranded until August 1930, when Bill Spence ferried it to Waterways. However, it seems that 'ARK never re-entered service. (W.J. McDonough Col.)

Chesterfield Inlet was a home away from home for NAME men and planes from 1928-30. This winter setting includes the NAME Loening and one of the company's Fairchilds. Then a contrasting summer scene. (J.P. Culliton Col.)

Three handsome Fairchilds on duty somewhere in the back country *circa* 1930. CF-ABM of Consolidated Mining and Smelting is nearest, NAME's G-CATT farthest. With nature's snow white, coniferous green and stunning sky blue, what a picture this would have been after adding the yellow, orange and red of the Fairchilds. (W.J. McDonough Col.)

While on staff at Fairchild in 1929-30, McDonough fell in love with the 3-seat KR-34, a gorgeous descendant of the mid-1920s "Challenger" designs by Ammon H. Kreider and Lewis E. Reisner of Hagerstown, Maryland. In 1929 this duo made a joint venture with Sherman Fairchild, who had the capital to stabilize their operation. The Challengers then became the "KR" series. Ten KR-21s and KR-34s soon were on the Canadian civil aircraft register, including one owned by Jack McDonough. His machine, CF-AJZ, is seen at Fairchild, Longueuil in the spring of 1933. McDonough sold 'AJZ to Doc Oaks in 1934. It lasted until September 19, 1939, when it crashed at Cordingly Lake in northern Ontario. In 1937 McDonough briefly owned KR-34 CF-AMW. (all, W.J. McDonough Col.)

Jack McDonough's long-dormant archive included rare views from his 1929-30 Fairchild sojourn. Shown in flight is Model 71 NC145H, likely shot prior to delivery to Colonial Airways. In 1944 it became CF-BXI with Northern Airways of Carcross, then later served Central BC Airways and PWA. On August 8, 1956 it was wrecked while landing at Kitimat.

At the factory in Farmingdale, Long Island, Jack McDonough flew many Fairchild types. Typical would have been these pictured in an 8 x 10 found in the McDonough collection: Model 42 "Foursome" X9183, Model 51A NC6800, a pair of KR 21 Challengers (X576E nearest), with Moth "A1" in the distance. With a 300-hp P&W Wasp Jr., the "51A" evolved from the 200-hp FC-2. The RCAF converted several FC-2s to 51 and 51A status, i.e. with a 300-hp Wright J-6 or P&W Wasp Jr. These RCAF conversions endured into WWII, after which most had civilian careers as bushplanes.

Jack McDonough while on his Fairchild sojourn.

He continued instructing until January 10, flying anywhere from two to five times daily.

Another McDonough student was Frank Fisher. Born in England in 1905, he used to tell people about boyhood days as German Zeppelin raiders flew overhead. Fisher emigrated in 1920, sailed three years on the Great Lakes, then was an Ontario Provincial Air Service radio operator. He met Doc Oaks at Gold Pines in 1928, asked him for a chance to get flying, and was bowled over when Oaks replied, "OK. You look eager enough." Fisher went on to a stellar career, flying for National Air Transport, then Austin Airways. In 1944 he was a Mosquito test pilot at Central Aircraft in London, where his boss was company president – Jack McDonough.

In January 1929 McDonough was sent to Sioux Lookout to fly FC-2s G-CARA and 'ARE supporting prospectors around Pickle Lake. He began on the 14th, flying 560 lb freight to Pickle Lake in 'ARA, a return trip of 3:30 hours (on one trip of February 9 he hauled 1000 lb, probably a fair overload). On the 14th he had a flight to a camp called Collins (80 miles east of Sioux Lookout) to help salvage a Fokker. Meanwhile, he was instructing at Sioux Lookout on G-CARU, Brian C. Blasdale, Frank Fisher and Kel Mews being his students.

Jack McDonough's fifth log book ends with an entry for February 19, 1929. That day he flew Moth G-CARU for 15-minutes, logging that with the comment "Froze face -25°. Test only". He now had a grand flying total of 2521:55 hours. (Unfortunately, McDonough's log books from here until into WWII are missing. His next available book commences January 6, 1940 at 4985:00 hours and opens with a flight in an RCAF Delta, seemingly at de Havilland in Toronto. So, from February 1929 and January 1940 he had doubled his flying time. This is easy to realize, considering his involvement with NAME, then with his own company, Spence-McDonough Air Transport.)

Some time in 1929 McDonough left NAME for a new flying job with Fairchild Flying Services. Any reasons for this move are unknown. In July 1929 he took part in a major airshow, likely as an official Fairchild representative. The Red Bank, New Jersey *Register* reported on the show under the headline "Big

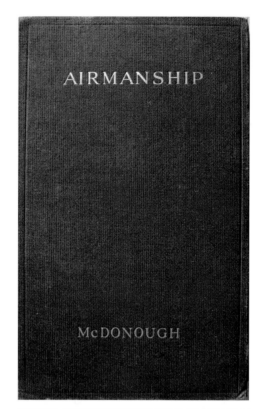

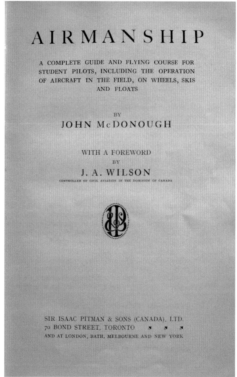

W.J. McDonough's *Airmanship* was a practical guide to flying in Canada, and remains a gem in the "aviation literature" genre. A copy occasionally appears for sale on the internet. (J.P. Culliton Col.)

The author's inscription in Jay Culliton's copy of *Airmanship*. (J.P. Culliton Col.)

Event for Aviators". For four days starting on July 3 some 30,000 spectators swarmed to the Red Bank Aero Club. VIPs on hand included Grover Loening, Amelia Earhart and Clyde Pangborn. Among the 60 planes were Standard Oil's Lockheed Vega and Tide Water Oil's OX-5 Challenger (a popular sport plane from the Fairchild stable). Flying a Gipsy Moth, Jack McDonough came first in the opening day 25-mile relay race. Next day he competed in a 25-mile "free for all", but didn't place. He competed again on July 5, taking the $250 first place prize.

In April 1930 McDonough returned to Canada and a partnership with ace bush pilot Bill Spence. By this time Dominion Explorers and NAME were faltering under the grave losses incurred by the McAlpine search. McDonough and Spence saw this as an opportunity and bid on bases and equipment from both companies. Also this year, Sir Isaac Pitman & Sons (Canada) Ltd. published McDonough's book *Airmanship*. The first comprehensive Canadian guide to aeronautics and practical flying, *Airmanship* illustrates McDonough's literary skills and practical sense of aviation. Besides all the usual theory of flight, he included such valuable opinions as:

Any man or woman with average intelligence can learn to fly an aeroplane sufficiently well … but flying is an art and as such will always show grades of proficiency. The man who plays the piano is not necessarily a musician; likewise the man who flies an aeroplane is not always a pilot in the strict sense of the word... Flying is like music, an endless study. The longer you fly, the more you should realize how far away you are from attaining perfection in the accomplishment of the art. An egotistical pilot is a menace.

Even for the 2000s *Airmanship* is a relevant handbook, and a useful philosophical guide for the thinking pilot. It is no surprise that in November 1931 pilot/author/philosopher McDonough was invited to address the Royal Aeronautical Society about Arctic air operations, nor that the great J.A. Wilson agreed to pen his foreword.

Spence-McDonough Air Transport

As was everyone in 1930, Jack McDonough and Bill Spence, former RAF pilots, were worried about the Depression and about losing their jobs. But these were not wimpy men – their solution to hard times was to go out and take a risk. McDonough described their big gamble in his unpublished 1948 memoir:

The renowned bush team of Spence and McDonough on a page lifted from their company prospectus.

Candid snaps of Jack McDonough with full kit on the trail, then Bill Spence in a relaxed mood. (W.J. McDonough Col.)

Bill had been chief pilot of Dominion Explorers. He was an engineer and one of the finest exploration pilots in Canada. "Things are grim", he told me, "so what about joining forces? MacAlpine might sell us those planes he has, if we could borrow some money to operate them." So back into the bush it was. This time as Spence-McDonough. Back to Great Bear, that mad rush of '32. Fortunes won and lost.

With it main base near Fort McMurray (formerly Dominion Explorers' base) the company thrived during a Great Bear rush, but also in selling exploration companies on the economics of chartering air transport, compared to the sky-high costs of water or overland options. "The aeroplane," said McDonough, "requires no ground preparation, and in most cases, not even landing facilities at its destination. There is thus no capital tied

FC-2W-2 CF-AAO on winter gear showing how the wings folded for storage. In his log book, Jack McDonough refers to G-CART as a "Super Fairchild". Notice the rough surface, one that would have been very unkind to any bush plane. 'AAO had begun with Dominion Explorers in February 1929, then went to Spence-McDonough in 1930. It survived with Canadian Airways into the late 1930s, then faded from the scene. In his book *Fifty Years of Fairchild Aviation*, Theron Reinhart credits demand from Canadian operators for development of the FC-2W-2. The first example G-CAIQ went to Quebec in January 1928. (W.J. McDonough Col.)

A typical scene (place unknown,) featuring Fairchild FC-2W-2 CF-AKZ in which Bill Spence later died at Moose Lake, Manitoba. Several RCAF aircraft are present, including two Vedettes and a Bellanca. (W.J. McDonough Col.)

up in roads, portages and intermediate camps which will, in the end, have to be written off as a loss." The main issue, however, was speed, McDonough explaining, "The value of any money which is kept idle through slow transportation facilities is actually a direct charge against the freighting."

In 1931 Spence-McDonough compared transportation modes between Edmonton and Great Bear Lake, the heart of a staking rush. In "Case 1" a traveller might ride two days by train Edmonton-Fort McMurray (275 miles), thence fly 785 miles to Great Bear in about eight hours air time with en route stops. Total cost for transportation? $1487. In "Case 2" one might spend nine days by rail and water, ending at Fort Rae at the top end of Great Slave Lake. From here it was a 250-mile, 3-hour plane trip to Great Bear. Total cost? $670. "Case 3" was a 1425-mile, 5-week rail and water trip from Edmonton to Echo Bay on Great Bear Lake via Fort Norman. Total cost?

Winter and summer views of Spence-McDonough Fairchild 71 CF-AKY. Its colours are said to have been yellow with red. With Canadian Airways, 'AKY snagged a tugboat cable while landing at Vancouver on August 6, 1935. Rebuilt by Boeing of Canada, it re-emerged as CF-AOP, but its affinity for trouble continued. On May 20, 1941 it was wrecked after colliding with a motor boat at Beauchesne Depot, Quebec. (W.J. McDonough Col.)

$489. As far as Spence-McDonough was concerned, a few days by air was well worth $1487, compared to the weeks to reach Great Bear by land and water.

Spence-McDonough Air Transport Statistics

	1931	1932
Hours flown	603	1350
Miles flown	54,375	126,125
Tons of freight	25	190
Passengers carried	300	779
Total flights both years		900
Forced Landings due to weather		8

Spence-McDonough Advice to Prospectors

A proper outfit of supplies and equipment suitable for the particular needs of Northern mining and exploration is of the utmost importance. These can be obtained in Edmonton from business houses experienced in equipping Northern parties for over a hundred years. The following is a suggested list of supplies necessary for two men for 100 days in the field:

Previously unpublished views of Spence-McDonough Super Universal CF-AJH over the 1932 season in the NWT. While the open cockpit Standard Universal had a 200-hp Wright J-4B, the "Super" used a 420-hp P&W Wasp. With an all-up weight of 5500 lb, CF-AJH could carry about a 1000-lb payload. It last served with Dominion Skyways at Noranda, where it was scrapped at the end of its career *circa* 1936. (W.J. McDonough Col.)

Camp Equipment for Base

Heavy canvas tent
Mosquito netting
*Collapsible camp stove with pipes
    and asbestos ring*
Two eiderdown sleeping bags
*Spools of copper wire, nails,
    auger and bit, bucksaw*
*Pots and pans, frying pan, tea pot,
    coffee pot*
*Pitch, copper rivets, canvas,
    thread and awls*
Pick or mattock and shovel
Box of explosives, fuse and caps
*A few dozen small canvas bags,
    heavy duck*

Small assay outfit, including blow torch
Candles, electric torch and batteries
First aid kit and a few drugs
*Snowshoes and extra babbich
    for filling, duffle*

Field Equipment

Sheath knife, compass, aneroid
One pair field glass, camera
*An automatic pistol, .45, .22 rifle,
    30.30 carbine*
2 light haversacks, 2 heavy pack bags
*Geological picks, fish hooks and
    trolling spoons and fish line*
Collapsible canoe with outboard motor
Hardwood material for sleigh, heavy

webbing for harness
*Aluminum cooking outfit, primus stove
    with oil*
*Magnifying glass, small mosquito-
    proof tent*

Clothing

*Canvas parka, summer work; fur parka,
    winter work*
Heavy socks, moccasins
Boots, heavy underclothing
Overalls, leather
Light, rubber canvas shoes
Sweater, light underwear, windbreaker
*Hat, fur cap, mitts (several pairs),
    light cotton gloves (several pairs)*

Fairchild FC-2 G-CARH of Spence-McDonough Air Transport in a typical winter scene somewhere along of the treeline. This aircraft had served Dominion Explorers in 1929, then joined SMAT the following year. Col MacAlpine purchased it in April 1932, sending it that summer to the NWT. C.F.K. "Kel" Mews was flying it on July 31 when he cracked it up about 60 miles east of Great Bear Lake. (W.J. McDonough Col.)

Food Supplies

Flour	180 lb
Rolled oats	18
Rice	12
Cornmeal	10
Whole wheat flour	20
Split peas	6
Bacon	120
Sugar	75
Tea	8
Coffee	6
Butter	30
Cheese	10
Milk Powder	20
Beans	50
Potatoes (des.)	26
Onions	14
Baking powder	4
Salt	10
Pepper	8 oz
Yeast	8 boxes
Baking soda	1 lb
Soap	10 bars
Dried fruit	34 lb
Raisins	8
Currants	2
Jam	12
Matches	2 cartons
Mustard	8 oz
Macaroni	7 lb
Tobacco	7

Spence-McDonough Air Transport fared well against Canadian Airways until fate stepped in. On January 12, 1933 Bill Spence had a trip from The Pas to Norway House with Fairchild CF-AKZ. After picking up RCMP Cpl P. Greaves, prisoner Buster Whiteway (charged with shooting the postmaster at Ilford) and prospector Ernest Robinson, he opted to return to The Pas. This normally would have taken about 90 minutes but, by the time Spence and engineer W.L. "Bill" Cooke got rolling again, the light was waning and the weather touch-and-go.

Spence flew low in blizzard conditions, hugging the tree-lined edge of one lake after another, keeping visual reference. After about an hour he decided on a precautionary landing on Moose Lake. Likely due to a white-out, however, Spence crashed disastrously. He died outright, the others were badly injured. In its January 19, 1933 edition, the *Northern Miner* eulogized the great Bill Spence, referring to him as the quintessential "Jack Canuck":

Acknowledged by other airmen as one of the most skilled in Canada … Spence piled up a tremendous air mileage since he started as a war pilot. He was a graduate of Queen's University and on his return to Canada practiced for a few years his calling as Civil Engineer. The coming of aerial photography drew him back to flying. He joined Dominion Explorers in 1928... It is doubtful if a better-liked man existed in the north...

Bill Spence on arrival with CF-AKZ at some NWT settlement. His passengers were missionary priests, likely Oblates of Mary Immaculate – the religious order that "ruled the roost" in the Roman Catholic missions all the way down to Aklavik. The missionary crowd was quick in the 1920s to recognize the importance of aviation in furthering their work. The Oblates eventually had their own Beaver, CF-OMI. (W.J. McDonough Col.)

An exceptionally skilful pilot, he had the advantage of engineering training and woods experience.

Unfortunately, "The Miner" didn't have all the facts so, in the style of the press, made them up to get the desired effect. It stated that the crash was caused by engine failure, and of Spence having to make a downwind landing. "Caught in a blizzard," the *Northern Miner* wrote, "Spence was circling the lake for a landing, when his engine failed." Fortunately, in his superb 2006 book *Bent Props and Blow Pots* Rex Terpening, in 1930 a Spence-McDonough air engineer, clarified this: "On his last flight, there is nothing to indicate that there was any mechanical problem with the aircraft … the motor was functioning normally until the final moment of flight." In his own memoir, Jack McDonough described how the passengers came out alive after discouraging hours in Arctic conditions:

The dreadful post-crash scene at Moose Lake. (W.J. McDonough Col.)

"The rescue of the survivors was an amazing epic of human courage and fortitude. The half-breed prisoner, taking the handcuff keys from the policeman, freed himself. Then, despite a compound fracture of the leg and terrible face injuries, crawled on hands and knees for six miles through the bush, guided by the howling of dogs, to bring aid to his companions."

In the aftermath of this tragedy, men made the most of it. By 1933 the going in air transport was not improving – small companies were hurting. Before the accident, however, McDonough and Spence had a buy-out offer from James A. Richardson. McDonough now accepted this and left the business. He later mentioned how Buster Whiteway was recognized for his heroics and reprieved as to the charges against him. But engineer Cooke lost his hands to frostbite. All he could do was return to England where, last heard of, he was running a small store. Cpl Greaves recovered, returned to Norway House, but further aviation woes lay ahead for him.

Nothing has surfaced about W.J. McDonough's relationship with Bob Noorduyn, but when Noorduyn's Norseman was ready to fly, Jack McDonough and Leigh Capreol did the test flying honours on November 14, 1935. It is likely that McDonough had met Noorduyn at Fokker in New Jersey in the late 1920s. However, there might have been a McDonough-Capreol connection – such characters would have known each other. Here is the Norseman on the day of its first flight off the St. Lawrence River. Visible in the *La Compagnie Aérienne Franco-Canadienne* hangar at Pointe aux Trembles are two disassembled "Compagnie" Schreck flying boats. (W.J. McDonough Col.)

Rough and ready Latham Island at Yellowknife as Jack McDonough would have known it in the mid-1930s. The Corona Inn (2ⁿᵈ shack from the right) was established by Pete Raccine, Ted Hickmont and Gordon Latham. There also was a government liquor store here and, doubtless, a fewer bootleggers. For 5 cents, Watt's Water Taxi would ferry a passenger the stone's throw from the mainland. (W.J. McDonough Col.)

Jack McDonough leaning on an Anson during his important "war effort" days at DHC and Central Aircraft. He's in some cozy-looking cold weather kit that looks like it was straight out of the box. (Fred Hotson Col.)

In 1935 Jack McDonough joined a conglomerate with such Thayer Lindsley companies as Ventures Ltd. and Falconbridge Nickel. Mining now was his chief passion and, in the coming years, he had interests from Peru to the NWT. From long experience he knew that the latter was rich in minerals and couldn't wait to get moving there. In 1939 he joined the RCAF, but was prevailed upon by P.C. Garratt to move to de Havilland Canada as a senior manager. Garratt soon named him to head Central Aircraft in London, a repair and overhaul base for many types of RCAF aircraft. Employment there rose to 4000 and business by war's end would total $50 million.

In 1945 there was an mineral rush around Yellowknife. Some thought that this was too distant from civilization to be profitable, but Jack McDonough needed no convincing. As far as he was concerned, Yellowknife was in Bay Street's backyard: "It is 3,450 miles by public carrier from Toronto, but only 24 hours in time, since one can leave here at 2 o'clock on any afternoon and be in Yellowknife the next afternoon between 1 and 2 o'clock." By comparison, he pointed out, one would be lucky to make Red Lake from Toronto (a quarter the distance) in three days. And nobody thought that Red Lake was too far.

Gold brought steady development to Yellowknife. Here is the town as it was evolving in early post-WWII days. The view is northeast up 50ᵗʰ Ave. At the top of the street is Old Town, dating to about 1935. Just across from Old Town is Latham Island, with Back Bay on the left, Yellowknife Bay on the right. This area was the town's aviation hub. Joliffe Island is to the right of Old Town, and the road to the Giant Mine heads off centre left between Niven Lake (above) and Frame Lake (lower). (W.J. McDonough Col.)

When Jack McDonough got into prospecting and mining in 1945, he acquired this Fairchild 71. CF-BKP was a resurrected version of FC-2W-2 G-CAIW, which had been reduced to spares by Canadian Airways in 1937. 'BKP was busy during development of the North Inca Gold Mine at Indin Lake north of Yellowknife, but was wrecked in a take-off accident near there on September 26, 1946. (all, W.J. McDonough Col.)

In March 1944 McDonough established Trans-America Mining Corporation, which staked its first claims at Indin Lake, NWT north of Yellowknife. In 1945 these became the basis for North Inca Gold Mines which, within two years, raised $660,000 in development cash. Drilling results were promising so, via tractor train from Grimshaw, Alberta and planes from Yellowknife, over the winter of 1945-46 North Inca brought in everything needed to start a mine. A telling remark in its first annual report (December 31, 1946) concerns air transport: "The largest commercial aircraft at present operating from this base have a payload of four and one-half tons. Such planes at the present contract rates of $100 to $110 per ton from

Jack McDonough (left) underground with some of his men at the North Inca mine.

Yellowknife are competitive with tractor haulage over the most direct 140 mile ground route." For its first year North Inca paid $14,950 for surface transport, $30,800 for air. It used its own Fairchild 71 CF-BKP and D.H.87 CF-DIP (registered to Trans-America Mining), but also hired Norsemans and DC-3s.

In 1948 Jack McDonough produced a brief memoir – "Destination Dubious", which appeared in *The Northern Miner* beginning on March 4, 1948. He pursued mining and aviation interests into the early 1950s, although he sold his Trans-American/North Inca interests in the US in 1949. Business kept him on a gruelling road schedule then, while in New York on June 19, 1954, everything suddenly caught up with him – at age 55 he suffered a fatal heart attack. A few days later his ashes were spread from a Beaver on a woodlot north of Downsview airfield. This was done according to a pact between himself and his great pal at DHC, P.C. "Phil" Garratt. They agreed that, whomsoever went first, the other would see to it that the ashes were spread over a certain woodlot. From WWI France to postwar Egypt and Appalachia, and on to the Canadian Arctic, William John McDonough had eagerly pursued his "Destination Dubious", perhaps to its inevitable conclusion.

William John and Winifred McDonough with sons Stephen (left) and David at home in Toronto in the mid-1930s.

Fairchild 71C CF-BVK replaced CF-BKP. Here it is at the North Inca mine in 1946. 'BVK had begun in April 1929 as RCAF G-CYYB. It was sold to Dominion Skyways in 1942, then to McDonough's Trans-America in December 1946. When McDonough sold his mining companies in 1949, 'BVK went to Central BC Airways. On November 13, 1955 it was damaged after running over a deadhead on takeoff at Ocean Falls. While being towed ashore, it sank.

Legendary planes and men were the hallmark of the Ontario Provincial Air Service. Here is a fine 1925 close-up of an OPAS Curtiss HS-2L with observer (later pilot) Giff Swartman ready for work. Mounted in the nose is the huge aerial camera which Swartman wielded all summer long, shooting oblique photos, as he stood in the open air at 80 mph. Each OPAS member seems to have been a character in his own right, as was Swartman. Besides being a professional on the aviation scene, he also was an accomplished musician, leading a band at the Nickel Range Hotel in Sudbury. (Ontario Ministry of Natural Resources)

The Ontario Provincial Air Service

In 1919 the Ontario government teamed with the Canadian Air Board to study the uses of aircraft in the realm of natural resources. This study indicated that, with a fleet of 18 planes, 30,000 sq.mi. of forest could be patrolled at a seasonal cost of $12.50 per sq.mi. Ontario viewed that as too pricey for immediate implementation. The following year, however, aircraft were chartered, especially for forest sketching and photography. The sketcher was a skilled professional. Perched in the nose of something like an HS-2L, he could view the forestscape for miles around. As he absorbed all of this, he began to transfer it – waters, the limits of various tracts,

OPAS observers King Crosbie and Ben Greenwood in their bulky leather flying gear. Such outfits were needed for duty in the nose of an HS-2L on a chilly day at 5000 feet. (*The Firebirds* Col.)

From 1925-27 the OPAS operated Loening Air Yachts G-CAOO and 'AOT. Describing these hot cabin monoplanes in *The Firebirds*, Bruce West wrote how "... they were the joy and pride of Roy Maxwell, who utilized them at every opportunity for VIP and other specialized flights..." However, neither machine lasted long. 'AOO was lost in a strange incident. As pilot H.C.W. Smith, who had never flown a Loening, taxied speedily on Ramsay Lake on July 21, 1926, 'AOO inadvertently became airborne, then plunged into the water. Neither Smith nor engineer Ed Ahr were hurt, but Sudbury car dealer Alex McLeod and his daughter, Myrtle, and their friend Mrs. H.K. Clements of Chicago, all were hospitalized. The Toronto *Star* reported how "Mr. McLeod is severely injured ... The plane is a complete mass of twisted wreckage." G-CAOT met its end at Ramsay Lake on July 1, 1927 as it attempted a dawn-to-dusk return flight from Toronto to Moose Factory, Jack Caldwell and Roy Maxwell being the crew. This was a special event – not only was it Dominion Day (Canada's national holiday), but also the Diamond Jubilee of Canadian Confederation. While landing for fuel at Sudbury, however, pilot Caldwell hit hard and 'AOT broke into pieces. Happily, neither crewman was injured. The great aviation hound, C. Don Long, took this fine view of 'AOT at rest on some scenic lake.

Since 1924 aircraft of the CGAO/RCAF, Laurentide Air Service, OPAS and others proved their worth in controlling the annual forest fire scourge. Jack McDonough photographed this major fire *circa* 1930.

etc. – onto his map sheets. Occasionally, his pilot might set down to let him examine a specific tract. Later, he would submit his sketches and notes, which became the basis for detailed topographic maps prepared by the provincial cartographic office.

In 1921 Ontario's Provincial Forester, E.J. Zavitz, was pushing for greater use of aircraft. That season he chartered a flying boat from which R.N. "Reg" Johnson and Frank Jenkins did forest sketches. On one flight they spotted a fire near Cliff Lake in northwest

In pre-provincial air service days, CGAO/RCAF Wright-powered Avro 504 G-CYGK was typical of government forestry patrol planes, as was HS-2L G-CACW of Laurentide Air Service, an important commercial operator. (William J. Wheeler Col.)

H-boats plus D.H.61 Giant Moth G-CAPG await the beginning of the flying season at Sault Ste. Marie. G-CAOJ (at the hangar door) served until wrecked in a storm at Fort Frances in August 1931. (CANAV Col.)

The spacious and usually busy shop floor in the OPAS hangar. H-boats, Moths, even a Loening can be seen, with G-CAOP nearest. With so many aircraft on hand, this likely was in the off season, when the fleet was in for overhaul. The large sign at the right urges "Safety First", then continues with a warning that these days certainly would be considered politically incorrect for its perceived sexism and harsh clarity: "The wife of a careless man is almost a widow." (Ontario Ministry of Natural Resources)

Dead of winter in the Soo in 1924-25. Eight HS-2Ls are staked out in cold storage awaiting completion of the OPAS hangar. (Ontario Ministry of Natural Resources)

Ontario, flew to a forestry base, collected some rangers and equipment and returned to the fire, which was successfully quelled. Johnson then proposed to Zavitz that Ontario employ aircraft routinely. In 1923 the Ontario Department of Lands and Forests gave Laurentide Air Service Ltd. a contract involving 12 HS-2Ls patrolling between Lake-of-the-Woods and James Bay at rates of $125-$150 per flying hour. That season 550 passengers were carried and 400 fires reported. At the same time LAS surveyed 39,000 sq.mi. of Ontario timber for the Spanish River Pulp and Paper Co.

Ontario requested tenders for 1924 for 2500 flying hours, the best offer being $95 per hour. Queen's Park (seat of the Ontario government in Toronto) felt that it could best this, so established the Ontario Provincial Air Service. In practical terms this resulted in transferring LAS personnel, aircraft and equipment to the Ontario payroll. Roy Maxwell of LAS, a former RFC pilot,

barnstormer, James Bay aviation pioneer, pilot for Canadian Aero Film of Hamilton, etc., was appointed director. Initially, 16 pilots, 19 engineers and 13 HS-2Ls were on strength and a modern base was established on the St. Marys River at Sault Ste. Marie.

HS-2L in OPAS Service

All the details of the magnificent Curtiss HS-2L are covered in the aviation literature, especially in the superb Molson-Shortt book, *The Curtiss HS Flying Boats*. The HS-2L was a typical performer of its day. Those who knew it would joke about how it took off, flew and landed at 65 mph. Powered by a 360- or 400-hp Liberty (an engine designed on short notice for wartime service), an HS-2L didn't always make it back to base by day's end. But no one would panic – they knew that the crew likely was on some lake tinkering with their engine. Almost invariably, they would turn up in a day or so. OPAS old-timer

Jack Dillon described a typical HS-2L predicament, the aircraft being stranded on a small lake:

The HS-2L needed more takeoff run than the lake provided, so we simply had to create room. To accomplish this, an axe crew moved in to cut a swathe through the standing timber on the opposite shoreline wide enough for the boat to fly through ... This meant dropping every tree for about a quarter of a mile along a 200-foot wide strip... the boat was pulled, tail up, nose in the water and pointed toward the opening being created. Then, a 2-inch rope was firmly attached to the bowsprit, threading back through the fuselage, out the tail assembly, and tied to a spruce tree about chest high ... the right amount of gas was carefully measured into the tank, with allowance made for warm-up. Every item of equipment that could possibly be removed from that craft was dismantled, and just enough water was left in the radiator... The pilot then

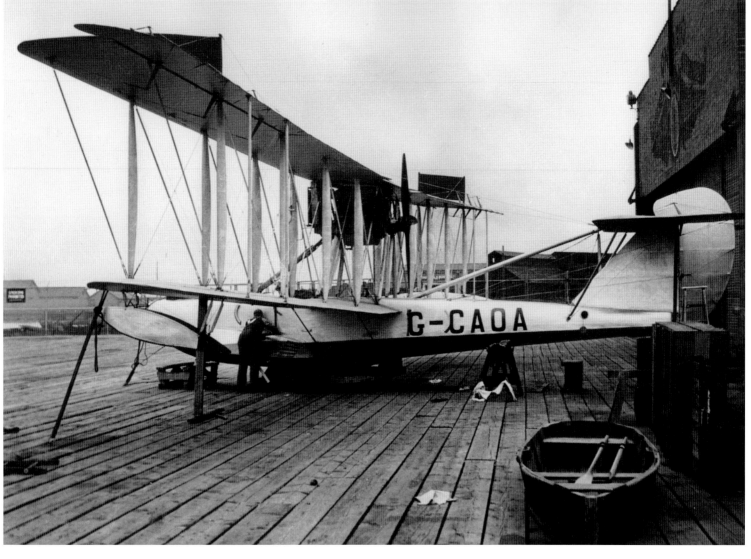

OPAS HS-2L G-CAOA *Albatross* on the slipway at Sault Ste. Marie. Few such pioneer flying boats had lengthy careers. This was assured by their vulnerability to everything from encounters on the water with deadheads and rocks, to fire and perpetual rot. Nonetheless, several OPAS "H-boats" survived years of toil. The days of *Albatross* stretched from 1924-32, after which it was reduced to spares. (CANAV Col.)

selected for the takeoff was picked because he was competent and did not weigh too much...

When all was ready, the motor was started. A ranger with a razor-sharp axe was stationed at the tree anchor. The pilot would hand-signal when he was ready and the restraining rope would be severed. As the revs increased to takeoff

H-boats at Sault St. Marie *circa* 1931. Of these, G-CAOQ *Quail* served to a normal retirement following the 1932 flying season. 'APE *Eagle* crashed disastrously at Pays Plat in May 1931, while 'APF *Finch* suffered hull damage in August 1932 and was written off. (J.P. Culliton Col.)

power, the spruce bowed and waved from the pull and the prop backwash. The rope was cut and, with a few skips and bounces, the lightened boat skimmed across the lake, passed through the trough in the trees and lifted into the sky.

In its first season the OPAS flew 899 patrols covering 2,870,000 sq.mi., reported 598 fires and logged 2597 hours. Aircraft reliability was rated at 96.3% (899 flights despatched, 866 completed). The Department of Lands and Forests calculated that, due to the expeditious reporting and fighting of fires by air, the government had banked the wages of 390 men over the 5-month fire season and saved $250,000 compared to chartering air services.

Fifteen HS-2Ls were on strength in 1924, six allotted per district. Main bases were Sioux Lookout in the west (J.R. Ross superintendent) and Ramsay Lake at Sudbury in the east (G.A. Thompson). Meanwhile, 152 lookout towers reported 851 fires. On a typical operation, pilot F.J. Stevenson and engineer L.H. Briggs in HS-2L G-CAOI carried 900 feet of hose, a pump, tools and spare parts, two 3-gallon cans of fuel for the pump and a tent and food to the site of a fire at Obashingkaka Narrows. After the load was ashore, they assisted in fire fighting for the next eight hours, then returned to Temagami having flown 2:05 hours for the day. G-CAOI flew the most in 1924 – 255:55 hours. Pilot C.J. Clayton logged the highest time in one day – 10:40 hours. Not surprisingly, 'OI had the longest list of technical snags – from broken oil pipes to carburetor, camshaft and crankcase problems. In 1926 Terrence Tully of the OPAS summarized the HS-2L's general performance:

In the warmer weather of July and August when the HS-2L is heavily laden it often takes a mile or more before leaving the water... the average rate of climb with full load is about 3,000 ft. in 30 minutes ... its best average height is about 4,000 ft. with its effective operating load... The HS-2L is comparatively slow as its average speed is about 65 mph. The machine has a steep gliding angle and the speed necessary to maintain good maneuvering control without the engine is slightly more than the average level speed with the engine on. Owing to the steep gliding angle and low serviceable

Curtiss HS-2L Specifications

Upper wing span	74'
Lower wing span	64' 1"
Length	38' 6"
Height	14' 7"
Empty weight	4350 lb
Gross weight	6223 lb
Fuel	153 US gal
Oil	13.3 US gal
Max. speed	91 mph
Stall speed	55 mph
Range	575 mi.
Number produced	1034

ceiling of the machine the margin of safety ... is governed by the route followed to ensure remaining in gliding distance of a lake ... It is necessary to carry an air engineer on operations particularly owing to the size and unwieldiness of the HS-2L on the water, and the difficulty in approaching and tying up to docks or shorelines in awkward wind conditions.

The annual report concluded with several recommendations, mainly that the OPAS needed a more modern type, one with better takeoff, climb and cruise performance, plus a modern, reliable, economical engine. The report also urged that the OPAS begin training pilots and air engineers for future service – the

original cadre already was moving on to other opportunities. In this period, senior pilots received a base pay of $215 monthly, "Junior A" pilots $175 and "Junior B" pilots $125. Pilots received an additional $2.00 per flying hour. Senior engineers were paid $185 plus $1.00 per flying hour. Through 1924 superintendents Ross and Thompson earned $250 monthly.

In the Fall 1974 edition of the CAHS *Journal*, Hugh A. Halliday described typical OPAS H-boat operations:

In the third week of June 1924, a fire was reported near Dog Lake. Duke Schiller, flying "Buzzard", flew in two rangers and their equipment from Kashabowie on the 22nd, then spent two days flying in additional men, pumps and hoses from Port Arthur. Again, early in July, a major fire was reported near the Manitoba boundary. G-CAOJ and 'OL and three pilots (Carter Guest, J.R. Ross and J.P. Roméo Vachon) flew from Sioux Lookout to Minaki where they loaded up with fire fighters, food supplies, pumps, etc., all of which were despatched directly to the outbreak...

On 21 July, Fred Stevenson and his engineer, L.H. Briggs, flew a pump, 900 feet of hose, a tent, food supplies and assorted other items to a fire that was raging near Obashingkaka Lake. That done, they remained for eight hours

An idyllic scene of G-CAOC although, in the end, this HS-2L came to a non-idyllic ending. On August 16, 1924, while searching for H-boat 'AOB, it crashed near Savanne Lake (west of Fort William). Crewmen V.C. Gilbert and E. McBride died and pilot E.C. "Ed" Burton was injured. Originally from the album of OPAS pilot J. Carter Guest, this photo cropped up in 2009 in the pages of one of William J. "Bill" Wheeler's magnificent aviation photo albums. Few did as much as Bill over the decades to advance Canada's aviation heritage. A founding member of the Canadian Aviation Historical Society, from 1963 to 2009 he edited the CAHS *Journal*, producing nearly 200 priceless editions.

helping the ground party to combat the blaze... About 7:30 A.M. on 31 July 1926 an HS-2L crew en route from Bear Lake to Longlac spotted a major fire. By good fortune they were able to locate the chief ranger at Bluffy Lake. The HS-2L landed and the fire was reported. Thereafter the aircraft ferried in fire fighters, the first contingent arriving at 10:30 A.M... 35 flights were made to the fire over the next ten days during which time 27 men and 6420 pounds of equipment were flown in. On 10 August the fire was declared extinguished ... In his report Maxwell noted, proudly, "The fire, which was inaccessible by canoe, was handled entirely by aircraft"

Each HS-2L carried its own small stock of tools and parts. A 1925 report listed a typical load as ordinary tools – 16 lb, engine tools – 4 lb, engine parts such as washers, screws, rocker arms – 31 lb, such repair items as wire, fabric and emery paper – 11 lb, plus a blow torch. All this was necessary since any HS-2L was prone to mechanical failure or to damage on the water. In the first OPAS season there were 43 forced landings due to engine failure. A description of HS-2L communications was provided by OPAS observer James A. Bartlett in the Fall 1982 CAHS *Journal*.

We did not carry a radio in 1927 and I don't know of anyone who did. If a fire was seen we would fly over to it and I would estimate its size, distance from water, best route in for a fire-fighting crew, plus a guess as to how many men, what pumps and hose would be needed. All of this was written down on a sheet of paper held well down out of the wind and put in the pocket of a message bag. This was a canvas pocket with a button-down flap, sewn to two brightly-coloured strips of bunting about six feet long ... The message bag itself was nailed to a block of pine ... The bunting tails were wrapped around the block ... as we headed for the nearest railroad station. We circled it until the agent on duty came out to see us, where upon I waved to him, leaned over the side a bit, and heaved the message to him... It was the agent's job to get it PDQ and telegraph my message to the District Forester ... Our method was crude by modern standards, but it worked and out of it grew the modern Ontario Provincial Air Service.

The OPAS began its 1930 season with six HS-2Ls for the heavier work, and 14 D.H.60 Moths for lighter duties. A Giant Moth, Vedette and Fairchild KR-34 rounded out the fleet. In this 1931 scene at The Soo sit five Moths, Vedette CF-OAB, Hamilton CF-OAH and Fairchild 71 CF-AHC. As usual, most of these were associated with odd bits of history. Lower left Moth CF-OAF, for example, served into 1944, then was sold to prospector Norb Millar of Bridgenorth, Ontario. He sold it in 1954 to Ron Hayashi, but 'OAF was destroyed at Toronto Island Airport, when Hurricane Hazel blasted through on October 15 that year. Moth CF-OAG (lower right) was damaged following engine failure near White River on July 31, 1934. It later was resurrected as a new Moth, CF-OAO, which itself was lost in a subsequent accident. Fairchild 'AHC joined the OPAS in June 1931, but cracked up on Arrow Lake 60 miles SSW of Fort William on that July 16. Pilot F.J. "Fred" Dawson and engineer P.M. Vooges were uninjured. (Ontario Ministry of Natural Resources)

The OPAS in 1930

The OPAS mainly excelled in detecting and controlling forest fires. This was essential in a province where, in 1923 alone, fires burned 2,120,000 acres of trees. The 1930 OPAS annual report shows how busy and useful the service had become. For the year it logged some 14,200 flying hours on 11,955 flights (previous year-end figures indicate a steady growth in OPAS activity: 1925 – 2739:52 hours, 1926 – 3529:22, 1927 – 4861:03, 1928 – 6102:40, 1929 – 11,602:00). For 1930, 4506:00 hours went towards fire detection, 3659:40 to fire suppression, and 2537:50 to transporting men and supplies to the fire lines. Many other tasks were listed, however, from sketching and photography to ferrying, flight instruction and carrying 9821 passengers.

By September 1930 the OPAS fleet totalled 14 Moths (9297:45 hours logged that year), 6 HS-2Ls (3122:40), 3 Hamiltons (1204:40), Hamilton NC878 on a lease (66:10), 1 D.H.61 Giant Moth (343:10), 1 Vedette (174:40) and 1 Fairchild KR-34. With 2756:50 total hours, HS-2L G-CAOK was the high-time OPAS aircraft by year's end. KR-34 CF-AOJ, acquired in September, was the lowest-time machine with 39:35 hours. Pilot R.R. Smith held the season's record for most time logged in a day – on June

18 he was airborne for 18:10 hours.

Throughout the season the fire hazard across Northern Ontario was usually severe, so the OPAS was relieved at having added three large Milwaukee-built Hamilton H-47 Metalplanes. The annual report discussed the new type, praising its speediness and adding: "The all metal structure ... reduces the annual reconditioning costs which are to be met in overhauling wood and fabric machines... It is particularly adapted to winter flying as it can be left out in the elements." The Hamiltons were described as capable of carrying "a complete crew and equipment consisting of five men, one pump, hose, food and equipment for one week ... many such suppression flights were carried out." It also was noted that a Hamilton could carry 12 men, or six sectional canoes.

The OPAS also was pleased with the season's results with its Giant Moth: "This particular machine has a remarkable pay-load, as much as 2200 pounds being lifted from the water at one time." Although six HS-2Ls had been scrapped the previous winter, the remaining six performed well. However, they were becoming harder to maintain. As to the much-loved Moths, the annual report observed: "The continuing success and sturdiness of the Moths is manifest by the splendid work they accomplish year by year and the severe treatment to which

In 1930 the OPAS selected an HS-2L replacement – the all-metal, 8-passenger, Milwaukee-built Hamilton H-47 Metalplane, powered by a 575-hp P&W Hornet. (By this time Thomas Foster Hamilton's company, which had operated briefly in Vancouver in 1914, was a subsidiary of Boeing.) Of OPAS H-47s CF-OAH, 'OAI and 'OAJ, 'OAI crashed. The others were sold in 1945 to Northwest Air Service in Alaska. CF-OAJ operated to July 1947, then was shipped to Minneapolis in 1951 for restoration, which Jack Lysdale undertook. Resplendent, NC879C, formerly CF-OAJ (right), flew again on August 12, 1975. In 2009 it remained serviceable with Eriksson Aircraft of South St. Paul, Minnesota. H-47 specs included: length 34' 9", wing span 54' 5", empty weight 3450 lb, all-up weight 5750 lb, fuel 140 US gal, cruise speed 120 mph, fly-away price $25,000. (William J. Wheeler Col., Jon Eriksson)

they are subjected." The year ended with not so much as one Moth engine failure. By this time the Moths had switched their 80-hp Cirrus engines for 100-hp Gipsies, so were considerably faster.

For the year the Vedette was the OPAS dedicated photo plane, but the service looked forward to replacing it with a plane that had a comfortable, heated cabin – Vedette men were fed up with flying in their open cockpits in whatever weather nature had to offer. To their rue, however, the Vedette would be around the OPAS for many more years. For 1930 it covered 1744 sq.mi. doing vertical photography and 3500 doing oblique photography. Some 47:05 hours were devoted to sketching, using various aircraft. Sketching proved its value when tracking a fast-moving forest fire.

Through 1930 the OPAS trained six new pilots. Most had been selected from the air engineer ranks, for the service had a long-range plan to have only pilot-engineers. One rookie pilot was third in

hours flown (731:20) and none had any difficulties on assignments. The annual report concluded with some personal remarks about activities at the OPAS Port Arthur base. Pilot E. Waller was chastised for showing no interest in his machine: "Never saw him give assistance to secure machine on the beach... Did not set good example. Does not pay Mess debts.

Leaves everything to his engineer, phones to enquire if machine is ready." Pilot E. Hodgson, however is described as "An excellent H.S. pilot. Shows uncanny judgment in every phase of flying and seamanship ... keen and ambitious... Pays particular interest in his machine and camp life. Never fails to assist his engineer ... Pays Mess debts promptly."

With the pilot ready to start and a crewman holding the tail steady, Giant Moth G-CAPG loads passengers at Ranger Lake near Sault Ste. Marie. As usual, a few well-wishers and sightseers are on hand. Powered by a 500-hp Bristol Jupiter XI engine, 'APG joined the OPAS in August 1928. In 1934 it was upgraded to a 550-hp P&W Hornet, which kept it going productively through the 1940 season. Thereafter, it was a ground training aid at the Galt Aircraft School and around war's end went for scrap. Only 10 Giant Moths were built, three of which served in Canada, others in the UK and Australia. All-up weight was 7000 lb, just between the later Norseman and Otter. (Ontario Ministry of Natural Resources)

Powered by a 300-hp Wright J-6, Vedette CF-OAB joined the OPAS in August 1929. In 1934 it was converted to a 420-hp P&W Wasp – as such it was a one-of-a-kind Vedette. It's seen on its beaching gear (location unknown), then in Montreal en route to Halifax to assist in a rescue operation at the Moose River Mine. (C. Don Long, William J. Wheeler Cols.)

When damaged on Lake Nipigon in August 1940, CF-OAB required major repairs. The OPAS purchased dormant Vedette G-CAND in Montreal, then combined the best of both machines to create a born-again version of 'OAB. Here 'AND is transported from the railway station in Sault Ste. Marie to the OPAS hangar. The new airplane seems to have operated through the 1943 season before going for scrap. (Norman Etheridge Col.)

OPAS Moth: The Daily Grind

In 2009 the following reminiscences about Moth operations were found in the unpublished memoir of veteran OPAS pilot J.P. Culliton:

George Phillips and I were the only pilots based at the Soo in 1932-34. We would alternate in carrying out the flying requirements of the district, and once in a while we would accompany one another. While on fire detection, we had quite a long patrol. A full patrol would take seven hours of flying and almost a full day. In the morning, we'd leave the dock at the Soo with supplies and mail for the various places we would be visiting. Our first stop would be Sand Lake, then over Michipicoten to Puckasaw Harbour. Landing at Puckasaw was often a ticklish matter. The heavy waves and swells off Lake Superior made it extremely hazardous most of the time. The long swells were very deceptive from the air, and it was difficult to judge their size until the aircraft was ready to touch down.

From Puckasaw we'd cut back to Wawa on a course a bit north of the track we came in on. From Wawa we'd fly across country to Kendigami or Aubrey Falls. We'd then head south to Lauzon Lake, near Blind River. From there we were flying into the sun until we landed back at the Soo.

Most of our flying was charged to fire detection work, even though we carried loads or passengers to various locations. When we had fires, however, we had to concentrate on fire suppression work. There were a few towers in the District,

A trio of OPAS Moths with canvas engine covers in place to keep out moisture, dust and birds. Having begun in May 1928, G-CAPB (nearest) was one of the earliest in the OPAS fleet. Then, CF-OAA in a summer setting. Having joined the OPAS in 1929, it endured until June 19, 1946, when it was wrecked in a mishap. In 2009 Ellis Culliton, who grew up in Sioux Lookout where his father was OPAS superintendent, recalled the usual OPAS paint schemes: "All the Moths I saw were yellow with black trim. I'm certain all the Buhls were the same, being built in the Soo shops. The Fairchild 71 I was most familiar with was yellow and black. I remember Hamiltons in silver or, perhaps, bare metal." (William J. Wheeler Col.)

and they were always helpful in reporting smokes...

While on a July 1932 detection patrol with observer Don Start, I flew close behind a group of lightning storms, plotting their course for my report. I flew a series of zigzag legs to keep behind and away from the lightning. We witnessed one vicious strike hit a large tree on a peninsula in one of the lakes. We dropped back and flew along the rear of the storm. After about 15 minutes we flew back to look at the strike, saw smoke coming up, so landed to investigate. The tree was starting to burn at its base. Using our little cooking pail from our emergency kit,

we carried water to douse the fire. After innumerable trips we got the fire out...

On March 15, 1933 I took a load to the Forestry station at Ranger Lake, where chief ranger Vince Prewer had an appropriation to build a cottage for his station. I was taking in some drill bits, amongst other things – they were having to go through a lot of rock to provide a basement for the home. I flew straight in and landed close to the shore near the cottage site. My Moth had hardly come to a stop on the ice when there was a terrific dynamite blast. I scrambled out of the cockpit and onto the lower wing, waiting with bated breath for the rock and debris

In 1932 the OPAS acquired Fairchild 71Cs CF-OAL and 'OAM. These were on lease from Hugh M. Pasmore of Montreal. CF-OAL, shown in a fine in-flight portrait, served to the end of 1934, then became CF-BAL of Great Lakes Airways based in Sault Ste. Marie. CF-OAM was damaged in an accident near The Soo on March 6, 1935. Following salvage, it re-emerged as CF-OAP *Pelican*. (William J. Wheeler Col.)

Winter views of CF-OAP during some forestry operation in Northwestern Ontario. (J.P. Culliton Col.)

to descend. One large chunk, about the size of a football, went right through the lower right wing, tearing out all the inner bracing and about two feet of the spar. With some wire and a couple of large bed sheets, I was able to make a bit of a repair. We then laid a large sheet of plywood from a packing crate over that, and tacked it well. Vince wanted to go out to the Soo, and was willing to ride out on my return trip. We took off and all seemed well until I noticed Vince pointing down at our repair job. It was only then that my mind registered the markings on the up side of the plywood. In quite large letters it was marked "do not drop".

Sioux Lookout became Jay Culliton's base in 1934. There he would fly all the OPAS types over the years, those for 1934 being mainly Fairchild 71s CF-OAM and 'OAP, and Hamilton 'OAJ. Each season would be full of variety, whether working on forest fires, supplying camps, flying photo and mercy missions or transporting government VIPS. On May 15, 1935 Culliton passed the 1000-hour point in his career. He first flew the air service's new Stinson SR-9 on August 16, 1937. SR-9s CF-OAW and 'BGM then became his main Sioux Lookout planes. Early in 1939 he flew 'BGM on an important photo survey that was to determine the route of a new road to connect Kenora with Fort Frances. Early in WWII Culliton joined the RCAF where he was extremely busy over 3½ years doing test and development flying from Rockcliffe.

Other Equipment

Other types would serve the OPAS in these years. The Buhl CA-6M proved ideal when a larger machine was needed, so four were built by the air service in Sault Ste. Marie in 1936-37. In a memo of March 19, 1937 George E. Ponsford reviewed the ideal qualities for any such OPAS bushplane. It would have " a

Buhl CA-6 Airsedan CF-OAR on the beach at Port Arthur. Then a new-looking CF-OAQ at Rockcliffe. Under its agreement with Buhl in Michigan, the OPAS built four CA-6s at Sault Ste. Marie. OPAS head George Ponsford was criticized for selecting this aging type. But Ponsford knew his stuff better than most, and the Buhls served the OPAS well. In *US Civil Aircraft Series*, Vol.2, Joseph P. Juptner describes the CA-6 as "quite sprightly and very manuverable ... asking no favors from the pilot or the landing strip". CF-OAQ and 'OAR both met untimely ends in 1945, CF-OAQ capsizing in a storm on Caribou Lake on July 23 and 'OAR being wrecked on October 23 after a hard landing on Mishabashu Lake. (William J. Wheeler Col., RCAF HC7387)

Stinson SR-9 Reliant CF-OAY served the OPAS from April 1938 to August 1949, when it moved to Chukuni Airways of Red Lake. In 2009 CF-OAY was a restoration project at the Alberta Aviation Museum in Edmonton. (W.J. McDonough Col.)

disposable load of about 1600 pounds, a smart water performance, quick take-off and initial climb, large, roomy cabin with large doors, reasonable speed and preferably [be] of the high-wing monoplane type to facilitate loading." As far as some critics were concerned, the Buhl did not meet all these specs, but Ponsford defended it, especially due to its performance on small lakes. In a September 22, 1936 letter to Deputy Minister of Lands and Forests, W.C. Cain, he reiterated that no one had expected the Buhl to be a rocket. "Service," he wrote, " is the acid test of these aeroplanes and … I am fully of the opinion that the ship has and will live up to our expectations."

In 1937 the OPAS was ready for further re-equipment, but at first found no suitable type. Sales agents had planes to offer, but none that met standards. The Beech 17 and the Bellanca were appraised and rejected. Beech's agent, Canadian Car and Foundry of Fort William, was quickly turned down, mainly due to a shoddy proposal, which gave no specs for seaplane operations. Besides, with the 285-hp Jacobs engine proposed by CCF, the Beech was underpowered. In spite of good performance and payload, the Bellanca, as offered by Aviation Service Corporation, was seen for what it was – a 1920s design about which George Ponsford noted, "to the best of my knowledge … modifications have been instituted since then". He added how the Bellanca's door "is very small at the bottom and not conducive for easy loading."

Finally, Stinson in Michigan offered the SR-9 Reliant. Ponsford informed his minister how Stinson already had delivered 700 of its speedy cabin monoplanes, how Stinson would add mods to meet OPAS requirements, but that an order should be placed quickly, before the world rush to re-arm curtailed deliveries to civil operators. The first of five OPAS SR-9s arrived in July 1937.

Mercy Missions

From its inception the OPAS provided air ambulance services – "mercy missions" as these were termed. This service greatly enhanced health care across Northern Ontario, where medical assistance normally was scarce. Several mercy missions were reported in 1935. Late in July a saw mill worker was injured at Nakina. Flying the OPAS Giant Moth G-CAPG, Dale Atkinson rushed the man to hospital in Port Arthur. In another case, just before freeze-up, there was an urgent call from Wawa about a gravely injured miner. The OPAS despatched pilot George Phillips and the victim was in hospital in Sault Ste. Marie about six hours later.

When word came of a critically ill patient at Fort Hope on the Albany River, the OPAS again stepped in. George Ponsford wrote of this in a memo of September 23, 1935: "The Department of Health at Toronto advised us to go in … Doctor Bell of Sioux Lookout accompanied the flight. The case was diagnosed as tuberculosis and the man is now in the sanitarium … at Orillia with a reasonable

chance of recovery. The entire flight was made under very hazardous conditions." Also that summer, pilot Frank MacDougall flew two mercy missions carrying gravely ill children. Such flights reinforced the value of the OPAS beyond its usual natural resource duties.

Staff Policy

In 1936 OPAS director George Ponsford was concerned about losing pilots to the commercial operators. His main point in a July 21 memo to his deputy minister involved pay rates: unless the government upped pilot pay from the present $150 to $180 monthly, to compete with commercial operators, the OPAS would suffer. He explained how just as OPAS pilots with years of training and service "reach a point where they are of value to us, they slip through our fingers". The air service then had to hire replacements "of unknown qualifications and little or no knowledge of forestry work." His recommendation was an increase of $200 a month, considering how $350 was typical for a commercial pilot. Ponsford's sense was that, without a pay raise, "the finest Service of its kind in the world" would begin to crumble.

The Price to Pay

Flying on the edge of civilization in basic airplanes was bound to bring mishap, even tragedy. The first OPAS annual report (by pilot Terrence Tully, dated February 14, 1925) noted that an HS-2L on patrol northwest of Goulais Lake had

OPAS HS-2L G-CAPE *Eagle* is readied at the Soo for its May 4, 1931 mission. Later that day pilot Earl Hodgson (age 26) and engineer Lloyd Mewburn (age 19) crashed at Pays Plat on the Lake Superior north shore. Mewburn died and Hodgson was injured after the plane hit wires while about to alight. On October 8, 1926 Hodgson had survived a near-disastrous ditching in Lake Superior with Leigh Brintnell in HS-2L G-CAOB *Buzzard*. In his album, Jay Culliton captioned this photo "Earl Hodgson and Lloyd Mewburn ready to leave on last trip on PE".

On June 8, 1936 pilot R.G. "Doc" Reid and observer Norman "Red" Cross took off from Port Arthur in Moth CF-OAC. Fifteen minutes later the plane was seen flying erratically, then crashed. Reid's body was found some distance from the wreck, while Cross was under the rubble. Clutched in Reid's hand was a note asking Cross if he was comfortable with proceeding, since rough weather loomed ahead. It seems that, as Reid stood to pass the message ahead, he was thrown from the plane. Cross had no parachute, nor any way to control the plane. (J.P. Culliton Col.)

suffered engine failure on July 7: "The engine was so badly damaged that it needed a complete overhaul, which was accomplished in the bush ... Machine unserviceable 21 days." On July 25 HS-2L G-CAOI *Ibis* had its own problems: "While flying off Lake Temagami there was an explosion in the crankcase, necessitating a new engine."

Other woes this season included several cases of hull and sponson damage, usually from running over submerged rocks. Tully describes damage to 'AOH in Toronto Bay on April 27 after it struck a deadhead: "In taxying in, forward portion of machine sank as far as pilot's cockpit. Hull was written off by crew of dredge during salvage operations, a rope placed around the hull behind the main planes severing machine in two." The *Daily Star* observed the next day how "the pilot [F.J. Stevenson] did not observe the log until a hole was stove in the bottom of the frail craft and it started to sink ... he managed to bring the boat into shallow water off the east end of Centre Island where the ship took a neat nose dive to the bottom." The annual report commented that "Toronto Bay did not lend itself to instructional flying ... owing to an abundance of floating debris which was quite natural after spring break-up."

On August 16, 1924 the OPAS suffered its first fatalities, when HS-2L G-CAOC, searching for 'AOB, crashed near Sudbury. Lost were pilot E. "Ken" McBride and observer V. Gilbert. E.C. Burton, who had been instructing McBride, survived. Many other mishaps would follow. On October 8, 1926 pilot Leigh Brintnell and engineer Eric Hodgson were en route from Orient Bay to Sault Ste. Marie in 'AOB *Buzzard*, when their engine quit, forcing them to alight. Hugh Halliday later noted: "Within 20 minutes a squall swept out of the east, blowing the HS-2L nine miles out into Lake Superior. At this point a freighter, the SS *Henry Cort*, appeared and the aircrew hailed her. As the ship maneuvered ... she rammed *Buzzard*, practically cutting her in two. Brintnell and Hodgeson scrambled onto the freighter, but the H-boat went down ..." In another case, on June 27, 1929 HS-2L 'AOF burned to the water line while refuelling near Lac Seul, northwest of Sioux Lookout (refuelling fires were common in the early days of flying).

The ill-fated OPAS Hamilton, which took Phil Hutton and his three companions to sudden death. In a letter to Fred Hotson of October 26, 1980, pioneer bush pilot W.F. "Bill" Shaylor noted of Hutton: "He was a Sergeant Pilot in my flight in Iraq in 1924. We met again at Camp Borden when he joined the instructional staff. An excellent pilot." (Ontario Ministry of Natural Resources)

On June 26, 1930 the famous wartime pilot, J.O. Leach, age 35 of Barrie, Ontario, crashed fatally at Port Arthur in Hamilton NC878. All his wartime survival skill and instincts seem to have failed him, as he decided to do some extreme manoeuvres in the non-aerobatic Hamilton. The Toronto *Daily Star* reported on June 30: " Major Leach had been thrilling his watchers for about fifteen minutes with spirals, banking, gliding and looping, and was just completing the third loop [when] his machine failed to make the upturn and plunged into the water." The OPAS was saddened by this loss, but referred to Leach's air display as "contrary to our regulations". There also were six minor scrapes in 1930, including a Hamilton damaged while taking off and two Moths overturned on the water.

On August 17, 1931 a furious storm swept across Rainy Lake, forcing two OPAS planes to seek haven. First, Moth pilot George Delahaye set down at Brulé Narrows, but his aircraft quickly flipped in the wind and was driven ashore in pieces. Delahaye spent about three hours floating with his life belt. Some canoeists picked him up, then they all over-nighted on an island. Meanwhile, HS-2L G-CAOJ *Jackdaw*, crewed by pilot Don Mahon and air engineer Claude V. Greer, also had made a hasty landing. Pounded by the storm, their plane started to come apart, forcing them into the water. Mahon helped non-swimmer Greer 300 yards to shore. That evening they reached Fort Frances by boat, only to hear of Delahaye's plight.

On the 18th Philip A. Hutton reached Fort Frances from Kenora in Hamilton CF-OAI. With him were pilot Al Runciman, air engineer Greer (fresh from his close encounter) and district forester W.W. Cram. When a search was organized, Greer volunteered. He, Hutton, Runciman and Cram soon were airborne. After several hours searching, they returned for fuel. District forester J.V. Stewart then replaced Cram. They set off and this time located Delahaye on the island but, as Hutton banked to land, 'OAI stalled and dove straight into the water near shore. All four men were killed, then Delahaye had the grim task of helping to recover them.

An Englishman, Hutton had served in the RFC in France, Mesopotamia and Russia. Before joining the OPAS, he had

The ruins of Giant Moth CF-OAK. This useful big airplane joined the OPAS in June 1932, then proved its worth in carrying hefty loads of men and equipment needed in fighting forest fires. On May 23, 1935 'OAK came to grief while landing in thick smoke at Gander Lake east of The Soo. (J.P. Culliton Col.)

instructed at the Toronto Flying Club. From Stratford, Ontario, Runciman was a junior pilot who had trained at Hamilton, Ontario. "Nip" Greer, from a large Sault Ste. Marie family, had sisters who were married to renowned bush pilots Al Cheesman and Duke Schiller.

On March 6, 1935 OPAS pilot R.M. "Bob" Smith was taking off with a light load from Rankin Field near Sault Ste. Marie in Fairchild 71C CF-OAM. By the end of the takeoff run, he found his machine "loggy, as if it were heavily loaded". Smith quickly ran out of sky and crashed into bordering trees. He later explained his decision to proceed, rather than abort: "The runway was fast, the engine giving full revolutions and the machine was heading directly into a brisk East wind." Smith suspected that his problem was a layer of light snow that froze to the upper wing over night. CF-OAM was badly damaged, but later was rebuilt as CF-OAP.

The crash of Giant Moth CF-OAK at Gander Lake in Northwest Ontario on May 23, 1935 brought a query from Sault Ste. Marie: why was Giff Swartman flying a plane assigned to R.M. Smith? In answering this question, J.P. Culliton in Sioux Lookout explained how Smith had been fairly worn out with the previous day's work, so he had allowed him to rest, while Swartman took the assignment, scheduled for 0300 hours. He took off from Swain's Lake at 0330 to assist in a fire near Gander Lake, 25 miles away. However, on approach Swartman entered some low morning fog

and smoke. As he flew out of this, his aircraft landed into some rocks beside a small island and was wrecked. All aboard escaped with minor injuries, but CF-OAK was a loss, as noted by Culliton: "… the fuselage appears to be in fair condition [but] the location of the accident and the absence of any kind of roads or trails in that area, makes it very doubtful if we shall be able to salvage any more of the machine other than the engine, instruments, and some of the fittings."

Political Circus

In 1934 the Liberal government of Mitch Hepburn swept into power in Ontario. High on its list in "house cleaning" was investigating the big-spending, fiscally (sometimes) unaccountable OPAS. The Liberals had a field day embarrassing their Conservative opponents. Commissioner Daniel Webster Lang spent days in Toronto digesting testimony about Roy Maxwell. He began by claiming that Maxwell had been running the OPAS as a one-man show: "His duties were not defined … he was given a free hand by the Minister."

Few faulted Maxwell personally or as an administrator – under his direction the OPAS was serving its purpose. But the purchase of H-boats in 1924 was revealed to have been from Laurentide Air Service, which Maxwell previously managed. The selling price was $5500 per machine, while Laurentide had acquired them from US surplus for as low as $3000. The aircraft were sold to Ontario as new,

Other Moth woes. G-CAOW *Wren* had a shocking time at Mattagami Post on July 20, 1927. As mechanic Knobby Clark swung the prop for pilot Jack Hyde, the engine caught, but a sudden flame ignited Clark's gas-soaked clothing. He immediately tossed the flaming rag in his hand into the water. Floating gas erupted and 'AOW soon was fried. The damage, however, was repairable and 'AOW served to season's end 1948. Then, CF-OAD half-sunk, maybe after an incident of May 4, 1944, when it capsized in winds at Cross Lake. The plane was deemed "damaged beyond repair". (Ontario Ministry of Natural Resources)

OPAS Aircraft and Crew Assignments 1936

Base	Aircraft	Pilots/Engineers
Algonquin Park	1 Fairchild KR-34	MacDougall/Hughes
Sudbury	1 Moth	Overbury/Phillips
Biscotasing	2 Moths	Crossley
		Woodside/Fleming
Remi Lake	1 Moth	Billington/McPhail
Fort Frances	1 Fairchild 71	Delahaye/Day
Port Arthur	1 Hamilton	Dawson
	1 Moth	Reid/Herald
		Buckworth/Denning
Orient Bay	1 Vedette	Heaven/Tyrrel
Oba Lake	1 Moth	Westaway/Hughes
Sault Ste. Marie	1 Moth	Phillips/Doan
Twin Lakes	1 Buhl	Twist
	1 Moth	Trussler/Wright
Kenora	1 Giant Moth	Delamere/Hallatt
	1 Moth	McIntyre/Batchelor
Caribou Lake	1 Moth	Cairns/Decourey
Goose Island	1 Moth	Gillard/Taylor
Sioux Lookout	1 Hamilton	Weller/Chapman
	3 Moths	Swartman/Failles
		Culliton/Milling
		Harvey/Humble&Harju

which none were. Also, Maxwell had purchased Liberty engines at $2850 from his friend, F.G. Ericson, who had paid only $300. Some were delivered with the warning "Not to be flown", so had to be overhauled at $2000 each.

Maxwell also was accused of over-buying Liberty spares at a time when the HS-2L was slated to retire. Besides all this, he was taken to task about buying the Loenings in 1925, then for trying to blame his boss for this deal, which was shown to be a poor one. Lang also argued that Maxwell had "squandered" money in having the Wright engine on a Vedette replaced by a P&W Wasp for $5737.50. In another case, he was queried about having dipped into public funds for his personal spending. When asked by counsel D.J. Coffrey, "Misappropriated for your own use?" Maxwell replied, "Well, OK." He also authorized the use of OPAS planes to assist H.A. "Doc" Oaks on a 1926 Red Lake mining venture for which, it seems, Oaks paid Maxwell $500 under the table. Other shady dealings were brought to light, such as how Maxwell purchased fuel for the OPAS from a Sault Ste. Marie company in which former Minister of Lands and Forests, James Lyons, was a partner; and used an OPAS plane to fly cronies on a fishing trip (the plane crashed while retrieving a canoe at the end of this swan).

Lang also revealed how de Havilland Canada had allowed Maxwell to buy company shares at $1.50; these he later sold at $5.00 - $20.00. As far as Maxwell was concerned, this transaction did not influence him in his extensive dealings with DHC. Complaints even included one about how employees used the OPAS hangar to repair personal automobiles, and helped themselves to fuel, parts and tools. There also was this remark: "The sum of $1,100.00 was expended in building a pigeon loft at the hangar. The expenditure was unwarranted and the money entirely wasted." In another case, when Maxwell was criticized for paying too much for four Hamiltons ($38,000 each), Lang said, "I do not find that the price paid was improvident." Lang's October 1934 report did its job in publicly shaming Maxwell, who soon retired. Premier Hepburn then hired his friend and chauffeur, George E. Ponsford, to run the OPAS, which he did (also as a private empire) for years to come.

The provincial hangar at Lac du Bonnet with Stinson SR-9 CF-MAJ awaiting a mission. 'MAJ served the MGAS from July 1937 to December 1948. On July 17, 1954 it burned on Lower Twin Lakes in eastern Ontario. (William J. Wheeler Col.)

Manitoba Government Air Service

Several Canadian provinces eventually followed Ontario's example by establishing air services. The first was Manitoba, which commenced operations in June 1932 with five ex-RCAF Vedettes. The province now could conduct its own forestry patrols – forest sketching and photography, and fire detection and suppression, and such general air transport needs as supplying fire watch towers, changing pigeons at towers, or caching canoes. For 1934 the service flew 646 hours, 87 for ministries other than Mines and Natural Resources. At season's end in 1934 two aircraft showed badly rotted hulls, so two Vedettes were added. A Fairchild FC-2 was purchased in April 1935. While the MGAS seemed to be functioning well and at a fair price to the public purse, commercial operators grumbled regularly and loudly through the years about revenue being lost to government planes.

MGAS Statistics 1934

Forestry hours flown	546.40
Test and training flights	22:55
Hydro	16:10
Surveys branch	15:45
Mines	15:05
Game and fish	11:45
Health	8:10
Indian Affairs	6:05
Provincial officials	4:10
Passengers	311
Freight (lb)	31,010
Average mph	64.19
Staff	7
Salaries	$13,746
Total costs incurred*	$21,696

*year ending April 30, 1935

Canadian Vickers Vedette CF-MAA was the first plane registered to the Manitoba Government Air Service. It was one of an eventual seven ex-RCAF Vedettes with the MGAS. The last example persevered into September 1937. In this same period, Saskatchewan also formed a provincial air service, likewise equipped with ex-RCAF Vedettes. (William J. Wheeler Col.)

The Forest Watcher

Over lake and pine-clad forest,
Over river flashing by,
Sails the white-winged
   forest watcher,
Softly in a cloud-swept sky.

Softly drones the distant engine,
Over virgin timberland,
Speaking peace unto the forest,
Where the mighty giants stand.

Onward then o'er tracts
   scarce charted,
Over cataracts asweep,
Over mountain, plain and valley,
Over glades that lie asleep.

Far into the western twilight,
Flashing wings against the sun,
Hums the softening song
   of engine,
Throbbing until day is done.

F/L Francis Vernon Heakes, RCAF, 1928

Two of the Fokker Universals that toiled on the 1929 search for the missing MacAlpine Expedition. Both eventually met tragic endings. On June 29, 1932 CF-AFL crashed in the NWT killing Andy Cruickshank, and engineers Horace W. Torrie and Harry King. G-CASM was lost in a March 4, 1931 hangar fire in Winnipeg. (Al Martin Col.)

Danger on the Fly

Destination James Bay: US Navy Balloon A-5598 is launched at NAS Rockaway Beach, Long Island on Decemebr 13, 1921. (US Navy NH90097, LCDR Waldo B. McLead Col.)

US Navy Misadventure

Although airplanes soon overshadowed lighter-than-air flight, balloons and dirigibles remained popular in the 1920s, one being especially newsworthy. On December 13 US Navy balloon A-5598 ascended from Rockaway Point, Long Island, apparently to some upstate destination. Aboard were three experienced men – Lts Walter Hinton, Louis A. Kloor (mission commander) and Stephen A. Farrell. (Farrell would later explain: "It was just a little balloon hop for us to get practice and experience.")

Hinton, on his first balloon flight, had piloted the *NC-4* on the first Atlantic airplane crossing. As the Atlantic had tried to beat him then, so would the elements in 1920. A-5598 soon entered cloud and was blown northward. The first town the crew could identify was Wells, north of Albany, NY. A momentary stop was made in a field, where the men got their bearings from a local fellow, then proceeded. They flew through the night, passed a city (later said to have been Ottawa), decided to press on "and make it a decent flight", but next day could see only wilderness. As the hours passed, the USN at Rockaway Point became

Located on the southern tip of Long Island, NY, Naval Air Station Rockaway, seen in a 1919 aerial view, was one of the US Navy's original air stations. (US Navy)

alarmed. The Oneonta *Daily Star* of Oneonta, NY, reported on the 16th:

A terrific gale swept the Adirondacks during the last two nights, making an air trip across the forest extremely perilous... It is possible that the airmen have been forced to land at a point far from human habitation. If such is the case, the three naval officers, who set out on the trip without rations, are waging a hard fight against the rigors of the Adirondack winter weather.

It was bad enough having poor visibility throughout the region, but the regular Adirondacks fire spotters (who would have reported any balloon sighting) recently had gone home for the

season. How-ever, when the weather lifted, US Army planes began scouring the mountains and the public was urged to report any messenger pigeons, as these might be from A-5598.

In the belief that the balloon may have drifted into Canada, the US Navy despatched Lt Albert W. Evans to Ottawa to direct search efforts. Meanwhile, one search plane crashed near Albany, but the two crew were safe. Ultimately, A-5598 ended far from the Adirondacks with its lift gradually waning. To keep aloft the crew tossed over all excess weight, even coffee thermoses. When they heard a dog barking, Kloor released some gas. They went on for a few more miles then, after flying for 24:20 hours, made a rough

(*The New York Times* January 3, 1921)

landing through some trees and were spilled from their basket. They estimated their position at 51°N, 80°W in the James Bay region. If so, they had covered some 850 miles.

Appreciating their circumstances, they set out towards the barking dog, making sure to take their three remaining pigeons (which they ate next day). With almost no survival equipment or food, they kept moving, reached a large river (the Moose) and headed downstream. By now they were weakening, especially Farrell, who begged his mates to kill him for food. On the fourth day came salvation – they met a local Cree, Tom Marks, whom they followed for some miles, then reached Moose Factory. A scout was despatched on the 175-mile route up the Moose and Missinabi rivers to the railroad at Mattice, there to deliver news of the Americans and letters to their families. This trip, commencing about Christmas Day, took until January 2.

Meantime, the survivors recuperated, then hit the trail on December 28. The local Hudson's Bay Co. factor noted in his records: "A fine cold day, 24 below zero this morning. The US naval officers left this morning with Oliver Mack and Lawrence Wesley. Oliver returned this evening saying that they would like two more dogs, as they could not get along very fast." The trail proved brutal, as each man helped push the sleds. The miserable group made Mattice on January 11. Here, to the delight of reporters, the story took a new slant, becoming a 1920 version of reality TV. Hinton and Farrell fell to fisticuffs when Farrell learned that Hinton had written

his wife about his plan for death. She then released the letter to the press.

Mercifully, the balloonists left Mattice on the 12th and were home in two days. Hinton continued in naval life until retiring in Florida, where he passed away in 1981 at age 90, but not before he had enjoyed a trans-Atlantic flight in the Concorde – less than four hours compared to his original 19-day mission in the NC-4.

(Lighter-than-air flight in Canada's north henceforth was rare. In 1958, however, a US Navy ZPG-2 blimp completed a 4700-mile science and recce mission from Weymouth, Massachusetts to Resolute Bay, NWT. With a crew of 12 plus passengers, it departed on July 27, steered northwestward to Kingston, Ontario. Then came a detour to the Goodyear airship base in Akron where, due to high temperatures, the vessel was lightened. The mission continued to Fort William for fuel. Churchill was reached on August 4, then wind delayed progress. On the 7th the ship flew 24 hours up Hudson Bay to Resolute, then a sortie was made to science base "Ice Island T-3", where some mail bags were dropped. The ship returned to Churchill on August 10, then proceeded to Weymouth next day. The senior navigator on this mission was an RCAF exchange officer, W/C Keith Greenaway, renowned for his knowledge of Arctic navigation. Only in the 2000s was there serious talk of further Arctic airship operations, when De Beers considered an airship to explore for diamond formations. On September 20, 2007, however, their only ship was badly damaged in Botswana.)

Stranded on the Tundra

No general history of Canadian aviation is complete without mention of the 1929 MacAlpine Expedition. Since Frank Ellis' coverage in his 1954 *Canada's Flying Heritage*, this story has been well told in such books as *Canadian Aeronautics: A Chronology 1840-1965*, *Pioneering in Canadian Air Transport* and *Air Transport in Canada*, as well as in the *Journal* of the Canadian Aviation Historical Society. Readers wishing a fuller story, must consult these sources. The MacAlpine drama commenced on August 24, 1929, when a Dominion Explorers party left Winnipeg to inspect the company's interests in the Northwest Territories as far down as Bathurst Inlet. Aboard Super Universal G-CASP was pilot G.A. Thompson (who had flown out the Wilson party), engineer D.A. "Don" Goodwin, LCol MacAlpine and Richard Pearce. 'ASP was followed by Fairchild FC-2W-2 CF-AAO with pilot Stan McMillan, air engineer Alex Milne and mining engineer E.A. Boadway.

Two days later both planes were at Churchill, where things turned sour with the loss on Hudson Bay of the expedition supply ship *Morso* and, on August 26, of Fokker G-CASP in heavy swells while moored. The plane was found submerged by a coast guard vessel and was a total loss. Western Canada Airways despatched replacement Super Universal G-CASK.

On August 28 'AAO flew MacAlpine to Tavani, NWT, his main base in the region while, on September 6, Roy Brown delivered 'ASK to Churchill. It proceeded next day to Baker Lake via

The MacAlpine party while stranded at Dease Point, NWT from September through November 1929: E.A. Boadway, S.R. "Stan" McMillan, A.D. Goodwin, A.J. "Alex" Milne, Col C.D.H. MacAlpine, Joe (local Eskimo), G.A. "Tommy" Thompson and Maj Robert F. Baker. Since Richard Pearce is not in the group, he may have been the man behind the lens. (NMST 25915)

Tavani, thence on the 8th towards Bathurst Inlet in company with 'AAO. After about 125 miles, however, weather forced them to land on Beverly Lake. Next day they made Pelly Lake, but were hit by more weather. Everyone appreciated that freeze-up was imminent – ice was forming on the lakes. They again set off, hoping to reach the Arctic coast by following a north-flowing river. En route they alighted at an Eskimo camp on Dease Point (68º 50'N 105º 50'W) to learn that Cambridge Bay was within reach.

On September 12, after transferring from 'AAO about 16 gal. fuel, 'ASK (now with about 55 gal.) attempted to get away, but carburetor troubles developed. Its meager fuel now went back into 'AAO, which set off with Stan McMillan, Alex Milne, Dominion Explorers official Robert Baker, and Eskimo guide, Joe. Unsuccessful in their reconnoiter, they returned. Without fuel, they were grounded, but were in safe hands with the Eskimos. They began building a shelter using stone, muck for chinking and a tarp for a roof. Food wise, no caribou were found. Only a few fish, ptarmigan and small rodents were taken, but the Dease Point Eskimos shared what they had. Food was doled out at 5 oz. per day per man. Passing locals also contributed, before continuing on their way. In late September two hunters trekked back with some meat. Of this type of treatment, G.A. Thompson later wrote:

This incident gives an insight into the sterling qualities typical of the Eskimo character... he is probably considered a heathen by the churches but, personally, I have never met truer Christians nor more truthful, honest, generous people... if we had been their own children, they could not have mothered us with greater care... The Eskimos are the whitest people collectively that I have ever met.

In his own story as told decades later to the Toronto chapter of the Canadian Aviation Historical Society, Alex Milne recalled how a fish net set out at Dease Point was shredded by crab-like creatures and how, when hunting with a .22 rifle, a ptarmigan's natural camouflage and high speed made it a difficult target. He also praised the Eskimos for contributing their best portions of fish and seal blubber. Even so, the whites could not stomach this fare. Meanwhile, reporters far to the

Dominion Explorers FC-2W-2 CF-AAO which, along with WCA Fokker G-CASK, flew the MacAlpine party from Baker Lake on September 8, 1929 to begin a fateful expedition. CF-AAO was crewed by pilot S.R. "Stan" McMillan and engineer A.J. "Alex" Milne. With them were Col MacAlpine and E.A. Boadway. (CANAV Col.)

south, having few real details about what was happening, concocted their own information, some from W.R. Mitchell, a former Hudson's Bay Co. man. They claimed that Mitchell said it was unlikely that one of the planes had crashed but, if it had, the other would have rescued those men, then gotten word out. He was quoted as saying that the whole party likely was safe and busy staking claims on some huge new mineral find, and keeping quiet to maintain secrecy about their fortune. He was correct, however, in stating that the Eskimos would care for anyone whom they found stranded, then added: "The deer are moving up through the lake regions for the winter and would supply an army, let alone a party of this size. The natives … most assuredly have food." Even though the Eskimos often starved to death in winter, such newspaper malarkey was gobbled up by the public. Richard Pearce's diary puts the issues of food, weather, etc. into simpler, more realistic focus:

October 11: *This was the day we were supposed to start for Cambridge Bay. The thaw is no doubt responsible for the delay in the return of the Eskimos. This has gradually lowered the morale of the party. We seem to be able to talk of*

nothing else. It tried to snow last night, then switched to rain for a while, but it is now colder again. Most of the boys are very pessimistic, but the colonel sticks to his prophesy that we will leave by the 17th. I have a hunch he is saying this to keep up our spirits.

I couldn't make the grade with the whitefish again to-day. The first piece I got was bad, that seems to be my luck. Bob [Major Baker] ordered me a second half slice of bacon instead. We had a route march today - a walk of eight or ten miles, and we all feel in better shape. Boadie [E.A. Boadway] stayed in and made a few biscuits. The colonel broke through the ice again today. In the late afternoon it suddenly turned very cold and the morale of the party jumped sky-high... Charlie and his young brother Jimmie, the Eskimos we have been waiting for, came in at six o'clock with their dog team. Were they welcome? I'll say they were. They brought part of a caribou and a lot of fish … A full stomach once more; what a glorious feeling. Charlie got my watch as I had promised and he was tickled to death…

October 12: *To-day is Alec's [Milne] birthday, the third event of its kind we have had at Dishwater Point, as we have*

Salvaging G-CASQ at Burnside River, where it went through the ice on October 25, 1929. In spite of brutal Arctic conditions, the job was a success. 'ASQ then forged on until damaged beyond repair while landing at Disappointment Bay, BC, on November 17, 1938. (A.J. Milne Col.)

named this place ... fuel gathering was a great success and the boys have promised to keep ahead of the cook's requirements. Bob again asked Charlie about going to the post. Charlie said it would be impossible to go overland to Bathurst and that we would have to make for Cambridge Bay. He thought a couple of cold nights would freeze the straits. We are tied down to the Eskimos for we haven't the clothing and equipment to make the trip alone.

October 14: *It is still stormy outside. Charlie tells us the straits between here and Cambridge will freeze before Bathurst Inlet, and that a trip across country to Bathurst is out of the question. There is not enough snow, he says, and fast rivers would have to be crossed... This business of having lots of grub on hand is wonderful. To think that we have lived for a month on five ounces per day each, and then have plenty, brings out the smiles.*

On October 21 the party finally set out for Cambridge Bay with three dog teams and Eskimo guides. The trip was expected to take three days. Thompson noted in his diary: "The first day we covered about 25 miles which, considering our condition, was good going. The next day a heavy fog set in and we were able to cover six miles only before the dogs and the whitemen were worn out." After resting in igloos for two days, they pushed across Kent Peninsula, then faced open water. With food low, one Eskimo hurried back to Dease Point for supplies.

A search for the overdue party had not immediately begun, likely because of MacAlpine's instructions: according to the *Manitoba Free Press* of November 5,

1929, "no relief plane should be despatched for ten days after they were due at Bathurst Inlet." Besides that, the radio operator at Bathurst Inlet had been unable to get a message out until late September. By then it was time to start searching. Placed in charge was Guy Blanchet. Having begun in 1906 with the Topographical Survey of Canada, he had more than 20 years of Arctic experience. A Canadian Press report of September 26 described what was transpiring by then: "Search for the Dominion Explorers' party, which includes the company President, Colonel C.D.H. MacAlpine, took definite shape today with the arrival from Toronto of a party of Eastern air officials. Thayer Lindsley and Brig-Gen D.M. Hogarth, directors of Dominion Explorers, are the executive officers in charge of arrangements here. With them from Toronto came H.R. Nosworthy, chief engineer of the company; Captain H.A. Oaks, Flying Director of the Northern Aerial Minerals Exploration Company, and W.L. Brintnell, Operating Manager of Western Canada Airways."

Aircraft soon were winging north, while a support operation began ferrying up fuel, provisions, etc. First on the search was Punch Dickins, who left Fort McMurray on September 26 in 'ASM with engineer W.S. "Bill" Tall. On the 29th they reached Dease Bay on the northeast shore of Great Bear Lake, then began scouring the tundra as far as Coronation Gulf. Nothing was found, but Dickins did carry a stranded Dominion Explorers party to Fort Fitzgerald on October 1. He continued searching almost to Bathurst Inlet, but weather intervened. He returned to Fort Fitzgerald on the 7th, but was out again next day.

Other aircraft were busy, including 'ASQ, which Andy Cruickshank ferried 1000 miles from Prince George. On September 27 Roy Brown and Paul Davis in 'ASO, and Bill Spence and Ernest G. Longley in Fairchild 'ACZ, landed on Beverly Lake to find the first solid clue – the MacAlpine camp of September 8. Other machines were at Stony Rapids awaiting weather and more supplies, as from the RCAF station at Cormorant Lake. Supplies went down to Churchill by rail, thence by the coastal vessel *Ocean Eagle* to Baker Lake, arriving October 7. Dr. D.L. Bruce, medical officer for the operation, also arrived aboard *Ocean Eagle*. Aircraft reaching Baker Lake changed from floats to skis, but this was tough work. Engineer Tommy Siers recalled: "... a bad storm sprang up from the south-west on the night of the 17th ... the NAME Fokker had its elevators and rudder irreparably damaged by the action of the waves and the floating ice." Much other excitement ensued, such as the engineers at Baker Lake fabricating ski fittings by using scrap metal.

On October 25 four aircraft took off from a roughed-out strip at Baker Lake and headed for Bathurst Inlet. They overnighted, then made Pelly Lake next day and continued north, searching line-abreast as they advanced. On landing on rubbery ice at Burnside, the Dominion Explorers camp 60 miles up the Burnside River from Bathurst Inlet, Cruickshank's 'ASQ sank to the wings in shallow water. Everyone started in to raise the plane. As it edged up, the skis, propeller, engine and instruments were progressively removed. T.W. Siers later reported:

The dismantled engine was taken into the house ... and all hands turned to helping remove all traces of damage due to the action of salt water. Magnetos had to be baked in the oven before they could be revived. The propeller ... had to be shortened and balanced before it could be of further use. By the time these parts were put into condition for assembly, the ice under the machine had become firm enough for the use of jacks... Working slowly and gently, the machine was jacked up and blocked until such a time as the undercarriage without skis could be fitted... A large tarpaulin was thrown over the machine to make a nose hangar. In this a coal stove made out of a

small gas barrel was placed and the engine, instruments and propeller were assembled and installed in the machine.

Meanwhile, 'ACZ, 'ASL and 'ASO searched on and the radio station at Bathurst Inlet kept the world informed. In one dramatic-sounding news report, the searchers were centred out as almost superhuman: "The rescuing Canadian airmen are distilling the best known mixture of intrepity, prudence and temerity for their task. But they have strict instructions not to be foolhardy… heroic men, birdmen of the new north, risk life and limb as generously and heroically as ever did the soldier battling his country's foes."

Finally, on November 5 an Eskimo dog team brought word to Burnside Camp that the MacAlpine party had reached Cambridge Bay two days earlier. This news had been relayed from Amundsen's old exploration vessel *Bay Maud*, iced-in at Cambridge Bay, to Bathurst Inlet HBC post, the historic wording being "MacAlpine and party found. All well. Located Cambridge Bay". Next day planes flew to Cambridge Bay to assist the beleaguered party. All eventually gathered back at Burnside on the morning of November 12, then set off for Fort Reliance. Weather obliged an overnight stop on Muskox Lake. Next morning three machines got away, but 'ACZ had to hold for repairs with pilot Bill Spence and mechanics E.G. Longley and Tommy Siers.

As the days passed, only 'ASQ, which had had its dunking, remained serviceable. Personnel were stranded in scattered locations, even near starvation after the MacAlpine party had reached Fort Reliance. So it was with CF-ACZ. Reporting on January 19, 1933 about Andy Cruickshank's reaching Muskox Lake to rescue the Spence party, *The Northern Miner* wrote:

Super Universals G-CASO and 'ASL at Cambridge Bay with the frozen-in *Bay Maud* in the background. Along with CF-ACZ, on November 6, 1929 these aircraft carried the MacAlpine party out to Bathurst Inlet and Burnside Camp, thence southward to a warm welcome in Winnipeg on December 6. Along the way CF-ACZ was damaged at Muskox Lake, then 'ASO was wrecked at Aylmer Lake (10 miles from Muskox Lake) while en route to assist 'ACZ. The crew of Brown and Davis was unhurt. In the end, it was up to water-logged 'ASQ to fly the Aylmer Lake crew out to Fort Reliance. (A.J. Milne Col.)

Aircraft of the MacAlpine Expedition search: Super Universal G-CASM with which Punch Dickins and Bill Tall were the first crew involved. Then, Super Universals 'ASO (F. Roy Brown, Paul L. Davis and Guy Blanchet), 'ASL (Herbert Hollick-Kenyon and W.B. "Bill" Nadin) and 'ASQ (A.D. "Andy" Cruickshank and Alfred H. Walker) at Baker Lake with FC-2W-2 "Super Fairchild" CF-ACZ (Bill Spence and Ernest G. Longley). October 22-25 this quartet pushed on to Bathurst Inlet/Burnside River, where 'ASQ broke through the ice. Finally, NAME's "Super Fairchild" G-CATL, crewed during the search by T.M. "Pat" Reid and W.E. Brown. On January 31, 1933 this plane would carry Paul Calder and Bill Nadin to their deaths near Cameron Bay, Great Bear Lake. (K.M. Molson Col.)

Upon arrival they found Spence and the two mechanics eating fox stew, all other food having been exhausted. They also learned from the mechanics that Spence …in the 16 days of waiting, had taken upon himself the duties of cook, which included the lighting of the tiny gasoline lamp to warm up the tent … So quietly did Bill go about these chores, carried on in the darkness of the Arctic nights, that he rarely wakened his partners until breakfast was ready.

Repairs underway at Muskox Lake on Fairchild CF-ACZ. A ski, previously given a "band aid" repair at Baker Lake, needed repairs here. But the ski failed on a take-off attempt on November 28. The plane had to be abandoned until the following March. (A.J. Milne Col.)

All three men were watching how the small supply of food was holding out and it seemed to be lasting much longer than should have been the case. Becoming suspicious, his associates watched Bill ... frying the bacon. When he said, as usual, "Here's breakfast," adding, "I've had mine", they verified a suspicion Spence had been stringing out the small food supply at the expense of his stomach...

Ultimately, the MacAlpine personnel made it to Stony Rapids, then Cranberry Portage on the Hudson Bay Railroad, where the first arrived on December 2. Only J.D. Vance and B.C. Blasdale were still north – stranded with Super Universal 'ARK in Baker Lake. They were to head for Churchill by dog sled, a trip of several weeks (they set out, but conditions forced them back, so they spent Christmas at Baker Lake). All involved in this great adventure survived and, in spite of the odds, there had only been minor injuries. Of 17 commercial and RCAF aircraft involved in the odyssey, only 'ASO, abandoned at Aylmer Lake, was totally lost. Sadly, by 1933 pilots Cruickshank, Spence, Sutton and Vance has lost their lives in other mishaps.

All along from September through December the North American press had avidly covered the MacAlpine story. The Syracuse, NY, *Herald* of December 22, 1929, for example, headlined a full page "Eight Men Who Laughed at Death". It presented a good quality of reporting with excellent photos and a map. The *Manitoba Free Press* offered some of the best writing, as these excerpts from November 5, 1929 show:

From the Mackenzie River in the west, from Stony Rapids at the east end of Lake Athabaska, from Cranberry Portage north of The Pas, from Churchill on the shores of Hudson Bay, and from Baker Lake in the north, at one time or another planes or boats were despatched or were in readiness to join the search for the MacAlpine expedition. Even from far distant New York a giant Sikorsky Amphibian plane, equipped with long-range wireless, was engaged ... As weather conditions changed, so did the immediate base from which the search pilots were sent out, or were held at readiness, all of this work being directed from a headquarters in Winnipeg, which was hastily established and placed in charge of men who knew thoroughly the conditions to be met ...

The change from fall to winter is normally very close to a month in duration, that being the time when waters of the high north begin to freeze and when the waters of the lower north at Cranberry Portage have received an ice covering sufficient to sustain the weight of ski-equipped planes. The advantage of the Baker Lake base was that it was probable that this point would be in the full grip of winter at least two or three weeks prior to Cranberry Portage, allowing the search to proceed that much earlier...

One of the best known of those who were engaged in the earliest part of the search is C.H. Dickins ... a Manitoba man who was born in Portage la Prairie in 1899. He was educated at the University of Alberta and has a wife and son. During the war he enlisted as a private in the 196th Universities battalion, with which he served during 1916-17. From 1917 to 1919 he served first with the Royal Flying

corps and later with the Royal Air Force, and won the Distinguished Flying Cross in 1918.

In 1928 he was awarded the McKee trophy for meritorious flying, his outstanding flight being in the later summer months of the year when he piloted Col. MacAlpine over 3965 miles in just over 37 flying hours. The party was absent from civilization only 12 days.

The first planes to undertake the search were two Super Fokkers chartered from Western Canada Airways and piloted by Herbert Hollick-Kenyon and Francis Roy Brown, and two other airplanes belonging to Dominion Explorers and piloted by William Spence and Charles Sutton. Mr. Hollick-Kenyon was born in London in 1897. He is married and has two children. His education was received at Archbishop Tenison's school and the London Polytechnic. During the war he served with the British Columbia Horse and the Second Canadian Mounted Rifles. He holds the 1914-15 Star, the Victory and General Service medals. He attended a special school in flying, and took the central flying school's instructors' course, and night flying and parachute courses.

Francis Roy Brown is a Winnipeg man, born in 1898. He is married and has one child. He enlisted in August 1914, and had 30 months active service in France. He holds the 1914-15 Star, General Service and Victory Service medals, and was a lieutenant in the Royal Air Force. All his post-war flying has been done with Western Canada Airways, which he joined in February 1928.

J.D. Vance is a Toronto man and about 32 years of age. He is an old Royal Flying Corps and Royal Air Force pilot, flying with the Independent Air Force on long-distance bombing raids. He did a lot of post-war flying abroad, and was one of the pilots who flew the four Handley Pages on the record flight from England to Egypt. He joined the Northern Aerial Minerals Exploration staff in June 1928...

T.M. (Pat) Reid is an Irishman now aged about 33 years. During the war he served with the Royal Naval Air Service on the North Sea patrol. He joined the Province of Ontario air service as an air engineer in 1924, and became a pilot in 1928. He joined Northern Aerial Minerals Exploration in June 1928, and in the opinion of his company is "a very

Pilots of the MacAlpine Expedition

Punch Dickins (top left), shown as a young soldier during WWI, was the first pilot involved in the MacAlpine search. Then others who played a role: Leigh Brintnell, who organized search requirements from WCA HQ in Winnipeg; Herbert Hollick-Kenyon (G-CASL), W.A. "Bill" Spence (CF-ACZ) and G.A. "Tommy" Thompson (G-CASK). (National Museums of Canada AC33-74-2, K.M. Molson Col., next two CANAV Col., DND RE19550)

resourceful man and one on the north's outstanding pilots."

Andrew David Cruickshank was born in England in 1898, and was a lieutenant in the Royal Air Force. He was educated in the Oxford Technical school and Bristol University School of Aeronautics. He possesses the Territorial, General and Victory medals.

There are two pilots in the missing MacAlpine party. G.A. Thompson and C. MacMillan. Unfortunately, no particulars are available regarding Capt. MacMillan, who is a Dominion Explorers pilot. George Anson Thompson was born in Niemuch, India and had an English public school education. He has the 1914-15 Star, and the Victory and General Service medals. His category is A1, Gosport, England. He has been flying continuously since 1916 and had probably over 4000 flying hours to his credit. He has flown in every province in Canada, and the length of his flying experience may be gauged from the fact that his pilot's licence number is 19 and his engineer's licence number is 11. He has been on the Western Canada Airways staff since February 1928.

Guy Blanchet received much of the credit for the party's survival. Col MacAlpine explained how he had made one wise decision after another. On

December 7, 1929 the *Manitoba Free Press* summarized Blanchet's retrospective thoughts:

In the first place the wreck of one machine at Churchill at the outset of the expedition caused the loss of a precious week – just how precious can be seen now in the light of what subsequently happened. Then, fall conditions set in a week earlier, and were followed by a late date for the setting in of winter. Normally in those northern latitudes flying can be kept up until Sept. 15. This year the

season was shortened to Sept. 7. The result of this was that the first condition made flying with pontoon-equipped machines difficult, and later, impossible, owing to the small lakes freezing... Their food shortage on Queen Maud gulf was caused by two conditions that were due to the lateness of the season, Mr. Blanchet noted. The first was that the caribou already had migrated south, and the second was that the usual fish runs had stopped. Two native food caches were invaluable in staving off actual starvation.

MacAlpine personnel back in Winnipeg with Fairchild CF-AAN on December 6, 1929: pilot Charles Sutton, Col R.H. Webb (mayor of Winnipeg), Col C.D.H. MacAlpine, Maj Robert Baker (Dominion Explorers), C.J. Rogers (Dominion Explorers), pilot Bill Spence and air engineer A.J. "Alex" Milne. (*Canadian Aviation* magazine Col.)

Little Red River

Some of the most famous 1928 Canadian headlines involved mercy missions to remote settlements. A key figure in one story was the renowned Wilfred Reid "Wop" May. Born in Carberry, Manitoba in 1896, he had served in the infantry, transferred to the RFC, joined 209 Squadron in March 1918 and soon was in the fray around Amiens, where the Germans were routing the British 5th Army. On his first combat mission in a Sopwith Camel, May was pursued by Baron von Richthofen, but evaded the great ace long enough for Allied sharp-shooters to bring the German down. In August, May was wounded while strafing the enemy, but recuperated and returned to his squadron. Back in Canada, in 1919 he and his brother, Court, formed May Aeroplanes Co., flying surplus JN-4s on the barnstorming scene. In 1928 he helped found the Edmonton and Northern Alberta Aero Club and, with associate, Vic Horner, formed Commercial Airways.

In December 1928 Mrs. Logan, wife of the Hudson's Bay Co. manager at Little Red River (some 350 miles north of Edmonton), alerted Dr. Harold A. Hamman about 50 miles west in Fort Vermilion, that her husband, Bert, was deathly ill. Suspecting diphtheria, Hamman set out by dog team carrying 5000 units of anti-diphtheria vaccine. He reached Little Red River after two nights on the trail and immediately treated Logan. Aiming to prevent an epidemic, he then began vaccinating as many of the 900 people in his district as he could. He

In a photo taken in Edmonton on January 2, Dr. M.R. Bow hands a package of diphtheria anti-toxin to pilot W.R. May. He and his partner Vic Horner then took off to deliver the much-needed medicine to Fort Vermilion, arriving there on January 3. (W.R. May Col.)

also wrote to the provincial health ministry urgently requesting vaccine. This message was carried by Bobbie Gray by dog team to Fort Vermilion. Next, mushers Joe La Fleur and William Lambert continued 280 miles further to Peace River, a trip of 11 days. From there the message went out by telegraph.

When Mr. Logan died, Dr. Hamman and Mrs. Logan burned their clothes, getting replacements from the HBC post, but both were shunned. Meanwhile, on January 2, 1929 "Wop" May and Vic Horner set out in their Avro Avian with the vaccine. In duff weather they followed the railroad to McLennan, overnighted,

then flew next day to Fort Vermilion, where Dr. Hamman met them. May and Horner returned to Edmonton, arriving on January 6 to be greeted by many well-wishers. Dr. Hamman spent 25 days vaccinating everyone in his district, sledding some 300 miles in the process. He later concluded that the disease likely had come west from Quebec, where Mrs. Logan had visited relatives, some of whom had diphtheria. She returned with clothing donated for the Indians in Peace River country. It is likely that her husband contracted his illness when unpacking the clothes. Understandably, this story became news, even in the

The May-Horner Avian on a refuelling stop at Peace River on January 2. (Glenbow Museum NA1258-62)

US and overseas. The Oakland, California *Tribune*, for example, ran a front-page headline on January 4, 1929, "Fliers Speeding Cargo of Antitoxin to Far North":

Edmonton, Alta., Jan.4 (AP) With a precious cargo of antitoxin, two Edmonton aviators had vanished today toward the frozen edges of Canadian civilization ... to carry relief to 200 persons who it was feared were suffering the ravages of diphtheria.

Captain "Wop" May and Vic Horner left Peace river shortly before noon yesterday on the last stage of their flight to Fort Vermillion and Little Red river, the trading post which may be suffering from an epidemic. They stopped at Peace river less than 15 minutes.

Whether the pair completed their flight will not be known until they fly back or until a dog team brings out word of their arrival. If they do not find ice or a solid emergency landing field on which they can land safely and again take off, they would be forced to return by dog team, an arduous two week's journey to the end of the railway. If they arrived at Fort Vermillion yesterday it is probable that antitoxin was taken to Little Red river by dog team relays, as the two trading posts are only 50 miles apart.

In later years Dr. Hamman travelled by snow machine in his district and set up his own 2-way radio station. He practiced medicine into the 1970s and died in 1987. To commemorate the 50th anniversary of the May-Horner flight, sons Denny May and Bob Horner flew a Fleet Finch to Fort Vermilion on June 21, 1979, where they were met by Dr. Hamman. For this occasion 1000 first day covers were produced. These sold at $50 each and raised enough money to purchase a Cessna 185 for the Lutheran Association of Missionaries and Pilots, doing good works in the North. Then, on January 2, 2004 an RCMP PC-12 piloted by SSgt Jerry Klammer re-enacted the original flight, carrying Denny May, Bob Horner and others. A banquet was held in the Canadian Legion in Fort Vermilion, about which Denny May commented, "It became very clear to us in Fort Vermilion how important this event was to them – many would not be alive today had the original flight not taken place."

The famous Junkers CF-AMX in which Paddy Burke made his fateful last flight. In the second view Burke is at the left, while engineer Emil Kading is centre and helper Johnny Jack is right. (NMST 5037, via Brian Burke)

More Junkers Adventures

In 1930 the Air-Land Manufacturing Co. of Vancouver purchased CF-ALX, a new Junkers F.13, a type known worldwide as a superb workhorse. The F.13 was a direct descendant of trench-busting fighters produced by Junkers during the war. Air-Land also added a used F.13 CF-AMX and a 2-seater Junkers sports plane CF-ANJ. The aircraft reached Vancouver from the US east coast by sea.

CF-AMX (F.13 No.663) was built in 1923 for one of the airlines from which, eventually, Lufthansa evolved. It began on the German registry as D-288 christened *Würger* and initially operated in Russia. In 1924 it went to the US for the Dayton International Air Races at Wilbur Wright Field, Ohio. In this period it was flown by Eddie Stinson between Detroit and Dayton, but apparently did not race. Back in New York, home of the Junkers Corporation of America, No.663 received a new 185-hp BMW engine and was Junkers' demo plane. Edward Stinson and/or Frederick Melchior flew in the 1925 Ford Air Tour either as contestant No.6 or as the tour pathfinder plane (two F.13s took part, but details are

ambiguous about which did what). According to a February 3, 1927 letter from J. Otto Scherer of Junkers in New York to the Secretary of Commerce in Washington, from November 1, 1926 No.663 had flown only 28:30 hours. "The plane is today," said Scherer, "in perfect condition, having been carefully maintained and always kept in a hangar, except when on tours." No.663 ultimately was registered in Canada as CF-AMX on May 29, 1930.

With pilot E.J.A. "Paddy" Burke, an ex-pat Brit and former RFC pilot, and engineer Emil Kading, 'AMX operated in northern BC from early June; while Wilhelm A. "Bill" Joerss had 'ALX at Prince George, flying for mining man Dick Corless. Joerss advertised some stated rates: he would take up five passengers on a local joyride at $5.00 a head; do a cross-country charter at $1.50 a mile; and charged an extra $50.00 for each overnight involved.

In October, Burke was to fly prospector Bob "Three Fingers" Martin from Lower Post on the Liard River on the BC-Yukon border to his claims near Atlin. But only a long silence followed their October 11 departure on the 200-

Emil Kading, Bob Martin and Joe Walsh in a photo taken by Ev Wasson soon after the rescue. Then, the rescuers – Walsh and Wasson. (Frank H. Ellis Col.)

mile flight. Burke's wife, waiting in Atlin, had been briefed to stand by for a few days should 'AMX not show. Even so, there was no effort to begin a search until it had been overdue for a week. Meanwhile, Northern BC and Alaska flyers kept their eyes peeled when anywhere near Burke's intended course. Finally, Donald R. MacLaren of Western Canada Airways was named to head a search.

Air-Land quickly sent 'ALX from Prince George to assist. First it reached Thutade Lake, where it was beset by freezing conditions. Each time the crew attempted takeoff, the plane became layered in ice. Finally, pilot Joerss, who had flown for the Kaiser, got airborne, while his mates, pilot R.J. Van der Byl and mechanic Ted Cressy, waited on the shore for 16 days. Then they joined some local Indians on the trail. This proved miserable, with blizzards and hunger due to a lack of game. Finally they reached the trading post at Takla Lake to hear that a rescue party, sent by Joerss, had been there in mid-November. Van der Byl and Cressy now trekked through the bush, covering 350 miles in 20 days to reach Fort St. James. Joerss himself had returned to Vancouver, confident that his friends would be safe.

Meanwhile, many aircraft were searching. This led to misadventure, as aircraft were wrecked or stranded, and men injured or killed, as with an American-registered Lockheed Vega, lost on October 28 with Vancouver pilot

Robin "Pat" Renahan, engineer Frank Hatcher and mining developer Sam Clerf of Seattle. A big air-sea search came up empty. Late in November few resources still were involved, but Frank Dorbant and Ev Wasson were always on the lookout, Wasson in FC-2 G-CARM. This paid off on November 24, when he and his prospector friend, Joe Walsh, spotted a snow-covered 'AMX on the Liard River. A few days later the weather improved enough to let Wasson land, although the nearest safe spot was 15 miles distant. He and an Indian companion then trudged to the river to find 'AMX abandoned and a note – "Leaving for Wolf Lake. Food low."

Wasson now made several flights between 'AMX and Wolf Lake until spotting two men. He dropped some food and a message, then landed 10 miles away and trudged back with his companion. Next day they rendezvoused with Martin and Kading. Word was that Burke had died on the trail on November 20. The duo was flown to Whitehorse, then Wasson and Sgt Leopold of the RCMP returned on December 16 to recover Burke's body. There they found a rueful note left by Martin and Kading:

Paddy Burke died November 20, 6:30 p.m., cause: sickness from lack of food, having been 23 days without same. Please pardon our poor efforts as we are in a sinking condition. Expect to leave here Saturday, November 23, for Wolf Lake, following the Liard River until

Caribou Creek. Hope we can make same. Snow very deep and no snowshoes. Bob Martin, Emil Kading.

A news item of December 11, 1930 in the Toronto *Daily Star* summarized the poignant events as finally learned. Having set out on October 11, Burke met harsh weather, so made a precautionary landing:

Later the same day they attempted another flight but were forced to land. The pontoons of the aeroplane struck floating ice and were badly damaged. They remained for almost a week ... On October 17 they started on their way on foot in an attempt to reach Wolf Lake. All were becoming exhausted because of scarcity of food and heavy travelling through deep snow... They camped often. Burke began to lose strength and his companions knew he could not keep up much longer. On November 8 he made his last entry in his log and wrote a letter to his wife ...

A week later Kading shot a caribou. This revived him and Marten, but Burke was too week to eat. They made soup for him but it did no good and on November 20 he died. The other two buried him and stayed nearby. On November 25 they saw an aeroplane fly overhead. It was Wasson. He was out of sight before they could light a fire... The next time they were prepared, having collected a pile of fuel. When they heard the drone of the aeroplane they started the fire and this

CF-AMX as found by Ev Wasson and Joe Walsh. Then, it's seen looking like a beached whale while awaiting salvage. Finally, 'AMX ready in June 1931 to be barged down various waterways from Bulkley House and across Takla Lake to Fort St. James. A detailed narrative of this exciting project appears in Peter Corley-Smith's *Bush Flying to Blind Flying*. (Frank H. Ellis, Ted Cressy and Elwood White Cols.)

Registered to V. Spencer of Vancouver, CF-ALX continued in mining in BC until July 23, 1933. That day Bill McClusky was taking off from McConnell Lake some 120 miles north of Takla Landing. He later wrote: "A nice south wind was blowing on the lake. I cleared the end … at about 650 feet. About a mile from the lake I ran into a strong downward current …" He fought this, lost a float skimming too low to the trees, then lost the battle altogether and crashed to the rocks. Somehow, he and passengers Fred Stanes and W.S. Harris came out OK. (On July 30, 1935 McClusky's own luck ran out – he died with two of his three passengers when he crashed Boeing 204 CF-ALD on takeoff at Alta Lake, BC, about 50 miles north of Vancouver.) In 1981 what wreckage remained of CF-ALX was recovered through the efforts of a Western Canada Aviation Museum salvage team.

CF-AMX years after surviving its appointment with the Grim Reaper. This advertisement appeared in the February 1937 edition of *Canadian Aviation* magazine. It seems that the only interested buyer was a scrap dealer.

was seen … But there was no place within miles for a safe landing. The fliers made their landing ten miles away and came back on snowshoes.

They struck a blizzard and walked several miles past the camp of the two survivors. Night fell and they also camped. Sunday morning they took up their search on foot. Martin and Kading were too weak to shout. They had one cartridge left. This Kading fired and the shot was heard … So the lost were found.

Both F.13s were salvaged, CF-AMX in January 1931 by the seasoned team of Van der Byl, Cressy and Joerss. The floats were changed for skis, then, wings removed, 'AMX ran under its own power to a lake, where it was left until spring. In May, Ted Cressy and William R. McClusky trucked a pair of floats from Vancouver to Fort St. James, then barged these to the stranded Junkers. But the floats had the wrong mounts, so Cressy and McClusky rafted the entire operation out to Fort St. James. There 'AMX was reassembled, put on wheels and flown out by Joerss. He landed in Vanderhoof for fuel, set off on the final leg to Vancouver, but had a forced landing at Boston Bar after engine failure. From there 'AMX completed its journey by rail, arriving at the Air-Land hangar in July. Refurbished, it flew some years with Pacific Airways doing many trips to mining camps, and lots of hunting and fishing charters.

Junkers F.13 Specifications

Length	31' 6"
Wing span	58' 2¾"
Wing area	473.6 sq.ft.
Empty weight	2535 lb
Gross weight	3814 lb
Useful load	1600 lb
Engine	6 cyl. BMW 185 hp
Cruise speed	87 mph
Accommodation	pilot +
	5 passengers
Cost 1930	$30,000

Canadian Colonial FC-2W-2 G-CAVL at St. Hubert with the first official air mail on the New York-Albany-Montreal run, October 1, 1928. This beautiful Fairchild was lost in a hangar fire at Newark on August 4, 1930. (LAC PA59962)

Widening Prospects, Hard Times

Air Mail Evolves

Although Canadian aviation headlines usually focused on northern aviation, there were developments in the south, especially in air mail. The first officially noted Canadian air mail was flown on June 20, 1918 by Capt Brian A. Peck from Montreal to Toronto (see *Canada's Flying Heritage* and *Aviation in Canada: The Pioneer Decades*). Another early flight involved the American, Katherine Stinson. On July 9, 1918 she flew 259 letters 175 miles from Calgary to Edmonton. These bear the cachet "Aeroplane Mail Service. July 9th, 1918. Calgary – Alberta". Later that summer there were three other official JN-4 trips carrying some 3000 letters between Leaside and Ottawa. On March 3, 1919 Eddie Hubbard, flying a Boeing Model C floatplane, carried Canada's first known international air mail on a Vancouver-Seattle flight.

When Laurentide Air Service Ltd. of Montreal began its 1924 scheduled service in the Ontario-Quebec Gold Belt, it applied to the Post Office to carry mail. This was approved in August. In the *Air Post Bulletin* of November 1926, Alan Turton explained how Laurentide, "entered into an arrangement with the Canadian Postal Authorities ... who allowed them to collect a fee of 25 cents for each letter ... the company issued labels and these had to be affixed on the back of the envelopes ... The stamps were bound up in vertical pairs, and rouletting was adopted as a means of separation... This was a genuine attempt to supply a

The DeVere Aviation School JN-4 in which Capt L.E.D. Stevens and Lt J.M. Stevenson carried the first known Nova Scotia-Prince Edward Island air mail (Truro to Charlottetown) on September 24, 1919. On the 29th Capt Stevens and Lt I. Logan Barnhill flew the same plane in 1:45-hours in the opposite direction with the first Post Office-approved air mail between the two provinces. JN-4 C-118 still wears its RAF (Canada) markings. It later became G-CAAV and served into early 1924. (Frank H. Ellis Col.)

This historic marker at Brentcliffe and Broadway avenues in the former Toronto suburb of Leaside summarizes the details of Canada's first official air mail flight. (Larry Milberry)

CANADIAN AVIATION JULY, 1935

· VIA AIR MAIL ·

1918

One of the earliest air mail flights in Canada was made on August 27th, 1918, when Lieut. A. Dunstan flew from Ottawa to Toronto with a consignment of His Majesty's mail. Imperial gasoline and oil were used in the Curtiss Biplane flown on this occasion. Then, as now, Canadian airmen recognized the superior qualities of Imperial Aviation Products.

Imperial Marvelube Motor Oils are refined to British Air Ministry Standards of Quality

IMPERIAL OIL PRODUCTS

- IMPERIAL ETHYL AEROPLANE SPIRITS "80"
- IMPERIAL MARVELUBE GREASES
- IMPERIAL AEROPLANE SPIRITS "71"
- IMPERIAL MARVELUBE MOTOR OILS

MANUFACTURED AND GUARANTEED BY CANADA'S OLDEST AND LARGEST PRODUCERS, REFINERS, DISTRIBUTORS OF PETROLEUM PRODUCTS

postal service by air in a difficult country." The inaugural flight operated Haileybury-Rouyn on September 11, 1924. That season Laurentide carried 425 passengers, some 55,000 lb freight and more than 15,000 letters and telegrams. From the winter of 1925-26 into 1927 Jack Elliot's JN-4s, Patricia Airways and Exploration's Curtiss Lark, and Western Canada Airways' Fokker Universals also carried semi-official air mail throughout Northwestern Ontario and Northern Manitoba using their own postage stamps. Mail was carried on many other local flights, the details of which are best covered in the newsletter of the Canadian Aerophilatelic Society. This avid group of collectors and researchers is fascinated by the history of air mail stamps, first day air mail covers and all the associated lore. The CAS has done much to clarify the early history of commercial aviation in Canada.

In the July 1935 edition of *Canadian Aviation*, Imperial Oil recognized an Ottawa-Toronto flight made shortly after Capt Peck's inaugural. In those early decades Imperial Oil showed an enthusiastic interest in Canada's aviation heritage and in 1954 financed publication of Frank H. Ellis' masterpiece, *Canada's Flying Heritage*. (CANAV Col.)

Eddie Hubbard and William E. "Bill" Boeing at Seattle on March 3, 1919. Flying a Boeing Model C powered by a 100-hp Hall-Scott engine, they had just arrived from Vancouver with the first official Canada-US air mail. Originally in timber, furniture and boat building, Boeing got "the flying bug" in 1914, following a flight with a barnstormer. He produced his own aircraft in 1915 and soon won a US Navy order for 50 of his Model C trainers. Hubbard, a US Army flight instructor during the war, flew for Boeing in 1917-20, then operated the Seattle-Victoria Air Mail Line for several years. (William J. Wheeler Col.)

The Boeing B-1 which Hubbard flew on October 15, 1920 for the inaugural Seattle-Vancouver daily route with mail connecting to trans-Pacific steamers. Normally powered by a 200-hp Hall-Scott, the B-1 was 31' 3" long with a wing span of 50' 3". All-up weight was 3850 lb. N-ABNA was a re-build of N-CADS, which Hubbard had crashed on March 29, 1923, but now it had a 400-hp Liberty. "N-C" registrations were sometimes used on commercial planes operating in Canada and the US in the early 1920s. In 1928 Boeing produced the C-204 – a refined B-1 with a 410-hp Wasp engine. Several C-204s would serve throughout British Columbia. (William J. Wheeler Col.)

Patricia Airways and Transportation's reliable Curtiss Lark G-CAFB carried much air mail during its year and a half at Hudson. (William J. Wheeler Col.)

In 1927 Ottawa budgeted $75,000 for official air mail trials. Many inaugural flights ensued, as on May 10, 1927, when J.F. "Fred" Stevenson of Western Canada Airways flew mail bags from Rolling Portage to Gold Pines and Red Lake return. On September 9, 1927 J.H. Tudhope and crewman Gerry La Grave loaded 35 mail bags (500 lb) onto a Canadian Vickers Vanessa floatplane at Rimouski. This would be the first of a series of flights carrying mail transferred from ocean liners. This system would pare 24 hours off delivery times, as the planes rushed ahead to Montreal. On this occasion the one-of-a-kind Vanessa would carry the mail from the Canadian Pacific liner *Empress of France*, but it cracked up on takeoff from the choppy St. Lawrence River. Crew and cargo were rescued, and the mail went on by train, reaching Toronto late on the same day. Undeterred, the Post Office initiated regular air mail between Rimouski and Montreal, shaving from one to four days off usual times.

In the CAS newsletter for March 1997, Murray Heifetz described the air mail service connecting with the trans-Atlantic liners. The Toronto-Montreal-Rimouski service was twice weekly in each direction. The distance from Toronto to Montreal was 310 miles (3½ hours flying time) and from Montreal to Rimouski 350 miles (4½). The first Toronto-Montreal flight (May 5, 1928) was flown by J.H. St. Martin of Canadian Transcontinental Airways in a Fairchild; the first Rimouski-Montreal flight was flown by Roméo Vachon on May 5.

Another air mail service commenced on December 25, 1927 when pilot Charles Sutton with Dr. Louis Cuisinier, owner of Canadian Transcontinental Airways of Quebec City, took off in Fairchild G-CAIP from Lac Ste-Agnes near La Malbaie to drop mail by parachute to several remote North Shore communities as far down the St. Lawrence as Sept-Îles. Sutton left CTA to join Patricia Airways and Exploration, so Duke Schiller, then Roméo Vachon, took over to make several more North Shore mail runs in January-February 1928. On February 8 he carried the first air mail to Anticosti Island. Already a household name in Canadian aviation, Vachon had been born in Quebec in 1898. In WWI he was a mechanic in the Royal Canadian Navy, then took further courses at Camp Borden, including flying lessons on the JN-4.

The isolated Magdalens in the Gulf of St. Lawrence, and Pelee Island in Lake Erie, soon were added to Post Office routes. Normally, Canada's mail planes operated on skis in winter but, for the Magdalens, Canadian Transcontinental Airways had Fairchild of Long Island develop a float with a recessed ski. This was done since the CTA mail plane would have to operate over long stretches of open water in the dead of winter. Fairchild FC-2W G-CAIQ was assigned to this service. Based at Moncton, it would fly first to Charlottetown, thence to Grindstone in the Magdalens, the whole route being some 176 miles. The first trip was made on January 11, 1928 by Edward J. Cooper. Six more followed by March 20, after which supply boats resumed mail delivery. Several air mail flights had to be curtailed due to winter weather. Pilot Cooper could not give high grades to the float-ski invention. Due to trouble with it, his Fairchild was unserviceable for 28 of the 68 days of the contract.

The one-of-a-kind Canadian Vickers Vanessa, used experimentally on the 1927 steamship mail service. Designed by W.T. Reid, the Vanessa emulated Eddie Stinson's new Detroiter cabin biplane, but had an added feature -- wing flaps. Also, its unique Reid-designed strut system eliminated wire wing bracings, making cabin access more convenient. The Vanessa is shown with a 220-hp Wright J-5 engine and is marked as RCAF G-CYZJ. Following the Vanessa's accident, Canadian Vickers decided against pursuing this promising concept. (DND RE9356)

Cartierville airport on May 5, 1928, the occasion of the inaugural Montreal-Rimouski air mail. Three FC-2s and a JN-4 are seen. On the left is G-CAIQ, registered in Canada in January 1928 to Canadian Transcontinental Airways. On May 17 it flipped in the mud at Rimouski, but pilot H.P. Ayres was unhurt. However, when J.M. Clarke cracked up 'AIQ on the following January 9 at Chibougamau, the plane was wrecked. G-CANC of Canadian Airways (Old) had just been registered on this inaugural day. It would serve to April 29, 1930, when it crashed at St. Sylvère, Quebec. Then, a scene the same day showing the mail delivered to Rimouski. Roméo Vachon is fourth from the left. (T.M. McGrath Col., LAC C81888)

For Pelee islanders the winter mail traditionally had arrived on a sled-mounted boat. A hardy crew would brave ice, snow and wind for 12 hours in crossing the waters from the mainland. On 63 flights over the winter of 1927-28, London Air Transport carried eight tons of mail on the Pelee run. Meanwhile, Yukon Airways Exploration Ltd. had formed in October 1927. Flying Ryan Brougham CF-AHD, this company carried the first Whitehorse-Mayo-Dawson return air mail from November 11-16.

1928 Air Mail Routes[*]

Route	Distance (miles)
Rimouski-Montreal[†]	320
Montreal-Ottawa	110
Montreal-Toronto	330
Kississing-The Pas[?]	100
Lac du Bonnet-Bissett-Wadhope[?]	82
Sioux Lookout-Gold Pines-Red Lake-Narrow Lake-Jackson/Manion[?]	320
Leamington-Pelee Island	32
Quebec-Seven Islands	350
Seven Islands-Anticosti	120
Moncton-Magdalen Islands	200

[*]service was daily to weekly
[†] trans-Atlantic steamship service
[?] mining services

Canadian Colonial FC-2 NC4012 also was at Cartierville on May 5, 1925. It soon joined Fairchild Aviation Ltd. as G-CATA. (LAC PA61985)

A Ryan Brougham, the type used on the inaugural Whitehorse-Mayo-Dawson mail run in 1927. This Ryan is CF-ATA, operated by R.L. "Ginger" Coote from June 1932-33 until lost in a March 1, 1933 fire that started while pre-heating the engine. (Dr. A.E. Hill Col.)

The Post Office issued the first Canadian air mail stamp (5¢) in September 1928. On September 5 S/L A.E. Godfrey and FSgt M. Graham left from Ottawa in a Fairchild FC-2W-2. After 32 hours of flight, they reached Vancouver on September 8, completing the first trans-Canada air mail flight via such places as Lac du Bonnet and Edmonton. Their aircraft had been loaned by Sherman Fairchild, probably to promote his latest design (it was wrecked at Peace River while on the return flight). In such ways did industry and government

G-CAII, the London Air Transport Waco 9 that delivered the Pelee Island mail on November 30, 1927. Floyd I. Banghart is seated atop his plane. A native of London, Ontario, he had instructed at Camp Borden during 1918. Following his air mail days, he instructed at the London Flying Club, then was airport manager for the DOT at St. Hubert, Malton, Winnipeg and London. Banghart retired in 1957 and died on March 30, 1961 at age 68. In 1935 James C. Bell, later of Austin Airways fame, was flying it from Sudbury. In April 1938 the plane disappeared from the civil aircraft register. (*Toronto Star* "Pages from the Past")

form bonds in the early years. Air mail continued, providing the revenue that allowed commercial operators to pay their bills, add equipment and evaluate new routes.

On January 15, 1929 Western Canada Airways inaugurated NWT air mail, the first route being Fort McMurray-Fort Simpson. To kick this off, Punch Dickins and mechanic Lew Parmenter ferried Super Universal G-CASN from Winnipeg to Edmonton. The weather was iffy, so they did not leave Edmonton until January 18, but their engine quit with carburetor icing. Dickins force-landed 28 miles from Edmonton, his two passengers returned by car and 'ASN flew back next day for maintenance.

Dickins re-commenced on the 19th, but had to land at Lac la Biche due to weather, so only reached Fort McMurray late the next day. Now he could get to work. Besides furs to fly out to Edmonton from

points north, there was much second-class mail sitting at Fort McMurray, awaiting spring break-up: 733 lb for Fort Resolution, 517 – Fort Simpson, 194 – Hay River, 107 – Fort Providence. On the 23rd Dickins flew fully-loaded ('ASN had

a 1000 lb payload) to Fort Smith via Fort Chipewyan and Fort Fitzgerald. On the 25th he continued in poor weather to Fort Resolution (where a Post Office employee was dropped off) and Hay River. Even so, he made Fort Providence (where it was -62°F) and Fort Simpson next day, still in bad weather.

On the morning of January 27, 1929 Dickins started south with furs, some mail and one passenger. Then came a long silence, not broken until the 31st, when a musher brought word to Fort Smith that Dickins, stopping at Fort Resolution to pick up his Post Office passenger, had crash-landed. He and Parmenter now slaved in the cold to repair their undercarriage and bent prop. Finally, on February 2 they flew light to Fort McMurray. Dickins switched planes, taking the replacement back to Fort Resolution for his passenger and load – 11 bales of furs and 750 lb of mail. He was back in Fort McMurray the same day, having covered some 800 miles in 6:45 flying hours.

FC-2W-2 NX7572 in which S/L Earle Godfrey and FSgt Martin made the first trans-Canada air mail flight in September 1928. (CANAV Col.)

This "crash cover", originally destined from Victoria, BC to London England, bears one of Canada's original (1928) Post Office-issued, 5¢ air mail stamps. This singed letter was recovered from the crash of an eastbound US mail flight near Portland, Oregon on November 9, 1929. (Richard K. Malott Col.)

One of the many Canadian hardrock mines that began receiving air service in the 1920s. Everything from passengers to equipment, food and mail were the daily loads. (George F. Kimball/CANAV Col.)

Dickins made two further 1929 winter trips down the Mackenzie. These pointed the way to a solid future for NWT aviation. As to having bent 'ASN, Dickins was reprimanded by his boss, Leigh Brintnell, who also didn't think much of Dickins' complaining about the Mackenzie: "Furthermore, we do not see that the Mackenzie River is such a hazardous place to fly, as you have a certain amount of dog team travel up and down the river, with occasional cabins and a post every 150 miles or so. Conditions are really much worse north of Gold Pines or north of The Pas, as there are no definite routes of travel and no one is in the country." On December 30, 1929, Punch Dickins flew the first known air mail north of the Arctic Circle, making it all the way down to Aklavik. In July 1930 he raised some extra cash there, reporting about this to WCA head office in Winnipeg:

At Aklavik there were about 300 Eskimos that had never seen a plane and, together with about 300 dogs tied up, the din, when I shut off the engine and got out, was astounding. The Eskimos were very curious and I took some 35 of them up in the machine at $10 each for about 10 minutes. I could have taken more, but by the time I had made seven trips ... I was too tired and called it a day about 11P.M. The revenue helped the trip considerably... I have no doubt that after making one or two more trips down there we will get all kinds of passenger business.

The effect of such enterprise soon became clear, as in a testimonial from Dr. C. Bourget, a government agent. On March 2, 1929 he wrote to WCA praising the improvement in mail delivery: "We received more in January than we had in the last four winters combined," then explained further:

The passenger service has been a blessing to all ... Every winter I have to visit only once, due to the expense beyond reason, Providence and Hay River, a 150 mile trip with dogs at a cost of $400 with misery during the 12 days the journey takes ... This year I made it in three hours round trip at a cost of $135, including excess baggage ... I can visit my district three times in the next winter if this splendid service is maintained.

In June 1929 WCA was awarded the Prairie air mail route to operate (return by night): Winnipeg to Regina, Moose Jaw, Medicine Hat and Calgary. The company invested heavily, ordering six Fokker F.14s and arranging for the installation of rotating ground beacons by which pilots could navigate, and for emergency airfields to be set up en route. Service commenced in February 1930. Although the Prairie air mail would fall victim to Depression cutbacks, it proved the importance of commercial air transport in this region and impressed all observers with a 90% serviceability rate. Reporting on May 21, 1930 to A.D. McLean, the Civil Aviation Inspector in Regina, Leigh Brintnell of WCA described some of the challenges:

On the night of May 18 Mr. G.A. Thompson, Superintendent of the mail operations, left Moose Jaw for Calgary. Visibility was poor and it was necessary for him to navigate by town lights to Swift Current. About ten miles east of Swift Current he could not pick up any beacons nor town lights due to heavy snowstorms ahead. He did not think it advisable to land on any of the emergency fields, as they were not properly marked, so he had to return to Moose Jaw for fuel and start again. He left at 6:30 in the morning and flew through to Calgary

Mr. Thompson reports that the beacons between Moose Jaw and Swift Current are a disgrace, as only the occasional one can be picked up, and then, only if the pilot knew exactly where to locate it. All of our pilots on this run seem to feel that ordinary street lights placed every three miles apart would be better than the present lighting.

The promise of healthy mail contracts led Canadian operators to order such new equipment as this Fokker F.14A. CF-AIL of Western Canada Airways is seen at Saskatoon for the inaugural air mail service on March 3, 1930. Designed especially for the US market and built by Fokker Aircraft Corp. in New Jersey, the F.14A accommodated eight passengers, with the pilot seated in the open behind the cabin. Powered by a 525-hp P&W Hornet, the F-14A weighed 7200 lb all-up and cruised at about 110 mph. (LAC PA61662)

F.14A CF-AIK refuels at Stevenson Field, Winnipeg. Of six WCA F.14As three crashed and one burned in a hangar at Winnipeg. The two survivors were withdrawn from use in the fall of 1932. (T.M. McGrath Col.)

This view of Calgary airport was not taken in 1927, but a decade later. Little wonder that America aviators passing through Canada in these years were critical about the lack of modern facilities. Three RCAF Bellancas are seen and near the hangar is Stinson SR-7B CF-AZC of Canadian Western Natural Gas, Heat and Power. (National Air Photo Library A5737-68C)

Envisioning the future of air transportation, Edmonton began funding its new airport in 1924. Known as Blatchford Field in honour of the city's air-minded mayor, the place boasted this excellent hangar by 1929. Note the spotlights on the corners and the wind sock (also lighted), which aided the comings and goings of the night mail planes. (Provincial Archives of Alberta A11662)

Of Canada's early urban airports only one met modern European or American standards – Montreal's St. Hubert. This view from August 1930 shows the layout as the great airship *R-100* rests at its mooring mast. Had plans gone ahead for a British airship fleet, St. Hubert would have been part of an "Empire" system of airship ports, but this was not to be. (Inset) Canadian air mail pilot Stuart Graham checks the weather at St. Hubert. It has just come off the teletype, the first such machine in use with the DND Civil Aviation Branch. (LAC PA117691, LAC PA89142)

Montreal also had Cartierville airport, seen in this 1929 south-looking photo. Near the corner of Laurentian (N-S) and Bois-Franc Road (E-W) is the new Curtiss-Reid factory, then producing Rambler sport planes. This place became an airport in 1911, when Percy Reid began conducting aviation experiments. It also was used by Capt Peck on his famous 1918 air mail flight to Toronto. With WWII Cartierville was home to a Canadian Vickers PBY factory along the Laurentian side, while Noorduyn built on the Bois Franc side. All this was further added to in the 1950s as Canadair built everything from the F-86 to the Argus. Flying here ended in the 1980s. A Bombardier fabrication plant remained along Laurentian Blvd in 2009, but all other signs of aviation had given way by then to real estate development. In April 1931 the eminent James A. Richardson lambasted Toronto for its lack of a decent airport, concluding that, because of its negligence, Toronto was losing out aeronautically to Montreal: "Its flying facilities are not as good as those of cities of less than 20,000 on the prairies." In 2009 Toronto still had remnants of this backwards business mentality: its socialist mayor, David Miller, spent years opposing one of his city's finest transportation assets – Toronto City Centre Airport. (T.M. McGrath Col.)

(Left) Ottawa's bare bones Hunt Club Field on the occasion of Charles Lindbergh's July 2, 1927 visit. Thousands of locals thronged out for the occasion. Many such Canadian airports got started through the flying club movement, launched in 1927. Increasing demand by the public and business for improved passenger, freight and air mail created a gradual movement to expand and modernize airports. (LAC PA125898)

Halifax airport at the old Bluebell Farm on the west side of the Halifax peninsula. This view *circa* 1930 looks southward across the Northwest Arm. The Dingle Tower is about half way down the arm, beyond which is Halifax Harbour (the tower was built in 1912 to commemorate the convening of the first elected assembly in Canada). All this space today is residential and commercial. The airfield was roughly inside the area bounded by Connaught Ave. running southeast from the bottom left and Chebucto Rd. running east-west along the far edge of the airfield. The east-west road across the bottom with the southwest jog is about where today's Bayers Rd. runs. Flying here ceased in 1941. (LAC PA126608)

George A. "Tommy" Thompson is another towering figure from Canada's pioneer days in aviation. Born in India in 1894, he arrived in Canada in 1912 to study at the Ontario Agricultural College in Guelph. He enlisted in the Canadian Army in 1914, fought in the trenches, then remustered to the RFC in 1916, flying B.E.2s on 16 Squadron, then D.H.4s on 18 Squadron. Back home, he and Pat Cuffe barnstormed on the prairies using two JN-4s and five Avro 504s. When this enterprise folded, they joined the newly-formed CAF. In 1920 Thompson was one of the pilots on the inaugural trans-Canada flight. He rose to squadron leader, then resigned in 1921 to join the Imperial Oil expedition flying down the Mackenzie. From 1922 he was with Laurentide Air Service of Grand-Mère, flying HS-2Ls with such other pioneer bush pilots as B.W. Broach, C.S. Caldwell, Roy Grandy, Roy Maxwell and Roméo Vachon.

From 1924-28 Thompson was with the OPAS, where he rose to be Superintendent of Operations. In February 1928 he joined Western Canada Airways, pioneered in the Arctic, then excelled during the MacAlpine Expedition of 1929. When Canadian Airways formed in 1930, he ran all operations from Sault Ste. Marie to the Rocky Mountains and down to the Arctic. By 1935 he was general manager for all of CAL. In 1937 he supported Tommy Siers (CAL's Superintendent of Maintenance) in developing an oil dilution system for the work-a-day Canadian bushplane. For this Siers received the 1940 McKee Trophy.

With the rise of Canadian Airways after 1930, Ottawa accelerated the air mail, leading James A. Richardson to expand his fleet. The Depression, however, stymied the economy to such a degree that the government reduced the air mail, then cut it by nearly 100% in 1932. In the Fall 1973 CAHS *Journal*, F. Roy Brown, a wartime pilot and a founder of Wings Ltd. in 1934, described the Prairie service in this era. Lamenting the general slowdown in commercial aviation due to the Depression, he began:

Fortunately, in March 1930 there was an entirely new development, which gave us the boost we needed. This was the Prairie Air Mail which ran from 1 March 1930 to 31 March 1932 ... The routes covered were as follows: Winnipeg-Regina-Moose Jaw-Medicine

Services similar to those rendered today by such operators as FedEx and UPS were well provided in the 1920s-30s by a sophisticated combination of rail, road, sea and air carriers. This Canadian Pacific advert and CAL timetable from the January 1930 edition of *Canadian Aviation* magazine suggest that the airplane was finding its place in the transportation mix. (CANAV Col.)

Hat-Calgary each way, daily except Sunday; a side run from Regina to Saskatoon to Edmonton on the same basis. These were subsequently revised as follows: Winnipeg-Calgary was changed to include Lethbridge and Regina, and Regina-Edmonton to include North Battleford. This was soon altered further to link Calgary and Edmonton, and the link from North Battleford to Edmonton was dropped... The route from Winnipeg through to Edmonton via Calgary was equipped, more or less, for night flying, with a rotating beacon and an emergency landing field every thirty miles and, part of the way, additional glass blinkers every ten miles. The latter were not of very much help, but the landing fields with the rotating beacons were very handy. They did not have any night landing aids, but there were at least boundary lights to give some guidance. The fields themselves were strictly the grass type, but serviceable enough.

The aircraft were an assorted lot, all single-engined with the pilot sitting away back towards the tail. Some were strictly mail planes with no passenger accommodation, while others ranged from four to eight passengers. The passenger cabin was located between the pilot and the engine ... In looking back one finds it difficult to believe that the public were brave enough to patronize the service – only one engine, questionable weather reports, and no such thing as radio.

It is astounding to consider that, with the contract calling for well over 2,000 miles of flying per day, 97.5% of the trips were completed over the two years and one month that it was in effect... Schedules were set up on a 100-mph basis and the aircraft were mostly doing their best cruising at 110 mph... Prime Minister R.B. Bennett took an extra look at the postal budget early in 1932 and decided we were a luxury... all the pilots scampered back to the bush, some down the Mackenzie and the rest scattered between there and Sioux Lookout. Things were quiet, but picking up. There had been no drastic changes but, with business getting better and mining activity on the increase, independent companies sprang up ... About 1934 the two-way radio became an established fact and it was a great asset. Mail contracts were being let to remote areas, but competition was so keen that it is doubtful if any company made money out of them.

Commercial Aviation Summarized

In the March 1929 edition of the *Canadian Air Review*, Col. T.E. Gilmore, OBE, of Canadian Vickers, summarized advances in aviation in his article "Progress of Canada Is Aided by Aviation". He compared the scene in the United States and Europe, where activity was on a grand scale, then noted the limitations in Canada, e.g. the need for specialized equipment for summer and winter operations. He lamented how, not far north of Canada's great east-west railroads, flying conditions suddenly became extreme, with such essentials as fuel being scarce and expensive. Even so, Gilmore was optimistic and saw Canada as a rising player in commercial aviation:

Surveys which would take many years, and be incomplete, have been made by aeroplane in a matter of days ... surface details – river, lake, forest, marsh, rocky outcrop – are featured accurately and, through the intermediary of the stereoscope, contours stand out distinctly. Maps and plans for railway and road construction, water power schemes and drainage systems, unrivalled in accuracy, are produced from these aerial photographs; exact inventories of timber and calculations affecting lumber operations, on which contracts may be safely based, are easily made; boundaries, claims, etc., can be defined with certainty...

The group of industries based upon the forest resources of Canada – pulp and paper and lumbering – rank second among the industries of the Dominion, having an annual production of approximately $500,000,000 ... yet every summer fire destroys millions of feet of valuable timber. Federal and Provincial Governments are fighting this menace effectively and economically by aeroplane. In Ontario alone, where destruction of forests by fire amounts to 300,000 acres on an average per year, already by aircraft aid that average has been reduced to approximately 40,000 acres. Fires ... are spotted, viewed and reported promptly and, no matter how distant, fire fighting crews with pumps and other implements are placed on the location within a matter of hours...

The Northwest Territories ... the Hudson Bay region and Labrador lie

open to the explorer, the prospector and the engineer. In a few days personnel, camp equipment, canoes and implements can be placed on any spot ... and regular communications and supplies be maintained... In a year or two Canada will have no unknown districts ... No place will be remote and the dreary isolation of distant camp life will cease... Rich mineral wealth will be located, mining camps will spring up, railways will follow and water power will be harnessed a generation sooner because of the aeroplane... The airway companies of Canada without government subsidy have been successful undertakings and their future is assured. The year 1929 will make history in Canadian aviation...

Fighting the Depression

William F. "Freddie" Shaylor was an ex-pat Brit flying in Canada in the 1920s. Many such wartime veterans had served 5-year "short term" commissions in the peacetime RAF, then returned to "Civvie Street". They often gravitated to civil aviation, but that could mean going abroad for work. Canada benefitted greatly from this situation. Many of its work-a-day RCAF, bush, mail and flying club pilots had done a 5-year RAF stint. They then were turfed onto the street, and caught a steamer for Canada.

Freddie Shaylor had begun in the Royal Flying Corps in 1916, then served his 5-year postwar commission. He spent three years flying Snipes with No.1 Squadron in Iraq, then a year home at RAF Hawkinge instructing on the 2-seat Snipe on 17 Squadron. He left the RAF in June 1926, worked at the RAF Apprentice Training School at Halton, then decided to emigrate. He arrived in Ottawa on

P/O W.F. Shaylor in the cockpit of a Blackburn Nighthawk fighter that he was testing in Iraq in 1924. (Shaylor/Hotson Col.)

April 20, 1928 and next day joined the instructional staff at Camp Borden. This would be a pleasant sojourn and years later he still could name many fellow instructors and students. Among the latter were Ernie McNab, later to fight in the Battle of Britain, and Beverley Shenstone, who would become chief engineer at British European Airways. Shaylor also recalled many former RAF ex-pats who also had landed in Canada in the Twenties, from Cyril Arthur to Richard Bibby, Willis Hewson, Phil Hutton, C.E. Kelly, W.J. McDonough, Bill Pudney, Terry Reynolds, T. Sherlock,

Skyways' ill-fated Travel Air. Delivered to Toronto in June 1929, it crashed a few weeks later at St. Catharines. Beyond is Skyway's Moth G-CAUC in which R.C. Williams purportedly committed suicide in December 1929. He is said to have been despondent over the recent death in a plane crash of his friend Frank Soan. (Shaylor/Hotson Col.)

Douglas Joy who was a partner with Geoff O'Brien in Aircraft Limited. When the company folded, Joy was hired by the Department of Transport, where he soon rose to be superintendent in the Toronto office. (Fred Hotson Col.)

Charles Sutton, Peter Troup, J.H. "Tuddy" Tudhope, H.W. Westaway and Babe Woollett. Some of these would have distinguished careers in Canada, some eventually would pack it in and return to England, a few would give their lives in the cause, as did Hutton and Westaway while flying for the OPAS.

While instructing at Camp Borden, Shaylor was part of an RCAF aerobatic team and in a letter to Fred Hotson of November 23, 1979 recalled: "For the official opening of St. Hubert Airport on October 1, 1928, I was a member of the aerobatic team which flew four Siskins from Camp Borden to Montreal via Deseronto and Ottawa. The Siskins were all the RCAF could muster in those days: 1 Siskin III and 3 Siskin IIIAs. Dave Harding, the only Canadian among us, flew the III and Terry Reynolds, Cyril Arthur and myself the IIIAs. The IIIAs could be flown inverted for slow rolls. Fortunately, I had perfected slow rolling on the Snipe, which was quite simple. I found the Siskin not so easy, but managed to perform reasonably well at St. Hubert. Our performance was not as polished as F/L Beamish's later Siskin Flight, but good enough to please the huge crowd that came out that day."

Shaylor soon left the RCAF to join Aircraft Limited, then flying D.H. Moths at de Lesseps airfield in Mount Dennis on the northwest edge of Toronto. Most of his flying here would be instructional and one of his anecdotes is particularly startling. On December 15, 1929, Robert C. Williams rented a Moth for a local jaunt, but the plane soon was spotted diving at full power straight to earth. Years later Shaylor recalled of this event:

"This man had been taught to fly by us at de Lesseps and did us a great disservice when he deliberately committed suicide by crashing one of our machines right in the centre of de Lesseps field."

In leaving the RCAF, Shaylor's timing seems to have been off, for Aircraft Limited folded with the stock market crash of October 1929. He now became involved with William Van Horne's company, Skyways Ltd., also at de Lesseps, but suffering under shady management. Skyways lately had had a grave accident – the crash of Travel Air CF-ABE at St. Catharines on September 14, 1929. Flown by Frank M. "Doc" Bradfield of International Airways, the handsome green Travel Air recently had excelled in the Cleveland Air Races.

At St. Catharines, Bradfield took off with five fare-paying passengers on a short joy ride. Inexplicably, he failed to gain altitude and crashed just out of sight of the airport. All aboard perished. Civil lawsuits ensued and Skyways' reputation was besmirched. (Eventually, a $10,000

Killed in the fiery St. Catherines crash of CF-ABE, John L. Bond and his little son Allan lie at rest, along with John's wife Lillian, in St. John's Norway cemetery in east Toronto. (Larry Milberry)

Freddie Shaylor (right) with some unidentified flying buddies and a Skyways Rambler. (Shaylor/Hotson Col.)

settlement was made by Skyways' insurer to the victims' families. But the company apparently had no insurance to cover the $24,000 loss of the Travel Air. An inquest held into the accident concluded in December 1929 that no cause could be determined.)

Besides the crash, Shaylor had to deal with a business predicament. Unknown to Van Horne (whom Shaylor had taught to fly at Aircraft Ltd.), in 1929 his managing director E. Lothrop and secretary E.B. Manning had been spending money on a new airport in Long Branch a few miles west of Toronto. Land had been purchased and construction begun. Van Horne asked Shaylor to resolve this mess. Shaylor determined that the airport land was low-lying and, being mainly clay,

was poorly drained. At 1850 feet and 1350 feet, the planned runways were too short. Shaylor reported to Van Horne: "The airport was bounded on the North side by Queen Street and on the South side by a concession road and therefore no possible expansion could be made … in order to get the necessary length for runways." Shaylor got Skyways out of the $233-a-month lease with the landowner and convinced General Electric to cancel the Skyways contract for costly airport lighting. Meanwhile, Lothrop and Manning "flew the coop" to points unknown in the USA.

In August 1930 Skyways acquired Puss Moth CF-AGU, and also added two former Aircraft Limited Moths. Three Ramblers were bought from Curtiss-

Reid through that company's head of sales, J.A.D. McCurdy. On June 22, 1931 Shaylor presented his 2nd annual financial report to Skyways' board of directors. The picture was a shaky one:

During the past year, the Company had a turnover of $40,000.00 and made a profit of approximately 20% on the sale of aircraft and sundries. A total sum of $14,994.42 was taken in in cash from student instruction, passenger flights, etc. Photographic work, which had started late in the Fall, netted us during the short period available for this work, $670.04. Repair and labour charges to clients' machines netted the Company $1512.93. Our total revenue from all these sources apart from the sale of aircraft and sundries amounted to $22,354.11. After providing for depreciation … our gross trading loss amounted to $5769.67.

In 1930 Van Horne cleared off all Skyways debts and sold the company to Freddie Shaylor who, ever enthusiastic, kept the business functioning, especially by realizing the value of good public relations. He was prominently involved in the popular Tip Top Derby and in other such events, racing included. Once, while pylon racing at Brantford, near the end of the race he was first, Leigh Capreol second. Shaylor pushed his nose down, obliging "Cap" to descend right down to the tree tops. He later explained: "A dangerous manoeuvre and Cap and I had words about it afterwards. However, I gave him a bottle of scotch to soothe his ruffled feelings."

Shaylor's Fox Moth and a General Airways Bellanca at Beaulieu's Dock in Rouyn over the summer of 1933. (Shaylor/Hotson Col.)

Freddie Shaylor (right) with photographer H.L. Sellar, his cameras and Puss Moth CF-AGU during Skyways' important 1932 Toronto aerial mapping project. (Shaylor/Hotson Col.)

In his letter to Fred Hotson of September 30, 1980, Shaylor wrote of attending one of Norm Irwin's famous fly-in garden parties at Norm's Redwing Orchards in Whitby, Ontario. On departing in a Rambler with his wife Vivienne in the front cockpit, they had an frightful experience: "I decided to give them all a thrill by looping at somewhat a low altitude … at the top of the loop, much to my horror Vivienne came out of her seat but hung on … she hadn't fastened her seat belt. My recovery from the loop – much too close to Norman's apple trees – gave me a rash shock and later more than a few words from my ever loving." On another occasion Shaylor took off in a Moth at de Lesseps unaware that one of his wing lock pins wasn't in place. Realizing his predicament – the wing could fold at any moment – he made a careful circuit and landed: "Another of my aviation lives used up. I was beginning to run a bit short of them by then."

In 1932 Shaylor won a promising aerial survey contract. That year Toronto became the first Canadian city to use aerial photos in creating an accurate land use map. Skyways' Puss Moth was used on this project, and eventually covered 50

square miles from Eglinton Ave. south to the Lake Ontario shore. On clear days Freddie Shaylor and photographer H.L. Sellar would climb to 3600 feet. Shaylor would hold a pre-selected course at a steady speed, while Sellar, using a Fairchild K-4 aerial camera, took photos at precise intervals, overlapping each exposure. The K-4 was loaded with a 75-foot roll of film that produced a hundred and ten 7¼" x 9½" negatives. Sellers scale was at 300 feet to the inch, but once processed, the negatives were enlarged at 100 feet to the inch and worked into a base map prepared by ground surveyors using existing maps. Individual structures, house numbers, fence and lot lines, streetcar tracks and hydro lines were added by draftsmen referring to the aerial photos. One engineer noted, "In two hours Mr. Sellar and Mr. Shaylor do work that would take four surveyors over a year to perform, securing the same information by actual house-to-house measurement." Another Skyways contract was to photograph the refinery at Noranda, Quebec, but in flying the Puss Moth over the stack, there was such a severe updraft that the wing spar was cracked and Shaylor had to return to Toronto for repairs.

In spite of all Shaylor's efforts, Skyways folded in 1932, but he soon teamed with Mr. Cooper of Canadian American Coaches in Windsor, Ontario to acquired Fox Moth CF-APH from DHC. Shaylor now formed Northern Skyways in the hope of making a go of bush flying in the Quebec Gold Belt region. The Fox Moth was based at the Dominion Skyways dock at Rouyn and was flown through the summer by Bill Resseguier.

It was a tough go competing in the Gold Belt aviation market. At season's end Shaylor abandoned his idea, something that he described in a letter to Fred Hotson of November 23, 1979: "I had made my mind up that there was no future in bush flying without adequate capital behind you. As I had a small family dependent on me, I decided to seek a career in the aircraft manufacturing industry or Imperial Airways in England." In getting reorganized, Shaylor sold everything, "including a magnificent Rogers Majestic radiogram, which was the last word in radios … and one of our treasured possessions, with all our classical records acquired over the years…" He sold several Persian rugs that he had brought back from Iraq, but held on to others long enough to see the small ones eventually rise in value to £4000. Back home in 1934, he spent three years at Pobjoy Aircraft, then joined Airspeed in 1937. Here he marketed the Oxford to the RAF, winning a first contract for 86 aircraft in 1938.

In the 1960s Shaylor ended his aviation career with de Havilland, then retired in Gloucestershire. Reminiscing when he was in his eighties, he wrote of his time in Canada: "We did excellent work at de Lesseps in 1930 and 1931 despite the difficult financial conditions … Our cent-a-pound flights were a sell-out over the weekends and it enabled us to keep going for a time… We also visited the fall fairs in Ontario and generally did well. Monday morning would bring joy to our bank manager, when I was able to deposit hundreds, sometimes a few thousand dollars, all in dollar bills, most of them very grubby and moth-eaten!"

Meanwhile, the mining sector across Canada stayed generally healthy in spite of the Depression. In 1933 there was a gold rush in BC's Caribou Mountains. The trip inland from Vancouver took two days, but by chartered plane only 2-3 hours. One newspaper claimed that the gold rush had caused "the most sudden awakening to the merits of air travel in BC". Meanwhile, should business waver, those ever-adaptable commercial aviators could always fall back on their old standby – barnstorming. When otherwise not busy, they scoured the countryside for any opportunity to hustle passengers for a quick buck. For such pilots the motto, "Anyone with 5 bucks to spare is my best friend", fit perfectly. J.C. "Jack" Charleson, one of Canada's prominent Depression era pilots, described the situation: "Piloting aircraft in those days was a very dangerous and hazardous profession, as the risk of starving to death was ever present." In a CAHS *Journal* article, Murray Shorthill recalled those barnstorming days:

Then we used to have the cent-a-pound weekends at Edmonton quite often, usually with parachute drops as an added attraction... We usually did quite well financially on these special events ... Only once did we have a near fatal accident. The J5s on McConachie's Trimotor were just ticking over when a woman walked right through the turning port propeller without a scratch... We often had wingtips dig in, machines up on their noses, flat tires, low grade gas which overheated the engines, short field problems ... but in the final run, I feel that we always gave good value for the customer's dollar...

In another case, Punch Dickins explained to CAL head office in a letter of April 9, 1931 how complicated it could be to collect on invoices in the North. The chief problem was the scarcity of cash in the North, where commerce since the days of Samuel Hearne had been by barter or credit:

Settlement is made in numerous ways by orders against credit at either of the companies [HBC and Révillon Frères] or by turning in "Wolf Bounties", which are issued by the police and are orders on the Department of Interior in Ottawa and cashable there, or in fur ... credits or produce sold to the companies or in the open market in McMurray or Edmonton ... on my last trip on the 3rd of April I arrived back at McMurray with $15 in cash, $240 in "Wolf Bounties", $320 in beaver ... 400 muskrat, 2 red foxes, 2 cross foxes, 7 marten, 5 mink, 1 lynx and 50 extra muskrats ...

Even in the depths of the Depression, Consolidated Mining and Smelting of Trail, BC had aircraft supporting exploration and mine development. Here from the collection of D.H. "Doug" Burt are CMS D.H.80A Puss Moth CF-AVA and two Fairchild 71Cs. The latter were lost, CF-AVY on October 12, 1941 when it flipped on landing on Sylvan Lake, Alberta; CF-AWG on April 12, 1943 when it crashed in bad weather near Hay River, NWT, killing pilot Anderson.

Canadian Airways Develops

A fine portrait of Canadian Airways Fokker Super Universal G-CAWB at St. Hubert on May 15, 1930. Sitting on the tire is a young mechanic with Consolidated Mining and Smelting, D.H. "Doug" Burt, from whose collection this photo comes.

In 1930 the Canadian airline scene remained a shaky patchwork of small companies constantly appearing, struggling along, then failing or merging. In this unhealthy environment, the Aviation League of Canada, jealously eyeing the growth of commercial aviation in the US, Europe, Russia, China, Japan, etc., was moved to editorialize how "The Dominion finds herself in the anomalous position of being a pygmy among giants in the matter of civil aviation." Happily, there were exceptions including Western Canada Airways, with business in the North. Another success story was Canadian Colonial Airways (a US subsidiary). After two years its New York-Albany-Montreal route still seemed viable. In its October 4, 1930 aviation column, the Toronto *Daily Star* reviewed the results: "This service was the first foreign airmail contract issued by the U.S. Post Office Dept... The mileage flown to date totals 422,674 during 4,297 hours in the air, with 88 per cent of the mileage done on regular schedule. Sixteen hundred and two persons have so far been transported, with 292,574 pounds of mail and 4,836 pounds of express. The fastest trip between New York and Montreal was made ...

in two hours, eight minutes including a stop at Albany."

The general atmosphere soon would change with the emergence on November 25, 1930 of Canadian Airways. The new company, a bulwark against American inroads, comprised James A. Richardson's Western Canada Airways, and the Aviation Corporation of Canada. The CPR and CNR each invested $250,000. Richardson, a director of the CPR, was named president. Sir Henry Thornton of the CNR and E.W. Beatty of the CPR became vice presidents. The Board of Directors included the kingpins of Canadian business.

Canadian Airways had two chief districts: Eastern Lines and Western Lines, with most parts of Canada having service. However, the regions were not connected, and the Canadian Airways fleet comprised mainly obsolete, single engine planes. Without bigger, faster, multi-engine types, there was no hope of such a service as Winnipeg to Toronto. However, Canadian Airways began weeding out old planes. Meanwhile, well-established competitors like Mackenzie Air Service still were problematic, and, the whole sector was keeping up its traditional complaint

against the RCAF – how it robbed civil air carriers of revenue by servicing Ottawa's many government bureaus. The air carriers were adamant that they could just as well provide those services.

In Ottawa on December 3, 1930, Richardson explained his Canadian Airways vision – to serve Canada with a seamless coast-to-coast airway. Even as he spoke, his experts were studying a possible Winnipeg-Sudbury service. He pointed out how Winnipeg and Calgary already were served and that Calgary-Vancouver was inevitable. He also explained why the CNR and CPR were joining forces. Each knew that it would have to get into the airline business, but nose-to-nose competition over duplicated routes would be suicidal. Richardson optimistically described his sense of the situation: "We are not novices in this game. We know, if we do say it ourselves, something about flying, and we believe we can give Canada a fine service... You hear a lot about Imperial Airways, but we fly as far in one day as they do in a week." Air mail especially interested Canadian Airways and a Toronto *Globe* item of December 8, 1930 illustrates how competitive and alluring this market was growing:

Canadian Colonial Airways operated this FC-2W-2 on the Montreal-New York run from September 1928 until selling the plane to Canadian Airways on February 19, 1930. Incredibly, on that very day it was lost in a fire near Moncton. (CANAV Col.)

Glover was proposing trans-Atlantic service using aircraft in the Azores, Bermuda, New York (summer) and Charleston (winter) in order to speed the mails by as much as four days. Glover suggested that Toronto and Montreal could receive such mail within 24 hours of its arrival on the East Coast, Winnipeg within 36. As the *Globe* item put it: "While many regarded an all-plane service across the Atlantic as ambitious, if not chimerical, Mr. Glover pointed to the fact that for many months now United States mail planes were daily navigating the Caribbean Sea for 900 miles and giving regular mail delivery. The hop from New York or Charleston to Bermuda was approximately 900 miles, and from there to the Azores about 1,200 miles, so that a regular transatlantic mail flight was far from being an impossible feat." Such optimism certainly had its historic footing in the flight of the *NC-4* and again showed the farsightedness of J.A.D. McCurdy's 1910 comment following his Key West-to-Havana flight: "I am seriously impressed with the possibility of making intercontinental, transoceanic flights by aeroplane."

Regardless of Glover's urgings, Ottawa remained convinced that using small planes to speed the mail from trans-Atlantic liners made the most sense.

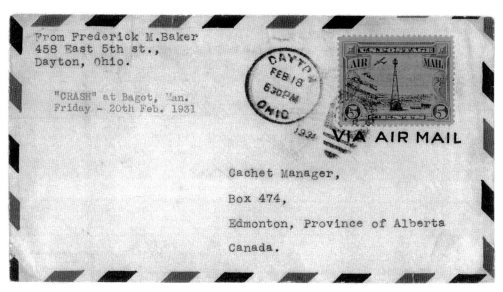

On February 20, 1931 CAL Fokker F.14A CF-AIH crashed near Portage la Prairie, Manitoba. Pilot Norman G. Forester survived, but passengers Dr. Allyn and George Lewis died. This letter, bearing a US air mail stamp and destined from Dayton, Ohio to Edmonton, was salvaged from the mail on board. To show the risk associated with the early Canadian air mail, in 1931 ten pilots and 16 passengers were killed, mostly in weather related crashes. (Richard K. Malott Col.)

Meanwhile, Glover was touting the proven New York-Montreal trans-border air mail, and Northwest Airlines' new St. Paul-Winnipeg service. He also was interested in splitting off a branch of Canada's Mackenzie Valley air mail to the Yukon and Alaska, and was impressed about recently successful German trials using mail planes cata-pulted mid-ocean from ships.

Unfortunately, accidents plagued Canadian Airways in these early times, most being related to foul weather – aviation meteorology was still in its infancy, and operating procedures usually favoured "getting through" regardless of conditions. On January 17, 1930 pilot R.H. "Dick" Bibby, en route with mail from Montreal to Toronto, met a fierce snowstorm, so he was forced to land on Alexander Jeffreys' farm near Whitby, about 30 miles short of Toronto. His mail bags then were rushed on by bus. In a worse case, on the morning of March 18, 1930 Travel Air SA-6000 CF-AJO crashed on the farm of W.F. Good of Tichborne, Ontario, about 30 miles north of Kingston. Pilot Hervé Simoneau

and radio operator Harold L. Robinson both died. They had been on the Toronto-Montreal airmail route when they got tangled up in the weather. On April 29 Harold Farrington crashed Fokker F.14 CF-AIJ soon after leaving Winnipeg at night with the mail, then getting into fog. On May 26 W.G. "Pat" Holden crashed in Boeing 40B CF-AIN. Out of Calgary at night and bound for Moose Jaw, he too encountered fog. Holden and both his passengers were killed. In spite of such trouble, Canadian Airways maintained a good record in 1930: of 4864 scheduled prairie mail flights, 4512 were safely completed.

Melville Good of Parham, Ontario then aged 9, was on the scene shortly after CF-AJO crashed. In June 2009 he recalled: "At the time my dad, William Franklin Good, and I were working close by and it was very foggy." Seven bags of air mail were gathered up and forwarded same day. "Mel" still was on his farm in June 2009, when Brian Milberry photographed him displaying a prop blade salvaged from 'AJO.

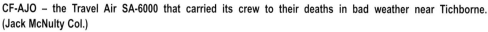

CF-AJO – the Travel Air SA-6000 that carried its crew to their deaths in bad weather near Tichborne. (Jack McNulty Col.)

Junkers Heavyweight

In 1931 Canadian Airways acquired its most famous airplane – Junkers Ju 52 CF-ARM. Sixty feet long and with a wing span of 96' 6", this mighty machine weighed nearly 16,000 lb all-up and boasted a revenue load of 5850 lb (about that of a DC-3). Other features included a 6' x 3' roof hatch for loading bulky cargo, and a 6' x 4' side door. Unfortunately, CF-ARM had an inauspicious beginning, mainly due to failures with its 685-hp BMW engine. It was stranded at Eskimo Point in September 1932, when the floats were damaged in a storm. Sheet metal, canvas and seal skin were used to patch the floats, then 'ARM flew to Winnipeg via Churchill and The Pas. With such woes it lost 297 days through 1932, so didn't earn Canadian Airways a penny.

Engine trouble persisted late into 1935, when the BMW was replaced by an 825-hp Rolls-Royce Buzzard. CF-ARM now came into its own, proving its worth in the bush. In 1936 a mass of freight was needed by Argosy Gold Mines at Casummit Lake, Ontario before freeze-up. Much of this materiel was barged from Hudson by the Patricia Transportation Co., but 780 tons of fuel, dynamite, lumber,

CF-ARM and one of its "baby brothers" at some northern dock. (NMST 1201)

Canadian Airways' Junkers Ju 52 CF-ARM reached Montreal by sea in November 1931. The great machine had been purchased in hope of new business from the Hudson's Bay Company. 'ARM was assembled at Fairchild in Longueuil (where it is shown) and test flown on November 27 by Alex Schneider. G.A. "Tommy" Thompson, accompanied by Schneider, ferried 'ARM to Winnipeg, arriving on December 28. (Jack McNulty Col.)

etc. had to go by air from Gold Pines, a return trip of about 140 miles. Several CAL planes were committed to this airlift, which began on September 28. The CAL newsletter *The Bulletin* later reported: "The Junkers 52 ... has carried regular loads of from two to two and a half tons. Although 20 tons has been an average day's performance, there have been occasions when flying conditions were good ... 24 tons were transported in one day..." By this time CAL was running its own radio stations and had 18 radio operators. On a job such as to Argosy Mines the radio was invaluable in co-ordinating air movements, especially in passing on weather reports. Another great project on which CF-ARM later flew was a 1941 dam project in northern Quebec. In one episode in May its engine had to be

One of Canada's famous planes of the 1930s – Ju 52 CF-ARM one sunny day at the Brandon Ave. base on the Red River. Thought to be at the left in the distance are Winnipeg's CNR yards. The steep-roofed building (centre) is a brick and tile operation, the Black Woods industrial area is to the right. The spire may belong to St. Augustine church. (William J. Wheeler Co.)

Some great beast, whether horse or ox, is manhandled at the door of CF-ARM, location unknown. (Lake of the Woods Museum)

Ju 52 specs / DC-3 specs

	Ju 52 CF-ARM (1931)	*DC-3 (1935)*
Wing span	96' 8"	95'
Length	60' 6"	64' 6"
Power	1 x R-R Buzzard 825 hp	2 x P&W R-1830 (each 1200 hp)
Empty weight	8410 lb	17,720 lb
Payload	5850 lb	6000 lb
All-up weight	15,900 lb	26,900 lb
Cruise speed	100 mph	160 mph

changed in the middle of a lake, since the plane could not be brought to shore due to shallow water. In another case 'ARM flew in a wing so that heavy repairs could be made to a Fairchild 82.

Canadian Airways also added some smaller Junkers. These proved to be delightful to fly, were fairly trouble free and made money wherever they went. Speedier Boeings and Stearmans replaced the Fokker F.14s and, for a time, Canadian Airways seemed to be flying high. Inevitably, however, the harsh realities of the times caught up. The government of R.B. Bennett cancelled the Prairie air mail routes in early 1932, forcing lay offs and pay cuts everywhere in commercial aviation. What was more infuriating was how Ottawa pressed RCAF aircraft into service carrying the mail. Then, it sold Manitoba several Vedettes. The province now had its own air service, so discontinued most commercial contracts in forestry, surveying, etc.

Even though Canadian Airways laid off staff and cut salaries, the loss for 1932 was $227,973. On August 31

company comptroller C.M. Forrest wrote to his boss, Wilfred Sigerson: "Have gone into the matter of cost and regret unable to find where savings can be effected ... appears to me the only solution is to endeavor to increase the volume of business or suspend operations entirely." Somehow, Canadian Airways kept the props ticking over. In 1935, for

example, it flew 17,869 hours, compared to 16,059 by the RCAF. It carried 5,275,745 lb express, 817,678 lb mail and 14,542 passengers. (For the story of this great company, two books are essential: *Pioneering in Canadian Air Transport* and *Double Cross: The Inside Story of James A. Richardson and Canadian Airways*.)

CF-ARM on duty at Onatchiway Lake, Quebec, during a 1940 dam building project. Soon after this job, 'ARM was laid up – it was a worn out old crate and modern planes were becoming available. "The Flying Boxcar", as people used to call 'ARM, soon was scrapped. (S.J. "Sid" Woodham)

A previously unpublished view of CF-ARM. The men on the dock give an idea of the size of this machine. (Norman Etheridge Col.)

"Small" Junkers W-33 CF-AQW at Norway House with Super Universal CF-AJF on April 5, 1932. 'AQW served Canadian Airways/CPA from late 1931 until sold 16 years later to Central BC Airlines. On August 10, 1959, soon after moving to Skyway Air Service, it was wrecked on Kootenay Lake. (NMST 6360)

Two newly-revealed photos from the W.J. McDonough collection show a freighter canoe being unloaded from atop W-34 CF-AQW, location unknown. A smaller canoe could be squeezed through the door, or lashed to a float. Over a 3-decade span, nine W-33s and W-34s flew in Canadian markings.

CF-AQB visiting Port Credit on the Lake Ontario shore west of Toronto. This W-33 served Hervé St-Martin in Quebec from 1931-42, then several other operators. It ended in BC with Skyway, then faded from the scene in 1959. In this photo it still had its original 310-hp Junkers L-5 water-cooled engine. While with Fecteau Air Service in 1959, it was converted to a 420-hp P&W Wasp, making it a W-34. Some of the W-33s and W-34s later had the 600-hp P&W R-1340 Wasp. These Junkers were 34' 5" long with a wing span of 58' 6". All-up weight was 6600 lb. (Jack McNulty Col.)

Canadian Airways operated CF-ABK (its first Junkers) from 1929 until it was reduced to spares in 1940. This scene is at Carcross on Lake Bennett in the Yukon, a bit north of BC's northern border. The stern wheeler at the dock is the SS *Tutshi*. Built in 1917, it served Carcross-Atlin into 1956. Restoration of this historic vessel commenced in 1984, but a 1990 fire ended those efforts. (K.M. Molson Col.)

Canada's last serviceable Junkers: CF-ATF is dug out and brushed clean of snow in a typical winter scene. 'ATF served CAL/CPA 1932-46, Central BC Air Airways, PWA, then was with Pacific Wings until retiring in July 1961. Soon afterwards, through the efforts of K.M. Molson, CF-ATF was acquired by the Richardson family of Winnipeg and donated to Canada's National Aviation Museum in 1962 where it is seen on the right. (William J. Wheeler Col., J.W. Jones)

From "The Bulletin"

Having a job with Canadian Airways was a real plum, especially during the Depression. Employees were in an exciting new industry and earning better than average pay. People got to know each other and a sense of family developed. The company newsletter, *The Bulletin*, helped keep "family members" informed, something that was good for morale in tough times. *The Bulletin* for July 15, 1932 (Vol.4 No.1), for example, described how Canadian Airways had already made its impact in Manitoba, especially on the Churchill project:

The Province of Manitoba is centrally located in the Dominion and extends 760 miles northward from the international boundary to lat. 60ºN... all railroads, with one exception, are confined to a belt some 160 miles wide along the southern boundary ... the agricultural area. The remainder of this vast territory is an expanse of bush, rivers and lakes without a single road. To negotiate it the traveller must have recourse to the canoe, steamboat, dog team or aeroplane...

At that time Churchill was more "off the map" than Aklavik on the Arctic Ocean is today. On March 20th, 1927, the first move was made in transporting by air 20,000 lbs. of equipment and 12 men from Cache Lake, near Kettle Rapids – the end of steel at the time – to Churchill, 200 miles distant. This work was to be done by

"break-up" and 27 trips were necessary to accomplish the job.

This was undoubtedly the greatest accomplishment in aerial transportation in Canada to that date. When the weather and the nature of the terrain over which the planes had to operate are taken into consideration, the achievement is all the more remarkable. The next outstanding demonstration of the utility of the aeroplane was the carriage of 40 men and 70,000 lbs. of freight from rail at Cormorant Lake to Sherritt Gordon in order to speed up development of the mine.

As to the West Coast, the same issue of *The Bulletin* reported on the success of the Vancouver-Victoria passenger run using the new Sikorsky flying boat CF-ASO. It added how a smaller salmon run was expected so, "fishermen are likely to take many chances in the way of violating regulations", implying that more fisheries charters might come out of this. Stan McMillan was busy on the coast doing charters into the Scurvy Creek placer gold properties, although CAL reported how this was an area much in the news, but lacking in any real signs of "the yellow metal".

The Bulletin also quoted fares and freight rates presently in effect. Vol.4 No.1 passenger fares included:

Charlottetown-Moncton	$10.00
Montreal-Quebec	$10.00
Toronto-Hamilton	$2.65
Toronto-Windsor	$15.25
(via Hamilton, Brantford, London)	
Winnipeg-Chicago	$40.00
(via Pembina, Grand Forks, Fargo, Minneapolis)	
Sioux Lookout-Gold Pines	$25.00
Gold Pines-Red Lake	$25.00
Winnipeg-Island Lake	$550.00
(airplane charter rate)	
Fort McMurray-Hay River	$120.00
Fort McMurray-Fort Norman	$280.00
Fort McMurray-Aklavik	$410.00

Each copy of *The Bulletin* also listed the disposition of the fleet with pilots and engineers. Samples for Vol.4 No.1 included: Charlottetown - G-CATR Fairchild FC-2, Moncton - CF-AAK Fairchild 71, Montreal - CF-ACO Fairchild 71, Senneterre - G-CANF Fairchild FC-2, Grand-Mère - G-CAVR Fairchild FC-2WC, Toronto - G-CATS Fairchild FC-2, Windsor - CF-AAT Fairchild 71, Sioux Lookout - CF-AMZ Junkers W.33, Winnipeg - CF-APY Laird, Lac du Bonnet - CF-ARM Junkers 52, The Pas - CF-AJQ Bellanca, Calgary - CF-AAL Lockheed Vega, Edmonton - CF-AIL Fokker F.14, Mackenzie - CF-AKI Bellanca, Vancouver - CF-ASO Sikorsky S-38, Takla Lake - G-CASQ Fokker "Super", Bella Bella - CF-ABA Boeing "B", Carcross - CF-ABK Junkers W.34. Also listed were current operating statistics. Vol.4 No.1 noted these for 1932 January to May inclusive:

CANADIAN AIRWAYS LIMITED AERIAL SURVEYS DIVISION DESBARATS BUILDING MONTREAL

During the past ten years the Surveys Division of Canadian Airways has mapped thousands of square miles by vertical photography and is fully equipped to advise on and undertake all mapping and survey engineering problems. Projects to which aerial survey have been successfully applied include:

RECONNAISSANCE SURVEYS

LOCATION SURVEYS
Highway, Railway
Transmission Line

CITY SURVEYS
Condition Maps
Town Planning
Assessment

GEOLOGICAL SURVEYS
Surface Study
Mining

TIMBER OPERATIONS
Forest estimates, cruising
Logging and cutting operations

POWER DEVELOPMENTS
Storage dams, drainage
Power house location
Flood lines

TOPOGRAPHICAL SURVEYS
Line Maps
Contact or precise mosaics
Contoured line maps or
Mosaics for all purposes
Models

Canada's Fokker Universals

Registration	Date	Registered/Owner	Fate
G-CAFU	6-10-26	Western Canada Airways	crashed 17-12-39 Fort St. John, United Air Transport
G-CAGD	22-2-27	Western Canada Airways	crashed 30-11-22 Edmonton, Independent Airways
G-CAGE	23-3-27	Western Canada Airways	crashed The Pas 5-1-28 killing F.J. Stevenson
G-CAHE	8-7-27	Dept. of Marine and Fisheries	Peace River Airways, had temporary certificate of airworthiness 7-40, fate unknown
G-CAHF	8-7-27	Dept. of Marine and Fisheries	J.R. McCowan, Sydney, NS, declared unairworthy 8-30
G-CAHG	8-7-27	Dept. of Marine and Fisheries	abandoned after forced landing while patrolling from Port Burwell 17-2-28
G-CAHH	8-7-27	Dept. of Marine and Fisheries	J.R. McCowan, Sydney, NS, declared unairworthy 8-30
G-CAHI	8-7-27	Dept. of Marine and Fisheries	J.R. McCowan, Sydney, NS, declared unairworthy 8-30
G-CAHJ	8-7-27	Dept. of Marine and Fisheries	Peace River Airways, Scrapped 1939
G-CAIV	23-1-28	Western Canada Airways	crashed Peace River 15-12-31
G-CAIX	10-2-28	Western Canada Airways	crashed Elk Lake, Ontario 12-3-31
G-CAIY	23-2-28	Western Canada Airways	burned while pre-heating at Reindeer Lake, Manitoba 6-3-28
G-CAIZ	23-2-28	Western Canada Airways	Arrow Airways, certificate lapsed 11-12-40
G-CAJD	11-4-28	Western Canada Airway	crashed through the ice Charron Lake, Manitoba 10-12-31, remnants recovered by Western Canada Aviation Museum in 2000s
G-CAJH	22-5-28	Western Canada Airways	destroyed in storm Gold Pines, Ontario 14-8-28
G-CASD	19-7-28	Western Canada Airways	burned while pre-heating at Winnipeg 23-12-29
G-CASE	3-8-28	Western Canada Airways	crashed Gull Lake, Alberta 10-6-33
G-CASF	20-8-28	Western Canada Airways	capsized Allanwater Lake, Ontario 2-6-30
CF-ABL	13-5-29	Yarrow Aircraft, Vancouver	crashed Toronto 2-9-30
CF-BID	23-9-37	O. Brieve, Roberval, Quebec	certificate lapsed 11-12-40

Canada's Fokker Super Universals

Registration	Date	Registered/Owner	Fate
G-CARK	19-7-28	Northern Aerial Mineral Exploration	declared unairworthy 18-3-31
G-CASJ	29-7-28	Western Canada Airways	crashed near Cat Lake, Ontario 13-7-29
G-CASK	17-8-28	Western Canada Airways	burned during refuelling Fort McMurray 31-3-33
G-CASL	20-8-28	Western Canada Airways	crashed Great Bear Lake area 29-6-32
G-CASM	28-9-28	Western Canada Airways	burned in hangar fire Winnipeg 4-3-31
G-CASN	17-12-28	Western Canada Airways	burned in hangar fire Winnipeg 4-3-31
G-CASO	5-1-29	Western Canada Airways	crashed Aylmer Lake, NWT 16-11-29
G-CASP	31-12-28	Western Canada Airways	sunk in storm Churchill, Manitoba 26-8-29
G-CASQ	16-1-29	Western Canada Airways	crashed Disappointment Inlet, BC 17-11-38
G-CAWB	28-1-29	Canadian Vickers	Canadian Airways crashed Takla Landing, BC 21-3-37
CF-AAM	11-2-29	Western Canada Airways	Northern Airways crashed Dawson, Yukon 5-12-37, restored by Clark Seaborn, et al, in Calgary, reflown for first time 1998, Western Canada Aviation Museum 2009
CF-AEW	28-12-29	General Airways, Toronto	burned on starting Amos, Quebec 25-7-30
CF-AEX	1929	Canadian Vickers	crashed Montreal 20-6-29
CF-AFL	9-8-29	Western Canada Airways	crashed through the ice Sydney Lake, Manitoba 12-33
CF-AFM	20-8-29	Western Canada Airways	crashed Reykjavik, Manitoba 22-9-29
CF-AFS	19-6-29	Pigeon Timber Co., Port Arthur, Ont.	collided with boat Port Arthur 8-7-39
CF-AJA	9-29	Canadian Vickers	Starratt Airways burned Hudson, Ontario 9-2-38
CF-AJB	9-29	Canadian Vickers	Starratt Airways withdrawn from use C of A expired 6-11-42
CF-AJC	25-6-30	Western Canada Airways	Northern Airways crashed Dazdeash River north of Whitehorse 19-6-42
CF-AJD	17-1-29	Western Canada Airways	destroyed by fire Winnipeg 27-6-30
CF-AJE	1929	Canadian Vickers	crashed Franz, Ontario 19-12-37
CF-AJF	7-1-30	International Airways	Canadian Airways wrecked when float collapsed Swan Lake, Manitoba 13-11-36
CF-AJG	8-1-30	International Airways	crashed Whitby, Ontario 7-1-30
CF-AJH	15-5-30	Canadian Airways	Dominion Skyways, withdrawn from use 26-1-36
CF-AJI	10-29	Canadian Vickers	Resort Airways, returned to Canadian Vickers and used in rebuild of CF-AJE 5-34
CF-AJJ	12-12-29	Canadian Vickers	Dominion Skyways, withdrawn from use 26-1-36
CF-ASZ	21-5-32	M.D. Nicholson, Toronto	burned Ball Lake, Ontario 10-1-38
CF-ATJ	3-9-32	Mackenzie Air Service	Northern Airways crashed Carcross, Yukon 7-11-38
CF-ATW	21-11-32	Mackenzie Air Service	crashed Cambridge Bay, NWT 20-4-34

CANADIAN AIRWAYS LIMITED

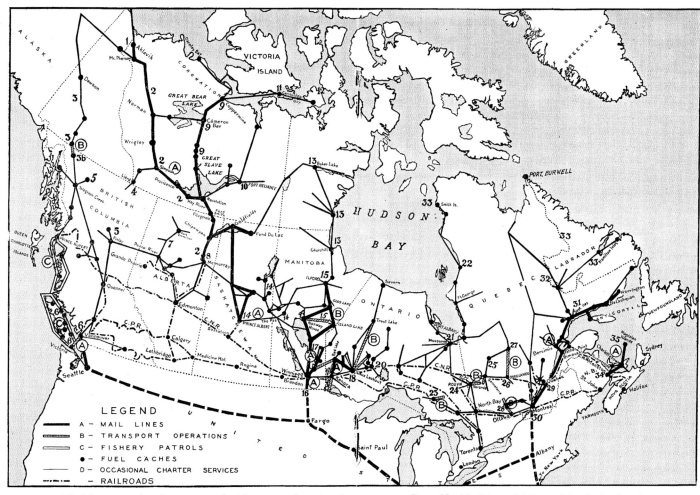

LEGEND
A – MAIL LINES
B – TRANSPORT OPERATIONS
C – FISHERY PATROLS
● – FUEL CACHES
D – OCCASIONAL CHARTER SERVICES
– RAILROADS

Schedules are numbered to correspond with routes and services shown on map. Route No. 31—**Rimouski–Seven Islands–Anticosti-Natashquan**—and Route No. 30—Mail, passengers and express—**Montreal–Rimouski**, connecting with incoming and outgoing Canadian Pacific mail steamships—are operated by Quebec Airways, Desbarats Building, Montreal; phone MArquette 4231.

Hours flown	6199.24
Miles flown	592,794.3
Mail, Freight, Express (lbs)	1,170,132.7
Passengers	2112

Another item in Vol.4 No.1 reported on Canadian Airways' growing aerial survey business:

Canadian Airways Limited has arranged to make an aerial survey of a block of approximately 150 square miles covering Echo Bay and Contact Lake in the Great Bear Lake area. The survey will be made by means of vertical photographs and the mining interests ordering this work will be furnished with a copy print of a matched mosaic photograph of the area on the scale of 800 ft. to one inch, together with the individual aerial photographs. The mosaic will be in sections of a convenient size.

So far as is known this is the first time an attempt has been made to adopt aerial survey to the actual work of prospecting and mineral development.

Use of the photographs with a stereograph will show the area in relief and will reveal all the surface features of the country covered. It will be possible to follow formations from one claim to another and, by using information obtained on the ground at various points, it ought to be possible to predict the possibility of further vein structure at different points as indicated by surface examination... The work will be proceeded with as soon as the snow is out of the valleys and Canadian Airways Limited expect to have the photographs back into the field for use during the summer... Canadian Airways Limited will also prepare wall mosaic maps, showing a composite photograph of the whole area at a scale of approximately 1600 ft. to one inch.

Vol.6 No.10 (June 1936) reported further about surveying, noting how 2777 sq.mi. had been covered through 1935 using vertical photography; 10,197 sq.mi. with oblique photography:

Included in the vertical photography were aerial photographs for the study of a power house location, flood lines and river control, also hydrographic data. Two other areas, each approximately 60 miles in length, were photographed for transmission line location. The towers were spotted to scale on the photographs, after stereographic study, and their positions were checked finally on the ground before commencing construction. An area of 636 square miles was photographed for a paper company for a study of timber types and conditions, and for planning of cutting and logging operations.

Canadian Airways Cargo Statistics 1931-34 (lb)

Year	Freight & Express	Air Mail
1931	764,449	459,458
1932	1,870,136	299,066
1933	2,522,233	328,618
1934	3,658,694	311,093

A CAL Fleet Gallery

The D.H.84 Dragon first flew at de Havilland at Stag Lane, Edgware, England, in November 1932. Designed for the low fare, cross-Channel market and carrying 6-8 passengers, the Dragon was an instant success. Although only three served in Canada, 115 were built in the UK, a further 87 in Australia. CF-APJ joined Canadian Airways in May 1933. For a decade it carried the Moncton-Charlottetown mail then, at the end of its career in 1942, was cannibalized for the rebuilding of CF-AVD. (CANAV Col.)

The Super Universal, 28 of which would serve Canadian operators, did more than any type to keep WCA/CAL operating in difficult times. CF-AJC was acquired by WCA in June 1930, served until sold to Northern Airways of Carcross in January 1938, then flew to June 19, 1942, when it was lost in a mishap 80 miles north of Whitehorse. CF-AJC was Canada's last known serviceable Super Universal. (Jack McNulty Col.)

This aircraft served Canadian Airways from January 1929 to June 1937, including on the MacAlpine search. It flew on with BC operator T.H. Jones until lost in a Vancouver Island crash of November 17, 1938. In his seminal book *Bush to Boardroom*, the great Duncan D. McLaren described daily Vancouver-Victoria operations using this very aircraft: "Each morning we would pull the Fokker Super Universal out of the hangar ... and tow it on its beaching gear to the top of the seaplane ramp that angled down into the river. The old Fordson tractor and towline would be detached from the front of the aircraft and reattached to the aircraft tailpost. The engine would be started, warmed up and the aircraft taxied on its beaching gear to the sloping ramp where it would gently roll down to the water, the speed and direction controlled by the driver of the tractor ... Upon entering the water, the towline would be released and the aircraft taxied to the dock where the beaching gear, consisting of two car wheels and an axle for each float, would be removed. Almost the reverse took place when the machine returned later in the day ... after towing to the hangar, the night shift ... would inspect, repair and service the airframe and engine. The interior and exterior would then be washed and polished. At the completion of the work, the ... log books would be signed off, certifying airframe and engine as being airworthy." (William J. Wheeler Col.)

Few in-flight photos exist from Canada's Golden Age of Flight in the 1920s-30s. Here is a rare example – Super Universal G-CASE, which served WCA/CAL from 1929-32. It later was wrecked with Independent Airways of Edmonton, when a float collapsed on landing at Gull Lake, Alberta on June 10, 1933. In *Bush to Boardroom*, Duncan McLaren describes how the mechanic started a Super Universal: "Prime the engine, crack the throttle, turn the magneto switch on, press the button to energize the inertia starter, engage the starter with the left hand and crank the hand magneto as fast as possible to the right. The three top cylinders that were primed each fired individually with a deep cough-like sound. Then, one by one the other six cylinders joined the first three. After verifying that the oil pressure was registering on the gauge, I nudged the throttle open to bring the power up to 1000 revolutions per minute. When the temperature rose to the operating range, I grasped the throttle and slowly opened it to about 1500 revolutions per minute, and checked the functioning of each of the two magnetos. All that was left was to throttle back to idle, switch off and call for the pilot." (Red Lake Museum)

Super Universal CF-AFL in a typical (if maybe "set up") northern setting. CF-AFL met its fate by going through the ice at Sydney Lake, Manitoba in December 1933. (Al Martin Col)

(Right) One can imagine this crowd of bush whackers gathered around the big blue and yellow WCA Universal, each man anxious for his flight out so he could start blowing his hard-earned wages on wine, women and song. G-CASD was short-lived as it burned on the ground at Winnipeg two days before Christmas 1929. (William J. Wheeler Col.)

Fairchild 71 CF-ATZ served CAL/CPA 1933-47, then was sold to Matt Berry for his Yellowknife operation, Territorial Air Service. 'ATZ lasted until a crash on Great Slave Lake on September 24, 1949. Decades later it was resurrected and today sits nicely restored in Canadian Airways markings in Edmonton's Alberta Aviation Museum. In this view, the fellows under the wing from the left are air engineers W.J. "Bill" Jacquot, Rudy Huess and Frank Kelly. Pilot Zebulon Lewis "Lewie" Leigh is second from the right. In his book *And I Shall Fly*, Leigh describes some typical flying on CF-ATZ with Bill Jacquot during 1935: "On August 17 I was back again on [CF-ATZ] ... We made a number of trips between Fort McMurray and Edmonton ... and on the 29th we went north along the Mackenzie with mail as far as Fort Norman. On the return I was instructed to unload ... at Fort Chipewyan and take on a special load to a new mineral area, Goldfields, on the north shore of Lake Athabasca, where a settlement had sprung up overnight... I was then sent back to Great Bear Lake with another load. A flight with Inspector Tom Reilly of the Post Office Department from Great Bear Lake to Coppermine ... followed on September 4." When CF-ATZ was unveiled at the AAM following restoration, the great Lewie Leigh was there in the crowd. (CANAV Col.)

From 1928-32 this beautiful Stearman C3B, G-CARR, carried the mail for Canadian Transcontinental Airways. When CTA was acquired by Canadian Airways, it continued until sold privately in 1940. It survived until wrecked at Rivière-du-Loup on January 2, 1947. By then it likely was the last aircraft in Canada still flying with a "G-C" registration. Writing of this classic biplane in his 1962 *U.S. Civil Aircraft Series*, the great Joseph P. Juptner notes that to fly a C3B "was just about the pinnacle of many a pilot's dreams". Built in Wichita in 1928, the C3B was powered by a 220-hp Wright J5 and cruised at about 110 mph. It was 24' long, had a wing span of 35' and weighed 2650 lb all-up. Fly-away price was about $9000. (William J. Wheeler Col.)

Canadian Airways owned four Stearman 4EM mailplanes. Shown is CF-AMB, which served from June 1930. Powered by a 420-hp P&W Wasp, the 4EM carried four passengers or 600 lb of mail at about 125 mph and, at 3950 lb all-up, was definitely the C3B's "big brother". CAL initially used the 4EM on its Montreal-Detroit air mail system. In 1965 John Paterson of Fort William acquired a 4EM that had begun life in 1930 with Standard Oil in the US. He restored it to flight status as CF-AMB in Canadian Airways black and yellow colours, then donated it to Canada's National Aviation Museum. (Jack McNulty Col.)

In June 1930 Canadian Airways added this Consolidated Fleetster 20-2, the only such on the Canadian civil aircraft register and Canada's fastest plane of its day. Built in Buffalo, NY, and powered by a 575-hp P&W Hornet, the 5900-lb (all-up) Fleetster accommodated 5 passengers, or 800-lb cargo/mail, or various combinations, and sped along at 125-140 mph. Fly-away price was $30,500. While landing at Calgary on the night of November 16, 1931, pilot Paul Calder lost control of CF-AIP when his brakes failed and the plane was wrecked. (Jack McNulty Col.)

First flown in January 1932, the 4- or 5-passenger D.H.83 Fox Moth was designed for the short-haul airline business that was developing worldwide. Powered by a 120-, 130- or 145-hp D.H. Gipsy, the Fox Moth enjoyed immediate success. In May 1933, prototype G-ABUO became CF-API, then went on to fly into 1950 with companies from General Airways to Ginger Coote Airways to United Air Transport. Eight "CF" Fox Moths served pre-war, then de Havilland Canada built 54 postwar "Canadianized" Fox Moths, some of which were sold as far away as Pakistan and New Zealand. Shown is CF-APG which was with Canadian Airways from February 1933 until wrecked in a wind storm at Cartierville on September 24, 1942. (Bert Phillips)

More photos of the amazing Canadian Airways workhorse CF-ARM. The in-flight view emphasizes its huge proportions relative to other commercial planes on the Canadian scene. Its 96' 9" wing span compares to 95' for the DC-3, which was just appearing as CF-ARM faded into the sunset. (C. Don Long, *Canadian Aviation* magazine Cols.)

Canadian Airways Junkers W-34s CF-AMZ and 'ARI. The former served in Canada 1930-45, then was picked apart for spares needed to rejuvenate CF-AQW. CF-ARI, which joined the CAL fleet in April 1933, had a bad ending. Soon after taking off from Waterways, near Fort McMurray, on January 25, 1940, its engine quit and it crashed. (William J. Wheeler Col.)

A classic bush scene from *Canadian Aviation* magazine of October 1934. Pilot Michael deBliquy is seen centre heading for the shore lunch that's being cooked up. His Junkers CF-AQV then was operated by Oaks Airways. Then, one of the finest Canadian Junkers photos – CF-AQV at Colby's Landing, Red Lake (Jackson Manion Mine) in July 1938. While near Gold Pines on September 1, 1939, 'AQV flew into trees and was wrecked. (*Canadian Aviation* magazine and K.M. Molson Cols.)

One of the most handsome and speediest planes of the Golden Age was the Lockheed Vega, the type flown by Wiley Post on his famous 1931 and '33 round-the-world flights. There was only one Canadian-registered Vega – CF-AAL was purchased by Wop May's Commercial Airways in April 1929. When Canadian Airways acquired Commercial Airways in May 1931, the Vega was part of the deal and remained in the fleet into the CPA era, finally being sold into the US in June 1944. (Glenbow Museum)

Summer and winter views of CAL Laird LC-B-200 CF-APY. In early 1931 Canadian Airways acquired four such "Laird Commercial" planes for air mail. CF-APW and 'APX were destroyed in the March 4, 1931 hangar fire at Winnipeg. Built in Chicago by Emil Matthew "Matty" Laird, this type flew at about 110 mph. Joseph P. Juptner once commented: "The Laird was usually built to suit the customer's particular fancies ... likened to a fine piece of precision machinery, they were built unhurried and with the greatest of care... sure-footed and delightfully responsive, they were a real joy to fly." CAL's Lairds had a 200-hp Wright J-5 (K.M. Molson claimed that, when CAL needed to bolster its capacity following some accidents, it chose the Laird mainly because it had a surplus of J-5 engines in its shops). In 1934 CF-APY was on the Winnipeg-Pembina air mail

route, then was fitted for blind flying. As such, Z.L. Leigh flew it to CAL bases from coast to coast to train pilots at this new art. In 1943 CPA pilot John T. Dart purchased CF-APY from his employer, then held on to it into the 1990s, always hoping to do a restoration. John died of old age before this happened. Happily, the Reynolds Alberta Museum acquired CF-APY and, in the early 2000s, restored it to its former glory in Canadian Airways colours. (Jack McNulty and William J. Wheeler Cols.)

Pitcairn PA-6 Super Mailwing CF-ACT originally served International Airways, then joined CAL with the great Canadian airline amalgamation engineered in 1930 by James A. Richardson. At 3050 lb all-up weight, a PA-6 was larger than a Laird LC-B-200. It carried 500 pounds of mail in a compartment ahead of the pilot. Cruising at about 110 mph, a PA-6 could haul its load some 600 miles. On September 27, 1930 CF-ACT was wrecked taking off from Detroit with the Toronto mail. (C. Don Long Col.)

Powered by a 300-hp P&W Wasp Jr., the sole Boeing of Canada A-213 Totem first flew at Vancouver in June 1932. A step advanced from the Boeing 204, this nifty little 4-seater had an aluminum hull. Its Canadian Airways era stretched from May 1935 to January 1938, when it flew mainly on fisheries duties. CF-ARF later was owned by W.J. Dyson of Victoria who, it is thought, let it go for scrap in 1942. (Jack McNulty Col.)

To bolster his Mackenzie Air Service fleet, Leigh Brintnell purchased this Super Universal from Fokker in New Jersey in November 1932. CF-ATW is shown in the spring of 1933 during change-over to floats at Fort Saskatchewan, Alberta. In April 1934 CF-ATW was wrecked in a mishap at distant Cambridge Bay, NWT. (LAC PA90895)

Mackenzie Air Service

Founded in 1932 by Leigh Brintnell, Mackenzie Air Service would be a thorn in Canadian Airways' side for years ahead. A wartime flier, later with the OPAS and Western Canada Airways, Brintnell had pioneered from Labrador to the Yukon. His history-making WCA/CAL flights included the first ever between Winnipeg and Vancouver – route-proving exercise in WCA's Fokker Trimotor. Flying westward via Regina, Edmonton and High River, Brintnell had on board several top aviation figures, the premier of Manitoba, etc. His return trip, which stopped only at High River, was made in a record flying time of 10:30 hours.

On another landmark trip, Brintnell departed Winnipeg on August 5, 1929 in Universal G-CASK with Toronto-based prospector Gilbert Labine and Dr. Bannerman of Winnipeg. Going via The Pas, Fort McMurray, Fort Smith, Fort Simpson, Fort Norman, they finally reached Labine's camp on the Sloan River on the east shore of Great Bear Lake. Brintnell continued to Aklavik, where he had a 780-mile charter to fly NWT administrator O.S. Finnie, two others and an official mail bag containing 83 letters to Dawson. This was the first known airplane flight between Aklavik and Dawson.

Brintnell found much of Dawson deserted. A town of 25,000 in "Trail of 98" days, only about 600 remained. "It gave one a peculiar feeling," recalled Brintnell, "to walk into a house with dishes on the table, just as the people had left them when they went out of the country." He flew on to Whitehorse, Prince Rupert, Prince George, Edmonton and The Pas, finally landing on the Red River in Winnipeg on August 29. He had covered some 9000 miles in 94 flying hours.

Pilot Leigh Brintnell completes some paperwork at Winnipeg just before he set off in WCA's Giant Moth. His passengers are standing by. (K.M. Molson Col.)

The famous Mackenzie Air Service Bellanca 66-75 Air Cruiser CF-AWR in a scene at Cameron Bay, NWT. This great machine survived with CPA until a forced landing near Sioux Lookout on January 24, 1947. In 2009 CF-AWR was being methodically restored in Winnipeg by the Western Canada Aviation Museum. (NMST 4710)

In 1932 Brintnell broke with Canadian Airways to form Mackenzie Air Service. His experience, vision and talent soon attracted top pilots from Matt Berry to Marlow Kennedy, Gil McLaren, Stan McMillan and Bob Randall. All would become legends in Canada's airline industry. Mackenzie Air Service began with such aircraft as Fairchild 71 CF-AKN and Fokker Super Universal CF-ATJ, then added such newer types as Fairchild 82s 'AXM, 'N and 'Q, Norsemen 'AZA, 'BAM and 'BFR, Beech 17 'BBB ("Brintnell's Bastard Beech"), and Bellanca Air Cruisers 'AWR, 'BKV and 'BTW.

CF-AWR, Canada's and Mackenzie Air Service's first Air Cruiser, was registered on March 14, 1935. Dubbed the "Eldorado Radium Silver Express", which would become famous hauling uranium ore from the Eldorado Mine at Cameron Bay on Great Bear Lake to Fort McMurray, the head-of-rail for the 900-mile Northern Alberta Railway. CF-AWR's first trip north left Edmonton on March 16. As would become its routine, men and supplies were carried north, then sacks of uranium concentrate were flown south. (Ore hauled by CF-AWR was processed at Eldorado's refinery in Port Hope, Ontario. It is said that Great Bear Lake uranium later fuelled the atomic bombs dropped on Japan in 1945.)

Many Canadian aviation operators had arisen in the "Roaring Twenties", each hoping for a share in what seemed to be mining, forestry and airmail bonanzas. Investors always began with high hopes, as if having an airplane, a chief pilot and a mechanic was some sort of a sure-fire recipe. In this atmosphere the sky really did seem to be the limit.

But commercial aviation proved to be an unforgiving master. By 1925 most of the original upstarts, usually bubbling with enthusiasm at first but under-capitalized and short on business sense, had succumbed. They were pretty well done once their cheap war surplus planes wore out. Even their successors, such seemingly well-financed and equipped companies as Commercial Airways, Dominion Skyways, Mackenzie Air Service, National Air Transport and Skyways Limited would be flashes in the pan. In the end, through risky investment and mergers, it would be up to big business to make any sort of success out of Canada's air transport sector. Even so, problems would continue into modern times as shown by the modern-day failure of such companies as Canadian Airlines International, Canada 3000, JetsGo and Zoom. Ironically, Canada's Centennial of Flight even found Air Canada again on the verge of bankruptcy.

St. Louis-built Curtiss Robin CF-ALZ began with Consolidate Mining and Smelting in April 1930, then served Mackenzie Air Service 1934-35. Note the long-range fuel tank above the wing. The Robin, 17 of which wore Canadian markings, always proved serviceable in the bush. (Douglas H. Burt Col.)

Other Small Operators

Another fly in the ointment for Canadian Airways' was Wings Ltd. of Winnipeg, founded in July 1934 by several experienced men, including wartime pilot Milton Ashton. Born in Brucefield, Ontario in 1894, Ashton enlisted in the Army and was overseas in 1915. Following the Battle of the Somme, he transferred to the RFC in 1916. He trained at the School of Aeronautics at Oxford, on Farman Short Horns at Thetford and was posted to 12 Squadron on R.E.8 observation planes on the Arras front. This was a hectic period during which Ashton scored three kills and himself was shot down.

Postwar, Ashton was a travelling salesman for an Ontario music and radio company. He took a CAF refresher course at Camp Borden, then bided his time. He didn't return to aviation until 1928, when he joined J.V. Elliott to instruct. When Elliott became International Airways, Ashton stayed on to fly the Windsor-Toronto-Montreal mail. In July 1929 he joined Western Canada Airways to fly the prairie airmail. When Ottawa axed most airmail contracts in March 1932, he continued on the Winnipeg-Pembina mail service. In 1934 he opened the Canadian Airways base at Kenora, then teamed with Roy Brown, Edward Stull and Jack Moar to form Wings.

In September 1936 Wings began a 1-year, 300-ton job for Newmont Mining Corp. of New York, which was developing the Berens River Mine at Favourable Lake in Northwestern Ontario. Two Fairchild 82s, a Fairchild 71

The fabulous Waco cabin biplanes proved a perfect fit for Canada's bush operators in the 1930s-40s. "Waco", shortened version of "Weaver Aircraft Co.", was founded by George Weaver and friends in the early 1920s. The first production Waco was the 3-seat, open cockpit Model 9 of 1925, two of which came to Canada in 1927 for London Air Transport. The first certified cabin Waco was the 4-seat "QDC", introduced at the 1931 Detroit Air Show. At $6000, the QDC sold well and many improved versions ensued. Waco ZQC-6 CF-BBO was acquired by Wings Ltd. of Winnipeg in December 1936 from Waco in Troy, Ohio. It served into the CPA era, then went in 1944 to Bill Sylvester's newly-formed BC Airlines. On September 20, 1946 it crashed after takeoff from Victoria. Happily, pilot Stan Berge and his three passengers survived. (CPA Col.)

Location unknown. CF-BBO taxis off as some men salvage the floats of a crashed plane. (Arthur Limmert Col.)

and a Norseman carried the loads on a 145-mile route from Berens River on Lake Winnipeg. Included were a sawmill, two crawler tractors, a 180-hp boiler plant motor with a 75-foot stack, a water pump, mine cage and hoist, drills, eight ore cars, steel rails for the cars, 30 tons of dynamite, 30 tons of fuel and oil, materiel to complete such buildings as the kitchen, power house, boiler shed and bunkhouse and 40 tons of food. As needed, the

sawmill, tractors, etc. were disassemble for shipping. Most such equipment had reached Berens River by coming down Lake Winnipeg by boat or (after freeze-up) tractor train. Seventy staff also went into the mine site by air. (The Berens River Mine would operate into 1948, by which time reserves had dwindled.)

That Wings was succeeding by 1937 is suggested by the location of its business offices in the swanky Marlborough Hotel

Wings Ltd. Waco YKS-6 CF-AYT in a typical cold weather scene at Red Lake. Then, the same plane salvaged after a mishap and ready for transportation on a horse- or tractor-drawn sledge. (William J. Wheeler and Arthur Limmert Cols.)

Wings Ltd. acquired Universal CF-ASZ in 1932. Here it is during a normal salvage episode. 'ASZ flew on until burned at Ball Lake, east of Kenora, on January 10, 1938. (Arthur Limmert Col.)

in downtown Winnipeg. But business really wasn't as rosy as the numbers made it look. For its May 1937-May 1938 fiscal year the company reported gross revenue of $214,460.60. It had carried 6611 passengers, 2,725,608 lb freight and 31,564 lb mail. However, for all this effort, profit for the year was a puny $913.33. This picture was typical from one small Canadian air carrier to the next.

In 1937 General Airways, Mackenzie Air Services and Wings Ltd. set up a loose affiliation called United Air Service to better compete with Canadian Airways, e.g. by having common purchasing, and sharing aircraft and staff. Following a brief burst of PR in early 1937, however, little further was heard of this partnership. Meanwhile, a new operator appeared in 1937 when Jack Moar, who had flown for Canadian Airways and Wings Ltd., was hired to manage Skylines Express of Montreal. This company had plans to link Montreal, Toronto and Winnipeg via northern gold mining centres (much of Canada's commercial flying still depended on gold – 1937 gold production alone totalled nearly $69 million). Skylines announced plans for five twin-engine Fairchild Sekanis. Service commenced with more standard equipment from Dryden into the Rowan Lake mining area under Harold Farrington, and from Winnipeg to Red Lake and Pickle Lake under D.W. "Scotty" Moire. A Waco inaugurated the Montreal-Kirkland Lake mining run, then Norseman CF-BDF was added. However, like so many ventures since "Day One" in commercial aviation, Skylines Express quickly folded. It looked as if the whole Canadian industry needed a saviour before it collapsed.

More Misery

On June 29, 1932 Super Universal G-CASL of Canadian Airways crashed 60 miles north of Fort Rae. The sad word came from CAL head office on July 5 that 'ASL had been found by Walter Gilbert and that pilot Andy Cruickshank and engineers Horace Torrie and Harry King were dead. Cruickshank was a famous figure. In his native England he had studied engineering before joining the RFC in 1915. He fought through the war over France and Germany, then emigrated to Canada, where he farmed, then joined the RCMP. Stationed in the Yukon, he eventually returned to aviation, barnstorming briefly in the US, then flying Ryan G-CAHR of Yukon Airways and Exploration until joining Western Canada Airways in 1928. Torrie had begun in the RCAF in 1925. Later he was with Commercial Airways, until it was absorbed by CAL in 1930. King had joined the company first on Prairie operations in 1928, then went north.

Another accident involved Canadian Airways Fairchild 71C CF-AET on October 6, 1934 at Norway House. At 0700 that morning pilot Edward Morris departed in 'AET with four passengers for the Island Lake Gold Mines camp 150 miles away. Morris had not flown in this country and, apparently, became lost among its innumerable lakes and islands. To get his bearings, at 0850 he decided to land at the RC mission in the Island Lake neighborhood. On final approach, however, he crashed into the water. Three passengers escaped, but Morris and one passenger drowned.

Meanwhile, aircraft piloted by Norman Forrester and W.R. May had flown to the

same destination from Norway House that morning. Upon returning, they got the word via the Island Lake radio operator that Morris was missing. On his next trip out, May spotted a signal fire from the RC mission, landed, got the bad news, then flew over to the mine camp. At 1135 news was radioed to CAL in Winnipeg, which immediately advised that Forrester should fly the survivors to their destination. The RCMP at Norway House was advised by Winnipeg to organize an investigation. Three Norway House officers flew out the same day on this duty. Next day a CAL plane took the two victims to Winnipeg.

Cpl Greaves of the RCMP (who previously had survived the Bill Spence crash) filed his report, which was Exhibit 1 at the court of enquiry held in Winnipeg on October 16. This placed no blame on pilot or employer. Edward Morris was described as a WWI pilot who had been in the CAF/RCAF 1921-32. One recommendation made was that men unfamiliar with a district should not be pilots in command until gaining experience there. Great credit was given to the effectiveness of ground radio stations in getting information relayed, putting the wheels in motion to effect the rescue, etc.

Another case with Canadian Airways resulted in the death of one of Canada's gold mining pioneers, Stanley E. Siscoe, who had been prospecting in northern Quebec since 1911 and whose gold properties remain productive to this day. On March 12, 1935 Siscoe set off early in the morning from Montreal with CAL pilot W.T. Wrathell in Puss Moth CF-AGV. They were headed for Senneterre, about 270 miles northward. Bad weather obliged Wrathell to set down only 25 miles short of destination.

General Airways' base at Rouyn and Noranda, Quebec *circa* 1935. The great copper mine here began production in 1927. Prospecting and other mining developments in this region kept aviation hopping for decades. Shown from the right are Bellanca CH-300 Pacemakers CF-AMO, CF-ATN and Clarke's ill-fated CF-AOL. Unidentified are a fourth Pacemaker and a D.H. Moth. (Bert Phillips)

An air search was organized with local bush pilots, and the RCAF sent two aircraft from Rockcliffe. Meanwhile, Wrathell and Siscoe found shelter in a trapper's cabin, but Siscoe insisted on March 24 on tramping off to seek help. Next day, Dick Burge of Prospectors Airways rescued Wrathell on the trail. Then, on the 26th, another pilot spotted a body on a lake – it was Siscoe, who had frozen to death. No explanation appeared in the press as to why Wrathell and Siscoe did not fly out in 'AGV. Did the weather not clear over the days, was 'AGV out of fuel, or had it been damaged on landing? In May 1935 the aircraft was sold back to de Havilland Canada.

Another of Canada's early air disasters involved a well-known and popular bush pilot, Wilson H. "Clarkie"

Clarke of General Airways. Clarkie grew up near Oshawa. He was a good student who spent summers working on Great Lakes cruise ships, and winters playing hockey. In 1927 he took his pilot's licence at H.P. Ayres' school in Peterborough. Such a sharp young man wouldn't have to look hard for a job – he soon was on the payroll with General Airways of Rouyn. Early assignments included mercy missions to Indian reservations and supplying camps in the mineral rich Chibougamau area in northern Quebec.

On May 23, 1936 Clarkie was doing his rounds to two or three camps in Bellanca Pacemaker CF-AOL. On his

final leg he had six passengers, including a famous prospector, Leo Springer. When Clarkie failed to reach his destination around noon, there was concern. Then the weather suddenly went down, holding up any search until the 25th. That morning fellow General Airways pilot Gath

Wilson Harold Clarke wearing his winter flying kit. (Fred Hotson Col.)

Edwards was searching along his route while delivering supplies to Springer's Opemiska copper mine: "We expected to find Clarke and AOL parked on a lake with engine trouble. Tony Bruneau and I kept a sharp lookout and, a few minutes after

General Airways' original pilots: Harold H. Langford, Wilson Clarke and Stuart L. Hill with the town of Amos, Quebec in the background. Then, a snapshot of Clarke's doomed Bellanca. (Fred Hotson Col.)

How the Toronto *Globe and Mail* shouted out news of the General Airways crash in its edition of May 26, 1936.

passing the east end of Lake Pusticamica, we picked up what looked like a red tent ..." The tent floating in Lac Lessard turned out to be the wreck of Clarkie's bright red Bellanca. No one survived what turned out to have been a violent crash about 80 miles west of Chibougamau, and 140 east of Rouyn. No cause for the tragedy was ever found.

General News

The Bulletin presented other news that kept everyone in Canadian Airways informed. There often was a list of "mercy flights" carried out and, when any employees were involved in an especially good show, this was covered. In 1935, for example, pilots Herbert Hollick-Kenyon and J.H. "Red" Lymburner were seconded to fly for Sir Hubert Wilkins on an Antarctic scientific survey. Upon their return to Winnipeg on May 9, 1936 they were treated like heroes. One great impression made upon the two Canadians had not so much to do with Antarctica, as with the tremendous progress in South American aviation. "In Canada", said Kenyon, "we have faint conception of the common use of air transport in the South American continent." He described how one could fly commercially from South America across the South Atlantic and on to Europe: "I was told that all these systems are assisted materially by the governments of the countries through which they pass."

A CAL 1936 contract saw Stearman

CF-ASF modified to dust acres of peas in the lower Fraser River delta. At first pilot Maurice McGregor made some test runs to check for serviceability. Adjustments were needed, e.g. dust was entering his cockpit from the 650-lb capacity chemical hopper ahead of him. The hopper was modified but, when some dust persisted, McGregor began using goggles and a respirator. He flew his runs at 10 feet at about 85 mph, each pass covering a 30-foot swath. From July 28-31 he dusted 75 acres.

In 1936 E.P.H. "Billy" Wells and Maurice McGregor became the first Canadian Airways pilots qualified on the Lockheed 10 Electra, introduced by CAL that year. Activity on the Montreal-Rimouski trans-Atlantic steamship mail for August 1936 included: incoming liners – *Duchess of Bedford* (Aug.7th), *Empress of Britain* (13th), *Duchess of York* (20th) and *Empress of Britain* (27th). Outbound – *Empress of Britain* (1st), *Duchess of Richmond* (7th), *Empress of Britain* (15th), *Empress of Britain* (29th).

Canadian Airways Stearman fitted with hopper and discharge tube for pea dusting in the Fraser Valley, then pilot McGregor equipped with goggles and respirator. (*The Bulletin*)

For 1936 Canadian Airways enjoyed solid growth: 47% increase in freight, 44% – passengers, 18.5% – mail. Northwestern Ontario was the busiest district, accounting for more than 5 million pounds of freight, nearly equal to the CAL's total freight carried in 1935. While mining mainly explained this, CAL also carried 267,000 lb of fish to

F.M. "Maurice" McGregor of Canadian Airways. (*The Bulletin*)

the railhead at Hudson. Other revenue came from the 20,163 miles of aerial photo lines covered, 36,000 lb furs and 140 mercy flights throughout Canada. The fleet grew by 2 Stinson Reliants, 2 Fairchild 82s, 2 Lockheed 10s, 1 Norseman and 1 Dragon Rapide, and totalled 42 aircraft, most by now radio-equipped. Pilot training in 1936 cost $20,000, including sending Z.L. Leigh on an instrument course. For 1936 CAL logged 21,789 flying hours and carried 7,749,926 lb freight, 955,214 lb mail and 20,948 passengers.

Hope on the Horizon

By now some in business felt that Canada was edging out of the economic doldrums. One optimist was funeral director George Speers. In May 1936 he teamed with the Regina Brewing Co. to establish Speers Airways, the first carrier on the prairies specializing in air ambulance work. In its first week, Speers' Waco CF-AYQ carried five medical cases. Meanwhile, in 1936 Canada's sanctioned carriers (mainly Canadian Airways) flew some 1.2 million pounds of mail. As had been the case since 1927, most was destined for isolated northern communities, for which volumes continued to soar. In the Lake Athabasca area, for example, air mail rose from 5400 lb in 1935 to 22,000 a year later. The busiest route in 1936 was Charlottetown-Moncton (245,500 lb), then came Winnipeg-Lac du Bonnet (109,899 lb), Kenora-Red Lake (89,540) and Fort McMurray-Aklavik (76,161 lb). For 1936 the Post Office collected $605,000 in air mail revenue for an outlay of $275,000.

Some of Canada's Commercial Types of the 1920s-30s

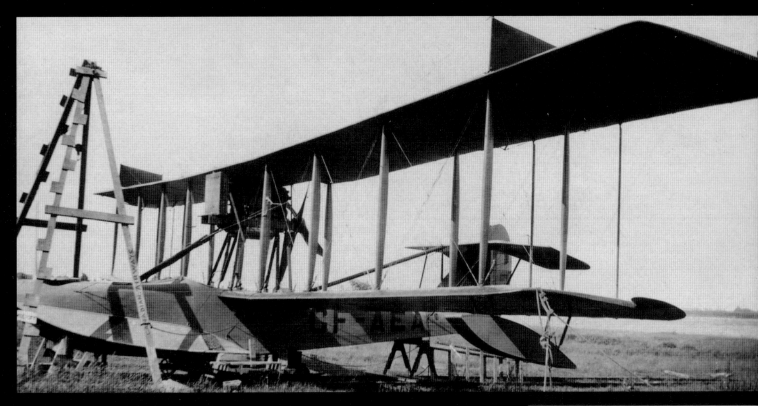

Out with the old. Wartime planes were the foundation of commercial aviation in Canada. By the late 1920s, however, most of these had been lost in crashes or were worn out. CF-AEA (above) was the only "CF" registered HS-2L. Originally with International Airways of Hamilton in 1929, it was exported to Bermuda the following year. Standard J-1 G-CAFT, originally a US Army trainer, served Toronto-based bush pilot and mining man, Howard Watt, from September 1926, until condemned two years later. Nearly all such aircraft were done in Canada by 1935, just as new commercial types were entering the market. (C. Don Long)

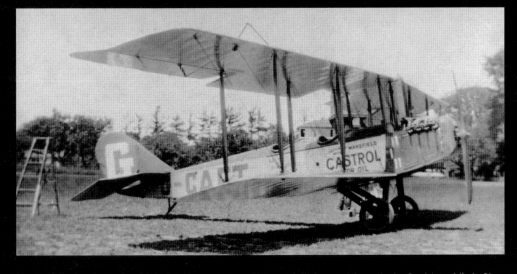

The International Airways advertisement in the May 1929 edition of *Canadian Air Review*. (CANAV Col.)

General Airways, formed under A. Roy Brown in June 1927, made its home at Amos in the Quebec goldbelt. Shown are the company's Super Universal CF-AEW and Stinson SR-8 CF-BAG in typical winter scenes. Both were eventually lost in fires, although 'BAG reportedly was salvaged and exported to South America during WWII. (Fred Hotson Col.)

(Top) Fairchild FC-2 G-CAJJ of General Airways on summer operations. Below, Super Universal G-CAWB, which was manufactured by Fokker's US subsidiary, Atlantic Aircraft of New Jersey. In March 1929 Canadian Vickers sold 'WB to International Airways. It's seen in contrasting settings: stuck in the spring gumbo, then sparkling on a frozen lake. 'WB joined Canadian Airways late in 1930, serving there to March 21, 1937, when it crashed on takeoff at Takla, BC, injuring pilot E.P.H. "Billy" Wells. Typical of CAL's top pilots, Wells had pioneered on the company's inaugural Vancouver-Victoria route with a Sikorsky flying boat. In 1935 he flew CAL's first Vancouver-Seattle air mail. When TCA formed in 1937, it hired 14 top CAL pilots, Wells included. On September 1 he and F.M. McGregor inaugurated TCA service, flying a Lockheed 10 on the Vancouver-Seattle route. (C. Don Long and Fred Hotson Cols.)

Super Universal CF-AJH was built by Canadian Vickers in May 1930. It worked initially on lease to W.J. McDonough, then went to A.G. "Tim" Sims and C.R. "Peter" Troup, who operated it from Rouyn. In this view 'AJH is delivering prospectors with all their kit. By the mid-1930s most Canadian Super Universals had been surpassed by the Fairchild 82 and Norseman. In 1928 a new Super Universal was priced on wheels at about $20,000 and sold far and wide, getting such key US airlines going as American Airways, Gulf Airlines, Mid Continent Air Express, National Parks Airways, Texas Air Transport and Universal Aviation Corp. (W.J. McDonough Col.)

One of Canada's few successful inter-urban passenger services from early days linked Vancouver and Victoria. All through the summer, year after year, aircraft profitably and safely plied this route. A Wells Air Transport Boeing 204, a type also used on this run by Canadian Airways, Coast Air Transport, Pacific Airways and Pioneer Airways, is seen delivering passengers at the dock in Victoria's inner harbour. This aircraft (CF-ALC) served from 1931 into 1939, when a cracked spar forced it into retirement. To this day the Vancouver-Victoria run is flown daily by such aircraft as the Beaver, Turbo Otter, Twin Otter and S-76. (Jack McNulty Col.)

In 1929 Commercial Airways of Edmonton, operated by Cy Becker, Vic Horner and Wop May, won the Post Office air mail contract for the Mackenzie Valley. This was a shock to Canadian Airways, which had pioneered the air mail in that vast region in 1928. These two companies now competed fiercely from Edmonton down into the Arctic. Depression conditions stymied both, but Canadian Airways prevailed, buying out Commercial Airways in May 1931. Shown on delivery to Edmonton from Bellanca of Canada in Montreal is Pacemaker CF-AIA. C. Don Long captured this scene as 'AIA was refuelling in Toronto.

The Commercial Airways fleet, dubbed "The Red Armada", looked impressive warming up for a day's work. Shown are Pacemaker CF-AIA, Lockheed Vega CF-AAL and Pacemaker CF-AKT. This airline carried the first fully official Arctic air mail. Piloted by Wop May and I. Glyn-Roberts, with engineers Sims and Vanderlinden, two Bellancas left Fort McMurray on December 19, 1930. They visited many posts before reaching Aklavik on December 30. Nearly all the mail – some 120,000 envelopes – was for philatelic

purposes, so was flown back to Edmonton! In the end, CF-AIA was lost on the ground at Fort McMurray on December 27, 1935 when spilled gasoline ignited. The Vega, sold in the US in 1936, last was heard of in Nicaragua in 1944, while Pacemaker 'AKT was wrecked while landing on Lake Athabasca on March 26, 1936. Happily, pilot W.J. "Bill" Windrum survived. (NMST 7168)

Mail being loaded in December 1928 at Fort McMurray for the first official air mail flight down the Mackenzie Valley to Aklavik. This classic photo was produced as a postcard by Sutherland's Pharmacy of Fort McMurray. (W.J. McDonough Col.)

Corporate Super Universals: Mining and forestry companies often operated their own aircraft. Here, bush pilot Al Cheesman stands at the dock on the Red River in Winnipeg in July 1928. He had just delivered G-CARK to Toronto-based Northern Aerial Mineral Exploration. (Below) CF-AAM during its time with Trail-based Consolidated Mining and Smelting 1929-35. Finally, CF-AFS of the Pigeon Timber Co. of Port Arthur. G-CARK was so badly damaged in a 1929 storm at Baker Lake, NWT, that it was finally scrapped. CF-AAM suffered a 1937 accident at Dawson in the Yukon. Eventually, it was salvaged and returned to flying status in 1998 by Clark Seaborn and friends, and today may be seen at the Western Canada Aviation Museum. While landing at Port Arthur on July 8, 1939, CF-AFS collided with a boat and was wrecked. (J.P. Culliton, D.H. Burt and CANAV Cols.)

Dominion Skyways of Montreal formed in 1935 to serve the northwest Quebec gold belt. Beginning in May with Waco YKC-S CF-AWK, the company added such modern aircraft as Fairchild 82 CF-AXB in August, and prototype Norseman CF-AYO the following January. In spite of being well equipped and well run, Dominion Skyways did not succeed and in 1938 was absorbed by Canadian Airways. CF-AWK ended a smoldering wreck when it force-landed in South Porcupine on August 8, 1949. CF-AXB was lost while landing at Trench Lake, Quebec on August 21, 1941. (William J. Wheeler Col.)

Prototype Norseman CF-AYO, first flown in November 1935, was delivered the following January to Dominion Skyways at Rouyn. Here it is fresh from the paint shop at Noorduyn. 'AYO served until the Dominion Skyways was absorbed by CPA. There it flew into late 1947. It last was owned by Orillia Air Services, which lost it in a crash on August 28, 1953. Its bones were recovered years later and today are on display in the Canadian Bushplane Heritage Museum at Sault Ste. Marie. In 2009 Fred Hotson, who flew in the old Dominion Slyways territory after WWII, recalled the paint job on this lovely bushplane: " 'AYO had a black fuselage with yellow wings and lettering. The black, as I remember, had a deep bluish tinge." (DND HC7452)

United Air Transport began in 1934 as the successor of Independent Airways. In both cases, a young Edmontonian, Grant McConachie, was a driving force. He barnstormed, did mining and prospecting work, hauled fish and eventually won some profitable air mail business. Here is one of his Fokker Universals sunk by a heavy snowfall; then, his speedy Stinson SR-7 Reliant (CF-AZC had originally been delivered to Dominion Gas Service of Calgary in 1935). McConachie later ran a Ford Trimotor between Edmonton and Whitehorse, amalgamated with BC-based Ginger Coote Airways to form Yukon Southern Airways and, ultimately, pulled many small Canadian companies together to form Canadian Pacific Airlines. (G.W. "Gil" McLaren, William J. Wheeler Cols.)

Grant McConachie looks on as some helpful northern Saskatchewan Indians patch up his broken ski mount using birch splints and caribou sinew. (LAC C61897)

Konnie Johanneson and Tom Lamb were upstart Manitoba air operators in the early 1930s. Here is Johanneson with his first plane, Moth CF-APM, on the Red River in 1933. Then, Stinson SR-5A CF-ANW owned first in 1935 by Johanneson, next by Bob Starratt, then by Tom Lamb. It later wandered to Red Lake, then to Nestor Falls, where it faded away in 1949. (Bruce Gowans Col.)

In 1934 brothers Chuck and Jack Austin, ambitious young men with an Ottawa Valley forestry background, used some of their inheritance to set up a flying service in Toronto. With an experienced partner, Leigh Capreol, in the midst of the Depression they acquired several Wacos, CF-AVN being the first. These formed the basis of a profitable air taxi service which led to a decades-long association with mining throughout Northern Ontario. Here is one of the company's speedy Wacos. (William J. Wheeler Col.)

Views of Austin Airways' Waco CF-BDN, which joined the company in 1937. In the second photo, the plane is without its propeller, which had flown off during a trip of October 14, 1938. Pilot Phil Sauvé landed safely, then he and his three passengers were rescued two days later by Chuck Austin. (Gordon Mitchell, Rusty Blakey)

Fairchild 51/71 CF-AWP served Austin Airways well from 1938 until it crashed at Nakina on June 17, 1949, killing the pilot, Felix Cryderman. (George Charity)

A wartime pilot from Chilliwack, Russell L. "Ginger" Coote returned to aviation in 1929. He soon acquired Golden Eagle CF-AKB, Ryan CF-ATA and Fox Moth CF-API. By 1933 he was operating as Bridge River and Caribou Airways (later called Ginger Coote Airways). He acquired a Hollywood-type reputation, which could not have been bad for business – one effusive reporter described Coote as "a hefty chunk of aerial dynamite". (William J. Wheeler Col.)

Fox Moth CF-ATX began with Toronto-based Prospectors Airways in 1933, but spent most of its days in Quebec with such operators as Arthur Fecteau and Phil Larivière, until fading away in 1951. Here it is after a successful bird shoot and moose hunt, then in a typical winter scene. (William J. Wheeler Col.)

Inspired by Fokker's Trimotor and introduced in the summer of 1926, the Ford Trimotor became synonymous with modern air transport. Powered initially by 200-220 hp Wright engines and carrying 12-14 passengers, Trimotors soon were plying America's passenger and mail routes. Made largely of aluminum, the early Model 4-AT-B had a wing span of 74', length of 49' 10", payload of 2200 lb and gross weight of 10,130 lb. It cruised at 95 mph, landed at 55 mph, carried 235 US gallons of fuel and could span 520 miles. Registered in Canada in May 1928, G-CARC was Canada's first modern airliner. Earlier that year it had assisted in the rescue mission, when the Junkers *Bremen* was stranded at Greenly Island, Quebec. Flying under the Sky View Lines banner from Oakes Airport at Chippawa, Ontario (inset), through the 1928 tourist season 'ARC carried some 12,000 passengers on joyrides over Niagara Falls. It then flew to Florida for a winter's worth of barnstorming. Here it sits at Chippawa. Now N1077, this Trimotor still was flying in 2009. (William J. Wheeler Col., Niagara Falls Public Library)

(Above) In 1935 G-CARC was sold to Grant McConachie's United Air Transport. In May 1935 oil man Robert Wilkinson offered McConachie $1000 to fly him from Calgary to Vancouver. This was an offer no operator could refuse, so on May 16 McConachie, co-pilot Gil McLaren and their passenger set off across the Rockies. Before long, severe icing had the pilots sweating and they were lucky to find safe haven at Grand Forks, BC. In Vancouver, McConachie and friends were feted but, by the time they paid their bills, they didn't have enough cash for fuel. A bit of impromptu joyriding took care of that and they returned to Edmonton. Always the hustler and PR man, McConachie palmed off this story as a major milestone in

Canadian airline history. Naturally, the newspapers bought his line. One report raved: "A daily aeroplane service could be operated between Calgary and Vancouver, Grant McConachie ... believes. He said the 1,000 miles of mountain flying had been uneventful ... The mountain barrier means almost nothing to modern machines, McConachie declared." (Below) G-CARC at Burns Lake in BC's northern interior in April 1935. A year later McConachie sold 'ARC to Northern Airways of Carcross, but the great machine was severely damaged at Telegraph Creek, BC on November 21, 1936, although it would be resurrected many years later. (NMST 6824)

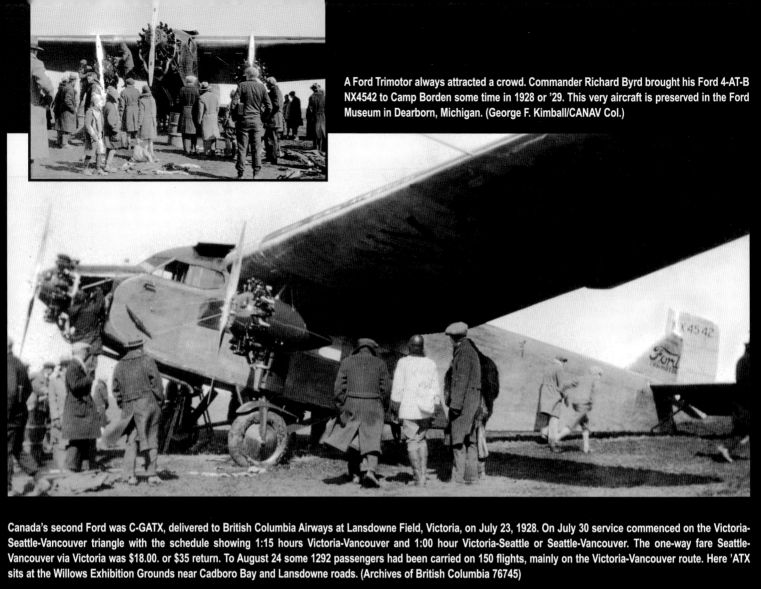

A Ford Trimotor always attracted a crowd. Commander Richard Byrd brought his Ford 4-AT-B NX4542 to Camp Borden some time in 1928 or '29. This very aircraft is preserved in the Ford Museum in Dearborn, Michigan. (George F. Kimball/CANAV Col.)

Canada's second Ford was C-GATX, delivered to British Columbia Airways at Lansdowne Field, Victoria, on July 23, 1928. On July 30 service commenced on the Victoria-Seattle-Vancouver triangle with the schedule showing 1:15 hours Victoria-Vancouver and 1:00 hour Victoria-Seattle or Seattle-Vancouver. The one-way fare Seattle-Vancouver via Victoria was $18.00. or $35 return. To August 24 some 1292 passengers had been carried on 150 flights, mainly on the Victoria-Vancouver route. Here 'ATX sits at the Willows Exhibition Grounds near Cadboro Bay and Lansdowne roads. (Archives of British Columbia 76745)

G-CATX runs up at Lansdowne Field. Note the company's motorcycle that was used to deliver luggage, express and mail. Sadly, this fine aircraft had a brief career. On August 25, 1928 it disappeared into the sea while on the Victoria-Seattle run. Capt Herald Walker, co-pilot Robert L. Carson and their five passengers all were lost. (NMST 1964)

In 1937 Grant McConachie purchased this ex-RCAF Trimotor, a 1929 Model 6-ATS-1. On July 5 1937 he and co-pilot Ted Field flew CF-BEP on the inaugural weekly service from Edmonton to Whitehorse, routing via Grande Prairie, Fort St. John, Fort Nelson and Watson Lake. On March 2, 1939 CF-BEP was wrecked when an out-of-control Hurricane smashed into it at Vancouver. (William J. Wheeler Col.)

In the early 1930s a boy named D.J. Cameron was immersed in aviation – building models, taking gliding lessons, photographing. Eventually, his photo albums went adrift, ending with a collector, but with no information about Cameron himself. He seems to have lived in the Quebec goldbelt, since the refinery at Noranda is in the background of many of his excellent photos. He also got around a bit – here is Ford Trimotor NC3041 which he photographed at Detroit in 1936. Built a decade earlier, NC3041 served in Ford's air cargo operation, then was sold in Kansas City. Others around the country had a turn with it, until it landed with the British Yukon Navigation Co. as CF-AZB. On August 8, 1941 its fuselage was buckled in a mishap at Whitehorse. Here it is damaged and pushed into the bush at Whitehorse, where it later was buried. (D.J. Cameron, M. Grant Cols.)

Selected Glossary

AEA	Aerial Experiment Association	**FTS**	flying training school	**NY**	New York
AFC	Air Force Cross	**gal**	gallon	**OPAS**	Ontario Provincial Air Service
BC	British Columbia	**G/C**	group captain		
BCATP	British Commonwealth Air Training Plan	**HBC**	Hudson's Bay Co.	**PEI**	Prince Edward Island
		HMA	His Majesty's Airship	**P&W**	Pratt and Whitney
CAF	Canadian Air Force	**H.P.**	Handley Page or horse power	**RAF**	Royal Air Force
CAL	Canadian Airways Ltd.			**R&D**	research and development
CAM	Canada Aviation Museum	**HQ**	headquarters	**RCAF**	Royal Canadian Air Force
CAS	Canadian Aerial Services	**Ju**	Junkers	**RCMP**	Royal Canadian Mounted Police
CCA	Controller of Civil Aviation	**LAC**	Library and Archives Canada		
CCF	Canadian Car and Foundry	**LAS**	Laurentide Air Service	**RCNAC**	Royal Canadian Naval Air Service
Col	colonel	**lb**	pound	**RFC**	Royal Flying Corps
Col.	collection	**LCMDR**	lieutenant commander	**RNAS**	Royal Naval Air Service
CAHS	Canadian Aviation Historical Society	**LCol**	lieutenant colonel	**Sgt**	sergeant
		Lt	lieutenant	**snye**	backwater or a channel joining two rivers
Capt	captain	**Maj**	major		
CEF	Canadian Expeditionary Force	**MBE**	Order of the British Empire	**spokeshave**	drawknife used on curved wood surfaces
		MC	Military Cross		
CMDR	commander	**MGen**	major general	**S/L**	squadron leader
CNE	Canadian National Exhibition	**mi.**	mile	**SSgt**	staff sergeant
		mph	miles per hour	**TAM**	Toronto Aerospace Museum
CPA	Canadian Pacific Airlines	**NAC**	National Aeronautical Collection	**U-boat**	German submarine
Cpl	corporal			**USAMS**	United States Air Mail Service
CNR	Canadian National Railway	**NAM**	National Aviation Museum		
CPR	Canadian Pacific Railway	**NAME**	Northern Aerial Mineral Exploration	**USAF**	United States Air Force
DFC	Distinguished Flying Cross			**USN**	United States Navy
D.H.	de Havilland	**NC**	Navy Curtiss as in *NC-4*	**VC**	Victoria Cross
DND	Department of National Defence	**NJ**	New Jersey	**WCA**	Western Canada Airways
		NMC	National Museums of Canada	**WCAM**	Western Canada Aviation Museum
DOT	Department of Transport				
DSC	Distinguished Service Cross	**NMUSAF**	National Museum of the United States Air Force	**W/C**	wing commander
DSO	Distinguished Service Order			**WWI**	World War I
FAI	Fédération Aéronautique Internationale	**NMST**	National Museum of Science and Technology	**WWII**	World War II
F/L	flight lieutenant	**NWT**	Northwest Territories		

A wide view of Moncton's first airport at Leger's Field. Taken in the early 1930s, some of the aircraft present were (2ⁿᵈ from the left) Fairchild 71 CF-AET of Quebec and Eastern Aviation and, on the right, Canadian Airways Moths CF-AAG and 'AHH. (via Don McClure)

Selected Bibliography

Blatherwick, John, *A History of Airlines in Canada*, Unitrade Press, Toronto, 1989.

Boyer, Chaz, *Handley Page Bombers of the First World War*, Aston Publications, Bourne End, UK, 1992.

Bungey, Lloyd, et al, *Pioneering Aviation in the West As Told by the Pioneers*, Hancock House, Surrey, BC, 1992.

CAHS Journal, Canadian Aviation Historical Society, Willowdale, Ontario.

Corley-Smith, Peter, *Bush Flying to Blind Flying 1930 – 1940*, Sono Nis Press, Victoria, BC, 1993.

David, Donald, *The Encyclopedia of Civil Aircraft: Profiles and Specifications for Civil Aircraft from the 1920s to the Present Day*, Amber Books, London, 1999.

Davies, R.E.G., *Airlines of the United States since 1914*, Smithsonian Institution Press, Washington, DC, 1998.

Davies, R.E.G., *Lufthansa: An Airline and Its Aircraft*, Orion Books, New York, 1991.

Dodds, Ronald, *The Brave Young Wings*, Canada's Wings, Stittsville, Ontario, 1980.

Douglas, W.A.B., *The Creation of a National Air Force: The History of the Royal Canadian Air Force, Volume II*, Toronto, University of Toronto Press, 1986.

Ellis, Frank H., *Canada's Flying Heritage*, Toronto, University of Toronto Press, 1954.

"Fairchild Aviation News", Vol.1, No.3, June 1929, Farmingdale, NY.

Fuller, G.A., Griffin, J.A., Molson, K.M., *125 Years of Canadian Aeronautics: A Chronology 1840-1965*, Willowdale, Ontario, Canadian Aviation Historical Society, 1983.

Griffin, J.A., *Canadian Military Aircraft Serials and Photographs*, Ottawa, Canadian War Museum, 1969.

Hammell, J.E., *Northern Aerial Mineral Explorations Limited*, Toronto, 1928.

Jackson, A.J., *De Havilland Aircraft*, Putnam, London, 1962.

Jefford, W/C C.G., MBE, *RAF Squadrons: A Comprehensive Record of the Movement and Equipment of All RAF Squadrons and Their Antecedents Since 1912*, Shrewsbury, England, Airlife, 1988.

Juptner, Joseph P., *U.S. Civil Aircraft Series*, Vols.1-9, TAB Aero, Blue Summit Ridge, Pennsylvania, 1994.

Keith, Ronald A., *Bush Pilot with a Briefcase: The Happy-Go-Lucky Story of Grant McConachie*, Doubleday Canada Ltd., Toronto, 1972.

Knott, Captain Richard C., USN, *The American Flying Boat: An Illustrated History*, Naval Institute Press, Annapolis, Maryland, 1979.

Kostenuk, S. and Griffin, J.A., *RCAF Squadrons and Aircraft*, Toronto, Samuel Stevens Hakkert & Co., 1977.

Leigh, Z.L., *And I Shall Fly, The Flying Memoirs of Z. Lewis Leigh*, CANAV Books, Toronto, 1985.

McDonough, John, *Airmanship: A Complete Guide and Flying Course for Student Pilots, Including the Operation of Aircraft in the Field, on Wheels, Skis and Floats*, Sir Isaac Pitman & Sons (Canada), Ltd., Toronto, 1930.

McGrath, T.M., *A History of Canadian Airports*, Lugus Publications, Toronto, 1992.

McLaren, Duncan D., *Bush to Boardroom: A Personal View of Five Decades of Aviation History*, Watson & Dwyer Ltd., Winnipeg, 1992.

Milberry, Larry, *Aviation in Canada*, Toronto, McGraw-Hill Ryerson, 1979.

Milberry, Larry, *Aviation in Canada: The Pioneer Decades*, CANAV Books, Toronto, 2008.

Mitchell, Kent A., *Fairchild Aircraft 1926 – 1987*, Santa Ana, California, Narkiewicz/Thompson, 1997.

Molson, K.M and Taylor, H.A., *Canadian Aircraft since 1909*, Stittsville, Ontario, Canada's Wings, 1982.

Molson, K.M. and Short, A.J., *The Curtiss HS Flying Boats*, Ottawa, National Aviation Museum, 1995.

Molson, K.M., *Canada's National Aviation Museum: Its History and Collections*, Ottawa, National Aviation Museum, 1988.

Parkin, John H., *Bell and Baldwin: Their Development of Aerodromes and Hydrodromes at Baddeck, Nova Scotia*, University of Toronto Press, 1964.

Rosenberg, Barry and Macaulay, Catherine, *Mavericks of the Sky: The First Daring pilots of the U.S. Air Mail*, New York, William Morrow, 2006.

Sullivan, Lt Alan, RAF, *Aviation in Canada*, Rous & Mann, Toronto, 1919.

Sutherland, Alice Gibson, *Canada's Aviation Pioneers: 50 Years of McKee Trophy Winners*, Toronto, McGraw-Hill Ryerson, 1978.

Swanborough, Gordon, *United States Military Aircraft since 1909*, Putnam, London, 1963.

Thetford, Owen, *Aircraft of the Royal Air Force since 1918*, Putnam, London, 1962.

Thetford, Owen, *British Naval Aircraft since 1912*, Putnam, London, 1962.

They Led the Way: Members of Canada's Aviation Hall of Fame, Canada's Aviation Hall of Fame, Wetaskiwin, Alberta, 1998.

Weicht, Chris, *North by Northwest, An Aviation History*, Creekside Publications, Roberts Creek, BC, 2004.

West, Bruce, *The Firebirds: How Bush Flying Won Its Wings*, Ontario Ministry of Natural Resources, Toronto, 1974.

White, Elwood, and Smith, Peter L., *Wings across the Water: Victoria's Flying Heritage 1871-1971*, Harbour Publishing, Madeira Park, BC, 2005.

Wise, S.F., *Canadian Airmen and the First World War: The Official History of the Royal Canadian Air Force, Volume I*, Toronto, University of Toronto Press, 1980.

Another of Canada's remarkable Loening amphibians, G-CARS first appeared in June 1928. Based at La Malbaie down the Quebec North Shore, it was in the Canadian Transcontinental Airways fleet. 'ARS went to Canadian Airways in January 1931 and ended its days in a takeoff accident at Quesnel, BC on March 16, 1933. Pilot W.J. "Bill" Holland walked away safely from this prang. This great West Coast pilot later flew for Ferry Command. In December 20, 1942 he was aboard Lockheed 14 CF-CPD when it crashed near Chilliwack killing all 13 aboard. (William J. Wheeler Col.)

Index

Canada's first Tiger Moth, CF-APL came to Canada in August 1931. It served de Havilland Canada until sold to Austin Airways in July 1934, where it did general duties for a year. CF-APL ended as a WWII-era training aid at Toronto's Central Technical School. (William J. Wheeler Col.)